Progress in IS

"PROGRESS in IS" encompasses the various areas of Information Systems in theory and practice, presenting cutting-edge advances in the field. It is aimed especially at researchers, doctoral students, and advanced practitioners. The series features both research monographs that make substantial contributions to our state of knowledge and handbooks and other edited volumes, in which a team of experts is organized by one or more leading authorities to write individual chapters on various aspects of the topic. "PROGRESS in IS" is edited by a global team of leading IS experts. The editorial board expressly welcomes new members to this group. Individual volumes in this series are supported by a minimum of two members of the editorial board, and a code of conduct mandatory for all members of the board ensures the quality and cutting-edge nature of the titles published under this series.

More information about this series at http://www.springer.com/series/10440

Horst Treiblmaier · Trevor Clohessy
Editors

Blockchain and Distributed Ledger Technology Use Cases

Applications and Lessons Learned

 Springer

Editors
Horst Treiblmaier ⓘ
Department of International Management
Modul University Vienna
Vienna, Austria

Trevor Clohessy ⓘ
Department of Enterprise and Technology
Galway-Mayo Institute of Technology
Galway, Ireland

ISSN 2196-8705   ISSN 2196-8713 (electronic)
Progress in IS
ISBN 978-3-030-44339-9   ISBN 978-3-030-44337-5 (eBook)
https://doi.org/10.1007/978-3-030-44337-5

This Springer imprint is published by the registered company Springer Nature Switzerland AG
The registered company address is: Gewerbestrasse 11, 6330 Cham, Switzerland

Preface

Only a decade ago, who would have thought that the decentralization of databases would turn into a topic not only of interest to computer scientists and technicians but also to C-level managers, politicians, and the general public? Back in 1991, the idea of connecting data blocks via hashed data was conceived by cryptographers Scott Stornetta and Stuart Haber. Since 1995, their technique can actually be found in The New York Times. Similarly, the release of the seminal Bitcoin paper in 2008 and the first working client in 2009 by the pseudonymous Satoshi Nakamoto did not immediately put blockchain into the mainstream spotlight. Only a handful of cryptographers and technology-savvy people, many of whom were affiliated with the cypherpunk movement, started to exchange value in a peer-to-peer network. It was not until 2015 that Bitcoin turned from a sleeping beauty into a global phenomenon of interest embodying a multitude of positive and negative attributes. Even more important, its underlying technology became an object of scrutiny, which triggered an enormous hype in which blockchain was envisioned as a potential solution for almost any conceivable problem. The hype was short-lived but what remained is a technology that, albeit not being a silver bullet, has the potential to solve numerous pending and highly relevant problems that cannot be tackled equally well with traditional centralized database solutions. The blockchain hype has also left its mark on academia, and numerous papers were published that describe potential use cases, relevant theories, and technological advancements. Creative solutions were propagated ranging from transforming supply chains toward creating new forms of national governance. We are now witnessing a second wave of academic research, and the time is ripe for the rigorous investigation of existing and novel blockchain use cases and blockchain case studies. Researchers, equipped with an arsenal of different methods, now critically investigate blockchain applications and report its advantages and use case applications.

With this book entitled, *Blockchain and Distributed Ledger Technology Use Cases: Applications and Lessons Learned*, we fill a gap in the market and present a wide selection of use cases, analyzed with academic rigor. This book contains conceptual papers, case studies, literature reviews and technical perspectives which traverse topics as diverse as health care, finance, smart cities, public administration, and supply chain management. We hope that the different angles and approaches will be inspiring for other researchers as well as practitioners and can serve as the basis for further rigorous blockchain research. We start this book with an introductory chapter from *Horst Treiblmaier*, which is a reprint from a paper published in "Frontiers in Blockchain." In this chapter, he lays the foundation on how to design and report blockchain case studies. Next, *Thomas Osterland* and *Thomas Rose* develop a maturity model for the engineering of distributed ledgers that distinguishes between different capabilities and functional scopes. *Trevor Clohessy* and *Saima Clohessy* use an inductive grounded theory approach to investigate pharmaceutical use cases and present a multilayer pharmaceutical blockchain vigilant information system model. Another example from the healthcare industry stems from *Rhode Ghislaine Nguewo Ngassam, Roxana Ologeanu-Taddei, Jorick Lartigau*, and *Isabelle Bourdon*, who design a blockchain-based allergy card that registers, shares, and traces information about users' drug allergies. Since blockchain was popularized by a cryptocurrency, it is not surprising that this book also contains use cases from the financial industry. *Marco Crepaldi* outlines the legal landscape for information exchange and establishes several desirable principles to which information exchange should adhere. *Andrew Le Gear* navigates the regulatory landscape for digital security offerings and presents a compliant blockchain solution, on the way to discussing the key compliance concerns of know your customer (KYC), anti-money laundering (AML), custody, tokenization, and secondary trading as part of a distributed exchange. When it comes to blockchain, privacy naturally is a big issue and blockchain has been heralded both as a potential threat to privacy and as a privacy-preserving technology. *Wolfgang Radinger-Peer* and *Bernhard Kolm* describe the application of blockchain technology to fulfill the GDPR documentation requirements for a log management system (LMS). *Matias Travizano, Carlos Sarraute, Mateusz Dolata, Aaron M. French,* and *Horst Treiblmaier* tackle the issue from a marketing perspective and present a solution which not only allows Internet users to preserve their anonymity but also enables them to capitalize on their private data.

Blockchain has also been announced as a technology that might help to create sustainable solutions. One such example is presented by *Ushnish Sengupta* and *Henry Kim*, who highlight the potential of smart contracts to provide a layer of assurance that agreements between indigenous communities and the natural resources industry will be honored. *Esther Nagel* and *Johann Kranz* present blockchain-based smart city applications and identify start-up archetype domains such as the sharing economy, privacy and security, and the Internet of things. This leads straight to application scenarios in the public sector as demonstrated by *Horst Treiblmaier* and *Christian Sillaber* who examine a use case in the state government of South Tyrol in Southern Italy. *Dominik Röck, Felix Schöneseiffen, Michael Greger*, and *Erik Hofmann* critically examine whether distributed ledger technology can be a useful addition to the smart factory concept within the context of Industry 4.0. Moving to the private sector, *Patrick Schneck, Andranik Tumasjan,* and *Isabell Welpe* scrutinize the applicability of blockchain technology for sharing economy platforms to challenge incumbents' business models. *Bikram Shrestha, Malka N.*

Halgamuge, and *Horst Treiblmaier* present the result from a literature review and illustrate which platforms and features are offered by blockchain-based multimedia platforms. Finally, *Wout Hofmann* ends this book with a plea for using distributed ledger technology to increase supply chain visibility.

We hope that the readers will find the wide range of use cases, investigated with different methods, inspiring and useful. The chapters in this book not only highlight what can be done with blockchain but also demonstrate several limitations. The second wave of blockchain applications and research is already here, and we enjoy being part of this exciting development. We encourage the readers to study these use cases and case studies and to use them as an inspiration for their own research and application development.

Vienna, Austria   Horst Treiblmaier
Galway, Ireland   Trevor Clohessy

Contents

Toward More Rigorous Blockchain Research: Recommendations
for Writing Blockchain Case Studies 1
Horst Treiblmaier

From a Use Case Categorization Scheme Towards a Maturity Model
for Engineering Distributed Ledgers 33
Thomas Osterland and Thomas Rose

What's in the Box? Combating Counterfeit Medications
in Pharmaceutical Supply Chains with Blockchain Vigilant
Information Systems....................................... 51
Trevor Clohessy and Saima Clohessy

A Use Case of Blockchain in Healthcare: Allergy Card 69
Rhode Ghislaine Nguewo Ngassam, Roxana Ologeanu-Taddei,
Jorick Lartigau, and Isabelle Bourdon

International Exchange of Financial Information on Distributed
Ledgers: Outlook and Design Blueprint 95
Marco Crepaldi

A Blockchain Supported Solution for Compliant Digital Security
Offerings.. 113
Andrew Le Gear

A Blockchain-Driven Approach to Fulfill the GDPR Recording
Requirements 133
Wolfgang Radinger-Peer and Bernhard Kolm

Wibson: A Case Study of a Decentralized, Privacy-Preserving
Data Marketplace... 149
Matias Travizano, Carlos Sarraute, Mateusz Dolata, Aaron M. French,
and Horst Treiblmaier

**Business Process Transformation in Natural Resources Development
Using Blockchain: Indigenous Entrepreneurship, Trustless
Technology, and Rebuilding Trust** 171
Ushnish Sengupta and Henry Kim

**Smart City Applications on the Blockchain: Development
of a Multi-layer Taxonomy** 201
Esther Nagel and Johann Kranz

**A Case Study of Blockchain-Induced Digital Transformation
in the Public Sector** 227
Horst Treiblmaier and Christian Sillaber

**Analyzing the Potential of DLT-based Applications
in Smart Factories** 245
Dominik Roeck, Felix Schöneseiffen, Michael Greger, and Erik Hofmann

**Next Generation Home Sharing: Disrupting Platform Organizations
with Blockchain Technology and the Internet of Things?** 267
Patrick Schneck, Andranik Tumasjan, and Isabell M. Welpe

**Using Blockchain for Online Multimedia Management:
Characteristics of Existing Platforms** 289
Bikram Shrestha, Malka N. Halgamuge, and Horst Treiblmaier

Supply Chain Visibility Ledger 305
Wout J. Hofman

Editors and Contributors

About the Editors

Horst Treiblmaier is Professor in international management at MODUL University Vienna, Austria. He received a Ph.D. in management information systems in 2001 from the Vienna University of Economics and Business in Austria and worked as Visiting Professor at Purdue University, University of California, Los Angeles (UCLA), The University of British Columbia (UBC), and the University of Technology Sydney (UTS). He has more than fifteen years of experience as Researcher and Consultant and has worked on projects with Microsoft, Google, and the United Nations Industrial Development Organization (UNIDO). His research interests include the economic and business implications of blockchain, cryptoeconomics, methodological and epistemological problems of social science research and gamification. Currently, he serves on the board of the "City of Blockchain," an association promoting blockchain and cryptographic technologies. His research has appeared in journals such as *Information Systems Journal, Structural Equation Modeling, DATA BASE for Advances in Information Systems, Communications of the Association for Information Systems, Information & Management, Journal of Electronic Commerce Research, Journal of Global Information Management, Schmalenbach Business Review, Supply Chain Management: An International Journal, International Journal of Logistics Management, and Wirtschaftsinformatik (Business & Information Systems Engineering).*

Trevor Clohessy is Assistant Professor in business information systems and transformative technologies at GMIT School of Business since September 2018. Prior to this post, he was Assistant Professor at the National University of Ireland Galway Business School and Postdoctoral Researcher with Lero. His research interests include blockchain, business analytics, digital transformation, digital addiction, digital politics, and cloud computing. He has published in a number of academic outlets including the *Journal of Information Technology and People* and the *Journal of Industrial Management and Data Systems*. He completed his Ph.D.

from the National University of Ireland Galway. His doctoral thesis investigated the digital transformation impact of cloud computing on IT service providers. He has lectured business information systems, business analytics, databases, and cloud computing topics in traditional classroom settings and blended/online learning settings. He and his research associates conducted one of the first blockchain Irish organizational readiness reports in 2018 entitled "Organizational factors that influence the Blockchain adoption in Ireland."

Contributors

Isabelle Bourdon University of Montpellier, Montpellier, France

Saima Clohessy Fidelity Investments Ireland, Galway, Republic of Ireland

Trevor Clohessy Department of Enterprise and Technology, Galway-Mayo Institute of Technology, Galway, Republic of Ireland

Marco Crepaldi Université du Luxembourg, Esch-sur-Alzette, Luxembourg

Mateusz Dolata University of Zurich, Zurich, Switzerland

Aaron M. French The University of New Mexico, Albuquerque, USA

Michael Greger Institute of Supply Chain Management, University of St.Gallen, St. Gallen, Switzerland

Malka N. Halgamuge Department of Electrical and Electronic Engineering, The University of Melbourne, Melbourne, Australia

Erik Hofmann Institute of Supply Chain Management, University of St.Gallen, St. Gallen, Switzerland

Wout J. Hofman TNO, The Hague, The Netherlands

Henry Kim Schulich School of Business, York University, Toronto, ON, Canada

Bernhard Kolm University of Applied Sciences, FH Campus Wien, Vienna, Austria

Johann Kranz Ludwig Maximilian University of Munich, Munich, Germany

Jorick Lartigau Pikcio, Montpellier, France

Andrew Le Gear Horizon Globex Ltd, Zug, Switzerland

Esther Nagel Ludwig Maximilian University of Munich, Munich, Germany

Rhode Ghislaine Nguewo Ngassam University of Montpellier, Montpellier, France;
Pikcio, Montpellier, France

Roxana Ologeanu-Taddei University of Montpellier, Montpellier, France

Thomas Osterland Fraunhofer FIT, Sankt Augustin, Germany

Wolfgang Radinger-Peer University of Applied Sciences, FH Campus Wien, Vienna, Austria

Dominik Roeck Institute of Supply Chain Management, University of St.Gallen, St. Gallen, Switzerland

Thomas Rose Fraunhofer FIT & RWTH Aachen University, Sankt Augustin, Germany

Carlos Sarraute Wibson, Gibraltar, UK

Patrick Schneck Technical University of Munich, Munich, Germany

Felix Schöneseiffen Roland Berger, Munich, Germany

Ushnish Sengupta Schulich School of Business, York University, Toronto, ON, Canada

Bikram Shrestha School of Computing and Mathematics, Charles Sturt University, Bathurst, Australia

Christian Sillaber University of Innsbruck, Innsbruck, Austria

Matias Travizano Wibson, Gibraltar, UK

Horst Treiblmaier Department of International Management, Modul University Vienna, Vienna, Austria

Andranik Tumasjan Johannes Gutenberg University of Mainz, Mainz, Germany

Isabell M. Welpe Technical University of Munich, Munich, Germany

Toward More Rigorous Blockchain Research: Recommendations for Writing Blockchain Case Studies

Horst Treiblmaier

Abstract About a decade ago the fundamental operating principle of the Blockchain was introduced. It took several years before the technology gained widespread recognition in industry and academic communities outside of the computer science sphere. Since then many academic communities have taken up the topic, but so far no well-defined research agenda has emerged: research topics are scattered and rigorous approaches are scarce. More often than not, use cases implemented by industry apply a trial and error approach and there exists a dearth of theory-based academic papers on the topic following robust methodologies. Being a nascent research topic, case studies on Blockchain applications are a suitable approach to systematically transfer industry experience into research agendas which benefit both theory development and testing as well as design science research. In this paper I offer guidelines and suggestions on how to design and structure Blockchain case studies to create value for academia and the industry. More specifically, I describe Blockchain characteristics and challenges, present existing Blockchain case studies, and discuss various types of case study research and how they can be useful for industry and academic research. I conclude with a framework and a checklist for Blockchain case study research.

Keywords Blockchain · Blockchain characteristics · Distributed ledger technology · Case study · Use case · Theory development · Case study checklist · Case study framework

Originally published as Treiblmaier, H. (2019) "Toward More Rigorous Blockchain Research: Recommendations for Writing Blockchain Case Studies", Frontiers in Blockchain, Vol. 2, Article 3, pp. 1–15, https://doi.org/10.3389/fbloc.2019.00003.

H. Treiblmaier (✉)
Department of International Management, Modul University Vienna, Vienna, Austria
e-mail: Horst.Treiblmaier@modul.ac.at

1 Introduction

Within roughly a decade the Blockchain has shifted from a rather obscure and poorly understood topic into a phenomenon that has gained widespread mass media attention and attracts academics and practitioners alike. The growth in size of selected Blockchain networks, as measured by the number of unique addresses participating in daily activities, exhibits an exponential development following Metcalfe's law (Alabi 2017). In spite of a sharp drop in the prices of Bitcoin and other cryptocurrencies at the end of the year 2017, the general Blockchain market size is still estimated to grow from USD 242 million in 2016 to USD 7684 million by 2022, at a compound annual growth rate of 79.6% (MarketsandMarkets 2017).

The emergence of Blockchain publications in leading academic journals has shown a substantial time lag in comparison to industry adoption. Outside of the computer science and cryptography communities, the first academic journal publications discussing Bitcoin appeared around 2012, followed by papers dealing with the Blockchain and DLT (Distributed Ledger Technology) around 2015. This delay has partly to do with lengthy review cycles of top-tier academic journals, but also with the complexity of the technology in combination with poorly understood and unclear use cases. This situation has changed with the emergence of publications targeting a broader audience, in which the authors speculate about potential application scenarios for the technology (Swan 2015; Tapscott and Tapscott 2016; Iansiti and Lakhani 2017). Many of the suggested use cases are far-reaching in terms of their potential implications and cover a wide range of industries and applications, including financial services, transportation and supply chain management, media and entertainment, education, tourism, public services, consumer services, voting and academic peer reviews (Bahga and Madisetti 2017; Lacity 2018a, b; Önder and Treiblmaier 2018; Treiblmaier 2018; Treiblmaier and Beck 2019a, b; Yli-Huumo et al. 2016).

The relevance of the Blockchain for the Information Systems community is twofold. First, researchers with an interest in the implications of the technology may want to better understand the behavioral (on an individual, group, and organizational level) and economic impacts of the Blockchain as well as its antecedents. Second, design science researchers may want to focus on the application of Blockchain technology to design and implement novel and innovative artifacts, which also includes the potential transformation of software development and business processes (Sillaber et al. 2018). While academia focuses largely on enhancing and refining existing frameworks and theories, as well as creating new ones, the industry needs advice and practical solutions.

The current lack of long-term experience with the Blockchain is aggravated by the fact that the technology is not yet mature, and therefore still under development. In their search for barriers to Blockchain adoption, Holotiuk et al. (2018) identified the lack of Blockchain use cases as a key challenge. A well-structured research agenda that encourages the systematic and comprehensive documentation of the findings of Blockchain case studies is therefore needed to ensure the cumulative compilation of knowledge and to provide guidance for the industry. Ideally, such a research agenda builds on previous research and allows for the comparability and straightforward integration of new findings. Given the flexibility and broad applicability of case studies (Cavaye 1996), they are well-suited for investigating nascent phenomena and structuring a research domain. They have the potential to bring together academic rigor and practical relevance, while simultaneously ensuring a substantial amount of methodological freedom (Yin 2014; Ridder 2017).

Beck et al. (2017) suggest a list of Blockchain research topics for the IS community, including new business models, disruption, implementation types, sustainability issues, organizational implications, application development, Internet of Things (IoT) applications, challenges of implementing business logic, and limits of applications. Notably, all of these topics can be investigated with the help of carefully designed, executed and documented case studies. Existing Blockchain case studies are rare and are often published as anecdotes without a clearly defined structure, which makes it hard to critically evaluate them and to use them as a solid basis for further research or recommendations for the industry. It is therefore my goal to provide suggestions on how anecdotal evidence can be turned into systematic knowledge by considering the principles and guidelines of academic case study research.

In the next section I present definitions, characteristics and challenges of the Blockchain, to lay a foundation for the remainder of this paper. Subsequently, I differentiate between four types of theory-based case study research, each of which has its respective strengths and weaknesses, and provide an overview of existing Blockchain case studies, which cover one or more use cases respectively. Next, I present a generic framework for Blockchain case study research, followed by a proposed structure for systematic Blockchain case study papers. I end the paper with a brief conclusion.

2 Blockchain: Definitions, Characteristics and Challenges

The Blockchain is a technology, or rather a combination of technologies (Narayanan and Clark 2017), that is still under development. In a recent white paper the IEEE states that the "Blockchain, as an industry, has entered its Cambrian phase" (Peck 2017, p. 1), alluding to the rapid diversification of various life forms during that period.

The term Blockchain originates from the original description of Bitcoin by the mysterious author (or group of authors) identified as Satoshi Nakamoto (2008). Nakamoto never actually uses the term "Blockchain" in his/her/their seminal paper, but instead describes how transactions, hashes and nonces can be grouped together into a block-based data structure in which the single blocks are chained together by including the hash of a previous block. Since then, the term Blockchain has gained widespread public attention and is most commonly used to denote what can be more loosely described as "trustless systems", indicating that the amount of trust required of individual actors is minimized. Most authors, however, do not care so much about a chain of blocks, but rather about the underlying characteristics of the technology which facilitate the creation of decentralized systems whose functioning does not necessitate specific trustworthy entities. It therefore makes sense to also consider the broader term "Distributed Ledger Technology" (DLT) in any paper dealing with the Blockchain in order to also include technologies that do not exhibit a chain-like structure, such as, for example, Tangle, a directed acyclic graph (DAG) used by IOTA, which entangles a stream of individual transactions. Another solution based on directed acyclic graphs is Hashgraph, a DLT with a consensus mechanism that does not rely on an energy-consuming proof-of-work mechanism. The major advantage of avoiding a linear block chain lies mainly in the faster throughput of the transactions (Schueffel 2017).

Table 1 lists several Blockchain and DLT definitions. The core of every Blockchain/DLT system is the distributed storage of data across multiple ledgers that can be spread across institutions and countries. While Meiklejohn et al. (2016) specifically refer to the Bitcoin Blockchain, all other definitions are more generic. The key characteristics include the distributed nature of the Blockchain, the immutability of the data, and the necessity of achieving consensus on which transactions are to be recorded. Each of these characteristics, and several others, are discussed in more detail in the following section. To date, no generally accepted definition of the Blockchain has emerged. It is therefore necessary to clearly describe the type of Blockchain/DLT being used in a specific case study and to outline the reasons for that particular choice.

The characteristics of the Blockchain, some of which might be only assumed or are currently under debate for technological, economic, business-related or legal reasons (Hoelscher 2018; Kim and Justl 2018; Posadas 2018), enable a wide variety of applications across multiple industries. Table 2 lists important characteristics of the Blockchain that emerged from a review of the literature as well as from interviews I personally conducted with 24 experts between January and February 2018. The interviews each lasted between 12 and 23 min. All interviews were recorded, transcribed and analyzed according to recognized standards for qualitative content analysis and grounded theory development (Hsieh and Shannon 2005; Glaser and Strauss 1967). The experts were chosen from the member directory of a large Blockchain interest group in Austria and included representatives of organizations from various industries (e.g., finance, energy, transportation), interest groups, consulting agencies, governmental institutions and educational institutions. All of the interview partners had substantial previous experience with Blockchain technology, such as the implementation and evaluation of diverse use cases, industry consulting projects, or the mining of cryptocurrencies. More details can be found in Treiblmaier and Umlauff (2019).

The shown characteristics might not apply equally well to all types of Blockchain manifestations. A permissioned Blockchain run by members of a consortium, for example, represents a rather closed ecosystem with clearly defined participants and control structures that are (partly) centralized, which contrasts with permissionless Blockchains that offer free access for anyone. The inherent differences between

Table 1 Blockchain and DLT definitions

Author	Definition
Government Office for Science (2016, p. 17)	*Distributed ledgers* are a type of database that is spread across multiple sites, countries or institutions, and is typically public. Records are stored one after the other in a continuous ledger, rather than sorted into blocks, but they can only be added when the participants reach a quorum
Lacity (2018a, b, p. 41)	A *Blockchain application* is a distributed, peer-to-peer system for validating, time-stamping, and permanently storing transactions on a distributed ledger that uses cryptography to authenticate digital asset ownership and asset authenticity, and consensus algorithms to add validated transactions to the ledger and to ensure the ongoing integrity of the ledger's complete history
Meiklejohn et al. (2016, p. 87)	The *Bitcoin Blockchain* is "a replicated graph data structure that encodes all Bitcoin activity, past and present, in terms of the public digital signing keys party to each transaction"
Mougayar (2016, p. 4)	Technically, the *Blockchain* is a back-end database that maintains a distributed ledger that can be inspected openly Business-wise, the *Blockchain* is an exchange network for moving transactions, value, assets between peers, without the assistance of intermediaries Legally speaking, the *Blockchain* validates transactions, replacing previously trusted entities
Treiblmaier (2018, p. 547)	A *Blockchain* is "a digital, decentralized and distributed ledger in which transactions are logged and added in chronological order with the goal of creating permanent and tamper-proof records"

these systems have repercussions regarding issues such as privacy, throughput, and the choice of consensus mechanisms.

Immutability is frequently mentioned as the central characteristic of the Blockchain, since it allows for the transformation of the "Internet of Information", in which digital data can be copied without loss of accuracy, into the "Internet of Value", in which units representing value can be transferred between peers and double spending can be prevented. Immutability is also highly desirable if transactions need to be tracked along the supply chain. However, this property comes at a cost. If data needs to be changed, which might be due to legal reasons (Posadas 2018), the Blockchain does not pose the most efficient data structure to do so. Furthermore, participation in public Blockchains is pseudonymous (or pseudo-anonymous), not anonymous,

Table 2 Blockchain characteristics

Characteristic	Consequences	
	Positive	Negative
Immutability	Internet of Value, traceability	Inflexibility
Transparency	Efficiency of data retrieval	Privacy, information leakage
Programmability	Execution in a deterministic manner	Unchangeable source code
Decentralization	Disintermediation	Disintermediation
Consensus	Minimize necessary trust	Energy consumption (PoW), potential centralization of power
Distributed trust	Establish trust	Elimination of personal relationships

which raises privacy issues as it does not preclude identification (Meiklejohn et al. 2016).

The transparency of Blockchains is achieved by allowing users read-only access to previous transactions and to inspect the content of smart contracts. This is especially important if products need to be tracked along the supply chain (Kshetri 2018). Again, it is crucial to differentiate between permissioned and permissionless Blockchains, with the former being run by members of a consortium and access thus restricted. In contrast, permissionless Blockchains, such as Bitcoin, allow for the inspection of blocks by everyone. While transparency and accountability are desirable in many instances, this might not hold true for all use cases. For example, private users might be concerned about sensitive personal data, and organizations might fear the leakage of confidential financial information.

The programmability of the Blockchain has rapidly improved in recent years. Bitcoin uses a basic scripting language, called Script, which intentionally avoids complex operations such as loops. In order to overcome this perceived limitation, the platform Ethereum (Wood 2014) introduced a Turing complete language called Solidity, which is currently the most popular language for the creation of so-called smart contracts (Szabo 1997): self-executing computer programs that execute in a deterministic and pre-defined way. However, this deterministic execution frequently lacks the flexibility needed in legal contracts and highlights the difficulties of reducing contractual relationships and the complexities of the real world into computer code (Mik 2017).

One of the most frequently cited characteristics of the Blockchain is its decentralized nature. This is not only true for the storage of data, but also for decision making and governance. Again, differences between Blockchain types exist, but in general no central authority is needed to validate transactions between peers. This leads to disintermediation, which, depending on the perspective, can be seen as both an advantage and a disadvantage. New governance structures can help to create more effective and efficient organizational structures and to reduce transaction costs. At the same time, disintermediation may be seen as a major threat for incumbents who hold strategic positions in existing supply chains and value networks (Treiblmaier 2018).

Decentralization is made possible by innovative consensus protocols across a network of nodes. Such protocols make sure that the task of compiling transactions and creating new blocks follows strict rules which do not favor one peer over another. The most widely known consensus algorithm, which is implemented in Bitcoin, is called proof-of-work (PoW) mining and is based on solving a mathematically demanding puzzle with dynamically adjustable complexities (Yuan and Wang 2018). During the evolution phase of Bitcoin, which saw a soaring exchange rate, miners invested more and more resources and PoW became notorious for its excessive use of energy. It is noteworthy, however, that PoW is only one out of a multitude of potential consensus algorithms used for permissionless networks, and various alternatives exist (e.g., proof-of-stake (PoS), which can be used in a hybrid form together with PoW; Byzantine fault tolerance-based consensus; crash fault tolerance-based consensus) (Nguyen and Kim 2018). Summarizing, the Blockchain can lead either to the consolidation of existing or the creation of new power structures.

Finally, the Blockchain enables the distribution of trust, such that it does not necessitate high levels of confidence in single authorities. Greiner and Wang (2015) introduced the notion of trust-free systems which use the Blockchain to create a verified, immutable and available record of transactions that is governed by the system itself. However, as Hawlitschek et al. (2018) point out, the conceptualization of trust depends on the context, which is in their study the sharing industry, and will depend on creating trusted interfaces. However, the potential elimination of existing relationships and the emergence of an economy that is controlled by automatically executed processes is not without dispute, as the disappearance of personal relationships might lead to undesirable consequences.

I do not list all of the characteristics of the Blockchain mentioned in the (grey and academic) literature, such as the data being chronological, time-stamped, and cryptographically sealed (Deloitte 2017), since those are usually means to an end. However, such characteristics should also be discussed in case studies if they represent an important factor in the respective research project. I recommend that every case study contains some reflection on why the respective characteristics of that particular Blockchain configuration were chosen from among the alternatives, why they were important, how they were applied, and what (un)intended consequences arose from their application.

The substantial interest surrounding the Blockchain has been fueled by the great variety of possible use cases and its potential applicability in many industries (Tapscott and Tapscott 2016). However, actual implementations must be assimilated within existing complex social, economic, institutional, regulatory and physical systems (Lacity and Willcocks 2018), which can generate the numerous practical problems of implementation shown in Table 3.

Swan (2015) lists various technical challenges, such as throughput, which determine the scalability of the Blockchain solution. This is mostly an issue for public Blockchains that depend on an elaborate consensus mechanism between peers. The Bitcoin network with a theoretical maximum of 7 transactions per second (tps) lags

Table 3 Blockchain challenges (Swan 2015; Lacity 2018b; Kshetri 2017; Saad et al. 2019; Lemieux 2016)

Challenge	Description
Throughput	Number of transactions being processed within a specific period of time
Latency	Amount of time before a transaction is processed
Size and bandwidth	The Blockchain grows over time as new blocks are constantly added. This also consumes considerable bandwidth for downloading data
Wasted resources	Blockchain-intrinsic inefficiencies such as redundant data transmission, storage and energy-consuming consensus protocols
Usability	Users' interactions with Blockchain applications
Versioning, hard forks, multiple chains	A multitude of Blockchain versions and forks facilitate attacks and hamper cross-transactions
Privacy	The right to control access to (personal) information as well as to delete it
Evidentiary quality, Trustworthiness of records	Questions pertaining to the truthfulness of content on the Blockchain
Lack of Standards	No standards have emerged yet for access rights, data structures and allowable transactions
Regulations	Legislation is lagging behind technological development
Shared governance	Blockchain solutions call for new structures that might disrupt existing governance
Viable ecosystem	The attraction of a critical mass of adopters
Attack Surface	The Blockchain as a target of potential attacks

far behind the processing power of VISA (2000 tps), Twitter (5000 tps) and advertising networks (>100,000 tps). A performance analysis of Hyperledger Fabric and Ethereum, two popular Blockchain platforms, showed that the former consistently outperformed the latter, but the authors still conclude that "both platforms are still not competitive with current database systems in term of performances in high workload scenarios" (Pongnumkul et al. 2017, p. 1). Another related issue is latency, the processing time for a transaction in a network, which, in the case of Bitcoin, amounts to 10 min. This processing time has been chosen on purpose to avoid chain splits, and will not be reduced in the future. Furthermore, in order to increase security it is recommended to wait for several confirmed transactions, which further increases latency (Swan 2015). Again, the situation might look quite different for permissioned networks that are less prone to threats such as double-spending attacks due to deliberately chosen validators. Further challenges include the ever-increasing size of Blockchains, which consumes a considerable amount of bandwidth due to redundancies in data storage and transfer, and which constitutes a waste of resources, which is most obvious in the case of the PoW consensus mechanism that essentially trades energy for security. The proliferation of different Blockchains furthermore leads to an increasingly complex and hard to use infrastructure that hampers communication between chains and facilitates attacks on smaller chains.

Privacy and the Blockchain is a complex issue which arises mainly due to the immutability of data on the Blockchain. The situation is especially complex for personal data relating to an identified or identifiable natural person. The European Union's General Data Privacy Regulation (GDPR), which took effect on May 25, 2018, provides a set of regulations to ensure that individuals within the EU and those that conduct transactions within the EU can guarantee the protection of individual data. The GDPR, however, was written with a centralized entity in mind that has the power to control access rights, which is not case when Blockchain technology is used. It is thus unclear how Blockchain technology will comport with the GDPR (Posadas 2018). However, as Kshetri (2017) points out, the Blockchain also bears the potential to strengthen cybersecurity and privacy by deterring cybercriminals and unauthorized data manipulators. Additionally, it offers the possibility of allowing individuals to control their own private data. It does not, however, guarantee the reliability of information and has limitations as a solution for keeping trustworthy digital records (Lemieux 2016).

Lacity (2018b) lists various managerial challenges that include the specification of standards for access rights, data structures, and allowable transactions. Furthermore, she points out that current legislation lags behind technological developments, which creates insecurity on the side of organizations. A largely unexplored area is the need for new organizational structures that are able to cope with the idiosyncrasies of the Blockchain (see also Treiblmaier 2018). Additionally, a major success factor of any technological solution is the attraction of a critical mass of adopters beyond the core originators, which is currently unclear for many Blockchain solutions that are still in an embryonic stage.

Finally, it must not be forgotten that the Blockchain is a potential target for manifold attacks. Just because the current cryptographic system and the chain of transactions in Bitcoin have so far withstood external attacks does not mean that Blockchain systems in general are resistant to all kinds of attacks. Saad et al. (2019) differentiate between three different attack areas, namely cryptographic constructs, the distributed architecture of the system, and the application context. They discuss a variety of potential attacks, including Blockchain forks, stale blocks and orphaned blocks, selfish mining, the 51% attack, DNS (domain name system) attacks, distributed denial of service attacks, consensus delays, Blockchain ingestion, double spending, and wallet theft.

A comparison between Tables 2 and 3 reveals various challenges (which might turn into serious problems during implementation or runtime) that are inextricably linked to the basic characteristics of the Blockchain. For example, conflicting goals such as creating publicly available solutions that guarantee security and privacy pose major technological, legal and organizational challenges. The same holds true if legal regulations demand the removal of data upon request, which contradicts immutability as a basic characteristic of the Blockchain. These are just some examples out of many potential areas of conflict that need to be carefully documented in case studies.

3   Case Study Research and the Blockchain

In his seminal book on case study research, Yin (2014) gives a twofold definition for case studies in which he differentiates between scope and features. More specifically, he defines a case study as "an empirical inquiry that investigates a contemporal phenomenon (the 'case') in depth and within its real-world context, especially when the boundaries between phenomenon and context may not be clearly evident" (p. 16). Since the phenomenon and the context are sometimes hard to distinguish, the features of a case also need to be considered (p. 17): "a case study inquiry copes with the technically distinctive situation in which there will be many more variables of interest than data points, and as one result relies on multiple sources of evidence, with data needing to converge in a triangulating fashion, and as another result benefits from the prior development of theoretical propositions to guide data collection and analysis". Yin explicitly differentiates between rigorous case studies and teaching cases, with the latter having less strict formal requirements.

Burns (2000, p. 459) laments that "the case study has unfortunately been used as a 'catch – all' category for anything that does not fit into experimental, survey, or historical methods". Much too often, case study research is reduced to being exclusively exploratory without having a proper methodological foundation. As a potential solution, Ridder (2017) presents a comprehensive and differentiated perspective and introduces a portfolio approach in which he presents four case study research designs, each of which exhibits different strengths. These designs, labeled "no theory first", "gaps and holes", "social construction of theory" and "anomalies", provide different contributions for building, developing and testing theory, and are discussed in more detail in the following section.

Case studies have a long tradition in IS. Benbasat et al. (1987) introduce case study research as a viable alternative to quantitative techniques that offers several advantages, such as independence from large samples sizes or distributional assumptions, as well as the potential of case studies to analyze a phenomenon within its context (i.e., an idiographic research strategy). Lee (1989) presents a scientific methodology for case studies and identifies four major problems, namely making controlled observations, making controlled deductions, allowing for replicability, and allowing for generalizability. He then describes how the alleged shortcomings of case studies can be overcome by using "natural controls" (e.g., by observing one person in varying, naturally occurring external situations), using logical reasoning for making deductions, adapting predictions while keeping the same theory and, finally, replicating case studies in different settings to ensure their generalizability. Lee furthermore suggests four considerations that can be used for a general assessment: (1) Does the case study consider any predictions through which the theory can be disproven? (2) Are all the predictions internally consistent? (3) Does the case study corroborate the theory through empirical testing? and (4) Does the case study eliminate rival theories?

Cavaye (1996) investigates case study research in IS and concludes that "case study research can be used in the positivist and interpretivist traditions, for testing and building theory, with a single or multiple case study design, using qualitative or mixed methods" (p. 227). Dubé and Paré (2003) focused on rigor in information systems positivist case research by investigating contemporaneous practices. They identified and coded 183 case articles from seven major IS journals and concluded "that while modest progress has been made with respect to some specific attributes or criteria, the findings are somewhat disappointing and there are still significant areas for improvement" (p. 620). They especially lament the fact that descriptive case studies lag far behind explanatory and exploratory studies with respect to several attributes. The core of their paper comprises detailed recommendations on how to improve case study research designs, which include the use of clear research questions, a priori specification of constructions, discussion of theory and units of analysis, description of the study context and roles of investigators, elucidation of the data collection process, use of multiple data collection methods, data triangulation, clarification of the data analysis process, use of field notes, empirical testing, application of cross-case patterns, and a comparison with extant literature.

Wynn and Williams (2012) introduce principles for case study research from a critical realist perspective. They derive their principles directly from ontological (e.g., independent reality, open systems) and epistemological (e.g., mediated knowledge, unobservability of mechanisms) assumptions of critical realism and propose five methodological principles, namely the explication of events, explication of structure and content, retroduction, empirical corroboration and triangulation, as well as the use of multiple methods.

A completely different approach is proposed by Avison et al. (2017): the French New Novel tradition. They argue that this style presents the richness of the problem situation and leaves it up to the reader to discover meaning from the narrative. As such, their approach does not provide specific guidelines and the authors themselves state that "there is no consensus on the techniques required to develop a narrative of this genre" (p. 267). However, they also provide a detailed analysis as to how this approach can be simultaneously demanding as well as inspiring, and might provide an antidote to publications that blindly follow a "formula". In a similar vein, my intention in this paper is not to favor a particular style or technique, but rather to illustrate the full range of available possibilities. Understanding different types of case studies thus presents an ideal starting point.

3.1 Typology of Academic Case Studies

As indicated in the previous section, case study research is a far wider-ranging and more powerful approach than many researchers might realize. Ridder (2017) presents a comprehensive typology that is based on the seminal work of four authors, namely Eisenhardt (1989) (no theory first, NTF), Yin (2014) (gaps and holes, GAH), Stake (1995) (social construction of reality, SCR), and Burawoy (2009) (anomalies, ANO). In Table 4 I highlight the main features of the respective approaches. A more detailed comparison can be found in Ridder (2017).

The general motivation for a specific case study distinguishes the four academic approaches. Whereas an NTF study starts with a couple of preliminary variables and constructs, but no assumed relationships, the research question in GAH is based on existing theory and strives to answer "how and why" questions. The main driving force behind SCR is the researchers' curiosity to understand a particular phenomenon, while an ANO case study specifically investigates why a specific situation cannot be explained by existing theory. Data collection also differs based on the design. Purposive sampling, which is used in GAH as well as SCR, chooses members of a population for inclusion in a study based on the researchers' judgment. The sampling approach in GAH is highly dependent on the goal of the case study, which might suggest the selection of extreme or unusual cases as well as common or revelatory cases. In SCR the case is either of general interest or may help to better understand a theoretical issue. Theoretical sampling is a variation of purposive sampling with a

Table 4 Case study research designs and their theoretical contributions (cf. Ridder 2017)

	No theory first (NTF)	Gaps and holes (GAH)	Social construction of reality (SCR)	Anomalies (ANO)
Motivation	Preliminary variables and constructs, no relationships	Existing theory	Curiosity in the case	Curiosity, contradictions
Data	Theoretical sampling	Purposive sampling	Purposive sampling	Theoretical sampling
Analysis	Constructs and relationships	Pattern-matching, analytic generalization	Categorical aggregation	Structuration, reconstruction of theory
Methods	Case descriptions, interviews, documents and observations	Case descriptions, interviews, documents and observations	Learning from the case, rich descriptions	Observation, interviews, dialogue between observer and participants
Theory focus	Building theory	Developing theory, testing theory	Building theory	Testing theory

stronger focus on identifying important theoretical constructs and their relationships (Ridder 2017).

As far as data analysis is concerned, the focus of NTF lies on the identification of emerging constructs within the case or between cases. GAH, in which a tentative theory exists, focuses on the correspondance between the researchers' framework or propositions and the data. The goal of SCR is to learn from the case and to come up with a categorical aggregation. Finally, data is also aggregated in an ANO study with a focus of theory reconstruction. In each study type, the methodological approach closely follows the intended research goal. In NTF, interviews, documents and observations can be used to discover relevant constructs and relationships. Similarly, a GAH approach relies on the confrontation of existing theory-based constructs and relationships with case descriptions resulting from interviews, documents and observations. In order to understand construct reality, a rich description of a particular case is completed in SCR, while an ANO approach relies on observation, interviews and dialogue between observer and participants to better understand why existing theoretical explanations have failed (Ridder 2017).

Eisenhardt and Graebner (2007, p. 30) point out that "Theory building from case studies is an increasingly popular and relevant research strategy", which is closest aligned with the NTF approach. Similarly, SCR strives to build theory from the rich descriptions gained during the analysis process, while the focus of GAH is more on developing and testing theory, and the goal of ANO is to test theory by emphasizing contradictions between existing theory and reality.

Case study researchers also have a substantial amount of freedom as far as the mode of argumentation is concerned. Dubois and Gadde (2002) highlight the different strengths of deductive, inductive and abductive approaches. Deduction works best for developing propositions from current theory and making them testable, induction strives to systematically generate theory from data, and abduction can be used for the discovery of new variables and relationships.

3.2 Blockchain Use Cases

It is a salient feature of the Blockchain that its characteristics allow for the creation of a multitude of (potential) use cases (Dieterich et al. 2017; Morabito 2017; Tapscott and Tapscott 2016; Lacity 2018a, b; White 2017; Leonard and Treiblmaier 2019; Treiblmaier and Umlauff 2019): cryptocurrencies, examples for smart contracts, crowdfunding, prediction markets, energy markets, smart property, settlements, processing, authenticity, traceability of products along the supply chain and visibility in data exchange, trade financing, international payments, know your customer (KYC), identity management, provenance, property, ownership, rights management, governance, digital certificates, digital identity, digital asset registry, escrow transfers, electronic voting, verified corporate due diligence, verified customer reviews, performance management systems, betting, tokenized incentive economies, digital rights, derivates markets, remittances, sustainability. This non-exhaustive list of use cases illustrates the potential of the Blockchain to transform organizations and their relationships. A comprehensive description of the respective use case is at the core of every case study and determines the methods being chosen.

3.3 Blockchain Case Studies in the Literature

In order to identify existing Blockchain case studies, I followed the guidelines for systematic literature reviews as suggested by Tranfield et al. (2003) and Watson (2015) and applied in Ngai et al. (2008) as well as Ngai and Gunasekaran (2007). I performed a database search using the terms "Blockchain" or "Distributed Ledger Technology (DLT)", in any combination with "case study", "use case" or "case". The databases I used were Business Source Premier from EBSCOhost and ScienceDirect as well as publicly available information on Google Scholar and ResearchGate. Furthermore, I screened the references of the selected publications to identify further papers of relevance. During the identification and selection process, it turned out that it was difficult to differentiate between full-fledged case studies and the documentation of single use cases, since many use cases were performed in close cooperation with the industry and embedded within more comprehensive projects. Furthermore, the term "case study" is frequently used for any kind of report in which project findings are reported, regardless of whether a rigorous approach was applied.

To select existing Blockchain cases studies, I decided to use as a relevant criterion the development or thorough discussion of (a) a prototype or an application, (b) a solution for a specific company, or (c) a solution for a particular industry. I did not include any white papers, which are frequently used by so-called ICOs (initial coin offerings) to promote their product and occasionally also refer to use cases. Table 5 lists the case studies that fulfill those selection criteria. I describe the methodological approach used in each case and the degree to which each study fulfils my recommendations for Blockchain case study research: the description of relevant Blockchain characteristics (cf. Table 2), the description of potential challenges that needed to be overcome (cf. Table 3), the research design with a focus on the underlying theoretical approach (cf. Table 4), and an evaluation of the outcome.

It turned out that Blockchain case studies are highly fragmented. Hardly any of them apply the suggested procedures for case studies that can be found in the academic literature. For example, I found only two case studies explicitly referring to theory. One is from Albrecht et al. (2018), who apply Diffusion of Innovations theory, the Technology-Organization-Environment framework and institutional economics to investigate Blockchain use cases in the energy sector. The other one is from Pazaitis et al. (2017), who build their study about the Blockchain and value systems in the sharing economy on the theory of value. Nonetheless, all of the case studies provide some insight on topics of interest to the industry and from which some insights can be drawn.

Table 5 Blockchain case studies

Author	Topic	Description
Albrecht et al. (2018)	The impact of theory-based factors on the implementation of various Blockchain technologies using cases in the energy sector	22 interviews using open questions and a semi-structured design. Open coding to identify relevant variables and axial coding to connect these variables to general factors Description of the relevant Blockchain characteristics Identification and description of various challenges (e.g., market power, regulation) Creation of a framework connecting factors found in the literature, constructs from the interviews, the impact on various use cases (e.g., microgrids, grid services) and the technology being used Application of Diffusion of Innovations (DOI) theory, the Technology-Organization-Environment framework and institutional economics
Angrish et al. (2018)	FabRec: A prototype for a peer-to-peer network of manufacturing nodes	Creation of a system framework that allows a decentralized network of users and service providers to operate in a decentralized manufacturing eco-system Description of the relevant Blockchain characteristics Identification of industrial implementation challenges Detailed description of the system implementation, as well as of the prototype implementation and evaluation. Development of a prototype that demonstrates the feasibility of connecting computing nodes and physical devices on a decentralized and interoperable network
Auricchio et al. (2017)	Potential impact of the Blockchain on the pricing model and organizational design of Ryanair as well as the behavior of pilots	Conceptual analysis using market equilibrium graphs and qualitative discussions Brief description of how Blockchain can help to support dynamic pricing, organizational decision making and risk management as well as customer service

(continued)

Table 5 (continued)

Author	Topic	Description
Biswas et al. (2017)	Development of a wine supply traceability system	Description of the relevant Blockchain characteristics Identification and description of the challenges (e.g., authenticity, provenance) Development of a framework highlighting the roles and relationships of various entities along the supply chain. The system enables transparency, accountability, safety and security along the supply chain
Gräther et al. (2018)	"Blockchain for Education" platform which issues, validates and shares certificates	Description of the system, including the conceptual system architecture, and the prototype implementation Discussion of security and privacy challenges Implementation of a prototype which deals with counterfeit protection as well as the secure access and management of digital certification
Karamitsos et al. (2018)	Smart contracts in the real estate industry	Presentation of the design of a smart contract following a traditional waterfall approach (analysis – design – implementation) Discussion of the importance of various Blockchain "parameters" (e.g., consensus mechanism, programming language, authorization) and types of Blockchain In their analysis phase the authors collect requirements from different actors/ roles (e.g., externally owned accounts, contract accounts, miners), in the design phase they elaborate on the major functions and processes of the smart contracts and, finally, they present the structure of the smart contract used in the implementation phase

(continued)

Table 5 (continued)

Author	Topic	Description
Khaqqi et al. (2018)	A seller/buyer reputation-based system in a Blockchain-enabled emission trading application	Creation of an Emission Trading Scheme (ETS) model. Illustration of a typical buying process for emission trading as well as the process of collecting, selecting and combining offers and buyer bids Detailed evaluation using a multi-criteria analysis of environmental performance, political acceptability and feasibility of implementation. The authors further discuss various processes of their proposed solution as well as transaction outputs. They propose a novel emission trading scheme that uses Blockchain technology to address management and fraud issues. Additionally, the system utilizes a reputation system to increase efficacy
Li et al. (2018)	A Blockchain cloud manufacturing system as a peer to peer distributed network platform	Presentation of a distributed peer-to-peer network architecture that improves the security and scalability of cloud manufacturing Discussion of Blockchain characteristics with a focus on IoT and cloud manufacturing Presentation of the proposed system architecture, illustration of the communication between different layers as well as the data sharing procedures and the roles of different key components The authors illustrate how the Blockchain can be applied in the manufacturing industry to improve trust and flexibility of cloud manufacturing Quantitative evaluation of the platform, security, and Blockchain Network (BCN) performance

(continued)

Table 5 (continued)

Author	Topic	Description
Lucena et al. (2018)	Grain Quality Assurance Tracking based on a Blockchain Business Network in Brazil	A case study in combination with an experiment focusing on a grain exporter business network Scrutinization of the Blockchain's applicability for business networks The high level architecture is presented. A Blockchain-based certification will potentially lead to an added valuation of around 15% for non-genetically modified soy
McConaghy et al. (2017)	Ascribe.io: A solution to identify and authenticate ownership of digital property	The authors explicitly justify their case study approach to examine why and how phenomena occur in complicated contexts Detailed description of the problems related to the attribution, transfer and provenance of digital property They describe the design of the service, which started in April 2014 and went out of operation in September 2018, with a focus on the functioning of the transactions
Mengelkamp et al. (2018)	The Brooklyn Microgrid: A Blockchain-based microgrid energy market without the need for central intermediaries	Documentation of the case including a project overview, and the market mechanism Discussion of the relevant Blockchain characteristics with a focus on microgrid energy markets Presentation of the concept of a Blockchain-based microgrid that enables consumers and prosumers to trade self-produced energy in a peer-to-peer fashion on microgrid energy markets. The authors show a high level topology of their solution and match their solution against seven components of microgrid energy markets Evaluation of the Brooklyn microgrid against required components of microgrid energy markets
Morabito (2017)	Brief presentation of eight Blockchain practices	Short description of eight cases that share an identical structure: The goal of the case is outlined, followed by description of the developer and the application itself

(continued)

Table 5 (continued)

Author	Topic	Description
O'Dair and Beaven (2017)	The disruptive potential of the Blockchain in the record industry	Analysis of the challenges the record industry is facing Identification of Blockchain implementation barriers and challenges Detailed description of how the Blockchain can enable accurate and easily available copyright data, near-instant micropayments and transparency through the value chain
Olsen et al. (2018)	Architecture of Lykke Exchange, a marketplace for the exchange of financial assets	Presentation of Lykke Exchange, a global marketplace for the exchange of financial assets Discussion of the properties of Blockchain and Bitcoin Description of the design of Lykke and the underlying IT architecture in detail. Discussion of various design considerations and a comparative analysis of exchanges with different degrees of centralization pertaining to criteria such as trust, privacy, risks of hacks and speed of transaction execution
Pazaitis et al. (2017)	Backfeed: A three-layered system that allows for the production, recording, and actualization of value	Exploration of the Blockchain's potential to enable value systems that support the dynamics of social sharing Envisioning of Backfeed, a system that comprises three layers: (a) production of value, (b) record of value, and (c) actualization of value
Sikorski et al. (2017)	Application of the Blockchain to facilitate machine-to-machine (M2M) interactions and establish an M2M electricity market in the chemical industry	Exploration of Blockchain within the chemical industry. Proof-of-concept implementation that facilitates machine-to-machine (M2M) interactions Description of the relevant Blockchain characteristics Discussion of various challenges, such as security, privacy, wasted resources and usability Demonstration that it is possible to employ blockchain technology to facilitate M2M interactions and create an M2M electricity market in the context of the chemical industry via the IoT

(continued)

Table 5 (continued)

Author	Topic	Description
Strugar et al. (2018)	Study of electric autonomous vehicles that use DLT for microtransactions	Description of an electric autonomous vehicle charging and billing architecture as well as a proof of concept Discussion of DLT and Tangle, the underlying technology of IOTA Proposal of a new charging and billing mechanism for electric vehicles that charge their batteries while in a charging station or on the move. Their proof-of concept employs an IOTA based payment system with machine-to-machine communication to carry out microtransactions
Sullivan and Burger (2017)	Application of the Blockchain to e-residency in Estonia	Investigation of the potential of the Blockchain for e-residency Detailed discussion of the implications for Estonian E-Residency using the Blockchain as well as the security implications Examination of the legal, policy and technical implications of this development in Estonia
Treiblmaier and Zeinzinger (2018)	Austrian case study in which the Blockchain was used to play the game Go on the façade of a public building	Findings from six narrative interviews with Blockchain developers, managers and users. Use of a holistic and single case design Several implementation challenges and problems are reported The Blockchain was used for recording all moves of the ancient game Go, which was played on the façade of a public building. The goal of this study was to familiarize end users with the Blockchain and to create some public awareness for internet-related privacy issues

(continued)

Table 5 (continued)

Author	Topic	Description
Ying et al. (2018)	E-commerce platform of Hainan Airlines	Description of the implementation of the Blockchain in an e-commerce context at Hainan Airlines. Statements from qualitative interviews are included Value was created by (1) issuing cryptocurrencies, (2) protecting sensitive information and (3) eliminating institutional intermediaries Several lessons learned are discussed, including the creation of own cryptocurrencies, the protection of sensitive information and the elimination of intermediaries
Zhang et al. (2018)	FHIRChain: Applying Blockchain to securely share clinical data	Analysis of health-related requirements and their implications for Blockchain-based systems Detailed discussion of the technical requirements for Blockchain-based clinical data sharing Development of FHIRChain, a blockchain-based architecture designed to meet health-related requirements by encapsulating the standards for sharing clinical data. Illustration of the composition and structure of the architecture with modular components as well as two process workflows: (1) user registration and authentication and (2) data access authorization

4 Designing and Reporting Blockchain Case Studies

Figure 1 presents a framework illustrating how Blockchain use cases, case study research, the creation of artifacts and the creation, development and testing of theory are connected. The starting point is a specific phenomenon, most likely an envisioned Blockchain use case as listed above, embedded in its real-world context. In a first step, a careful preparation of the case is needed, in which it is crucial to outline the design of the study, including the motivation for applying Blockchain technology, data sources and the context. As is shown in this paper, case study research is a fairly flexible and multifaceted research approach that accommodates different methodological designs, but I still recommend to explicitly outline the basic structure and the goals of the project and how they influence the choice of methods. A crucial part of any Blockchain case study is the description of the relevant Blockchain characteristics (as shown in Table 2) and how they potentially contribute to the solution for a specific problem.

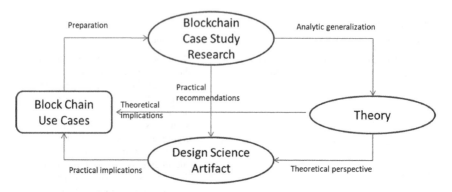

Fig. 1 A framework for Blockchain case study research

4.1 Blockchain Case Study Framework

After outlining the justification for why a Blockchain-based approach is used, there are two basic streams of research, which can be differentiated by their goals of either focusing on theory or creating an artifact. Yin (2014) writes that "some theory development as part of the design phase is highly desired" (p. 37), but, as was shown above, alternative academic case study designs exist (Ridder 2017), or researchers may decide to create a teaching or industry case. If the focus is on the creation of theory, analytic generalization is applied, which is a two-step process that involves the illustration of how the findings of a case study bear upon a particular theory, theoretical construct, or theoretical sequence of events as well as the application of the same theory to implicate similar situations (Yin 2010). If the goal is the creation of an artifact, practical recommendations are needed which enable replication studies to track and trace the design, development and implementation process.

Theory-oriented research aims at theoretical implications for further use cases, but does not necessarily preclude the creation of a design science artifact. In a frequently cited case study, Markus (1983) reports on the implementation of a financial information system, but also applies and evaluates three different theories of resistance in the same study. She thus illustrates how a theoretical perspective can actually help in the solution of a practical problem. The generation of a design science artifact, which in the case of Blockchain might be a prototype, a full-fledged application or the implementation of a smart contract, has practical implications for the final evaluation of the use case. Either the original goal is achieved—("success story"),—which calls for further replication studies in different scenarios, or the deviation from the originally specified project goals necessitates several modifications. Failures should therefore be documented, which is something that rarely happens in the industry, but should be a hallmark of academic research. It has to be noted, however, that design science research does not have to exclusively focus on design artifacts. As Baskerville et al. (2018) highlight, design theorizing is an expected norm in design science research, which implies that there is "some reflection on the advance in design knowledge that is being made" (p. 363).

A careful documentation of the deviations between initial expectations and concrete implementations is highly beneficial for future related studies. In the case of the Blockchain those experiences are especially important since, for example, the engineering process for smart contracts needs to be designed to account for the immutability of the Blockchain (Sillaber et al. 2018). Other than in traditional software design, Blockchain-oriented design needs to prepare for all contingencies already during the conceptualization phase of a project. Currently there is a lack of research that evaluates the extent to which this is possible. The goal of the framework shown in Fig. 1 is to give a rough overview of how case studies and their related methodological and epistemological approaches can be connected.

4.2 Blockchain Case Study Structure

The checklist in Table 6, which is loosely based on recommendations for systematic reviews from Moher et al. (2009), includes various sections (topics) to be included and discussed in a Blockchain case study. The actual structure clearly depends on the chosen design (e.g., research case, teaching case, industry case), but several principles might equally apply for different designs. As is the case in any academic paper, the abstract should highlight the major findings of the study in a nutshell, and will not be discussed any further herein.

In order to put a case study into context, researchers initially need to clearly outline the goal(s) of the project, as well as the justification for applying a Blockchain-based solution in this specific setting. Ideally, similar cases from the literature are considered. Defining and describing the type of Blockchain being evaluated and/or deployed (cf. Table 1) as well as the organizational context of the study is crucial to examining the fit between them. This includes all conditions and circumstances that are of relevance for the project, including internal and external driving forces as well as existing organizational structures and top management support. Numerous decision trees can be found in the literature that scrutinize the general applicability of the Blockchain. A recent white paper from the World Economic Forum (2018, p. 6) summarizes decisive filter questions that help organizations to identify those scenarios in which a Blockchain application may not be appropriate. Most importantly, these scenarios include settings in which there are no intermediaries or brokers that need to be removed, no digital assets are used, and no permanent authoritative record of a digital asset can be created. For a comprehensive description of a Blockchain project at a conceptual stage, Feig (2018) recommends asking the following ten questions: (1) Who are the users?, (2) What data do users input?, (3) Are any inputs irreversible?, (4) Who are the peers?, (5) How do peers create blocks?, (6) What do peers validate?, (7) How do peers validate?, (8) How do peers reach consensus?, (9) Is the Blockchain immutable?, and (10) How are peers incentivized? In short, the first part of any Blockchain case study must lay the foundation for the rest of the paper

Table 6 Case study checklist

Section/topic	Content
Abstract	
Structured summary	Background; objectives; case selection criteria; methodological approach; data sources; participants; major findings; limitations; conclusions and implications
Introduction	
Research and Application Goals	Description of goals being addressed and their relevance for academia and/or the industry
Case rationale	Rationale for the case study in light of previous research/studies
Blockchain rationale	Rationale for using the Blockchain
Blockchain definition	Definition of the Blockchain technology being used
Blockchain characteristics	Description of Blockchain characteristics
Methodology	
Methods	Justification and explanation of the methods being applied
Information sources	Description of information sources (e.g., company resources, databases, interviews) and date of information retrieval
Data collection process	Method of data extraction from primary and secondary sources
Variables and their relationships	Description of variables as well as their relationships. Frameworks or models might be used
Results	
Presentation of results	Detailed results of the case study
Study challenges	Description of Blockchain challenges and how they were dealt with
Discussion	
Summary of evidence	Summary of the main findings and consideration of their relevance for the main stakeholders
Evaluation	Validity assessment of the study
Limitations	Study limitations in light of the original research goals
Conclusions and implications	General interpretation of the results in the context of other evidence and implications for future research
Funding (if applicable)	
Funding	Funding sources for the case study; role of funders for the case study

by pinpointing the organizational setting as well as the technology and its intended purpose. Researchers especially need to document how they apply the respective characteristics of the Blockchain (cf. Table 2) and how they tackle the major challenges that arise during an implementation (cf. Table 3). Both industry and academia are at an early stage of Blockchain development and the careful description and documentation of case studies can help the industry to build on previous success stories and avoid pitfalls.

Subsequently, the methodology of the project needs to be introduced and explained, which differs significantly based on the role of theory. If the research is explicitly theory-focused, the four different designs shown in Table 4—NTF, GAH, SCR, and ANO—need to be described in detail. The respective selection obviously impacts the choice of methods and data sources as well as the interpretation of the findings. If the focus is more on the creation of artifacts, the traceability and documentation of the case are paramount. However, this does not preclude theorizing, which can be done in an "interior mode" (i.e., producing theory for design and action) and an "exterior mode" (theorizing about artifacts in use) (Baskerville et al. 2018). A comprehensive documentation of the data collection process is needed for all types of cases studies, while an in-depth description of the variables, which might include latent constructs, and their respective relationships is especially important for theory-related Blockchain studies. Independent of the type of case study, a certain amount of rigor is needed for the research design as well as for data collection and analysis processes (Darke et al. 1998).

The presentation of the Blockchain results, again, heavily depends on the chosen design, but I recommend the inclusion of an additional discussion on how the characteristics of the Blockchain (cf. Table 3) were applied and how the Blockchain challenges (cf. Table 3) were overcome. Depending on the overall goal of the case study, it might be useful to detail various business processes or the development of smart contracts which deviate from previous software engineering approaches. Sillaber et al. (2018) suggest an elaborated engineering process which takes into account the immutability of smart contracts and is not based on the traditional waterfall model, but rather details the following phases: conceptualization, implementation, approval, submission, execution and finalization. Elaborating on these stages helps readers of Blockchain case studies to reproduce the development and deployment of smart contracts.

The discussion summarizes the main findings and their relevance for major stakeholders. Additionally, a comparison with previous research is advisable, which especially includes the identification and description of "surprising" results. Lacity (2018a, b, p. 48) suggests structuring Blockchain applications around four major components: (1) the application interface or access point (e.g., digital asset exchange, digital wallet, bridge/gateway services, interfaces with existing systems, IoT devices), (2) use cases (e.g., track & trace, payments, voting), 3) code bases (e.g., Hyperledger Fabric, Ethereum, Corda, Multichain), and (4) Blockchain protocols (i.e. specific rules regarding access and how transactions are structured, addressed, transmitted, routed, validated, sequenced, secured, and added to the permanent record). Her framework provides a possible structure to systematically discuss the findings.

In order to provide a comprehensive quality assessment, Yin (2014, p. 45) suggests an evaluation of construct validity, internal validity, external validity, and reliability. This is especially crucial for studies that build on previous research, develop and test theory, or strive to create a new research agenda. Given that the Blockchain is an evolving technology, a thorough analysis of limitations in light of the original research goals will help to critically shed light on its possibilities. As I have already noted above, the careful documentation and analysis of unsuccessful projects will also benefit future Blockchain endeavors. Carefully drafted conclusions and implications, which extend previous research, will further help to build a comprehensive Blockchain research agenda. Finally, if applicable, funding sources and the role of funders have to be specified.

5 Conclusion

In this paper I summarize key principles of various types of case study research and propose guidelines on how to design, conduct, and report Blockchain case studies. However, the structure I provide in this paper, along with suggestions on how to incorporate theory and ensure validity, is not meant as an exhaustive checklist to be used by reviewers in order to assess the overall quality of a publication. In other words, it should not be the case that the guidelines "become more important than the study" (Holtkamp et al. 2019) or that the paper is "written according to a 'formula'" (Avison et al. 2017, p. 271). Instead, I concur with Klein and Myers (1999, p. 78) who write "while we believe that none of our principles should be left out arbitrarily, researchers need to work out themselves how (and which of) the principles apply in any particular situation". I therefore believe that researchers will benefit most from this paper by consulting it prior to designing their study and selecting those parts that they deem useful for their specific research goals.

In a nutshell, I recommend that researchers.

- provide a rationale for the use of Blockchain technology,
- define the type of Blockchain they use,
- describe the Blockchain characteristics that are relevant for their study and how they are implemented,
- discuss the Blockchain challenges encountered during the case study and how they influenced the outcome,
- justify the chosen case study type,
- outline the respective case study methodology,
- present and discuss the results appropriately for the specific case study type,
- provide a critical evaluation of their results,
- embed their results into a broader context, thus enabling incremental research.

Case study research provides a lot of freedom for academics and allows for the combination of various theoretical and practical approaches. By carefully designing their studies, researchers can ensure that they get the most out of this versatile approach. Blockchain technology is currently in its infancy and case study research provides many useful tools to systematically generate knowledge on which future research can build, be it theory-based or practically oriented. The recommendations I present in this paper are intended to enable such an incremental research agenda and I hope that many researchers will find them useful. Future research can easily adapt my recommendations to the investigation of other disruptive technologies.

References

Alabi, K. (2017). Digital blockchain networks appear to be following Metcalfe's Law. *Electronic Commerce Research and Applications, 24,* 23–29.

Albrecht, S., Reichert, S., Schmid, J., Strüker, J, Neumann, D., & Fridgen, G. (2018). Dynamics of Blockchain implementation—A case study from the energy sector. In *Proceedings of the 51st Hawaii International Conference on System Sciences*, Hawaii, USA.

Angrish, A., Craver, B., Hasan, M., & Starly, B. (2018). A case study for Blockchain in manufacturing: "FabRec": A prototype for peer-to-peer network of manufacturing nodes. *Procedia Manufacturing, 26,* 1180–1192.

Auricchio, A. Fontela, B., Goel, A., He, Yuxiang, Jungmair, C., & Roa, A. (2017). Ryanair: Impact of Blockchain on the organizational design of Ryanair, report. https://de.slideshare.net/AntonioAuricchio/the-impact-of-blockchain-on-ryanairs-dynamic-prices. Accessed July 14, 2018.

Avison, D., Malaurent, J., & Eynaud, P. (2017). A narrative approach to publishing information systems research: Inspiration from the French New Novel tradition. *European Journal of Information Systems, 26*(3), 260–273.

Bahga, A., & Madisetti, V. K. (2017). *Blockchain applications: A hands-on approach*. Berlin: VPT.

Baskerville, R., Baiyere, A., Gregor, S., Hevner, A., & Rossi, M. (2018). Design science research contributions: Finding a balance between artifact and theory. *Journal of the Association for Information Systems, 19*(5), 358–376.

Beck, R., Avital, M., Rossi, M., & Thatcher, J. B. (2017). Blockchain technology in business and information systems research. *Business & Information Systems Engineering, 59*(6), 381–384.

Benbasat, I., Goldstein, D. K., & Mead, M. (1987). The case research strategy in studies of information systems. *MIS Quarterly, 11*(3), 369–386.

Biswas, K., Muthukkumarasamy, V., & Tan, W. L. (2017). Blockchain based wine supply chain traceability system. In *Proceedings of the Future Technologies Conference* (pp. 1–7). Vancouver, Canada.

Burawoy, M. (2009). *The extended case method. Four countries, four decades, four great transformations, and one theoretical tradition*. Berkeley: University of California Press.

Burns, R. B. (2000). *Introduction to research methods*. London: SAGE publications.

Cavaye, A. L. M. (1996). Case study research: A multifaceted research approach for IS. *Information Systems Journal, 6*(3), 227–242.

Darke, P., Shanks, G., & Broadbent, M. (1998). Successfully completing case study research: Combining rigour, relevance and pragmatism. *Information Systems Journal, 8*(4), 273–289.

Deloitte. (2017). Key characteristics of the Blockchain. Deloitte Touche Tohmatsu India LLP. https://www2.deloitte.com/content/dam/Deloitte/in/Documents/industries/in-convergence-blockchain-key-characteristics-noexp.pdf. Accessed October 1, 2018.

Dieterich, V., Ivanovic, M., Meier, T., Zäpfel, S., Utz, M., Sandner P. (2017). Application of blockchain technology in the manufacturing industry. Working Paper, Frankfurt School Blockchain Center.

Dubé, L., & Paré, G. (2003). Rigor in Information Systems positivist case research: Current practices, trends, and recommendations. *MIS Quarterly, 27*(4), 597–635.

Dubois, A., & Gadde, L. (2002). Systematic combining: An abductive approach to case research. *Journal of Business Research, 55*(7), 553–560.

Eisenhardt, K. M. (1989). Building theories from case study research. *Academy of Management Review, 14,* 532–550.

Eisenhardt, K., & Graebner, M. E. (2007). Theory building from cases: Opportunities and challenges. *Academy of Management Journal, 50*(1), 25–32.

Feig, E. (2018). A framework for Blockchain-based applications. https://arxiv.org/abs/1803.00892.

Glaser, B., & Strauss, A. L. (1967). *The discovery of grounded theory: Strategies for qualitative research.* Chicago: Aldine Publishing Company.

Government Office for Science. (2016). Distributed ledger technology: Beyond block chain. A report by the UK government chief scientific advisor. London, GB: Government Office for Science.

Gräther, W., Kolvenbach, S., Ruland, R., Schütte, J., Torres, C. F., & Wendland, F. (2018). Blockchain for education: Lifelong learning passport. In W. Prinz & P. Hoschka (Eds.), *Proceedings of the 1st ERCIM Blockchain Workshop 2018* (pp. 1–8). Reports of the European Society for Socially Embedded Technologies, Amsterdam, Netherlands.

Greiner, M., & Wang, H. (2015). Trust-free systems—A new research and design direction to handle trust issues in P2P systems: The case of Bitcoin. In *Proceedings of the Americas Conference on Information Systems*, Puerto Rico.

Hawlitschek, F., Notheisen, B., & Teubner, T. (2018). The limits of trust-free systems: A literature review on blockchain technology and trust in the sharing economy. *Electronic Commerce Research & Applications, 29,* 50–63.

Hoelscher, J. (2018). Taking the lead on Blockchain: As the technology behind Bitcoin finds new uses, internal auditors must assess how the risks may impact the organization. *Internal Auditor, 75*(1), 19–21.

Holotiuk, F., Pisani, F., & Moormann, J. (2018). Unveiling the key challenges to achieve the breakthrough of Blockchain: Insights from the payments industry, In *Proceedings of the 51st Hawaii International Conference on System Sciences*, Waikoloa (pp. 3537–3546).

Holtkamp, P., Soliman, W., & Siponen, M. (2019). Reconsidering the role of research method guidelines for qualitative, mixed-methods, and design science research. In *Proceedings of the 52nd Hawaii International Conference on System Sciences*, Maui, Hawaii, USA (pp. 6280–6289).

Hsieh, H. -F., & Shannon, S. E. (2005). Three approaches to qualitative content analysis. *Qualitative Health Research, 15*(9), 1277–1288.

Iansiti, M., & Lakhani, K. R. (2017). The truth about Blockchain. *Harvard Business Review, 95*(1), 118–127.

Karamitsos, I., Papadaki, M., & Barghuthi, N. B. A. (2018). Design of the Blockchain smart contract: A use case for real estate. *Journal of Information Security, 9,* 177–190.

Khaqqi, K. N., Sikorski, J. J., Hadinoto, K., & Kraft, M. (2018). Incorporating seller/buyer reputation-based system in blockchain-enabled emission trading application. *Applied Energy, 209,* 8–19.

Kim, K., & Justl, J. M. (2018). Potential antitrust risks in the development and use of Blockchain. *Journal of Taxation & Regulation of Financial Institutions, 31*(3), 5–16.

Klein, H. K., & Myers, M. D. (1999). A set of principles for conducting and evaluating interpretive field studies in information systems. *MIS Quarterly, 23*(1), 67–94.

Kshetri, N. (2017). Blockchain's roles in strengthening cybersecurity and protecting privacy. *Telecommunications Policy, 41*(10), 1027–1038.

Kshetri, N. (2018). Blockchain's roles in meeting key supply chain management objectives. *International Journal of Information Management, 39,* 80–89.

Lacity, M. (2018a). *A manager's guide to Blockchain for business: From knowing what to knowing how.* Warwickshire, UK: SB Publishing.

Lacity, M. (2018b). Addressing key challenges to making enterprise Blockchain applications a reality. *MIS Quarterly Executive, 17*(3), 201–222.

Lacity, M. C., & Willcocks, L. P. (2018). *Robotic process and cognitive automation: The next phase.* Steve Brooks Publishing.

Lee, A. S. (1989). A scientific methodology for MIS case studies. *MIS Quarterly, 13*(1), 33–50.

Lemieux, V. L. (2016). Trusting records: Is Blockchain technology the answer? *Records Management Journal, 26*(2), 110–139.

Leonard, D. & Treiblmaier, H. (2019). Can cryptocurrencies help to pave the way to a more sustainable economy? Questioning the economic growth paradigm. In H. Treiblmaier & R. Beck (Eds.), *Business transformation through Blockchain—Volume I.* Cham, Switzerland: Palgrave Macmillan.

Li, Z., Barenji, A. V., & Huang, G. Q. (2018). Toward a blockchain cloud manufacturing system as a peer to peer distributed network platform. *Robotics and Computer-Integrated Manufacturing, 54,* 133–144.

Lucena, P., Binotto, A. P. D., da Silva Momo, F., & Kim, H. (2018). A case study for grain quality assurance tracking based on a Blockchain business network. *Symposium on Foundations and Applications of Blockchain (FAB '18),* Los Angeles, California, USA.

MarketsandMarkets. (2017). Blockchain market by provider, application (payments, exchanges, smart contracts, documentation, digital identity, supply chain management, and GRC management), organization size, industry vertical, and region—global forecast to 2022, Market Report, MarketsandMarkets.com.

Markus, M. L. (1983). Power, politics, and MIS implementation. *Communications of the ACM, 26*(6), 430–444.

McConaghy, M., McMullen, G., Parry, G., McConaghy, T., & Holtzman, D. (2017). Visibility and digital art: Blockchain as an ownership layer on the Internet. *Strategic Change, 26*(5), 461–470.

Meiklejohn, S., Pomarole, M., Jordan, G., Levchenko, K., McCoy, D., Voelker, G. M., & Savage, S. (2016). A fistful of Bitcoins: Characterizing payments among men with no names. *Communications of the ACM, 59*(4), 86–93.

Mengelkamp, E., Gärttner, J., Rock, K., Kessler, S., Orsini, L., & Weinhardt, C. (2018). Designing microgrid energy markets. A case study: The Brooklyn microgrid. *Applied Energy, 210*(C), 870–880.

Mik, E. (2017). Smart contracts: Terminology, technical limitations and real world complexity. *Law, Innovation and Technology, 9*(2), 269–300.

Moher D., Liberati A., Tetzlaff J., Altman D. G., The PRISMA Group. (2009). Preferred reporting items for systematic reviews and meta-analyses: The PRISMA statement. *PLoS Med, 6*(7), e1000097. https://doi.org/10.1371/journal.pmed1000097

Morabito, V. (2017). *Business innovation through Blockchain: The B^3 perspective perspective.* Cham, Switzerland: Springer.

Mougayar, W. (2016). *The business Blockchain: Promise, practice, and application of the next internet technology.* Hoboken, NJ: Wiley.

Nakamoto, S. (2008). *Bitcoin: A peer-to-peer electronic cash system* (pp. 1–9). Self-Published paper.

Narayanan, J., & Clark, J. (2017). Bitcoin's academic pedigree: The concept of cryptocurrencies is built from forgotten ideas in the research literature. *ACM Queue, 15*(4), 1–30.

Ngai, E. W. T., & Gunasekaran. (2007). A review for mobile commerce research and applications. *Decision Support Systems, 43*(1), 3–15.

Ngai, E. W. T., Moon, K. K. L., Riggins, F. J., & Yi, C. Y. (2008). RFID research: An academic literature review (1995–2005) and future research directions. *International Journal of Production Economics, 112*(2), 510–520.

Nguyen, G. -T., & Kim, K. (2018). A survey about consensus algorithms used in Blockchain. *Journal of Information Processing Systems, 14*(1), 101–128.

O'Dair, M., & Beaven, Z. (2017). The networked record industry: How blockchain technology could transform the record industry. *Strategic Change, 26*(5), 471–480.

Olsen, R., Battiston, S., Caldarelli, G., Golub, A., Nikulin, M., & Ivliev, S. (2018). Case study of Lykke exchange: Architecture and outlook. *The Journal of Risk Finance, 19*(1), 26–38.

Önder, I., & Treiblmaier, H. (2018). Blockchain and tourism: Three research propositions. *Annals of Tourism Research, 72* (September). https://doi.org/10.1016/j.annals.2018.03.005.

Pazaitis, A., De Filippi, P., & Kostakis, V. (2017). Blockchain and value systems in the sharing economy: The illustrative case of Backfeed. *Technological Forecasting and Social Change, 125*, 105–115.

Peck, M. (2017). *Reinforcing the links of the Blockchain.* IEEE: IEEE Future Directions Initiative White Paper.

Pongnumkul, S., Siripanpornchana, C., & Thajchayapong, S. (2017). Performance analysis of private Blockchain platforms in varying workloads. In *26th International Conference on Computer Communication and Networks (ICCCN)*, Vancouver, Canada.

Posadas, D. V. (2018). The internet of things: The GDPR and the Blockchain may be incompatible. *Journal of Internet Law, 21*(11), 1–29.

Ridder, H. -G. (2017). The theory contribution of case study research designs. *Business Research, 10*(2), 281–305.

Saad, M., Spaulding, J., Njilla, L., Kamhoua, C., Nyang, D.-H., & Mohaisen, A. (2019). Overview of attack surfaces in Blockchain. In S. S. Shetty, C. A. Kamhoua, & L. L. Njilla (Eds.), *Blockchain for Distributed System Security* (pp. 51–66). Wiley-IEEE Press, Hoboken, New Jersey, USA.

Schueffel, P. (2017). Alternative distributed ledger technologies: Blockchain vs. Tangle vs. Hashgraph—A high-level overview and comparison. *SSRN Electronic Journal*, 1–8.

Sikorski, J. J., Haughton, J., & Kraft, M. (2017). Blockchain technology in the chemical industry: Machine-to-machine electricity market. *Applied Energy, 195*(C), 234–246 (Elsevier).

Sillaber, C., Gallersdörfer, U., Waltl, B., Felderer, M., & Treiblmaier, H. (2018). Toward an integrated process model for smart contract engineering. In *Pre-ICIS Workshop on Blockchain and Smart Contract* (pp. 82–86), December 13, San Francisco, USA.

Stake, R. E. (1995). *The art of case study research.* London, Thousand Oaks: Sage Publications.

Strugar, D., Hussain, R., Mazzara, M., Rivera, V., Lee, J.-Y., & Mustafin, R. (2018). On M2M micropayments: A case study of electric autonomous vehicles. *IEEE International Conference on Blockchain* (Blockchain-2018), July 30–August 3, 2018. Halifax, Canada.

Sullivan, C., & Burger, E. (2017). E-residency and blockchain. *Computer Law and Security Review, 33*(4), 470–481.

Swan, M. (2015). *Blockchain: Blueprint for a new economy.* Sebastopol, CA, USA: O'Reilly Media.

Szabo, N. (1997). The idea of smart contracts. Nick Szabo's papers and concise tutorials. https://www.fon.hum.uva.nl/rob/Courses/InformationInSpeech/CDROM/Literature/LOTwinterschool2006/szabo.best.vwh.net/idea.html. Accessed May 1, 2018.

Tapscott, D., & Tapscott, A. (2016). *Blockchain revolution: How the technology behind bitcoin is changing money, business, and the world.* New York: Penguin.

Tranfield, D., Denyer, D., & Smart, P. (2003). Towards a methodology for developing evidence-informed management knowledge by means of systematic review. *British Journal of Management, 14*(3), 207–222.

Treiblmaier, H. & Zeinzinger, T. (2018). Understanding the Blockchain through a gamified experience: A case study from Austria. In *25th European Conference on Information Systems*, June 23–28, Portsmouth, UK.

Treiblmaier, H., & Beck, R. (2019a). *Business transformation through Blockchain—Volume I.* Cham, Switzerland: Palgrave Macmillan.

Treiblmaier, H., & Beck, R. (2019b). *Business transformation through Blockchain—Volume II.* Cham, Switzerland: Palgrave Macmillan.

Treiblmaier, H. (2018). The impact of the Blockchain on the supply chain: A theory-based research framework and a call for action. *Supply Chain Management: An International Journal, 23*(6), 545–559.

Treiblmaier, H., & Umlauff, U. (2019). Blockchain and the future of work: A self-determination theory approach. In M. Swan, J. Potts, S. Takagi, P. Tasca, & F. Witte (Eds.), *Blockchain economics: Implications of distributed ledger technology* (pp. 105–124), New Jersey, USA.

Watson, R. T. (2015). Beyond being systematic in literature reviews in IS. *Journal of Information Technology, 30*(2), 185–187.

White, G. R. T. (2017). Future applications of blockchain in business and management: A Delphi study. *Strategic Change, 26*(5), 439–451.

Wood, G. (2014). Ethereum: A secure decentralised generalised transaction ledger. Ethereum Project Yellow Paper, 1–32.

World Economic Forum. (2018). *Blockchain beyond the hype: A practical framework for business leaders.* White Paper, World Economic Forum, Geneva: Switzerland.

Wynn, J. D., & Williams, C. K. (2012). Principles for conducting critical realist case study research in Information Systems. *MIS Quarterly, 36*(3), 787–810.

Yin, R. (2010). Analytic generalization. In A. J. Mills, G. Durepos, & E. Wiebe (Eds.), *Encyclopedia of case study research* (pp. 21–23). Thousand Oaks, CA: SAGE Publications, Inc.

Yin, R. K. (2014). *Case study research: Design and methods.* Thousand Oaks, California: Sage.

Ying, W., Jia, S., & Du, W. (2018). Digital enablement of Blockchain: Evidence from HNA group. *International Journal of Information Management, 39,* 1–4.

Yli-Huumo, J., Ko, D., Choi, S., Park, S., & Smolander, K. (2016). Where is current research on blockchain technology? A systematic review. *PLoSONE, 11,* 1–20.

Yuan, Y., & Wang, F. -Y. (2018). Blockchain and cryptocurrencies: Model, techniques, and applications. *IEEE Transactions on Systems, Man, and Cybernetics: Systems, 48*(9), 1421–1428.

Zhang, P., White, J., Schmidt, D. C., Lenz, G., & Rosenbloom, S. T. (2018). FHIRChain: Applying Blockchain to securely and scalably share clinical data. *Computational and Structural Biotechnology Journal, 16,* 267–278.

Horst Treiblmaier is a professor in international management at Modul University Vienna, Austria. He received a Ph.D. in Management Information Systems in 2001 from the Vienna University of Economics and Business in Austria and worked as a Visiting Professor at Purdue University, University of California, Los Angeles (UCLA), University of British Columbia (UBC), and the University of Technology in Sydney (UTS). He has more than fifteen years of experience as a researcher and consultant and has worked on projects with Microsoft, Google, and the United Nations Industrial Development Organization (UNIDO). His research interests include the economic and business implications of Blockchain, cryptoeconomics, methodological and epistemological problems of social science research and gamification. Currently he serves on the board of the "City of Blockchain", an association promoting blockchain and cryptographic technologies. His research has appeared in journals such as *Information Systems JournalStructural Equation Modeling*, The *DATA BASE for Advances in Information Systems,Communications of the Association for Information SystemsInformation & ManagementJournal of Electronic Commerce ResearchJournal of Global Information ManagementSchmalenbach Business ReviewSupply Chain Management: An International JournalInternational Journal of Logistics Management, andWirtschaftsinformatik (Business & Information Systems Engineering).*

From a Use Case Categorization Scheme Towards a Maturity Model for Engineering Distributed Ledgers

Thomas Osterland and Thomas Rose

Abstract This contribution focuses on the maturity of the engineering of business applications for a *trusted collaboration in business networks*. Distributed ledgers emerge as technology enabler for establishing trust across business partners while *blockchain* is often used as a synonym. Hence, mature knowledge for application engineering and quality assured methods for selecting technology platforms for distributed collaboration are essential. When choosing a *Distributed Ledger Technology (DLT)* it is difficult to compare the different technologies in order to identify the one technology best suitable for a specific use case. Platforms' maturity for distributed ledgers cannot be assessed sufficiently. Detailed knowledge about the technological details of platforms and functional characteristics are sometimes sparse. To start with, we propose a characterization approach for distributed ledgers based on various classification schemas. This characterization is founded in an evaluation of use cases and prototypical implementations as well as a record of projects conducted. The approach allows one to sort out unsuitable technologies at an early stage. Since the automation of business cooperation is one of the core benefits of DLT, *Smart Contracts* for the automation of business processes and *Distributed Autonomous Organizations (DAO)* for the specification of collaboration networks furnish a key benefit for business re-engineering with DLT. Levels of maturity for collaboration specification are defined to distinguish different computational and organizational powers in contract enforcements.

Keywords Platforms for distributed ledgers and blockchain applications · Blockchain decision trees · Governance · Engineering maturity · Correctness of smart contracts · Validation of DAO

T. Osterland (✉)
Fraunhofer FIT, Schloss Birlinghoven, 53754 Sankt Augustin, Germany
e-mail: Thomas.Osterland@fit.fraunhofer.de

T. Rose
Fraunhofer FIT & RWTH Aachen University, Schloss Birlinghoven, 53754 Sankt Augustin, Germany
e-mail: Thomas.Rose@fit.fraunhofer.de

© Springer Nature Switzerland AG 2020   33
H. Treiblmaier and T. Clohessy (eds.), *Blockchain and Distributed Ledger Technology Use Cases*, Progress in IS, https://doi.org/10.1007/978-3-030-44337-5_2

1 Introduction

Ledgers are a well-established principle for a reliable governance of organisational processes. A ledger basically maintains and controls the consistency of records of transactions. A core organisational principle of ledgers is *centralisation*. A ledger manages all transactions for a specific purpose, e.g., land & property registry or driving licenses. All processes run in light of a specific governance with centralized processes in terms of data management, control and authority.

Once moving towards distributed ledger technologies (DLT) the concept of centralisation is replaced by *distribution* with an essential need for *consensus*. Hence, DLT or blockchain technology is considered as a new means for cooperation management. Cooperation is not any longer governed by centralised authorities, i.e. the *intermediaries*, but a network of participating nodes seeking consensus on the transactions that are mutually *believed* in a networking partnership. Thus, DLT is an enabler for new kinds of business collaboration.

On the one hand, DLT serves as enabler for the distribution of transaction management. Rather than following a centralised approach for data management as in prevailing data base technology, DLT goes beyond decentralisation and fosters a distributed maintenance of transactions in a peer of networking nodes. *Consensus* among participating nodes emerges as new requirement for network maintenance. Yet, methods and algorithms with their laurels and darts are known. However, consensus building is still an open research challenge with respect to the different collaboration characteristics. Yet, there is an array of methods for establishing trust with different service levels.

On the other hand, DLT is also a concept for defining process collaborations and the certification of partnerships in open business networks. *Smart Contracts* allow for a specification of business collaboration—not only in light of Electronic Businesses (Subramanian 2018) but also for the automation of cooperation patterns—in terms of rules and process descriptions that cannot be tampered, i.e. the execution of any of these cooperation processes is authentic and immutable. Hence, Smart Contracts come as enabler for establishing networks of cooperating partners that are governed by collaboration rules embarking an *Decentralised Autonomous Organizations (DAO)*. Osterland and Rose presented such a DAO for a full-scale automation of the business process for a *Smart Replenishment Box* as well as *Vehicle Control*[1] at the International Industrial Fair in Hannover in 2018, which illustrates the automation of collaboration processes as well as the immutability of transaction records for revision safety. Thus, the Smart Replenishment Box presents a value generating business opportunity with secured processes in an open partnership.

A core ingredient to these approaches is distributed ledger or blockchain technology. DLT comes with a transactional account for distributed data management as well as trust in the automaton of business processes via Smart Contracts or chain code as named in some systems. However, DLT should not be considered as the *Silver Bullet*

---

[1]A description of the demonstrator can be found at: https://www.fit.fraunhofer.de/en/fb/cscw/blockchain/smart-contracts.html.

for mass data management in operational scenarios for production processes such as fine blanking in mechanical engineering. Such processes often generate Mega Byte of data every second, which certainly out parses any performance realities as well as visions of DLTs.

DLT rather focus on certification matters for the correctness of data and respective production processes, i.e. a certificate of the last production slot will be maintained by a blockchain rather than the entire data set of product assessment. Thus, management of operational data remains the turf of production management systems while audit certificates of such processes will be maintained by DLT. Moreover, the automation of business collaborations including trust is considered as key for embarking on new business opportunities. DLT is no more considered disruptive but as key enabler for new business opportunities and networks. Hence, DLT surfaces as new intermediary raising two essential questions: (1) what is the maturity of blockchain platforms and (2) how to engineer business collaborations following ideas of *Capability Maturity Models (CMM)*, which have boosted the engineering of software solutions (Humphrey 1989).

This paper is organised as follows. In Sect. 2 we review categorizations of use cases for distributed ledgers as proposed in literature. Our own proposal of a use case categorization scheme is elaborated subsequently. In Sect. 3 we discuss an array of attributes of DLT platforms that allow one to distinguish different instances. This is based on our work on sustainability engineering as reported in Osterland and Rose (2018), but extended by a discussion considering the relations of use case categories and DLT attributes. Section 4 surveys methods and tools for quality assessment. It starts with product quality and then elaborates on processes for the engineering of quality. Based on these quality review of engineering Sect. 5 presents our maturity model for the engineering of distributed ledgers. Finally, Sect. 6 summarizes the major findings and pencils the application perspective of our approach towards a mature engineering perspective for DLT applications.

2   A Categorization of Distributed Ledger Use Cases

There exists a large body of papers and surveys discussing the potential of DLT in different application areas. Although several approaches for the suitability of certain application designs for DLT are known under the label of *Blockchain Decision Flowcharts*[2] no overall classification scheme for application and implementation platforms have emerged until now. We analyse classifications of use cases that other

---

[2]A keyword search in the net unveils many proposals for deciding the suitability of DLT for certain use cases. Some of these proposals come from consulting companies such as Deloitte while others come for platform vendors such as Hyperledger Fabric or academia to stress the difference between databases and DLT (Chowdhury et al. 2018). Common to most of these proposals is a structured flowchart to build a decision tree for the suitability.

authors propose and elaborate on the use cases commonly related with DLT. This survey furnishes the basis for our core categories as introduction to the characterization model of DLT in Sect. 2.2.

2.1   Overview of DLT Classification Schemes

Classification schemes intend to characterise different use case and technology opportunities according to application domains, functional services, stakeholder networks or anchor objectives such as tokenisation.

Tama et al. (2017) follow for instance a domain-oriented separation and propose the classification into four categories: *financial industry, healthcare, business and industry* and *other applications*. The first category contains primarily crypto currencies, as for instance Bitcoin (Nakamoto 2008). *Healthcare* applications are mostly operating and standardising platforms for a secure management and exchange of patient data, while the category *business and industry* comprises *Internet of Things (IoT)* applications, as well as DAOs, supply chains and micro payment systems for the fair settlement of cloud computing resource consumptions. The trailing category of *other applications* is further sub-divided into a mix of system classes: *(digital) rights management, reputation systems, digital content distribution, WiFi authentication,* and *IoT security.*

Pilkington (2016) discusses the uses of DLT as a cryptographic currency, as well as a token representing and proving the provenance and possession of valuable objects, i.e. real world artefacts are mapped to *tokens* serving as *digital twins.* Additional fields of applications include: *digital identity provider, voting systems, financial industry applications* (besides the currency applications, also the trading of securities) and *supply chain management.* Pilkington (2016) argues that the transparency of DLTs enables a more holistic and global version of a supply chain to which he refers as global commodity chain.

An additional use case in the financial field is the "Social Inclusion in the Developing World" (Pilkington 2016) for connecting the world population via mobile phones to the banking system and a stable currency system. Still two questions remain: who operates the DLT network and what entity guarantees economic stability? Unmanaged crypto currencies, as for instance Bitcoin are very volatile with serious stability issues due to its primary use for speculation (cf. Weber 2014). *Stable coins* are still in an infancy stage, but appear promising for online payment services. Overall, the classification of use cases is strongly related to financial applications, while other applications are neglected.

While authors like Pilkington (2016) and Crosby (2016) emphasize the potential of DLTs in financial services, others expose the *notarial certification* of documents as important use case. Within the financial perspective, companies and organisations are enabled to emit shares directly to potential shareholders, while DLT can uniquely identify assets as a notary system in order to track possessions and provenance. In this regard the authors refer to the music industry with the idea of automatically billing royalty dependent receivables.

Applications in cloud computing as well as IoT applications are also mentioned by the authors. They further raise counterfeiting as potential application, which strongly depends on the notarial certification of documents or the tracking of assets.

Another proposal beyond cryptographic currencies is given by Tsilidou and Foroglou (2015). They emphasize its role as base technology to securely store transaction-based activities and introduce several application categories: *currencies, contracting, voting systems, intellectual property rights, smart properties,* enabling a secure management of values and applications in the financial industry comprising the direct emission of company shares, but also other concepts as for instance crowd founding.

Casino et al. (2018) conduct a systematic literature review to identify categories that partially overlap with the categories of Tama et al. (2017): They propose two categories: *business,* what comprises financial applications and *healthcare* to collect use cases that for instance relate to the secure management of patient data. Apart from these two categories Casino et al. (2018) choose a more fine-grained classification schema: They introduce a single category for *supply chain* use cases and additional categories for the *internet of things* and *privacy and data management.* The latter category holds use cases, as for instance identity management, but also clearing house applications for tracking the usage of data.

Pompianu and Bartoletti (2017) conduct a data-based analysis of smart contract platforms regarding usage, application domains and characteristics of smart contracts being operational in the net. The authors analyse the smart contracts in detail and categorize them into 5 different groups: *finance, notary, game, wallet* and *library.* The finance category comprises for instance contracts that "manage, gather or distribute money as preeminent feature" (Pompianu and Bartoletti 2017) or the notary category, that comprises contracts "exploit[ing] the immutability of the blockchain" (Pompianu and Bartoletti 2017). The authors conclude that the financial categories comprise the most contracts, while the application of wallets is least populated.

An interesting aspect of this analysis is that it shows the current spread of smart contracts being operational in the net. Most contracts are related to the financial industry what might be explained by the fact that distributed ledger technologies initially started with the use case of crypto currencies (cf. Nakamoto 2008). However, the logistics of documents in inter-modal transportation has at least comparable challenges, but perhaps not found interested supporters. A similar argument explains the popularity of the notary category. Early use cases apart from currency were such applications, as for instance the concept of coloured coins on top of the Bitcoin blockchain.

Other categories are less populated and lead to the impression that smart contracts belonging to this category are merely on a prototype level. Limiting the survey to prevailing technologies like Ethereum and Bitcoin might distort the analysis, since often blockchain technologies claim their direction towards certain applications. Moreover, smart contracts that can be created on Bitcoin are very limited. One should keep in mind that by analysing the currently implemented smart contracts we only get an impression what is implemented right now, but this does not necessarily cover the full potential of the distributed ledger technology. Certain applications need time to be accepted by the users, while others cannot be implemented right now, since connecting points are missing regarding law and government, although the technology could handle it.

Following the discussion of the categorization schemes so far, it is a challenge to come up with a uniform and synchronized classification schema that is expressive and sufficiently fine-grained to enable a coherent separation of technologies, while on the other hand being coarse-grained enough to result in an observable amount of use case categories, with an categorization rule set that is easy to apply.

2.2 Lessons Learnt from the Various Approaches for Categorizing

Different application perspectives and use perceptions resulted in a manifold landscape of classification schemes as summarized before. Our approach extends some of the aforementioned categorizations, while promoting a different set of criteria to tell use cases apart. We also give sample use cases for each category to provide an intuition what flavours of use cases a category comprises. Please note, that we do not separate interacting smart contracts in our consideration. In contrast to Pompianu and Bartoletti (2017), we do not introduce a category library, since we consider a smart contract together its library as one smart contract and thus, as one application.

Our categories are founded in the basic characteristics and services of a distributed ledger rather than following application-oriented use cases as pivotal discriminator. Please note that categories such as healthcare (as proposed in Tama et al. 2017; Tsilidou and Foroglou 2015) are too coarse-grained in our categorization system and hence refer to multiple categories. In a bird's eye perspective our categories are itemized below while each category will be elaborated in detail afterwards:

- **Finance**—Crypto currencies, as Bitcoin (Nakamoto 2008), micro payment systems, the trading of securities—*replacing intermediaries in classical finance networks*;
- **Notary**—Digital rights management, patent management, personal certificates for capabilities such education or vocational training (Gräther et al. 2018)—*immutable management of capabilities and privileges*;
- **Processes**—business process engines, decentralized autonomous organisations (DAO), supply chain—*automation of cooperation logics and business processes in distributed partner networks*;
- **Provenance**—supply chain, proof of ownership, tracking of responsibilities—*monitoring the life cycle of assets be they hard or soft*.

Finance: The finance category describes use cases that rely on the *distribution of properties that a distributed ledger can maintain*, i.e. the usage of currency itself, but also the creation of representative currencies, as gift certificates or incentives programs. It also includes the use of blockchain as a market place for trading goods or securities with direct payment.

Notary: The notary category describes use cases that *utilize the signature and timestamping mechanism of the blockchain*. Examples include the proof of the original publishing of a song or movie. Please note that we do not consider the requirement of a transactional update history to this category. Thus, use cases in the notary category comprise problems, where a value must be securely stored, but it is of no interest, how this value is updated throughout its lifecycle.

Processes: This category comprises use cases that employ the characteristics of distributed ledger technology to *securely execute program logic* (smart contracts). For instance, all use cases that depends on the automated execution of processes are part of this category.

Provenance: DLT stores a transaction history and some of these transactions depend on each other. So for instance a certificate that proofs the ownership of a house can be moved to another person by adding a transaction to the distributed ledger. By retracing the transactions one can explore the history of an element on the ledger. All the use cases that depend on the *immutable transaction-based history* of an element or person are also part of this category. This is an extension of category *Notary*.

Often use cases might refer to multiple categories. This is in particular the case for complex use cases. Also one might argue, that the implementation of a currency, which is a use case of category *finance*, requires *provenance*, since one needs to comprehend the account balance to ensure other's creditworthiness. However, we argue that there are applications where provenance is required without the need of maintaining a currency system. Therefore, we distinguish these categories. Similar arguments can be found for other connections between the proposed categories.

3   Comparing Distributed Ledger Technologies

In this paper we compare and emphasize important characteristics of implementation platforms of DLT in order to enable the selection of a technology for a concrete use case, i.e. what platform fits best to specific application requirements. In Osterland and Rose (2018) we discussed a number of distributed ledger characteristics for reasons of comparison. We re-formulate these attributes here and extend them to suit the more general idea of the final goal of our approach to furnish the grounds for a maturity model for engineering DLT applications (Fig. 1).

The **Permissioned/Public** attribute indicates, whether the considered technology can be used for the creation of public or permissioned networks. Permissioned networks are restricted in the sense that it is not possible for a party to join the network without the consent of other network participants.

Note that public ledgers can be always elevated to permissioned systems, by using additional technologies such as VPN. However, we do not consider such approaches

Fig. 1 Characterizing
attributes of DLT platforms

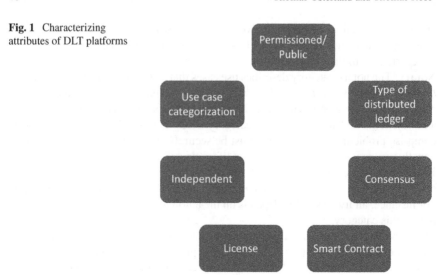

in our rating but evaluate, whether a permission system is part of the ledger's core functionality.

The **Distributed Ledger Type** attribute shows the ledger type. Possible types are blockchain, hash graphs and DAGs. Of course, there exists subtypes and hybrids. A mere move from a list structure towards "more powerful" data structures has significant impacts on data access and retrieval as well as paralyzing input operations and maintaining their consistency.

The **Consensus** field answers the question of the utilized consensus protocol applied on the ledger. Examples include *proof-of-work* or *proof-of-stake*, which are popular in public ledger networks or *Practical Byzantine Fault Tolerance (PBFT)* and *Raft (selecting a leader for consensus building)* on the other hand, which are often used in permissioned networks. Note that a clear categorization of consensus algorithms can be difficult, since they are often combinations of multiple protocols to inherit the advantages of different approaches. Consensus algorithms are often even not disclosed.

We do not compare consensus protocols or discuss their potential issues in this section. An overview and a discussion of practically applied consensus algorithm is given by Cachin and Vukolic (2017). The authors compare different consensus algorithms and consider the distributed ledger consent from the viewpoint of replication research. They reduce proposed consensus protocols to well-researched variants and try to determine potential issues in the actual implementation. They also argue that many proposed protocols do not follow proper cryptographic best-practices in their development, as full-disclosure reviews or formal verification.

The **Smart Contract** attribute indicates, whether smart contracts are supported on-chain, that is, contracts are executed within the blockchain nodes. If so, it is important to consider the supported languages for the development of smart contracts. This can help in deciding, whether smart contracts can be developed in house or if it is necessary to employ external competence. The group of EVM (Ethereum Virtual Machine) based development languages describe smart contracts that can be developed with languages in the Ethereum eco system, as *Solidity* or *Viper*. Another popular approach for implementing smart contracts is to utilize virtual machines for executing smart contracts and allows the use of arbitrary languages. This is for example the case in *Hyperledger Fabric* with *Docker*.

The **License** attribute covers the license of the technology. Sometimes there is no license information provided or there are scenarios where multiple licenses exist. One for commercial use and one for private use. However, knowledge about the used licenses is important for running distributed ledger applications in production.

The **Independent** attribute is used to indicate, whether a technology is based on another technology, as for instance by utilizing pegging. *Pegging* refers to the publication of specific certificates about the state of one blockchain in others blockchains—typically open ones—as *proof of content*. Hence, a manipulation becomes unfeasible because the public blockchain needs also to be manipulated. Some technologies are sidechains of more popular ledgers, as for instance Bitcoin.

The **Use Case Categorization** attribute contains the use case categories, that are supported by the considered technology (cf. Sect. 4 for more information).

Selecting these attributes for categorizing distributed ledger technologies is a result of our experience from implementing different distributed ledger use cases and thereby assessing different technologies. An approach to identify a distributed ledger technology based on the requirements and constraints of a specific project has been discussed in a former publication by Osterland and Rose (2018). But others also rely on this collection of attributes for characterizing distributed ledger technologies as well as fostered under the label of *Blockchain Decision Flowcharts*.

Pompianu and Bartoletti (2017) compare 6 different smart contract platforms with respect to criteria: as whether the technology works independently or in combination with another distributed ledger technology, if it is a public or a permissioned ledger, the employed consensus protocol and the programming languages of the smart contracts. We correspond with the selected criteria for assessing distributed ledger technologies and build upon it. However, we extend the collection of considered characteristics by the provided license, the question, whether a platform supports smart contracts at all—so in contrast to Pompianu and Bartoletti (2017) we are not solely interested in smart contract platforms, but in distributed ledgers in general. We also consider the distributed ledger types not limited to blockchains, but also considering alternative data structures, as for instances directed acyclic graphs (DAG).

Finally, one remark to a general constraint in selecting the analysed technologies. As an additional filter criterion we only consider technologies, where the source code is publicly available. If one does not have access to the source code to potentially analyse it, one can never fully trust it what questions the reliability of this ledger technology in first place.

Based on these technology attributes we are able to assess different technologies.

4 Evaluating Software Maturity—Various Approaches for Assessing the Quality of Software and Engineering Processes

This section firstly surveys software quality and maturity models for assessing the quality of software in order to evaluate their applicability to the engineering of distributed ledgers, which is the prime focus of our research. To start with, we first review measurements for software quality. Then, we turn towards the engineering process as decisive criterion.

Measuring the quality of software is an open research topic for decades. First approaches concentrate on the evaluation of complete programs, while in the early century with the broad use of component libraries, the specific evaluation of software components gained focus. Miguel et al. (2014) denote models of the former category as basic models, since they evaluate a software program as a whole, while the latter are denoted as tailored quality model. A tailored quality model evaluates the quality of a functional component and is often adapted to suit its particular characteristics.

In general, there are a variety of different schools of how to approach the quality measurement of software. While some rely heavily on code measurements (cf. Samoladas et al. 2008), others approach it by taking the perspective of a user and evaluate the software with respect to different categories (Miguel et al. 2014; Samarthyam et al. 2013). Software usability is also a research topic with a strong relation to software quality evaluation.

More recent approaches measure particularly the quality of open source projects. The fact that the source code is accessible enables the use of code measures and in addition, when considering open source projects hosted on open platforms, as e.g. Github,[3] it is even possible to consider the dynamics of the community (e.g. number of issues, contributions, average commits per contributor, etc.) that develops a software program or a component library.

Remarkable is the huge number of survey papers (Miguel et al. 2014; Jung et al. 2004), that compare different approaches to measure the quality of programs and program components. It indicates the interest in this topic and emphasizes the long history of research resulting in different approaches for measuring software quality. Continuously developed over the time these approaches represent changing perspectives in software engineering, verifiability, the emergence of open source code repositories (as for instance Github), the development of new code measures and so on. It also indicates a certain lack of consensus regarding the usability and efficiency of these approaches. So in the eyes of the research community it seems that there is no ultimate one-fits-all approach.

The evaluation of software quality has great importance from a business perspective as well as for practical applications. So standards are provided to organize the quality measurement procedure. The *ISO SQuaRE* standard (2011) for the evaluation of software quality differentiates five categories of quality features: Functionality,

---

[3]https://www.github.com.

Reliability, Usability, Efficiency, Maintainability and Portability. Every category has subcategories, which must be individually rated on a scale when testing the software. The ISO SQuaRE standard (2011) is the succeeding standard of the *ISO/IEC 9126* standard Software Engineering (2001) which introduced the categories in a first quality model. Jung et al. (2004) evaluated the application of the quality model introduced in Software Engineering (2001) by polling companies and discuss the problems of such a static approach. So it is not proven that certain procedures determined by the standards are actually efficient or purposeful for assessing the quality of software and as a second argument the evaluation of different subcategories depends on the provided scale. The assessment is subjective and influenced by the shape of the scale as for instance, whether a person can differentiate between three divisions or five. Choosing a suitable scale is a non-trivial task.

Recent approaches are particularly interested in measuring the quality of open source projects for determining their maturity and providing a decision guideline, whether it should be used in a project or not. The different evaluation procedures vary widely. Approaches already exist that strive to automate the evaluation process as much as possible (Samoladas et al. 2008), while other lay their focus on a reliable decision whether it is usable in the environment of a specific organization (Taibi et al. 2007).

Samoladas et al. (2008) build upon the claim that the quality of a software directly depends on the quality of the underlying source code. The authors evaluate the source code with respect to a number of quality features, as maintainability, reliability and security. For the evaluation procedure the authors partially rely on the quality model described in the ISO/IEC 9126 standard (Software Engineering 2001). A number of established software measures are used to automate the evaluation of source code. The authors point out, that the development of new code metrics is an ongoing process, while the evaluation of their efficiency and results is controversial. So they concentrated on the generally accepted metrics in their approach. As an example the authors evaluate the number of critical bugs in the last six months of an open source project.

A popular recent approach that evaluates the software quality starting in the architectural design phase of a software project is *Method for Intensive Design Assessment MIDAS* (Samarthyam et al. 2013) proposed by SIEMENS, which evaluated their approach with various in-house software projects. It demarcates from other approaches by strongly weighting the freely and project-dependent selectable assessment goals. Thereby Samarthyam et al. (2013) introduce three perspectives that enable the project evaluation: The "Ility-Based View" breaks down the influence of specific design problems to quality of the resulting software, the "Design Principles-Based View" emphasises the relationship of design problems or the software quality with the disregard of design principles during development and the "Constraint-Based View" emphasises the relationship of the resulting software quality and the contempt of project constraints. The MIDAS approach is an evolution of existing approaches on which MIDAS is based and that, according to the authors, showed their qualities and efficiency in concluded projects.

When considering software quality models or maturity models that are specifically fashioned for the field of distributed ledger technologies the available approaches and papers covering this topic are remarkably sparse. There is the maturity model for blockchain proposed by Wang et al. (2016). It is based on the *Capability Maturity Model (CMM)* (Paulk et al. 1993), that tries to measure or deduce the quality and maturity of software by regarding the underlying software development process. It distinguishes five categories describing the software development processes of an organization: (1) *Initial*: No defined processes, (2) *Repeatable*: the process is informally defined so that process participants can execute it repeatedly, (3) *Defined*: the process is formally defined in standard definitions, (4) *Capable*: the process execution is evaluated and measured and (5) *Efficient*: the processes are continuously improved and optimized.

Wang et al. (2016) adapt the CMM to be applicable on distributed ledger technology and provide a guideline of aspects that allow organisations to evaluate the actual usability of blockchain technologies. Thereby they introduce analogously to the CMM five different levels: (1) *Initial*: describes the non-organised beginning of a ledger implementation, (2) *Repeatable*: which describe Wang et al. (2016) as phase "wherein some experiences are borrowed from similar" implementations (3) *Defined*: which covers the question of the documentation quality of an implemented technology, (4) *Managed* stage: where the quality of the implementation is tested using software engineering methods and finally the 5'th stage *Optimizing*, in which the implementation is continuously improved.

Although we agree that these aspects will give a good idea of the software quality of blockchain implementations we are concerned that the proposed organizational levels are partially vague and impossible to analyse thoroughly. So the differences between the first and the second phase is particularly blurry. Aspects and concepts of other technologies are used, as early as one considers the implementation of a similar software (as for instance another blockchain variant) or in case a project uses a library as for instance a crypto library. Measuring the documentation quality in advance is also very elaborate. Just by considering the amount of available documentation gives no clue about its quality. We personally experienced this in a project, where we used Hyperledger Fabric early after the version 1.0 switch. The documentation was taken over from the earlier version, without adaption to the crucial changes in the software.

Another process maturity approach is described as *SPICE* (Software Engineering—Process assessment—Part 5, 2012). It proposes a reference model that entails a *process* and a *capability* dimension. The process dimension defines processes that if applied, lead to a mature software development process. These processes are ordered in five functional categories: *customer–supplier, engineering, supporting, management* and *organisation*. The capability dimension aims at the evaluation of the implemented processes. The evaluation is done using assessments and lead to a rating comprising 6 different levels: 0) *Incomplete process*, (1) *performed process*, (2) *managed process*, (3) *established process*, (4) *predictable process* and (5) *optimising process*. So an organisation that implements a software development rated as level 5 is considered to produce high quality software. Compared to other approaches SPICE is relatively strict in the assessment guidelines. Even the selection process of an accessor is determined. The maturity rating is derived from rating process attributes, as for instance *process performance* or *work product management*. Thereby the rating scale consists of four value: Not achieved, partially achieved, largely achieved and fully achieved. Since the evaluation results strongly depend on the ability and experience of the assessor there exists high requirements to the qualifications and competency.

All the discussed methods and automated evaluation approaches are very promising and our valuation model partially depends on them. We see some problems and challenges that come with their application on distributed ledger technologies. The required information for doing the evaluation is often not available or unambiguously interpretable. The efficiency and basic functionality of proposed metrics is controversial and evaluation results strongly depend on the experience and knowledge of the evaluating person. Although (partially) proven for the area of regular software there are no application or evaluation results of the proposed models on the field of distributed ledger technologies.

Our approach is based on concepts of existing evaluation models, but follows a slightly different path. From experience we learned that the information about the technologies that would allow a thorough evaluation is hard to come by. The documentation is often incomplete or outdated, the analysis of the source code by code measures is not very meaningful, since often technologies are directly based on the source code of other technologies. So for example the permissioned blockchain *Quorum*[4] is a fork of the *Ethereum*[5] blockchain and their node implementation, called *geth*,[6] is forked from the Ethereum geth node. The latter is a stable node implementation tested in hundreds and thousands of hours of production runtime, while the former is a comparatively new implementation developed and maintained only by a fraction of the people maintaining the Ethereum geth node. However, due to the large overlaps in source code, applied code measures might provide similar results.

Performance results are almost never reproducible and heavily depend on the employed benchmark environment due to network effects. Hence transaction throughput can hardly serve as classifier for different DLTs. The problem is, that almost every (permissioned) DLT application have different requirements on the production environment and often they differ also compared to other production environments. We experienced that throughput claims measured in a benchmark environment are limited to providing a rough estimation of potential transaction throughput. Yet, throughput will quickly decrease, when considering, real world network aspects, node shutdowns, due to maintenance tasks, software bugs in the node implementations or in other layers of the network stack of the operating system, extensive size of the ledger or simply because of limited bandwidth.

---

[4]https://github.com/jpmorganchase/quorum.

[5]https://www.ethereum.org/.

[6]https://github.com/ethereum/go-ethereum.

5 Maturity Modelling for the Engineering of Distributed Ledgers

Our maturity model for the engineering of distributed ledgers distinguishes different levels of capabilities and functional scopes. The model ranges from the mere use of DLT for application design via structured frameworks for a suitability assessment towards the use of smart contracts as means for automation towards the specification and implementation of self-governing business collaborations in terms of DAOs. Finally, the top level is characterized by the use of tools for assuring formal correctness of smart contracts and their inter-relations.

Hence, engineering capabilities extend from a mere of use of DLT via structured decision processes plus process automation towards the specification of collaboration networks by interacting smart contracts with model checking for assuring formal correctness.

Capability maturity models (Humphrey 1989; Paulk et al. 1993) typically distinguish five different levels:

1. *Initial*—Organisations are going to start the use of engineering processes and tools.
2. *Repeatable*—Basic engineering processes are practiced, but no overall coordination inside the organisation is in place, i.e. different projects might run different processes.
3. *Defined*—Deep knowledge about the engineering processes is available. Hence, processes can be designed at an organisation-wide scale in order to share processes across multiple projects. In addition, rules for project-specific customizations are known.
4. *Managed*—Engineering goals are formulated and different process areas have been defined and populated in order to raise the quality of engineering processes. Most of the measures are of qualitative nature and design rationales are known to achieve goals qualitatively.
5. *Optimizing*—The entire organization focuses on a continuous improvement of processes by searching for bottlenecks and formally analysing the performance of engineering processes. Quantitative measures are in place in order to steer change management for process improvement.

We do minic this upscaling of capabilities inside our maturity model for the engineering of distributed ledgers.

1. *Initial*—Organisations use blockchain technology just for the development of prototypes to assess the benefits of DLT. Minimal Viable Products (MVP) are built to explore the re-engineering the processes or changing governance structures due to a potential replacement of intermediaries. Border lines between prevailing database technology and DLT are blurred. Basic intention is to explore potential benefits and the selection of blockchain platforms is rather random.
2. *Structured*—The selection process of use cases to be implemented by a blockchain platform is structured such as by Klein et al. (2018), i.e. specific

criteria have been defined to distinguish blockchain from prevailing database technology. Moreover, the selection of a suitable implementation platform is governed by a technology assessment as presented in Sect. 3 while the design of a sustainable partner network also follows a structured course of action as presented by Osterland and Rose (2018). To-iterate, processes for deciding the suitability of use cases as well as technology selection and governance design are defined. Thus quality of the application is assured by well-defined processes.

3. *Automation (Smart Contracts)*—DLT is not any longer just considered as a distributed transaction manager with means for consensus building and trust enabling, but also understood as vehicle for process automation on the basis of smart contracts. Smart contracts are employed to represent the logics of business collaboration or an enforcement of complex data dependencies. Smart contracts represent in both cases enforcements. Yet, the scope of smart contracts refers to single dependencies between data or business processes.

4. *Business collaboration (DAO)*—Once smart contracts are inter-linked more complex relationships can be expressed. An entire network of business partners and their cooperating processes can be specified. In addition, rules for enforcement, punishment for violating agreements and the like can be established in terms of a DAO. Our Smart Replenishment Box with its smart contracts is only a starting point to illustrate the potential of DAO for automating processes in business networks.

5. *Verification*—The top level refers to the formal correctness of smart contracts and respective DAOs. Although many guidelines for the development of smart contracts are available and even consulting platforms for plausibility checking have been established, the verification of their correctness is still open. Verification can be accomplished by means of model checking. Osterland and Rose (2020) propose the translation of smart contract into a formal model, which can be assessed by known model checkers to verify the correctness towards specified test cases or derive counterexamples. Hence, formally proven automation is the main discriminator for level five.

Our maturity model spans a range of capability levels. It starts with initial capabilities for the implementation of use cases with some blockchain platform (level 1—initial). Then, decision processes become structured and defined at level 2 (level 2—structured). Organisations or implementation teams have knowledge about the characteristics of platforms and their benefits for certain usage scenarios. Decisions for the suitability of a use, the implementation platform best suited and a sustainable governance structures follows defined processes. At this stage, the distinction among a database and a blockchain is well understood and DLT is not any longer considered as storage medium for operational business data but rather seen as auditing tool for maintaining certificates in tamper-proof fashion. Hence, the division of labour between database and distributed ledger technologies are deeply understood and clarified. The next level (level 3—automation) represents the move from mere transaction manager for distributed transaction management towards a tool for a tamper-proof automation of business processes by smart contracts. While 3 focuses more on individual contracts the next level (level 4—business collaboration) includes networks of interacting smart contracts to represent business networks as DAO. Finally, the top level (level 5—verification) points to the correctness of smart contracts and respective DAOs. Hence, our maturity model mimics prevailing CMM by an increasing extensions of capabilities for the utilization of DLT for application design.

6   Conclusions

Although DLT is considered as key technology for digitalization and the design of eco systems for future business collaboration in the digital age, reports on engineering principles are sparse. Many papers present DLT applications from a use case perspective and the benefits of some DLT attributes such as private versus public solutions. This paper presents a comprehensive model for the comparison of different DLT technologies and a maturity model for the engineering of distributed ledgers. Popular *Blockchain Decision Flowcharts* for deciding the suitability of an application for DLT is only one starting point. Such decision paths rather scratch on the surface of core elements of a blockchain such as distribution or trusted process consistency. Available DLT platforms however unveil a much broader spectrum of technological as well as organisational options. Hence, the decision process needs to be structured according to elaborated categorization schemas. On the one hand, suitability of an application for DLT and the benefits materialised thanks to the blockchain has to be checked. However, there is not one standardised pattern for comparison. Hence, the heart of our contribution is an assessment methodology for DLT applications, DLT technologies itself as well as the governance options for sustainable collaborations.

In addition, we have developed a schema for the categorization of applications that builds upon a review of other classification schemas and is founded in the core functional services of DLT. It basically builds upon the core services for *finance*, *notary*, *process* and *provenance*, which are founded in DLT attributes and opportunities rather than contrasting usage scenarios.

Finally, we proposed a maturity model for blockchain platforms that builds upon existing maturity models for common software engineering. Hence, the blockchain community is now equipped with a comprehensive tool box for the assessment of an application's suitability, the assessment of the maturity of the blockchain platform, the assessment of the collaboration's sustainability and process guidance for conducting projects to re-engineer corporations and foster the beauties of DLT.

References

Tama, B.A., Kweka, B. J., Park, Y., & Rhee, K. H. (2017). *A critical review of blockchain and its current applications* (pp. 109–113). https://doi.org/10.1109/ICECOS.2017.8167115.

Cachin, C., & Vukolic, M. (2017). Blockchain consensus protocols in the wild. CoRR, abs/1707.01873, [1707.01873].

Casino, F., Dasaklis, T., & Patsakis, C. (2018). A systematic literature review of blockchain-based applications: Current status, classification and open issues. *Telematics and Informatics*. https://doi.org/10.1016/j.tele.2018.11.006.

Chowdhury, M. J. M., Coman, A., Kabir, M. A., Han, J., & Sanda, P. (2018). Blockchain versus database: A critical analysis. In *17th Intl. Conf. On Trust, Security and Privacy in Computing and Communication*. https://ieeexplore.ieee.org/document/8456055.

Crosby, M., Nachiappan, Pattanayak, P., Verma, S., & Kalyanaraman, V. (2016). Blockchain technology: Beyond bitcoin. *Applied Innovation Review*.

Gräther, W., Kolvenbach, S., Ruland, R., Schütte, J., Torres, C. F., & Wendland, F. (2018). Blockchain for education: Lifelong learning passport.

Humphrey, W. (1989). Managing the software process. SEI Series in Software Engineering.

Jung, H. W., Kim, S. G., & Chung, C. (2004). Measuring software product quality: A survey of ISO/IEC 9126. *Software, IEEE, 21,* 88–92. https://doi.org/10.1109/MS.2004.1331309.

Klein, S., Prinz, W., & Gräther, W. (2018). A use case identification framework and use case canvas for identifying and exploring relevant blockchain opportunities. In *Proceedings of 1st ERCIM Blockchain Workshop 2018*.

Miguel, J.P., Mauricio, D., & Rodriguez, G. (2014). A review of software quality models for the evaluation of software products. CoRR, abs/1412.2977, [1412.2977].

Nakamoto, S. (2008). Bitcoin: A peer-to-peer electronic cash system. https://bitcoin.org/bitcoin.pdf.

Osterland, T., & Rose, T. (2018). Engineering sustainable blockchain applications. In *Proceedings of 1st ERCIM Blockchain Workshop 2018*.

Osterland, T., & Rose, T. (2020). *Model checking contracts for ethereum*. Special Issue on Blockchain Technology: Journal on Mobile and Pervasive Computing.

Paulk, M., Curtis, W., Chrissis, M.B., & Weber, C. (1993). Capability maturity model for software (Version 1.1). *Technical Report* CMU/SEI-93-TR-024, Pittsburgh, PA: Software Engineering Institute, Carnegie Mellon University.

Pilkington, M. (2016). Blockchain technology: Principles and applications.

Pompianu, L., & Bartoletti, M. (2017). An empirical analysis of smart contracts platforms, applications, and design patterns. https://doi.org/10.13140/RG.2.2.28086.09283.

Samarthyam, G., Suryanarayana, G., Sharma, T., & Gupta, S. (2013). MIDAS: A design quality assessment method for industrial software. In *2013 35th International Conference on Software Engineering (ICSE)*, pp. 911–920. https://doi.org/10.1109/ICSE.2013.6606640.

Samoladas, I., Gousios, G., Spinellis, D., & Stamelos, I. (2008). The SQO-OSS quality model: Measurement based open source software evaluation. In B. Russo, E. Damiani, S. Hissam, B. Lundell, & G. Succi (Eds.), *Open source development, communities and quality* (pp. 237–248). Boston, MA, US: Springer.

Software engineering—Process assessment—Part 5. (2012). An exemplar software life cycle processs assessment model. *Standard, International Organization for Standardization*, Geneva, CH.

Software engineering Product quality—Part 1. (2001). Quality model. *Standard, International Organization for Standardization*, Geneva, CH.

Systems and software engineering (2011)—Systems and software quality requirements and evaluation (SQuaRE)—Systems and software quality models. *Standard, International Organization for Standardization*, Geneva, CH.

Subramanian, H. (2018). Decentralized blockchain-based electronic marketplaces. *Comm. of the ACM, 61*(1), 78–84.

Taibi, D., Lavazza, L., & Morasca, S. (2007). OpenBQR: A framework for the assessment of OSS. In J. Feller, B. Fitzgerald, W. Scacchi, A. Sillitti (Eds.), *Open Source Development, Adoption and Innovation* (pp. 173–186). Boston, MA: Springer.

Tsilidou, A., & Foroglou, G. (2015). Further applications of the blockchain.

Wang, H., Chen, K., & Xu, D. (2016). A maturity model for blockchain adoption. *Financial Innovation, 2,* 12. https://doi.org/10.1186/s40854-016-0031-z.

Weber, B. (2014). Bitcoin and the legitimacy crisis of money. *Cambridge Journal of Economics, 40,* 17–41. [https://oup.prod.sis.lan/cje/article-pdf/40/1/17/8082287/beu067.pdf]. https://doi.org/10.1093/cje/beu067.

Thomas Osterland studied computer science at RWTH Aachen University and completed his studies with Master degrees in the field of prediction methods for travel planning in autumn 2016. Since 2017 he is research assistant at the "Risk Management and Decision Support" group at Fraunhofer FIT in Sankt Augustin. His research interest is directed towards the application of the blockchain technology for innovative transaction management, the engineering of blockchain enabled processes and resulting changes of governance structures. Thomas Osterland has relevant experience in the implementation of Ethereum and Hyperledger Fabric, us concerns the field of verification for securing the functional correctness of blockchain applications.

Thomas Rose is professor for media processes at RWTH Aachen University. He is also head of the research group on risk management and decision support at Fraunhofer FIT, Schloss Birlinghoven, Germany, and co-founder of the Blockchain Experience Lab of FIT. His research interests include process engineering while focusing on process support for emergency management and health care for the last years. Recently he focuses on distributed ledger technologies for the re-engineering of business processes and collaboration networks. He received his Doctoral degree in computer science from the University of Passau, Germany, in 1991. From 1990 through 1993 he was as a research associate with the University of Toronto, Canada. From October 93 until 2002, he has been a senior researcher with the Research Institute for Applied Knowledge Processing (FAW), Ulm, Germany. Over the past years, Thomas Rose has been managing several projects for industrial sponsors and publicly funded research projects at national as well as European level. These projects have been in the domains of environmental informatics, mechanical engineering, health care services, emergency management and logistics. Among others, he has been project coordinator of EC projects APNEE and APNEE-TU, which have been selected as a success story of European funded research projects in 2005 by EU Commissioner Viviane Reding.

What's in the Box? Combating Counterfeit Medications in Pharmaceutical Supply Chains with Blockchain Vigilant Information Systems

Trevor Clohessy and Saima Clohessy

Abstract Counterfeit medications, medication overprescribing and a slow anti-quated process encompassed in recalling batches of medications represent serious supply chain concerns for the pharmaceutical industry. Blockchain, the technology underpinning the Bitcoin cryptocurrency, has been touted as a possible solution and panacea for the pharmaceutical industry to overcome the aforementioned concerns. Vigilant information systems enable organisations to make quick decisions in real-time in dynamic supply chain environments. Currently, the concept of blockchain vigilant information systems and their impact on supply chain decision making has not been researched in the pharmaceutical industry. Consequently, using an inductive grounded theory approach, we investigate pharmaceutical blockchain use cases and present an emergent multi-layer pharmaceutical blockchain vigilant information system (PBVIS) model. The various capabilities of each layer for pharmaceutical supply chain stakeholders are discussed. Research implications and fruitful avenues for future research studies are also presented in this chapter.

Keywords Blockchain · Pharmaceutical supply chain · Counterfeit · Medication · Vigilant information system

1 Introduction

If there is insufficient product on the market, within days, the vacuum is filled with fal-sified versions…location doesn't matter. It's about just as risky to buy medications from a street market in Africa as it is to buy them from an unregulated website in North America…pharmaceutical supply chain vigilance is paramount

(World Health Organisation, 2017).

T. Clohessy (✉)
Department of Enterprise and Technology, Galway-Mayo Institute of Technology, Galway, Republic of Ireland
e-mail: trevor.clohessy@gmit.ie

S. Clohessy
Fidelity Investments Ireland, Galway, Republic of Ireland
e-mail: saimaclohessy@gmail.com

© Springer Nature Switzerland AG 2020
H. Treiblmaier and T. Clohessy (eds.), *Blockchain and Distributed Ledger Technology Use Cases*, Progress in IS, https://doi.org/10.1007/978-3-030-44337-5_3

Place yourself in the following scenario which is based on a real life case: Your partner has severe asthma. He/she must use two inhalers for the maintenance and rescue of the condition for the rest of their life. You have been recently made redundant and no longer have access to your company's medical insurance which provided a small subsidy for the inhalers. Without these two inhalers your partner could suffer a severe asthma attack which could result in their hospitalisation or even worse their death. You use Google to search for the following term: "Cheap asthmas inhalers". You are brought to an online pharmacy where you can purchase both inhalers for 40% cheaper than normal. The website looks legitimate and even states that it is Food and Drug Administration (FDA) and European regulator compliant. You purchase two months' supply of the maintained and rescue inhalers. The following month Sky News shows a documentary on counterfeit medications. The website that you used to purchase the inhalers is featured and identifies that a number of people have died using medications purchased from this fake pharmacy. Your partner's asthmas attacks have increased and worsened in the past month....

Trust is a cornerstone of the pharmaceutical industry in terms of ensuring the integrity of all medications which are circulated in the supply chain. Pharmaceutical supply chain stakeholders such as pharmacists and patients must have trust in the medications that are being dispensed and consumed. However, the scale and increasing trend of global falsified medicinal products is worrying both from financial and humanitarian perspectives. According to the World Health Organisation (WHO) 10% of medical products around the world are falsified (WHO 2017). Furthermore, the counterfeit medications have cost the global economy $250 billion-per-year (OECD 2019) and has resulted in the deaths of 250,000 children a year (Sample 2019). All of the aforementioned are compounded by the emergence of fake online pharmacies through which patients can order medications. Additionally, the process of mass recalls of medications is time consuming, laborious and costly. There is also another challenge in terms of opioid overprescribing which is one of the primary causes of opioid abuse. According to the organisation for economic co-operation and development (OECD) in the United States in 2015 there were 240 million opioid prescriptions (OECD 2019). Similarly, in the United Kingdom, there were 23.8 million opioid-based prescriptions in 2017, an increase of 10 million prescriptions since 2007. Currently, the following scenario is possible in the United Kingdom. A patient can order opioid prescriptions from two online pharmacies while also receiving a third prescription from the traditional NHS route. This patient is now in possession of a potentially lethal dose of the specific opioid.

Given the global scale of the increasing challenges being faced, pharmaceutical companies are now under increased pressures to: (1) ensure the authenticity and providence of medications; (2) prevent patient medicine over-prescription, and (3) ensure that the speed of medication recalls is targeted and fast. For example, the falsified medicinal directive (FMD) came into force in February 2019 in the European Union. The FMD is a legal framework which aims to protect the public against tampered, falsified and counterfeit medicines. Blockchain has been proposed as a technology which can add additional safe guards in terms of providing security, privacy and transparency to ensure the provenance of medications along pharmaceutical supply chains (Mettler 2016; Apte and Petrovsky 2016). Currently IBM, KMPG, Walmart, and Merck in collaboration with the FDA agency in the United States are piloting and evaluating blockchain technology's ability to enhance food and pharmaceutical supply chain security. The FDA will trial a shared permissioned blockchain network built on cloud computing infrastructure in order to track the lifetime history data of all manufactured medications in real-time.

Pharmaceutical supply chain stakeholders need to act faster and make quicker identifications of fake goods. Currently, there is a dearth of research which has examined the extent to which blockchain can assist a pharmaceutical company's decision making using real-time data which is stored on the blockchain. Consequently, the aim of this chapter is to bridge this gap in the extant research, and advance the concept of blockchain vigilant information systems. Consequently, we investigate the following research question:

How can blockchain vigilant information systems enable pharmaceutical supply chain stakeholders to make faster decisions to combat counterfeit medications?

This chapter is structured as follows. First, we discuss blockchain and the pharmaceutical industry. Next we provide an overview of vigilant information systems. Then we delineate our research approach and discuss how we collected and analysed our data. Next, we provide an overview of a proposed blockchain vigilant information system model that can be applied in the pharmaceutical industry. Finally, we present our conclusions and research implications. We also outline a number of future research areas.

2 Theoretical Background

2.1 Blockchain and Pharmaceutical Industry

Blockchain is a distributed ledger technology which underpins Bitcoin. However, blockchain is a more versatile beast with business use cases which go beyond securing and enabling cryptocurrencies (Clohessy and Acton 2019). Blockchain can be used for tracking and proving the provenance of a wide range of digital and non-digital products (Treiblmaier 2018a). For example, *Fishcoin* use blockchain to track fish all along the supply chain from the farm to the table. Also, Ailsa Bay use blockchain to ensure the provenance of all of their whiskey products from source to store. It is estimated that up to a third of all global whiskey products are counterfeit. From fermentation to the store, data is shared on the blockchain so that all supply chain stakeholders can have a real-time view of the whiskey making process. This real-time data is visualised via a generative artwork vigilant information system. Further details with regards to vigilant information systems will be provided in the next section.

In terms of the pharmaceutical industry, blockchain can also be used to track and ensure the provenance of medications and combat the use of counterfeit products

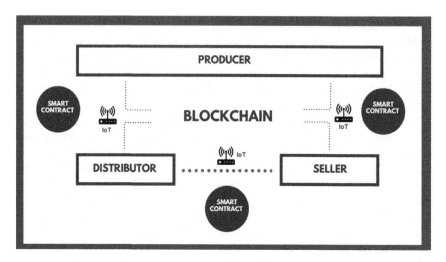

Fig. 1 Pharmaceutical blockchain use case

(Mettler 2016). Blockchain enables pharmaceutical companies to "enable end users to verify exactly how, where and by whom the product they intend to purchase has been assembled and made, thereby denying a market for illegal and counterfeit products… and provides a major advance for excipient supply chains, assisting in the delivery of unadulterated, source, process and transit verifiable drug product excipients" (Apte and Petrovsky 2016).

Figure 1 depicts a high-level overview how blockchain could be used in the pharmaceutical industry from source to store. This figure depicts a number of stakeholders which include producers (pharmaceutical companies), distributors (logistics companies) and sellers (pharmacists). Notice how smart contracts and smart internet of things (IoT) devices underpin the provenance process. Smart contracts are used to remove intermediaries and are used to automate the provenance authentication process. Smart IoT devices (e.g. sensors, QR codes) are used to monitor and record every data transaction along the supply chain. However, there is currently a dearth of research which has examined the manner with which the pharmaceutical industry could potentially use vigilant information systems underpinned by real-time blockchain data to enhance their decision making processes when combatting counterfeit medications.

2.2 Vigilant Information Systems

In an uncertain and cost-minded economy, organisations operating in fast and agile supply chains, particularly large-volume suppliers, find themselves in a constant battle to meet the constantly changing demands of customers. In such circumstances, vigilant information systems (VIS) are needed to make quick decisions. According to Houghton et al. (2008) in order for organisations to be effectively vigilant (e.g. alert) requires their decision making information systems to possess real-time sensing (e.g. detect changes and enhance managerial visibility) and real-time responding (e.g. capabilities that enable decision makers at each organisational level to execute effective actions). There are nuanced differences between real-time *sensing* capabilities and real-time *responding* capabilities. In terms of the former, organisations can deploy real time dashboards at specific operational locations within the company in order to be sufficiently vigilant. With regards to the latter, real-time means that organisational level managers are viewing and receiving synchronised data feeds which are free of noisy or meaningless data. Figure 2 highlights the differences between traditional information systems (e.g. the pull method) and VIS (e.g. the push method).

The observe-orient-decide-act (OODA) loop is a useful concept to highlight how VIS can be designed effectively. The OODA loop concept was first conceptualised by US Air Force Colonel John Boyd (Curtis and Campbell 2001). This OODA loop is used by the US Air Force to assess the mental processes of a fighter pilot. John Boyd

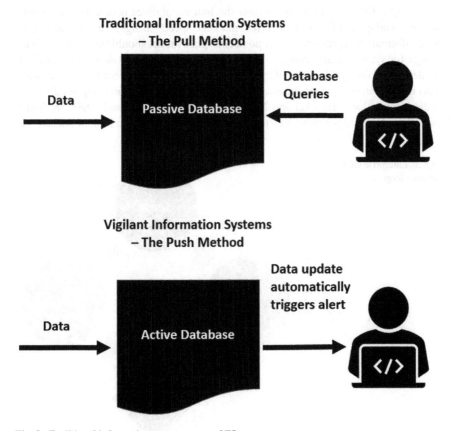

Fig. 2 Traditional information systems versus VIS

first noted how pilots in older aircraft were able to outmanoeuvre pilots in newer aircraft in an aerial battles conducted at close range (e.g. dogfights). The pilots in the older aircraft were said to be able to process much faster OODA loops. In this scenario OODA represented the following:

- Observe: Sense external signals;
- Orient: Assess and interpret those signals;
- Decide: Select the correct combat response;
- Act: Execute the selected response.

This OODA loop concept was adapted by Haeckel and Norton (1993) to create an iterative learning loop (Fig. 3) that could be used by organisations to create VIS that possessed the following sense and respond capabilities:

- Sense: See change signals;
- Orient: Interpret the signals;
- Decide: Formulate an appropriate response;
- Act: Execute the selected response.

By analogy, this learning loop contains the four capabilities necessary for organisations to adapt and thrive in uncertain markets: speed, change, variation and real-time information representation. A good enterprise model should incorporate a VIS design for systematically changing data models, forecasting models, or procedural models based on signals received by the organisation in its competitive environment. This model can prevent organisations from "running learning loops repeatedly over static information" (Haeckel and Norton 1993). In the 1980s and 1990s, Walmart and Wrangler used common VIS to communicate data between both companies to

Fig. 3 Enterprise OODA learning loop

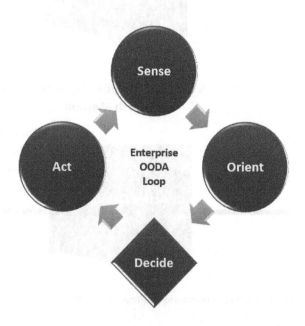

enable faster OODA learning loops. These learning loops resulted in reduced inventory and logistics costs and also reduced the risk of stock outs. Most significantly, the data models underpinning their common VIS adapted to changing fashion trends enabling both Walmart and Wrangler to also simultaneously adapt.

Fast forward to 2019 and a company called DeepMind is enabling companies to integrate artificial intelligent (AI) machine agents into their VIS and decision making processes. Working hand-in-hand with human decision makers, DeepMind uses sophisticated machine learning algorithms and neural networks to analyse and visualise large data sets in order to inform decisions in real-time. In test use cases, the time taken to make decisions under uncertain and complex conditions has been substantially reduced in comparison to traditional decision making. Decision making which is underpinned by AI will facilitate faster OODA loops. Consequently, it is envisaged that decisions making, which is augmented by AI products such as DeepMind, will seep into various organisations in the future.

3 Research Approach

We used Crunchbase (www.crunchbase.com) and Angle List (https://angel.co) to identify specific pharmaceutical, medical and healthcare blockchain applications and platforms. Our search elicited of total sample of n = 267. Following a process of elimination (e.g. removal of duplicates, companies focusing solely on crypto services, brokers, and non-active applications and platforms) we established a final sample of 50. We adopted a content analysis of online data sources which were available to the general public (e.g. white papers, case studies, web pages). Consequently, no anonymity of results applied. Content analysis encompasses the qualitative or quantitative analysing of verbal, written and visual communication (Cole 1988). It can be used in an inductive or deductive way. Given that blockchain is an early stage concept, we used an inductive qualitative content analysis approach. Content analysis enables researchers to investigate a new phenomenon in order to provide new insights, knowledge and a representation of facts. Ultimately, the aim of content analysis is "to attain a condensed and broad description of the phenomenon, and the outcome of the analysis is concepts or categories describing the phenomenon. Usually the purpose of those concepts or categories is to build up a model, conceptual system, conceptual map or categories." (Elo and Kyngäs 2008, p.108). The data was analysed using a qualitative research approach based on grounded theory (Corbin and Strauss 2008). Grounded theory provides a rigorous inductive approach which is suitable for dynamic environments (Glaser and Strauss 1967), such as the blockchain and the pharmaceutical industries. We adhered to the blockchain case study guidelines as advised by Treiblmaier (2018a, b). Table 1 illustrates ten specific examples of the 50 pharmaceutical blockchain use cases that were analysed.

Table 1 provides an overview of the study's blockchain use cases, its access privileges in terms of being permissioned or permissionless, the use cases' objective and finally the main value proposition associated with the use case. It should be

Table 1 Pharmaceutical blockchain use cases

#	Pharmaceutical use case	Description	Access privileges	Objective	Value proposition
1	SAP Information Collaboration Hub for Life Sciences	A public cloud network which enables customers to verify their medical product's serial number against pharmaceutical data stored on the blockchain	Permissioned	– Medication provenance	– Enables trading partners to exchange large amounts of serialization and associated traceability data – Real-time visibility
2	SAP Pharma Blockchain POC app	A digital ledger app which creates unique identifiers for pharmaceutical products to enable customers to establish provenance	Permissioned	– Medication provenance	– Real-time visibility with a global geographical view – Mobile scanning functionality
3	Novartis	Tracking and tracing of pharmaceutical data on the blockchain to establish proper provenance	Permissioned	– Medication provenance	– Real-time visibility – Track temperatures – Third party compliance
4	Exochain	A token-based blockchain ecosystem that medical providers can use to verify the secure identity of patients and doctors participating in clinical trials	Permissioned	– Protect patient data – Protect health care intellectual property – Provide smart contracts for clinical trials	– Secure and curated patient health records – Real-time visibility
#	Pharmaceutical blockchain use case	Description	Access privileges	Objective	Value proposition
5	MediLedger	Open and decentralised pharmaceutical blockchain network	Permissioned	– Record all supply chain transactions to ensure regulatory adherence – Medication provenance	– No business intelligence data is shared amongst business partners – Real-time visibility – Regulator compliant

(continued)

Table 1 (continued)

#	Pharmaceutical blockchain use case	Description	Access privileges	Objective	Value proposition
6	Machine Learning Ledger Orchestration for Drug Discovery (MELLODDY)	A blockchain federated learning network that protects each member's intellectual property data	Permissioned	– Using blockchain for research and development to bring pharmaceutical products to the market quicker	– No business intelligence data is shared amongst business partners – Digital ledger underpinned by an artificial intelligent training algorithm
7	LuxTag	Pharmaceutical track and trace blockchain tagging solution	Permissioned	– Medication provenance – Smart contracts for clinical trials	– Real-time visibility – Third party compliance
8	MediConnect	Tracking of pharmaceutical products on a private blockchain	Permissioned	– Medication provenance	– Real-time visibility – Alerts patients immediately for drug recalls – Prevents patients from ordering prescriptions from multiple pharmacies – Regulator compliant
9	Trust Your Supplier	A private blockchain network which improves supplier qualifications, and validation	Permissioned	– Supply chain goods and services provenance	– Real-time visibility – Life cycle information management – Regulator compliant
10	RxAll	A hyperspectral platform for authenticating and tracking quality of prescription medication	Permissioned	– Medication provenance	– Real-time visibility – A hand held mobile device is used to authenticate medications in real-time

noted that given the embryonic nature of blockchain, our search of pharmaceutical blockchain products and services only uncovered a small number of actual business use cases.

4 Data Analysis

In this section, we provide an overview of the grounded theory approach undertaken as depicted in Fig. 4. All data sources were imported into the qualitative data analysis software tool NVivo (v.12.1). It should be noted that NVivo does not automatically code imported data sources. NVivo was used to organise the various categories and codes that were identified during the first and second order analyses. NVivo supports different phases of qualitative data analysis.

The data was analysed in several steps. First, we engaged in a process of open coding which encompassed the identification of preliminary categories. No a priori coding was used. We also familiarised ourselves with the data prior to the identification of categories using the various features of NVivo. For example, the query function was used to ascertain the frequency of specific concepts contained within the data set. The text search function was used to create word trees to identify the context in which specific concepts were used. For the second step we developed the preliminary categories into themes as per the instructions of Corbin and Strauss (2008). Finally, we used selected coding in order to transform our categories into a coherent theoretical model. During the process of data collection and analysis, we reviewed the information systems and pharmaceutical literature to identify the potential contributions of our findings to the blockchain literature in the pharmaceutical domain. Throughout the coding process we embraced an iterative comparative method (Glaser and Strauss 1967) whereby all data sources were compared and contrasted. Consequently, this process enabled us to consider the diversity of the data

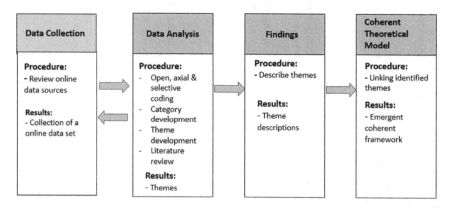

Fig. 4 Grounded theory research approach

set. We continued this process until no new categories were being formed and we reached a point of data saturation. We ensured trustworthiness in terms of credibility, transferability, dependability and conformability using the guidelines provided by Lincoln (1995). For instance, in order to address credibility, we used multiple methods and sources to ensure triangulation of the findings.

5 Discussion of the Emergent Theoretical Model

In this section, we present and discuss the emergent pharmaceutical blockchain vigilant information system (PBVIS) OODA layer model (Fig. 5), illustrating the various capabilities of each layer for pharmaceutical supply chain stakeholders.

Figure 5 shows a four-layer schematic view of the PBVIS model. Using the OODA loop core phases, we will describe how the model works from the bottom up. Starting from the bottom, in Layer 1 raw transactional data comes from various

Fig. 5 Emergent PBVIS OODA layer model

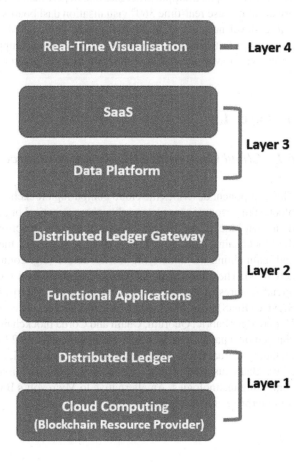

sources. The data flows into numerous functional applications (e.g. logistics, ERP systems, quality systems) in Layer 2. This is the *sense* phase of the OODA loop. The distributed ledger gateway enables any device with internet access to interact with the blockchain consortium network. This interoperability capability is a core feature of the PBVIS model and enhances the speed, ease of use and reliability of the PBVIS. Next in layer 3 the data platform encompasses business intelligence and SaaS systems which extract, transform, load (ETL) and analyse supply chain transactional data. This is the *orient* phase. The objective of layer 3 is to determine whether there are anomalies in the supply chain (e.g. counterfeit medications, over prescription etc.). This transactional data is verified with the data that has been entered onto the blockchain (e.g. matching of serial numbers). When an anomaly is detected in the data, an alert is sent to layer 4, the visualisation real-time dashboards layer. This is the *decide and act* phase. The ability for layer 4 to tap into the preceding three layers enables pharmaceutical organisations to make faster decisions than those organisations who do not have PBVIS models in place. Well-designed dashboards can assist pharmaceutical organisations to accelerate the OODA loops of supply chain activities that span multiple processes and departments. It is recommended that these organisations use real-time 360° visualisation dashboards which are underpinned by a three-level nested OODA loop structure as depicted in Fig. 6 to visualise and manage the fast cycles encompassed within dynamic supply chains.

We will now discuss each of the four layers in greater detail.

6   Layer 1

6.1   Cloud Computing (Blockchain Resource Provider)

This component describes the cloud computing blockchain resource provider. These blockchain resource providers enable pharmaceutical organisations to build and host their own blockchain decentralised applications, functions and smart contracts on the blockchain while the resource provider manages the complexities of creating and maintaining the underlying infrastructure (e.g. connected node setup, support activities). The pharmaceutical business user can then focus on leveraging the beneficial features of blockchain. For instance, the Microsoft Azure Blockchain-as-a-Service (BaaS) hosts blockchain on Linux servers. The service also uses Ethereum, Hyperledger Fabric, Quorum, Chain and Corda blockchain frameworks. Each user is charged on a pay as-you-go basis. There are currently 23 partner solutions available including Corda, BlockApps, and GoChain. Xbox, 3M, and Insurwave are listed as Azure BaaS customers. Users can scale their decentralised applications using cloud computing technologies. An alternative to Microsoft's BaaS is Dragonchain's BaaS for enterprise and developers.

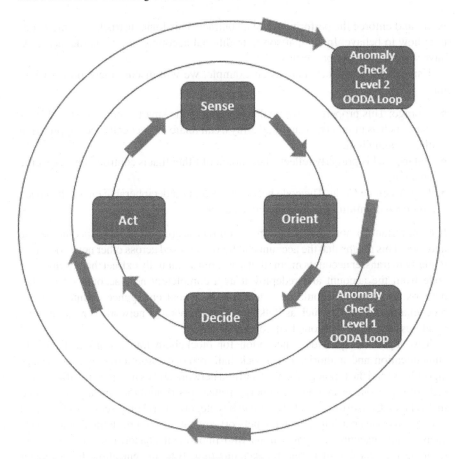

Fig. 6 Real-time visualisation dashboard OODA nested structure

7 Distributed Ledger

This component comprises the two core elements. First, it entails a cloud-based blockchain virtual machine (e.g. hosted computer) used for 3rd party digital ledger stacks and for deploying consensus, networking and database functionality. Second, it comprises a fully managed digital ledger (e.g. UTXO adapters). This layer is underpinned by smart contracts. Smart contracts are accounts which are not controlled by humans but are controlled by computer software code/protocols, that enforce the terms and conditions of a contract without the need for a third-party such as a legal entity. Digital smart contracts provide superior security, authentication, consensus, and traceability in comparison to existing traditional legal contracts. Smart contracts alter the state of the blockchain using conditional logic that enable stakeholders to verify and enforce the performance of a contract. This logic instructs the smart contract how to behave. In comparison to traditional accounts smart contract accounts have several different properties.

Using Ethereum blockchain as an example, we will discuss these properties in turn:

- Storage: This property is where data relating to the smart contract is stored. This data, such as numbers, strings and arrays, can relate to a decentralized application that is being built.
- Balance: This property reflects the amount of Ether that is controlled by a specific account.
- Raw Machine Code: The code becomes virtually indecipherable once it had been compacted within the Ethereum code editor.

It is important to note that these smart contract accounts are only specific to one network. This means that the account cannot be accessed across other networks. This inability to transfer accounts means that a user must manually extract the raw machine code from the account and redeploy it as a completely new account on another network. However, it should be noted that the recent emergence of interoperable blockchain applications such as Polkadot (https://polkadot.network/) are attempting to address the aforementioned interoperability issue.

This layer also provides encryption for blockchain transactions and identity authentication and authorization. Blockchain protocol proprieties (e.g. consensus algorithms) and the topology for a consortium network and its mapping to information technology resources in order to support private network activities are also configured in this layer. Consortium blockchains can be categorized as being semi-decentralised where consensus participants on the network are a group of pre-defined nodes. This enables pharmaceutical organisations who implement consortium blockchains to leverage the features of public blockchains (e.g. Bitcoin) but allow for a greater degree of control and security of the network.

8   Layer 2

8.1   Functional Applications and Distributed Ledger Gateway

This layer provides core services which enables organisations to create new blockchain applications and to connect to and integrate data flows to proprietary organisational or third party systems. Functional applications include enterprise resource planning (ERP) systems, customer relationship management and customer experience systems and supply chain management systems. For example, IBM has partnered with Walmart to combine a Hyperledger—based blockchain with Walmart's ERP system to track multiple shipments of retail products. Combining both technologies eliminates the need for additional shipping records and information while concurrently monitoring for abnormalities along the supply chain in real-time. SAP's Collaboration Hub for Life Sciences has also partnered with pharmaceutical companies to integrate ERP functionality with blockchain to track and trace medications. The distributed ledger gateway provides interoperability with other blockchains and third party applications, servers and services. This capability is known as application-to-blockchain or blockchain-to-blockchain integrations. Distributed ledger gateways are categorised as device agnostic and are designed on serverless principles meaning that they can be deployed on cloud platforms and on traditional locally hosted platforms.

9   Layer 3

9.1   Data Platform and Software as a Service (SaaS)

This data platform is concerned with business intelligence and machine learning capabilities (e.g. auditing, business analytics, rich data services). The Software as a Service (SaaS) element represents the various user/client terminals such as smart phones, tablets, PCs, laptops, scanning devices through which end users can read or write data. For example, many organisations are now complimenting internet of thing (IoT) devices and networks with blockchain along their supply chains (Rejeb et al. 2019). In this scenario, the data platform can store physical profiles, device owner profiles and environmental data. Oracle currently provides sophisticated blockchain cloud IoT enabled supply chain track and trace services for their clients. For instance, pharmaceutical companies can monitor and track medications and drugs which require cold storage from the manufacturer all the way to point of sale. IoT heat sensors provide real-time updates on the temperatures of products all along the supply chain.

Specific service levels agreements (SLAs) are agreed by all stakeholders via smart contracts. These smart contracts enable the monitoring of process parameters (e.g. vibration and temperature thresholds) and the automation of specific processes such as exception handling (e.g. sales and purchase order matching). Information is shared in a trusted and secured manner by all supply chain ecosystem partners, Oracle's blockchain cloud IoT services can easily integrate and connect with their own proprietary functional applications or 3rd party applications in layer 2 (e.g. ERP systems, customer experience systems, and supply chain management systems).

10 Top Tier Layer 4

10.1 Real-Time Visualisation

At this level, blockchain dashboards provide end users with real time 360° view of all supply chain processes. Key performance indictors (KPIs) are in place to ensure better planning and control. A well designed blockchain dashboard collects, organises and visualises an organisation's significant metrics in real time. Alerts can also be created to warn of any process parameter violations, bottle necks or the presence of defective or counterfeit produces. Some blockchain dashboard service providers provide chatbot functionality to allow end users to retrieve information and status updates at any given time. The ultimate objective of this layer is to enable management and supervisors to make quick, effective and collective decisions.

11 Conclusion

11.1 Research Implications

The recent literature suggests that blockchain possesses a multitude of benefits for adopting organisations (e.g. see Clohessy and Acton 2019). One aspect which has not been investigated is how blockchain vigilant information systems can create value for adopting organisations and assist in faster decision making along the supply chain. Given the impact of counterfeit medications, over prescribing of medications and the existing slow recall medication process, pharmaceutical supply chains represent an interesting context with which to examine the aforementioned potential of blockchain vigilant information systems. Using an interpretive grounded theory research approach, this study investigates pharmaceutical blockchain use cases. This research responds to the gap in blockchain research and makes the following contributions. First, it introduces an OODA multi-layer theoretical model (the PBVIS) that explicates how a pharmaceutical stakeholder could potentially implement a blockchain vigilant information system. A grounded theory approach provides a rich lens to understand how organisations can use blockchain vigilant information systems. Second, this research contributes to the recent call for interdisciplinary research by converging the research themes of both IS and healthcare informatics (Smith et al. 2011) and represents a comprehensive view of supply chain management (e.g. decision making, the use of new technologies and information systems) within the pharmaceutical domain.

11.2   Limitations and Future Research

This study has the following limitations which can be resolved through future research opportunities. First, it is worth noting the validity and the generalisability of the PBVIS model. Our study was focused solely on the pharmaceutical industry and the discovery of patterns for the purpose of theory building. Consequently, it would be reasonable to assume that the model can be used to guide future research using specific data collection methods in other industries in order to develop a more formal theory. Furthermore, longitudinal data would be useful so a better understanding of the benefits, challenges and lessons learnt can emerge. Second, given the embryonic nature of blockchain technologies, there are a dearth of actual pharmaceutical blockchain use cases which could be examined. This imposes a number of constraints. For instance, our selected use cases are located across disparate global locations. Therefore, there could be salient differences in legal structures and cultural differences with regards to adopting new technologies. Hence, another research opportunity would be a comparative study of how legal factors impact blockchain vigilant information systems taking into consideration country and cultural differences.

References

Apte, S., & Petrovsky, N. (2016). Will blockchain technology revolutionize excipient supply chain management? *Journal of Excipients and Food Chemicals, 7*(3), 76–78.

Clohessy, T., & Acton, T. (2019). Investigating the influence of organizational factors on blockchain adoption: An innovation theory perspective. *Journal of Industrial Management and Data Systems.* https://doi.org/10.1108/IMDS-08-2018-0365

Cole, F. L. (1988). Content analysis: process and application. *Clinical nurse specialist, 2*(1), 53–57.

Corbin, J. M., & Strauss, A. L. (2008). *Basics of qualitative research: Grounded theory procedures and techniques* (3rd ed.). Newbury Park: Sage.

Curts, R., & Campbell, D. (2001). Avoiding information overload through the understanding of OODA loops. *Proceedings of the Command and Control Technology Research Symposium.* Annapolis, Maryland, United States: U.S. Naval Academy.

Elo, S., & Kyngäs, H. (2008). The qualitative content analysis process. *Journal of Advanced Nursing, 62*(1), 107–115.

Glaser, B. G., & Strauss, A. L. (1967). *The discovery of grounded theory: Strategies for qualitative research.* New York: Aldine de Gruyter.

Haeckel, S., & Nolan, R. (1993). Managing by Wire. *Harvard Business Review*, 122–132.

Houghton, R., El Sawy, O. A., Gray, P., Donegan, C., & Joshi, A. (2008). Vigilant information systems for managing enterprises in dynamic supply chains: Real-time dashboards at Western Digital. *MIS Quarterly Executive, 3*(1), 4.

LuxTag. (2019). Everlasting legacy. Retrieved from https://www.luxtag.io

Lincoln, Y. S. (1995). Emerging criteria for quality in qualitative and interpretive research. *Qualitative Inquiry, 1*(3), 275–289.

Mediconnect UK. (2019). Safety net for patients. Retrieved from https://mediconnect.io

MediLedger. (2019). Blockchain solutions for pharma companies. Retrieved from https://www.mediledger.com

MELLODDY. (2019). Drug discovery platform. Retrieved from https://www.janssen.com/emea/new-research-consortium-seeks-accelerate-drug-discovery-using-machine-learning-unlock-maximum

Mettler, M. (2016). Blockchain technology in healthcare: The revolution starts here. In *IEEE 18th International Conference on e-Health Networking, Applications and Services (Healthcom)*, IEEE, pp. 1–3.

Organisation for Economic Co-operation and Development. (2019). Addressing the problematic opioid use in OECD countries. Retrieved from http://oecd.org/health/addressing-problematic-opioid-use-in-oecd-countries-a18286f0-en.htm

World Health Organisation. (2017). WHO global surveillance and monitoring system for substandard and falsified medical products. Retrieved from https://www.who.int/medicines/regulation/ssffc/1-10-med-prod-SF/en/

Rxall. (2019). *Drug anticounterfeiting*. Retrieved from https://www.rxall.net

Sample, I. (2019). *Fake drugs kill more than 250,000 children a year, doctors warn* . Retrieved from https://www.theguardian.com/science/2019/mar/11/fake-drugs-kill-more-than-250000-children-a-year-doctors-warn

Smith, J. H., Dinev, T., & Xu, H. (2011). Information privacy research: An interdisciplinary review. *MIS Quarterly, 35*(4), 989–1015.

Rejeb, A., Keogh, J., & Treiblmaier, H. (2019). Leveraging the internet of things and blockchain technology in supply chain management. *Future Internet, 11*(7), 1–22.

Treiblmaier, H. (2018a). Toward more rigorous blockchain research: Recommendations for writing blockchain case studies. *Frontiers in Blockchain, 2*(3), 1–15.

Treiblmaier, H. (2018b). The impact of the blockchain on the supply chain: A theory-based research framework and a call for action. *Supply Chain Management: An International Journal, 23*(6), 545–559.

Trust Your Supplier. (2019). *Digital identity platform*. Retrieved from https://www.trustyoursupplier.com

Trevor Clohessy is an assistant professor in business information systems and transformative technologies at GMIT School of Business since September 2018. Prior to this post, Trevor was an assistant professor at the National University of Ireland Galway business school and a post-doctoral researcher with Lero. His research interests include blockchain, business analytics, digital transformation, digital addiction, digital politics, and cloud computing. Trevor has published in a number of academic outlets including the Journal of Information Technology and People and the Journal of Industrial Management and Data Systems. Trevor completed his Ph.D. from the National University of Ireland Galway. His doctoral thesis investigated the digital transformation impact of cloud computing on IT service providers. Trevor has lectured business information systems, business analytics, databases, and cloud computing topics in traditional class room settings and blended/online learning settings. Trevor and his research associates conducted one of the first blockchain Irish organizational readiness reports in 2018 entitled "Organizational factors that influence the Blockchain adoption in Ireland."

Saima Clohessy is a Senior Software Engineer at Fidelity Investment, with a keen interest in blockchain and analytics and a big advocate for clean, modular, reusable design and coding standards. Having graduated with a Masters in Information Systems Management from NUI Galway, Saima first started her career as a Software Design Engineer with Ericsson. Over the last 10 years, Saima's has worked in different areas, across multiple platforms and coding languages. This has allowed her to gain valuable experience in business intelligence, analytics, data, mid-tier, UI, and back-end development. Saima is now working as a Senior Software Engineer in Fidelity Investments working on Innovation and Proof of Concept (POC) projects.

A Use Case of Blockchain in Healthcare: Allergy Card

Rhode Ghislaine Nguewo Ngassam, Roxana Ologeanu-Taddei,
Jorick Lartigau, and Isabelle Bourdon

Abstract Blockchain has often been mentioned in recent years as being a promising innovation for the healthcare sector in that it can ensure the secure exchange and traceability of information while respecting the regulatory framework for the confidentiality and portability of healthcare data. However, concrete cases remain very rare in the literature, and we investigate relevant use cases applying blockchain in healthcare. This chapter shows how we design a blockchain-based allergy card to solve real-life issues that is register, share and trace information about drug allergies. Therefore, we iteratively use action design research to determine the needs, design solution, develop the application and evaluate outcomes by involving stakeholders in the construction and evaluation.

Keywords Private blockchain · Allergy card · Traceability · Security · Healthcare

1 Introduction

In recent years, health information systems have faced several challenges in terms of accessibility (Omary et al. 2011) privacy and traceability (Cruz-Correia et al. 2013) of medical information. Indeed, these elements are decisive in the care of patient because they allow to ensure the continuity of care based on reliable information. This situation is obvious for drug allergies information whose difficult access and inaccuracy are very harmful for patients' care (Demoly et al. 2014). As a result,

R. G. Nguewo Ngassam (✉) · R. Ologeanu-Taddei · I. Bourdon
University of Montpellier, Montpellier, France
e-mail: rhode-ghislaine.nguewo-ngassam@etu.umontpellier.fr

R. Ologeanu-Taddei
e-mail: roxana.ologeanu-taddei@umontpellier.fr

I. Bourdon
e-mail: isabelle.bourdon@umontpellier.fr

R. G. Nguewo Ngassam · J. Lartigau
Pikcio, Montpellier, France
e-mail: jorick.lartigau@pikcio.com

© Springer Nature Switzerland AG 2020
H. Treiblmaier and T. Clohessy (eds.), *Blockchain and Distributed Ledger Technology Use Cases*, Progress in IS, https://doi.org/10.1007/978-3-030-44337-5_4

the community of researchers and practitioners in information systems are developing a greater interest in the design and implementation of digital tools aimed at optimizing the patient's care pathway and facilitating the work of healthcare professionals (Blumenthal and Tavenner 2010). Since, several medical software and applications projects have emerged. However, these solutions have revealed weaknesses in terms of adoption (Sligo et al. 2017), regulatory compliance and interoperability with existing systems (Omary et al. 2011).

Meanwhile, blockchain technology, after being applied to finance, has begun to attract the interest of researchers and practitioners from other sectors, including the healthcare sector, since 2015 (Hölbl et al. 2018). Therefore, many papers from academia and companies have been published to describe the potentialities of blockchain in healthcare as well as present some use cases tending to demonstrate that blockchain technology is a boon for all these technological challenges faced by the healthcare sector. The number of these papers has evolved rapidly, and we can cluster the content of all these papers into three groups: technical, reports, and applications (Agbo et al. 2019).

However, the ever-growing number of studies on the use of this technology in health contrasts with the number of studies related to successful implementation and evaluation of blockchain-based health solutions to meet the real needs of users (Agbo et al. 2019) because all these studies are mainly descriptive either of possible opportunities or of some developed tool (Hölbl et al. 2018). Evidence suggests that current blockchain studies in healthcare sector focus more on technological aspect than on other; while several other aspects such human factors must be also considered, for the solution to be successful (Sligo et al. 2017). Indeed, numerous studies have shown that human factors are mainly related to the utility (need-centric i.e. solve real-life problem) and ease of use (usability). To fill this gap, our study aims to answer the question:

How to build an effective blockchain-based health solution that deals with real-life issues?

The main objective of this chapter is to describe the building process of a blockchain-based allergy card to solve problems identified by allergists. To meet this objective, we use an action design research methodology to combine theoretical development, application through use cases and evaluation for improvement. The reminder of this chapter presents a background on blockchain in healthcare, the problem and relevance, the methodology, results, implications as well as conclusion and future directions.

2 Background of Blockchain in Healthcare

When blockchain is discussed in regard to the healthcare sector, several usages are prioritized, including electronic healthcare records, drug/pharmaceutical supply chain management, remote patient monitoring, biomedical/clinical research and insurance claims, among others (Agbo et al. 2019). Some authors go even further and describe in detail what can be done with this technology. In this sense, Rabah (2017) presents a list of opportunities for the application of blockchain in the healthcare sector:

- Drug traceability. Each transaction between drug manufacturers, wholesalers, pharmacists and patients can be tracked to verify and secure drug product information that is important for tackling issues such as counterfeit drugs,
- Improvement and authentication of healthcare records and protocols for record sharing,
- Detecting drugs that, by error, do not contain the intended active ingredients they are meant to and can lead to patient harm,
- Smart contracts in which certain rule-based methods are created for patient data access. Here, permissions can be granted to selected healthcare organizations,
- Clinical trials in which fraudulently altering or modifying data from clinical trials can be eradicated,
- Precision medicine through which patients, researchers and healthcare providers can collaborate to develop individualized care,
- Genomics research via access to genetic data secured on blockchain,
- Electronic health records,
- Nationwide interoperability,
- Recall management. One million people are killed each year worldwide from counterfeit drugs. Better tracking through the supply chain has a significant effect at the human level,
- Prescription drug abuse, which is often made possible by disconnected healthcare records across hospitals, walk-in clinics, physicians and pharmacies.

Through these use cases, the benefits of blockchain applied in healthcare can easily be deduced and presented in Table 1.

However, while this technology seems to have several applications in the healthcare sector to make data secure, traceable and portable, Table 2 presents some challenges and the solutions found in the literature.

Table 1 Key benefits of blockchain in healthcare (Kuo et al. 2017)

Key benefits	Description
Decentralized management	Patients can manage these healthcare records themselves; we can have real time processes, and data sharing is improved
Immutable audit trail	Data stored in the chain are immutable, enabling the detection of fraud or simply the accountability of all the users
Data provenance	The signature embedded in each information makes it possible to trace the source of this information
Robustness/availability	Data are not held by a single institution but can be shared among several organizations
Security/privacy	The encryption of data that can be decrypted only with a patient key increases the security of healthcare data

Table 2 Challenges of blockchain

Challenges	Proposed solution in the literature	References
Anonymity	Patients grant access to identified persons or institutions	Hölbl et al. (2018)
Security/confidentiality	Access control, right granted by patients	Hölbl et al. (2018)
Scalability and data management	Data are not stored in the chain but in a data lake (a data repository enabling the storage of diverse data types)	Linn and Koo (2016)

In short, the literature is only a reflection of the growing interest in applying blockchain to healthcare. Paradoxically, it lacks concrete elements to prove the real need of blockchain for the applications that are mentioned. Similarly, there is a lack of studies demonstrating implementations in a functional environment (Hölbl et al. 2018). The purpose of this chapter is to demonstrate how we have evolved from an existing need with regard to drug allergies to a blockchain-based solution. Therefore, we will show how current processes related to drug allergy information sharing will be impacted and how users will be involved to ensure the relevance of the application.

3 Problem and Relevance

Drug Hypersensitivity Reactions (DHRs) suspicions affect more than 7% of the general population (Demoly et al. 2014). DHRs can be life-threatening, even fatal, and may require a prolonged hospitalization, with changes in therapy. Thus, they represent an important public health problem (Demoly et al. 2014; Gomes et al. 2004). Globally, depending on the clinical history and the culprit drug, about 1 in 5 patients is confirmed to be allergic following allergy testing (Brockow et al. 2016). Therefore, in most situations, the label of drug allergy determines the therapeutic choices of the patient (Jones and Como 2003). Drug allergy is believed to be lifelong in many patients. Thus, a formal allergy work-up should be ideally performed, in order to confirm or rule out the diagnosis. Indeed, underdiagnosis (under-reporting) and overdiagnosis (suspicion of allergy, based only on the clinical history alone for example) lead to misdiagnosis which may affect future therapeutic options and lead to the use of more-expensive and potentially less-effective drugs (Golden et al. 2011). If the drug allergy is confirmed, the culprit drug (and potentially cross-reactive drugs) must be avoided. Re-administration of a drug the patient is allergic to is the most important risk factor for the recurrence of more severe and life-threatening reactions (Apter et al. 2004). However, this avoidance is not achieved in all patients (Jones and Como 2003), accidentally or intentionally. Most "errors" of prescription result from:

- Ignorance of a patient's allergy,
- Poor documentation (Villamañán et al. 2011),
- Lack of knowledge: the treating physician may not be aware that the prescribed drug is potentially cross-reactive or does not think that the allergy is real. The lack of knowledge may be caused by (Khalil et al. 2011): (i) failure to collect relevant information from patients, (ii) patients failing to report their allergy to physicians, (iii) patients forgetting their allergy, (iv) inability to recognize the allergy. The latter has been found to cause approximately 12.1% of medication errors that usually result in adverse drug events (Lesar et al. 1997),
- The re-administration was chosen despite the acknowledgement of the allergy and after assessing the risk/benefit balance.

On the other hand, it has been proven that even with clear drug allergy delabeling practices, up to one third of patients (or their prescribing physician) continue to erroneously report a drug allergy, rendering the delabeling process less effective. Patients and their care providers need adequate communication and education at the time of any change in allergy status, including clear documentation guidance. Actually, a drug allergy can be communicated orally or based on a written document which should ideally be universal (Khalil et al. 2011). Indeed, such a document should be available for domestic but also international use and fulfill several criteria: intuitive, readable, understandable abroad and with generic name of the drug. The main purposes of an allergy document are mainly related to the safety of patients by informing them as well as their physicians, the possibility for physicians to treat with possible alternative medication, the provision of expert information on reliability and the high lightening of previous life-threatening reactions. In 2016, a task force by the European Network of Drug Allergy/EAACI Drug Allergy Interest Group (Brockow et al. 2016) has analyzed the documentation provided by allergy centers in Europe (see Fig. 1).

This task force emphasized the fact that allergy documentation was not standardized, and that the information could be provided under different forms (allergy card,

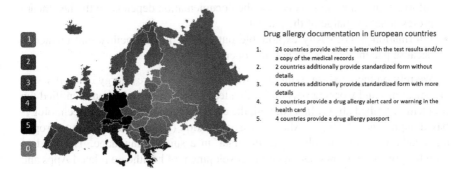

Drug allergy documentation in European countries

1. 24 countries provide either a letter with the test results and/or a copy of the medical records
2. 2 countries additionally provide standardized form without details
3. 4 countries additionally provide standardized form with more details
4. 2 countries provide a drug allergy alert card or warning in the health card
5. 4 countries provide a drug allergy passport

Fig. 1 Map of allergy documentation in Europe. Adapted from Brockow et al. (2016)

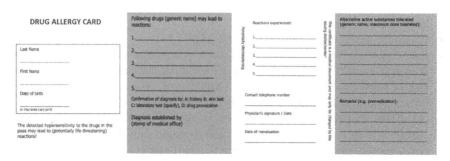

Fig. 2 Paper documentation of drug allergy. Adapted from Brockow et al. (2016)

allergy passport, medical letter, with or without details). A documentation was issued and selected by the members of the expert group as a usable drug allergy pass.

Figure 2 presents the selected paper-based documentation that carries information on patient identity, risky drugs, alternative drugs tolerated by the patient, details on reactions as well as the signature and stamp of the physician. Actually, this document is mainly used after the allergic investigation has been performed, whereas the information on potential drug allergies (and their grading as "confirmed", "ruled out", "possible or probable") is also needed beforehand. Usually, before meeting the allergist, the patients themselves will write a note or will give orally the information to their care providers or will obtain a letter mentioning the occurrence of the alleged allergic reaction. Paper documentation can be forgotten or lost, therefore leading to loss of information. Also, the multitude of information needed but not always essential cannot all appear on a paper documentation and having it available in electronic form is the solution. The existing solutions have the following weaknesses:

- Paper-based solutions are not are not sufficient to contain all important information on drug allergy,
- The risk of information loss is very high since an oral information can be forgotten and a paper-based solution such as an allergy card or letter can be easily lost,
- Information is not unified because the documentation depends on the healthcare professional in charge of the patient,
- Information is not easily exploitable outside the health facility that created it because patient records are not interoperable.

We rely on the need for a digital card to report and share allergy data after several meetings and working sessions with a team of allergists who had identified the problem described above. Indeed, with the development of information technology-based approaches, a Digital Allergy Documentation (DAD) could be the appropriate standardized tool involving all the data, in a suitable language. The field of mobile application grows fast, with the development of healthcare related Apps and devices whose main purpose is to improve patient care. A DAD would have several advantages compared to paper documentation (Table 3):

- It can be filled by different users (patients, physicians, nurses, any care providers),

Table 3 Comparison between a DAD and a paper documentation

Elements	Digital allergic documentation	Paper documentation
Medical content	Exhaustive memory, chronologic structure of the allergy follow-up Possibility to include a validation scale (tested and confirmed/ruled out/ not tested/possible/probable) Possibility to provide data on alternative medication Possibility to share specific medical advice (e.g., list of medications to avoid) and guidance	Instantaneous information because the physician should look for the information of a specific patient with a digital tool instead of only look directly at the paper presented by the patient Limited information (due to the limited size of the document)
Quality of the medical content	Same information, shared according to a clear chronology, available for multiple end-readers	lack of information, available (or not) according to their addition on the paper support
Availability	Anytime, anywhere, possibility to avoid data loss with backups	Only if carried by the patient, if the paper is lost, the information is lost as well
Course of the disease	Any additional information is structured chronologically and can capture the flow history of the allergy follow-up	Adding non-structured information is possible

- All the information (whether literal or photos which are essential in drug allergy diagnosis) can be registered and uploaded,
- The information is available anytime, in case of emergency,
- The information can be standardized,
- The contents can follow the recommendations of allergist' groups.

4 Methodology

Our project focuses on the construction of a blockchain-based mobile application for the reporting and sharing of allergy information between patients and their various healthcare professionals. The main purpose of this project is to use blockchain technology in a problem-driven user-centric approach. Therefore, we use the methodology of action design research to design an application that truly fits the needs of the final users. Action design research is a method that combines design science research and the interventions that the researcher or research team propose for the

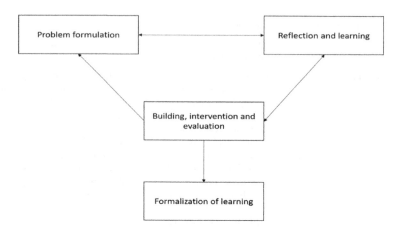

Fig. 3 Action design research. Adapted from Sein et al. (2011)

project as action research (Sein et al. 2011). In the case of our project, there is a multidisciplinary team composed of allergists who contribute to the clinical part of the tool, the company Pikcio, which develops a blockchain technology, and a university research team focusing on the information system for needs analysis and solution modeling. According to the action design research (ADR) principles, our project follows a three-step (Fig. 3) methodology before formalizing the outcomes as a mobile application for the reporting and sharing of information about patients' drug allergies (Sein et al. 2011).

Summarized in Fig. 3, this method shows how we iteratively refine the formulation of the problem or need, the proposed intervention, the evaluation, and the learning and its formalization.

4.1 Problem Formulation

In this stage, during many meetings, allergists describe the current operation of healthcare processes with regard to allergies, especially in France and we analyze this process to identify problems. Indeed, when an adverse drug reaction occurs, the patient can either keep the information to communicate it orally during his or her next care episode or directly report it to a physician. The physician can either directly consider the information as given by the patient or examine him or her to ensure consistency and the possibility of an allergy. The physician can then either record the information in the patient's file, draw up an allergy card or recommend the patient to an allergist for extensive testing. Note, the allergist can be directly contacted by the patient him or herself to schedule allergy testing. The allergist can either report the test results in the patient's file or establish an allergy card. Regardless of the situation, the information on the allergy, when it exists, must be communicated to prevent the administration of risky drugs to the patient (Brockow et al. 2016). The riskiest part of this process is the management of a patient when he or she is unconscious by a physician who does not hold information about his or her allergy history.

4.2 Reflection and Learning

The second stage allows us to think about different strategies and actions to address the identified problems and, in some cases, return to the previous step. Several authors have built a decision-making process around whether to use the blockchain (Pedersen et al. 2019; Wüst and Gervais 2018). Based on the model proposed by Pedersen et al. (2019) in Fig. 4, we design a decision process for the use of blockchain, and the type of blockchain to use. We have further matched this process with our project related to the use of blockchain technology to ensure the decentralized management of allergy information, the availability of the data and the secure exchange of this information.

Each number in this figure representing a step in the decision process, we explain them successively below by drawing a parallel with our case.

1. As we have many actors who are potential sources of information, there is a need for a common decentralized database to make it possible to save the entire audit trail of information, regardless of who is the author,
2. The parties affected by the information on allergies are patients; healthcare professionals, such as general physicians, specialists, pharmacists; and clinical research organizations,
3. Patients tend to abuse the term allergy by claiming to have an allergy following any adverse drug reaction. Similarly, physicians are divided between the obligation to take into account the information given by the patient (which is often not validated) and their forensic responsibility in case of medical errors. In this way, it can be said that while for patients the verifiability of the information is not of great importance, for physicians, it is very important, as their care strategy is strongly impacted,
4. There is no need for a trusted third party to manage this information because currently, there is no organization responsible for the validation of allergies. The only validators are physicians themselves who report the validated information in a paper document for the patient and/or in the internal file of the patient in the hospital. The aim is therefore to strengthen this existing data exchange structure that is made from physician to patient and vice versa. Moreover, international allergy organizations recommend to build patient-centric tools with patient empowerment over their health information,
5. The information coming from the patient has the value of only declared information, yet the physician has additional functionality allowing him to validate the information. Access levels are therefore different depending on the profile of the user,

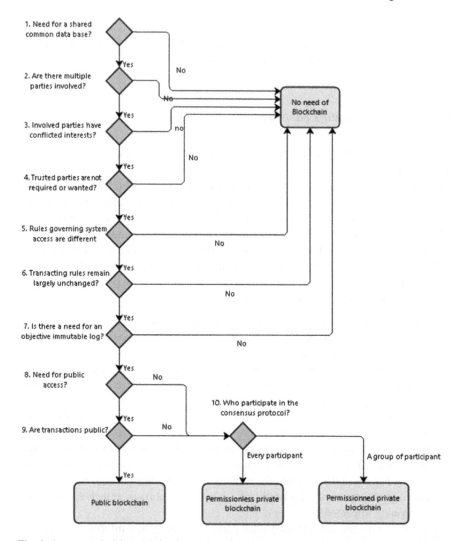

Fig. 4 A ten-step decision path for the choice of blockchain. Adapted from Pedersen et al. (2019)

6. Transaction stability is ensured because the registration, validation, and sharing of information about allergies are fairly defined processes,
7. The need to access information and chronologically organize allergy information and the importance of the source of information make an immutable log indispensable.
8. (9) and (10) are related to blockchain permission levels (e.g. private or public). The sensitivity of healthcare information makes it necessary to use a permissioned blockchain with interorganizational consensus.

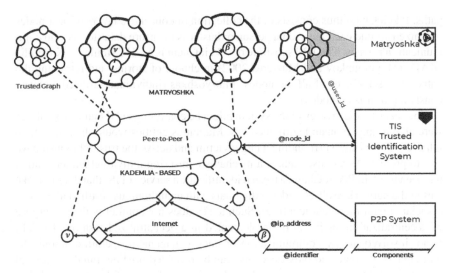

Fig. 5 PikcioChain main components

After concluding the need for blockchain technology in our project, we analyze the private blockchain that underlies our application. Indeed, we use a permissioned blockchain named PikcioChain in this project whose structure is displayed in Fig. 5.

PikcioChain achieves privacy by design in that it has been designed as a network addressing privacy from the very beginning (Lartigau et al. 2018). Privacy from centralized omniscient entities is achieved with the adoption of a decentralized P2P (peer to peer) approach. Privacy from malicious users is achieved with communication obfuscation through anonymous routing techniques such as matryoshka, data confidentiality through the use of encryption, and profile integrity through certified identifiers.

Indeed, most P2P networks suffer from a privacy problem that is due to the scheme itself. Since all the services interplaying among participants are executed in direct lines, tracing communications by very simple means would disclose the communication relationships in the network. When a blockchain is permissioned, for example, because of the legal requirements or the sensitivity of data, the addresses of miners and ledger hosts represent sensitive information, especially regarding network attacks. The adoption of anonymous communication techniques seems to be an obvious step towards the security objective of protecting trust links from community members. However, such anonymous communication techniques should be in line with the design principle of trust. Therefore, an individual node chooses his trusted contacts to act as intermediaries for the exchange of data, thus forming a concentric ring. Further rings are built through similar trust relationships, without requiring nodes on the same ring to have trust relationships with one another and without requiring the transitivity of trust. Data requests are then addressed to the nodes in the outermost ring and are forwarded to the nodes in the first ring along hop-by-hop trusted links. Data are served by nodes in the innermost ring, and replies are sent back along the same paths. PikcioChain thus consists of the collection of concentric layers of peer nodes organized around each individual person or business to ensure data storage and communication privacy. The P2P substrate of PikcioChain is a DHT similar to Kademlia (KAD) (Maymounkov and Mazieres 2002) in charge of storing and retrieving the entry point references of all the nodes' Matryoshkas (individuals' trusted pathway consisting of trusted nodes).

The security and privacy of the system might be compromised if malicious entities were able to impersonate legitimate ones. Malicious entities would then be able to intrude into the rings surrounding a target victim and derive the trust relationship we aim to protect. As a consequence, a mechanism ensuring individual authentication has been used. In PikcioChain, a trusted identification service (TIS) that does not take part in the network itself provides individuals with unambiguous certified identifiers associated with their real identities. Such a TIS does not conflict with the purpose of decentralization, as it can be implemented in a decentralized fashion. The TIS is not involved in any communication or data management operation among the participants, is contacted only once, and can be provided off-line. Finally, classical encryption techniques have been adopted to ensure data confidentiality and data integrity.

In addition to the detailed description of PikcioChain above, we have looked at this specific technique of blockchain compared to other existing ones on the market, and the table below explains the differences based on specific characteristics. Indeed, one of the marked advantages of PikcioChain for our application is the fact that it enables the certification of the users' identities, which is the first step towards true data security.

Several criteria are often used in the literature to describe the technical characteristics of a blockchain:

- The type: this characteristic defines whether a blockchain is public, private or permissioned,
- Block production time that defines the duration needed to close or validate a block,
- The duration of a transaction,
- The level of security.

Based on Hyperledger, Pikciochain differs from other blockchains on the market mainly in terms of identity management and the peer to peer approach. The rest of the comparison between Pikciochain and popular blockchains, such as bitcoin, Ethereum and Hyperledger, is described in Table 4 according to criteria listed above.

4.3 Building, Intervention and Evaluation

Based on the shortcomings of the existing tools for the reporting of drug allergies and based on the reflections carried out in the previous steps to clarify the problem and develop a clear strategy to remedy it, we have approached the intervention stage with the proposal of functional specifications. These specifications were discussed during

Table 4 Comparison of blockchains

Criteria	PikcioChain	Bitcoin	Ethereum	Hyperledger
Type	Permissioned	Public	Permissioned/public	Permissioned/public
Block production time	15 s	10 min	15 s	Transaction time
Transaction per second	200	7	17	3000

several exchanges among the different actors of the project before being validated. These exchanges took place between the allergists, the university research team in information systems and the company Pikcio, they consisted in sessions of work around specifications, analysis and mockups.

In terms of evaluation, we achieved usability evaluation with users. Indeed, usability, which is often called user experience by some authors (Albert and Tullis 2013), must be taken into account throughout the project cycle to avoid the extra costs of redeveloping new interfaces (Virzi 1992). During this project, one of the goals was to iteratively improve the interfaces of the application. Therefore, we undertook the evaluation of usability to identify potential errors or difficulties that users will face when they navigate the application. Heuristic evaluations of user interfaces (Scapin and Bastien 1997) and user tests (Bangor et al. 2008) are important and will be used in this project. However, at the mockup stage, we only conducted user tests with patients and physicians. All interviews were recorded and transcribed (Interview guide in the appendix). We interviewed approximately twenty (20) users, including five (5) physicians and fifteen (15) patients. We use content analysis method to analyze the outcomes and we clustered all the interviews in topics.

5 Results

The current process described above with regards to drug allergies shows that there are several actors who are potential sources of allergy information, and they must share information with each other to ensure patient safety. It can also be noted that, depending on the actor who reports the allergy, the rest of the process can be different. Starting from this process, we first present the problems identified before presenting the stages of reflection, building and evaluation that followed.

5.1 Problem Formulation

We can summarize the needs using three core topics based on elements related to the current process described above:

Table 5 From need to blockchain-based solution

Needs and requirements	Key benefits of PikcioChain
Empower every user	Decentralized management
Reliably access information when necessary	P2P transactions
Distinction between self-reported allergy and validated allergy	Data certification
Patient and healthcare professional identification and forensic responsibility and audit trail	Identity management
Data security	Permissioned blockchain, privacy by design

- Availability of data; at this level, it is important to keep in mind that the information can be emitted by any actor,
- Support of data with enough details,
- Process of sharing data among actors,

Since we have a problem-driven approach, Table 5 describes how the characteristics of PikcioChain meet the identified needs.

5.2 Reflection and Learning

Based on these needs and requirements, we have identified the following specifications distinguished by user's profile (see Table 6).

Therefore, these specifications lead us to conduct the analysis using Unified Modelling Language (UML). We designed the use case, class and sequence diagram as displayed in Figs. 6 and 7.

Figure 6 shows the structure of data that underlines the application. Therefore, it involves different classes to manage users, feedback, account management by trusted third parties and calendar management.

Figure 7 describes the use case of the declaration and validation of an allergy. The declaration consists in the recording of a new reaction and can involve any user, whether he or she is a patient or a physician. The validation part involves only physicians. Depending on whether there are test results, the information on the allergy will have a status "Declarative" or "self-reported". But before any action, the user must be authenticated.

5.3 Building and Evaluation

After the analysis phase, we designed interactive mockups with the software Balsamiq cloud (https://balsamiq.cloud). These mockups can show the appearance and content of each page and the general plan of the application. As a result, we were

Table 6 A summary of specifications

User profile	Use cases/scenarios	Description
Patient	Sign up/sign in	The patient is welcomed on his or her first use of the application by an identification form that is partially filled automatically after loading his or her identity document. This document is also used to certify the patient's identity and to recognize him or her in case of reidentification following the forgetting of his or her access codes. After signing up, the patient can sign in with a login and a password
	Report an allergy	At any time, the patient can report a reaction to a drug by specifying the elements such as date, the reaction time after taking the drug, and the type of reaction, and in the case of a cutaneous reaction, he or she has the choice between several images and the ability to load an image of his or her reaction
	Check his or her allergy information	Whether he or she is the author or not, the patient has access to the allergy information history. He or she can then consult, for example, the information added by physicians
	Grant access to identified healthcare professionals	The patient is the one who holds his or her allergy information on his or her device, and, if necessary, he or she can give access to a physician. There can be a case in which the patient responds to a request sent by a physician and another case in which he or she spontaneously seeks a physician to whom he or she assigns access rights, for example, on the eve of an appointment
	Choose trusted third parties to manage his or her account in case of emergency	Unconscious patients cannot manage their file to grant access to a physician, for example. In these cases, the patient is given the opportunity to choose trusted third parties who will be able to manage his or her file
	Manage trusted third-party account	Each patient has the opportunity to be the trusted third party of another patient

(continued)

Table 6 (continued)

User profile	Use cases/scenarios	Description
Physician	Sign up/sign in	At his or her first visit, the physician must complete an identification form. Physician's identity information are validated with the national directory of physicians
	Send an access request to a patient	To access the patient's records, normally, the physician must send a request that the patient can either refuse or accept. If accepted, the data are exchanged between the patient's device and the physician's device without going through a centralized server
	Check detailed information about patients' allergies	For effective patient management, the physician, when given permission, has access to detailed information about the patient's allergy record
	Report a patient's allergy	The physician can report a reaction to the medication if he or she has access to the patient's file
	Validate allergy information reported by a patient	Each physician has the opportunity to validate allergy information either based on the history of the patient or different types of test. He or she will then mention if the patient truly has an allergy or not by specifying the validation process used
	Access the patient file without prior authorization in case of emergency	In the case of a patient's unconsciousness, the law provides for the solutions of trusted third parties and emergency access by the physician without waiting for authorization, provided that this access is truly justified by an emergency

able to represent exactly how each user could navigate the application for each use case stated earlier in this chapter. The interactive mockups allowed us to put the links behind each button to simulate the functioning of the real application. According to usability best practices, we based our mockups on the interfaces of popular applications such as Instagram. Figure 8 presents some of these mockups for the patient registration process with all the buttons that are active so that the process can be executed.

In addition, these mockups enabled us to initiate the first usability evaluations. At the same time as the usability evaluations with users (patients and physicians),

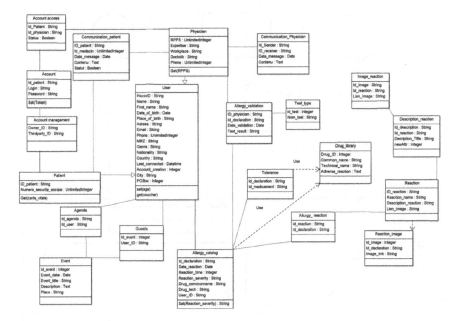

Fig. 6 Class diagram

we also initiated a qualitative study to ensure the clarity of the purpose, the different functionalities and the page contents of the application.

We performed a content analysis of the interview data that we synthesized in Table 7.

As a result, we have an application and a new process in the event of a drug hypersensitivity reaction. The menu of the application on the patient side is composed of tabs: allergy, healthcare professionals, messaging, agenda and trusted third party, as shown in Fig. 9.

On the professional side, there are tabs that include patient, other professional and the agenda, as shown in Fig. 10.

Regardless of the user profile concerned, the default homepage is a newsfeed of the different activities on the account. The process always implies that both the patient and the physician can rearrange allergy information but this time on a device that will allow complete traceability and the logging of all modifications. In this way, the application records the list of allergies as well as details related to each allergy. All changes regarding an allergy are also visibly recorded with the most recent information. The following figures present some visuals of the application in its current state of development.

Figure 11 is the page listing the allergies of a patient with a color code to distinguish the levels of validation of the information. Figure 12 presents the details page for an allergy with a history of the various changes that have occurred.

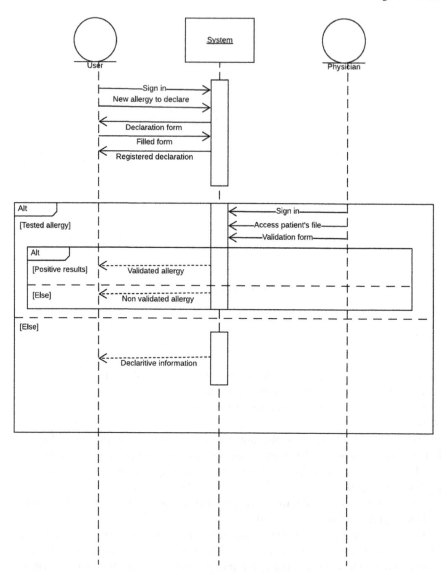

Fig. 7 Sequence diagram (declaration and validation of an allergy)

6 Implications

This project proposes the modeling and evaluation of the blockchain-based solution (PikcioChain) for the case of an allergy card using a problem-driven and user-centric approach, thus producing proofs of concepts and interesting axes of deployment for a solution that still seems to be missing in Europe.

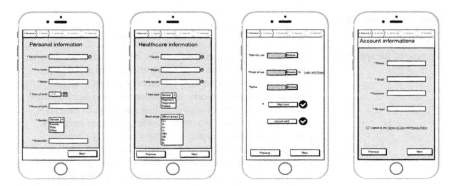

Fig. 8 Mockups for the sign up process

In addition, this chapter contributes to the blockchain literature, more specifically in healthcare by providing a real-life use case, built to solve real-life issues and involving stakeholder participation in both construction (allergists) and in the field of healthcare. Evaluation (patients and Physicians). Concretely, this application will empower patients in the management of their allergies. Patients can easily report suspicions and allergies, enable their physician to directly validate this information in the application and share this information when necessary by granting access to identified users. In this way, it will be possible to have a complete audit trail of information about drug allergies. Physicians will have quick access to their patients' allergy information with details on the level of validation.

7 Discussion

The solution that we have presented changes how allergy information management aims to enable an immediate report after a reaction, as well as the ability to easily share information with his or her physicians. From the point of view of physician, the solution allows easy access to detailed and chronological information on of their patients' allergies with the possibility of knowing the owner and the level of relevance of the information (Matricardi et al. 2019). The permissioned blockchain technology and the P2P approach used for data exchange ensure transparency in the system while respecting the confidentiality of patients' personal information. This feature is compliant with GDPR (General Data Protection Regulation) requirements and allows every information owner to delete his/her information when wanted (De Hert et al. 2018). In addition, the careful analysis of the components of our solution reveals the importance of user's identification. Actually, identities are first and foremost, a support for the problem of traceability that the application aims to solve in the sense that they make it possible to ensure that we deal with the right person. Second, user identities are important in the implementation of interoperability, which seems to be a major requirement of health information systems (Sligo et al. 2017). However, our

Table 7 Interviews analysis

Topics	Patients	Physicians
Purpose of the application	The first part of the questions about the purpose of the application was intended to understand whether patients had an understanding of what an allergy card is for. Two main profiles of patients emerged: those who currently suffer or have already suffered reactions to a drug and have an allergy card and those who have no idea of what an allergy card is. The first group of patients had a clear vision of what they expect of an allergy card as "a tool to report the allergies of a patient" After reviewing the mockups, some noted that it is good for patients to report information directly after a reaction, even at the risk of forgetting events at their physician's appointment	The interviewed physicians see an allergy card as a way to access a patient's allergy history to avoid administering high-risk drugs to patients. Some physicians have even reported having already experienced situations where, without knowing it, they have administered risky drugs to their patients, which has caused violent reactions
Contents	It would be good to allow the patient to actually describe the circumstances surrounding his or her reaction to give the most details to the physician	Regarding the content of the application, the physicians interviewed found some patient identity information useless such as information related to social security number. They also wished to have access to information sources to make it possible to obtain additional information if necessary, for example, by directly contacting this source
Interoperability	Patients who participated in the study were skeptical about building an application detached from the electronic medical records currently used, as they stated that it is better to have all their healthcare data in the same platform	The interoperability aspect was also important for the physicians since most of them want to access patient's allergy information directly from their medical software

Fig. 9 Home page of the application, patient side

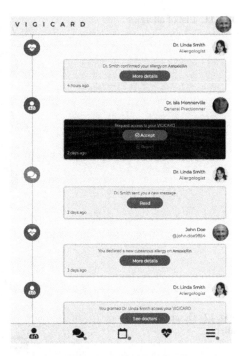

Fig. 10 Home page of the application, Physician side

Fig. 11 List of allergies

Fig. 12 Description of an allergy

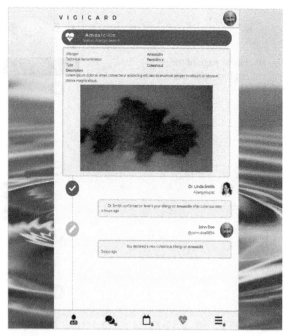

solution uses third-party services to validate user identities; these services also use centralized data structures. This feature may raise questions about the integrity of the identification data at the input. The highest risk in this situation of uncertainty concerns the identities thieves of physicians. Indeed, once the identification is carried out, the application save users logs (complete audit trail of their activity). The solution is the feature of access management that enable patients to grant access to only identified physicians, which still significantly limits impunity identities thieves. Concerning the accessibility of information, we relied on a mobile application taking into account the high adoption rate of smartphones in Europe and worldwide as well as recommendations of the World Health Organization concerning mobile applications for the management of drug allergies (Matricardi et al. 2019).

8 Conclusion and Further Developments

Throughout this chapter, we described how we used the action research design to develop a mobile allergy card application that allows the reporting, sharing and traceability of drug allergy information. The problem has been identified by allergists and clarified and resolved by an interdisciplinary team to target the real needs of users and respond effectively. Our approach is user-centered because, at each step, user assessments are carried out to ensure that the tool meets their expectations and that problems are solved. We then plan to perform other large-scale usability and quality assessments to improve the interfaces and the content of the application and thus make it easier for users to get started with the tool. Similarly, a clinical study will be conducted to evaluate the impact of the application on the well-being of patients. In addition to the existing functionalities, we plan to add the possibility for patients to agree to anonymously share their data for clinical research. This will have the advantage, in addition to advancing science, of providing a clearer idea of the prevalence of drug allergies through statistical studies.

Appendix. Semi-Directive Interview

1. Context

   What do you know about allergy card?
   What do know about applications in healthcare? Have you ever used them? What did you think?
   What do you think of the principle and the usefulness of Digital allergy documentation?

2. Ergonomics

What do you think about the interfaces of the application?
Is it simple or are there any difficulties in use? (intuitive use?).

3. Content

Are the fields to be filled understandable?
Are the different textual contents understandable
Would you like to add or remove any information?

4. Usage

Would you like to use it? Why? How?
Do you have anything to add?

References

Agbo, C. C., Mahmoud, Q. H., & Eklund, J. M. (2019). Blockchain technology in healthcare: A systematic review. *Healthcare, 7,* 56.
Albert, W., & Tullis, T. (2013). *Measuring the user experience: Collecting, analyzing, and presenting usability metrics* (Newnes ed.). Newnes.
Apter, A. J., Kinman, J. L., Bilker, W. B., Herlim, M., Margolis, D. J., Lautenbach, E., et al. (2004). Represcription of penicillin after allergic-like events. *Journal of Allergy and Clinical Immunology, 113*(4), 764–770.
Bangor, A., Kortum, P. T., & Miller, J. T. (2008). An empirical evaluation of the system usability scale. *International Journal of Human-Computer Interaction, 24*(6), 574–594.
Blumenthal, D., & Tavenner, M. (2010). The "meaningful use" regulation for electronic health records. *New England Journal of Medicine, 363*(6), 501–504.
Brockow, K., Aberer, W., Atanaskovic-Markovic, M., Bavbek, S., Bircher, A., Bilo, B., et al. (2016). Drug allergy passport and other documentation for patients with drug hypersensitivity—An ENDA/EAACI Drug Allergy Interest Group Position Paper. *Allergy, 71*(11), 1533–1539.
Cruz-Correia, R., Boldt, I., Lapão, L., Santos-Pereira, C., Rodrigues, P. P., Ferreira, A. M., & Freitas, A. (2013). Analysis of the quality of hospital information systems audit trails. *BMC Medical Informatics and Decision Making, 13*(1), 84.
De Hert, P., Papakonstantinou, V., Malgieri, G., Beslay, L., & Sanchez, I. (2018). The right to data portability in the GDPR: Towards user-centric interoperability of digital services. *Computer Law & Security Review, 34*(2), 193–203.
Demoly, P., Adkinson, N. F., Brockow, K., Castells, M., Chiriac, A. M., Greenberger, P. A., et al. (2014). International consensus on drug allergy. *Allergy, 69*(4), 420–437.
Golden, D., Moffitt, J., Nicklas, R., Freeman, T., & Graft, D. (2011). Joint Task Force on Practice Parameters, American Academy of Allergy, Asthma & Immunology (AAAAI), American College of Allergy, Asthma & Immunology (ACAAI), Joint Council of Allergy, Asthma and Immunology. Stinging insect hypersensitivity: a practice parameter update 2011. *The Journal of Allergy and Clinical Immunology, 127*(4), 852–854, e851–e823
Gomes, E., Cardoso, M., Praca, F., Gomes, L., Marino, E., & Demoly, P. (2004). Self-reported drug allergy in a general adult Portuguese population. *Clinical & Experimental Allergy, 34*(10), 1597–1601.

Hölbl, M., Kompara, M., Kamišalić, A., & Nemec Zlatolas, L. (2018). A systematic review of the use of blockchain in healthcare. *Symmetry, 10*(10), 470.

Jones, T. A., & Como, J. A. (2003). Assessment of medication errors that involved drug allergies at a university hospital. *Pharmacotherapy: The Journal of Human Pharmacology and Drug Therapy, 23*(7), 855–860.

Khalil, H., Leversha, A., & Khalil, V. (2011). Drug allergy documentation-time for a change? *International Journal of Clinical Pharmacy, 33*(4), 610–613.

Kuo, T.-T., Kim, H.-E., & Ohno-Machado, L. (2017). Blockchain distributed ledger technologies for biomedical and health care applications. *Journal of the American Medical Informatics Association, 24*(6), 1211–1220.

Lartigau, J., Bucamp, F., & de Casaubon, D. C. (2018). *PikcioChain: A new eco-system for personal data.*

Lesar, T. S., Briceland, L., & Stein, D. S. (1997). Factors related to errors in medication prescribing. *JAMA, 277*(4), 312–317.

Linn, L. A., & Koo, M. B. (2016). *Blockchain for health data and its potential use in health it and health care related research.* Paper presented at the ONC/NIST Use of Blockchain for Healthcare and Research Workshop. Gaithersburg, Maryland, United States: ONC/NIST.

Matricardi, P. M., Dramburg, S., Alvarez-Perea, A., Antolín-Amérigo, D., Apfelbacher, C., Atanaskovic-Markovic, M., et al. (2019). The role of mobile health technologies in allergy care: An EAACI Position Paper. *Allergy.*

Maymounkov, P., & Mazieres, D. (2002). *Kademlia: A peer-to-peer information system based on the xor metric.* Paper presented at the International Workshop on Peer-to-Peer Systems.

Omary, Z., Mtenzi, F., Wu, B., & O'Driscoll, C. (2011). Ubiquitous healthcare information system: Assessment of its impacts to patient's information. *International Journal for Information Security Research, 1*(2), 71–77.

Pedersen, A. B., Risius, M., & Beck, R. (2019). A ten-step decision path to determine when to use blockchain technologies. *MIS Quarterly Executive, 18*(2).

Rabah, K. (2017). Challenges & opportunities for blockchain powered healthcare systems: A review. *Mara Research Journal of Medicine & Health Sciences, 1*(1), 45–52. ISSN 2523-5680.

Scapin, D. L., & Bastien, J. C. (1997). Ergonomic criteria for evaluating the ergonomic quality of interactive systems. *Behaviour & Information Technology, 16*(4–5), 220–231.

Sein, M., Henfridsson, O., Purao, S., Rossi, M., & Lindgren, R. (2011). Action design research. *Management Information Systems Quarterly, 35*(1), 37–56.

Sligo, J., Gauld, R., Roberts, V., & Villa, L. (2017). A literature review for large-scale health information system project planning, implementation and evaluation. *International Journal of Medical Informatics, 97,* 86–97.

Villamañán, E., Larrubia, Y., Ruano, M., Herrero, A., & Álvarez-Sala, R. (2011). Strategies for improving documentation and reducing medication errors related to drug allergy. *International journal of clinical pharmacy, 33*(6), 879–880.

Virzi, R. A. (1992). Refining the test phase of usability evaluation: How many subjects is enough? *Human Factors, 34*(4), 457–468.

Wüst, K., & Gervais, A. (2018). *Do you need a Blockchain?* Paper presented at the Crypto Valley Conference on Blockchain Technology (CVCBT).

Rhode Ghislaine Nguewo Ngassam is an industrial Ph.D., candidate in management Information System (MIS) at the University of Montpellier, France. She received her Master Degree in MIS in 2017 at the Catholic University of Central Africa, Cameroon where she started to work on some research projects related to data mining and smart cities. She has presented her research in major international conferences as WorldCIST and R&D conference 2019. She is a co-author of a book chapter published by IET (Institution of Engineering and Technology). Her research interests include design science research and IT adoption and evaluation.

Dr. Roxana Ologeanu-Taddei, Ph.D. is an associate professor in management of information systems at University of Montpellier. Her research area is focused on digital transformation of organizations especially in healthcare sector. She is the research director of the E-health Chair, in University of Montpellier. She has published papers in international conferences and journals mostly related to the healthcare sector as BMC Healthcare Services Research for which she serves as associate editor. She is involved in several scientific programs as the European Conference of Information Systems (ECIS). Her research has appeared in peer-reviewed journals such as *Journal of Association for Information Systems, International Journal of Technology Assessment in Health Care, International Journal of Technology and Human Interaction, Systèmes d'information and management, Global Business*, and *Organizational Excellence*.

Jorick Lartigau, Ph.D. in computer science & technology from Harbin Institute of Technology, China, is one of the co-founders of Pikcio Services. He has a significant experience in information technology and services industry. He is extremely skilled in Java, Python, Optimization, Blockchain technologies, Distributed consensus, P2P, and Algorithms. He has designed and developed the premises of Cloud Manufacturing and recently PikcioChain technology. He published papers in several international conferences and journals around system interoperability, and optimization algorithms in distributed network. Currently, he coordinates the Pikcio's R&D team and all the research projects in collaboration with several research centers to bring expertise and continuous improvement to Pikcio using cutting edge technology.

Isabelle Bourdon, Ph.D. is associate professor in management of information systems at University of Montpellier. Her current research interests include information systems management and innovation. Her research consists of developing frameworks and tools for implementing, and evaluating complex IT projects to support knowledge and work that relate to the role of information technology in business models. She has published her work in numerous international journals. She regularly works with leading firms in Europe and presents her research at premier academic and practitioner venues. She has been elected member of the board of the French Association of Information Systems. Her research has appeared in peer-reviewed journals such as Systèmes d'information et management (SIM) and Global Business and Organizational Excellence.

International Exchange of Financial Information on Distributed Ledgers: Outlook and Design Blueprint

Marco Crepaldi

Abstract The international fiscal system is made by multiple entities that are struggling to establish sound mechanisms for co-operation. Policy initiatives are currently aiming at strengthening the information sharing of financial information for tax purposes across jurisdictions. In this work, I outline the legal landscape for the exchange of information and establish four desirable principles to which information exchange should adhere. Then, I argue that distributed ledger technology appears well-suited to address some of the challenges related to the exchange of financial information. I explore possible designs and lay the foundation for future discussion.

Keywords International taxation · Information exchange · Common reporting schema · XML · Distributed ledgers · DLT · SDR

1 Introduction

The technological innovation of blockchains and distributed ledger technology (henceforth, also DLT) is likely to impact the international fiscal system. It is likely that some of the properties of DLT would improve the existing paradigm by enabling reporting entities and regulators, as well as taxpayers, to share and access information on a single, distributed system. The benefits of DLT with regard to the exchange of information relate to critical attributes of the technology such as the maintenance of a single source of information, difficulty to tamper with information stored in the ledger as well as the possibility to trace the entire history of each entry. Moreover, DLT enables the verification of the time and order of events among adverse parties, this characteristic is appealing form the legal perspective where the verification of events plays a crucial role. Lastly, adopting a distributed ledger architecture may increase the reliability of complicated legal arrangements that establish the international exchange of financial information. When it comes to tax law and technology, scholars focus on three aspects. First, how tax law reacts to technological change,

M. Crepaldi (✉)
Université du Luxembourg, 4364 Esch-sur-Alzette, Luxembourg
e-mail: marco.crepaldi@protomail.com

© Springer Nature Switzerland AG 2020
H. Treiblmaier and T. Clohessy (eds.), *Blockchain and Distributed Ledger Technology Use Cases*, Progress in IS, https://doi.org/10.1007/978-3-030-44337-5_5

second, how taw law stimulates technological change, and, third, how tax administrations react or make use of technology (Cockfield 2017a, b). This contribution focuses on the last aspect. I investigate how tax administrations may leverage DLT at the international level.

Blockchain technologies—a species of the genus of DLT widely used in cryptocurrency projects—have been examined in the context of tax-related issues, mostly because of the properties outlined above (Vishnevsky and Chekina 2018). Proposals have been put forward to use the technology to prevent VAT fraud (Ainsworth and Alwohaibi 2017; Ainsworth and Shact 2016; Ainsworth and Musaad 2017); to shift the current paradigm from one based on the comparison of income and costs for the reporting period to a system based on the real-time accounting of income and costs (Vishnevsky and Chekina 2018), and to disrupt the payroll taxation area (Ainsworth and Viitasaari 2017). In this work, I focus on the issue of the exchange of financial information among tax authorities and financial institutions and on how the current state of affairs may benefit from DLT.

The exchange of information between national tax authorities has emerged as a central issue in the international policy debate. Tax policy, moreover, has been identified as a significant contributor to poverty and income inequality, arguably, two of the most pressing issues of current times, according to report UN Doc. A/69/297 of the United Nations Special Rapporteur for Extreme Poverty and Human rights. Several high-profile initiatives have been established in recent years to improve the exchange of information between jurisdictions (EoI). The prominence of EoI is likely due to the practical failure in the coordination of tax rates and policies (Bradbury and O'Reilly 2018; Keen and Ligthart 2006a, b).

Additionally, the rise of the digital economy has aggravated the issues of international taxation by allowing companies to exploit loopholes present in the current global framework, think, for example to the hybrid mismatches, i.e. arrangements exploiting differences in the tax treatment of instruments, entities, or transfers between two or more countries (Cockfield 2001, 2017a, b). This chapter proposes to use a distributed ledger data structure as the infrastructure for the EoI among tax authorities and reporting entities.

The argument is presented in the following structure. The next section provides a primer on the EoI by analyzing recent initiatives and establishing the scope of the problem before outlining the basic principles that ought to drive the design of an information-sharing infrastructure for financial data. Later it will be argued why a DLT-based system could be beneficial for the cross-border exchange of information. Then, different architectural choices proposed in the context of DLT will be examined; suggestions on which designs appear best suited for the international tax domain will be offered. The last section concludes.

2 Exchange of Financial Information: A Primer

This section provides the necessary notions to understand the issue of financial information exchange from the legal perspective. The complexity of the matter has been subject to some simplification due to the nature of this contribution. A necessary condition for any EoI to occur is the presence of a valid legal instrument. There are three types of EoI: upon request, automatic, and spontaneous (Keen and Ligthart 2006a). In recent years, there has been a considerable shift from the EoI on request to the automatic exchange, or AEoI.

The modern EoI system traces back to the initiative of the League of Nations in the post-World War I with the recommendation of the adoption of bilateral tax treaty provisions to lay the legal basis for the EoI. Such a recommendation evolved into the OECD model tax treaty (1963). Bilateral instruments are by far the most widespread ones, at the time of writing, over 3,000 bilateral agreements that contain an EoI provision based upon art. 26—rubricated exchange of information—of the model treaty have been signed (OECD 2017a). Other bilateral instruments are information exchange treaties, for example, the treaty between the U.S. and Barbados signed in 1984. In this case, countries enter an agreement with the principal and often the sole purpose of exchanging financial information. Bilateral agreements are not the only legal instrument that countries use to establish the exchange or to gather information about taxpayers; there are also unilateral and multilateral instruments. The proposed DLT-based infrastructure does not depend on the type of the instrument, but it appears that multilateralism is the best option.

If a single country enacts legislation to gather information from entities outside of its jurisdiction, such legislation is a unilateral instrument that triggers the exchange. The most prominent example of this approach is the Foreign Account Tax Compliance Act (FACTA) passed by the U.S. Congress in 2010 and entered into force since 2013. Unilateral legal instruments establishing an EoI are not widely diffused since they are reserved to prominent players in the global landscape and do not appear to promote co-operation as much as both bilateral and multilateral approaches. From the present perspective, a DLT infrastructure makes little sense in the context of unilateralism.

The third, and final, class of legal instruments to establish the EoI is multilateral. Due to the relatively high cost of negotiating a bilateral agreement and difficulties in addressing the so-called third country problem, several multilateral agreements have been established (Keen 2008). The third country problem refers to the circumstance that not all countries are part of a unified information sharing agreement, so that, a country external to the agreement may provide an opportunity to invest without declaring the proceeds. Of particular relevance is the directive on administrative co-operation adopted by the Council of Europe in 2011 (Directive 77/799/EEC) that establishes, in section II, the mandatory automatic exchange of information among the Member States regarding a plethora of financial information. Beyond the European context, a significant multilateral instrument is the Convention on Mutual Administrative Assistance in Tax Matters (onward, also, the Convention) developed jointly by the OECD and the Council of Europe (OECD and Europe

2011). The Convention is a comprehensive multilateral instrument for all forms of tax co-operation among fiscal authorities. At the time of writing 129 jurisdictions have taken part in The Convention. The OECD also established the Country-by-Country Reporting under action 13 of the G20 Base Erosion and Profit Shifting Project (BEPS). This instrument requires countries to mandate that multinational enterprises submit a report (so-called CbC Report) to allow national tax authorities to share automatically key indicators (such as profits, taxes paid, employees and assets of each subsidiary) between each other. The OECD also developed technical standards to facilitate the exchange of information.

The G20 has endorsed the Common Reporting Standard (CRS), developed within the Global Forum on Transparency and Exchange of Information for Tax Purposes in 2013 as the technical backbone of the EoI going forward. At the time of writing, there are close to 4000 exchange relationships committed to using the CRS. Due to its technical nature, the CRS can be established by different legal instruments. For example, the CRS is covered under art. 6 of The Convention by the establishment of the CRS Multilateral Competent Authority Agreement (the CRS MCAA). The CRS aims at providing more structured information to enable tax authorities to make use of it and enable data analytics. The present work investigates the opportunity of combining the CRS with DLT to foster co-operation among countries and enable new possibilities in the domain of international taxation. To do so, a brief exposition of the CRS is in order.

2.1 The Common Reporting Standard

The CRS sets out the financial account information to be exchanged, the types of accounts and taxpayers covered, and the due diligence procedures to be performed by financial institutions. While financial institutions are the source of information, it is envisioned that tax authorities will share such information according to the international legal framework under which the exchange is established. The standard consists of four parts: a model competent authority agreement (CAA), the CRS, the commentaries on the CAA and the CRS, and the XML schema (OECD 2017b).

The CRS establishes the information that financial institutions are required to report to national fiscal authorities, such information includes but is not limited to name, address, jurisdiction(s) of residence, taxpayer identification number (TIN), account(s) numbers, amounts at the last day of the calendar year and so on. The CRS is aimed at individual taxpayers and contains a broad range of financial information that reporting institutions must exchange automatically with fiscal authorities. For example, if a taxpayer resident in country A opens an account with the financial institution X, established in country B, X will inform country B which later will exchange the information with country A. In this simple example, the information is shared cross-border among three different entities.

The more technical side of the CRS is the XML schema. It heavily borrows from the FACTA schema and, hence, suffers some of the same issues (Bean and Wright

2014). The schema is intended to make the information computable with the use of an ad-hoc extensible mark-up language. Any tags can be created along with their description and permitted uses so that instructions on how to process information are included in the standard. An example of the resulting data structure is provided in Fig. 1.

While there are several problems with this data structure ranging from translation, disambiguation, and imprecise categories it suffices to note how the XML attempts to encode the data that financial institutions share with tax authorities. Interestingly, the XML schema could be used to model transactions within a DLT-based system.

Lastly, the CAA establishes the principles under which the EoI must occur. While specific implementations of the CAA might differ in some respects, the core tenets are the following. In the preamble, the CAA generally assumes that jurisdictions have in place "the infrastructure for an effective exchange relationship (including established processes for ensuring timely, accurate, and confidential information exchanges, effective and reliable communications, and capabilities to promptly resolve questions and concerns about exchange or request for exchanges and to administer the provision of Sect. 4 [Collaboration on Compliance and Enforcement]" (OECD 2017b, p. 224). Section 5 goes into more details stating that "[a]ll information exchanged is subject to the confidentiality rules and other safeguards provided for in the Convention/Instrument [...] to the extent needed to ensure the necessary level of protection of personal data" (OECD 2017b, p. 228). From Sect. 5, it is possible to extract two critical principles for the EoI, namely, confidentiality and data protection. In general, the CAA remains somewhat vague about the requirements on an effective EoI; however, the literature on the subject has identified several principles that should be pursued when exchanging financial information. The next section, then, discusses what makes a good EoI system.

2.2 How Should Countries Exchange Tax Information?

The challenges in implementing an efficient system to exchange tax information are significant. Not all of the following principles are explicitly mentioned in the various legal instruments that establish the exchange, yet these principles appear necessary toward a more transparent global financial system (Cockfield 2017a, b). The goal of this section is to highlight key design objectives before evaluating if a DLT system is suited to achieve them. A central issue in the EoI concerns the quality of the information exchanged. In this case, quantity does not necessarily lead to quality (ibidem). Tax authorities might be overwhelmed by the sheer quantity of data so that the real issue is whether the receiving country can make use of the information (Keen and Ligthart 2006a). A corollary of information quality is temporality. That is, the information exchange should occur readily and reflect the actual financial reality to avoid both false positives and negatives.

A second principle is taxpayer privacy. Taxpayers' information is one of the most sensitive forms of personal data as it can provide granular information of an

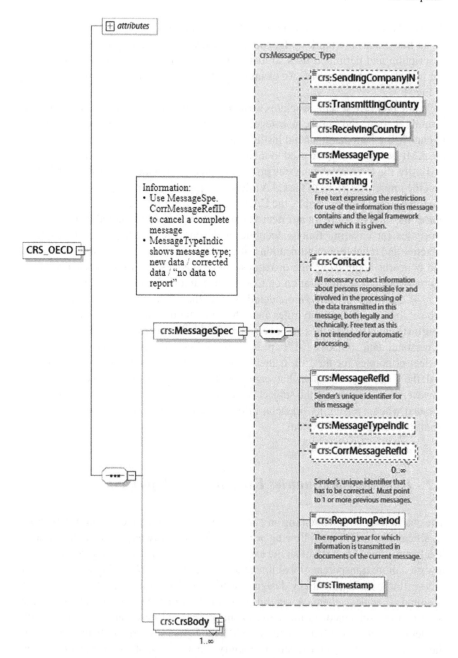

Fig. 1 Message header of the CRS XML schema (OECD 2017b, p. 274)

individual's behavior and identity. Consequently, taxpayers' data protection concerns might justify an injunction to stop the exchange of information to a country that does not implement adequate safeguards. This issue is particularly relevant when countries might misuse financial information for political reasons, thereby potentially infringing on an individual's human rights (Flora 2017). The third principle is data security. The EoI of bulk taxpayers' data represents a significant concern from the perspective of security. More precisely, several attack vectors might be possible when the exchange occurs with little regard to security standards. For example, the IRS suffers from one million weekly attempts to hack its information technology systems (Johnson 2016). The recent hack of the Bulgarian NRA tax agency reported by the Guardian that exposed the financial information of nearly 7 million people is another case in point.[1] Bad security practices from one single country might endanger the information of foreign taxpayers in the case of EoI. Data security appears to be especially challenging to achieve in this context as there is no standard infrastructure for both storage and transfer of the information. Therefore, data security hinges on the single state's resources and capabilities, which, of course, are unevenly distributed. Hence, states can be considered as single points of failure.

The last main principle that an effective EoI system should have is data traceability. While this aspect does not seem to have received much attention in the literature, it may have a significant impact on taxpayers' rights. More precisely, knowing where and by which entities the information originated and each subsequent transfer might strengthen taxpayers' protection. Further, the traceability of information might prevent tampering. Arguably, the successful implementation of the principle of data traceability would increase trust in the system itself by enabling effective auditing procedures and making each transmitting entity accountable. The principles are arguably at the core of an effective system for the exchange of financial data. They all demand a multidisciplinary approach and, require thinking about the available technical solutions. It does not seem enough to require that countries have "the infrastructure for an effective relationship" when it comes to the AEoI. On this basis, policy initiatives might consider evaluating specific technological means to achieve an effective and desirable EoI. On this basis, the next section examines if DLT can achieve the principles outlined above and, perhaps, even change the current paradigm.

3 Distributed Ledger Technology and the EOI

DLT gained prominence in the context of cryptocurrencies after the launch of Bitcoin in 2008 (Nakamoto 2008). The recent Libra project spearheaded by Facebook Inc. has contributed to the growing popularity of cryptocurrencies by bringing them to the spotlight. For our purpose, it is important to note that Bitcoin proved how a

---

[1] https://www.theguardian.com/world/2019/jul/18/wizard-hacker-charged-after-financial-records-of-nearly-every-bulgarian-exposed.

particular kind of replicated database—the blockchain—enables parties to exchange unique strings of code without a centralized third-party (Narayanan et al. 2016). While it is fair to argue that Bitcoin's design was mostly aimed at addressing the double-spending problem and at achieving Byzantine fault tolerance in a distributed environment, the resulting data structure has interesting properties that go beyond 'electronic cash.' The relevant properties of this data structure for this study will be discussed later. The blockchain is a particular distributed ledger in which data is organized in blocks linked together by hashing functions, i.e., mathematical functions used to map data of arbitrary size to a string of a fixed size (Glaser and Bezzenberger 2015). It is important to note that data might not be organized in linked blocks, but, for example, as elements of a directed acyclic graph (Benčić and Žarko 2018).

For our purposes, we need not indulge in whether blocks are present or not for the current argument is based on common properties of different designs (Shahaab et al. 2019). Beyond cryptocurrencies, later implementations proved that DLT could be used to handle general computations via a virtual machine, thus enabling the trusted execution of distributed programs, often referred to as smart contracts (Wood 2014). Due to the properties of blockchains and distributed ledgers more generally, a growing strand of research is aimed at adapting these technologies to other areas beyond cryptocurrencies, as, for example, corporate governance (Panisi et al. 2019; Yermack 2017), and e-government (Elisa et al. 2018). Some authors claim that blockchain technology is revolutionary and that the so-called 'blockchain revolution' will impact many aspects of modern economies (Swan 2015; Tapscott and Tapscott 2016). Without taking a stance on the debate on the nature of the innovation brought about by DLT, in this section, I examine its properties to assess whether this class of technologies might help in establishing a better system for the exchange of financial information. We start by defining DLT.

There are many definitions of DLT out there. Some present DLT as P2P, append-only, tamper-proof, ever-growing distributed, and decentralized networks that function as records for transactions (Glaser and Bezzenberger 2015). Others insist on the properties of the network that allow the nodes to agree on the order, validity, existence, and authenticity of all the transactions that ever occurred within the system (Iansiti and Lakhani 2017). Researchers argue that the relevant properties of DLT for the tax domain are: transparency, self-checking, near real-time information, and efficiency (Vishnevsky and Chekina 2018). By focusing on the data, DLT enables the nodes to agree on a single version of truth shared across the network. We need not delve into the technicalities of these features to evaluate their desirability in the context of EoI. In order to do so, I will examine the four principles for a good EoI mentioned in the previous section and how they relate to the common characteristics of DLT-based systems. It turns out that DLT might be highly desirable from the perspective of international taxation.

The first principle is information quality. In this regard, DLT do not offer significant advantages over other solutions. However, the challenge of ensuring the quality of data cannot be solved by any computer system. Richard Feynman put it eloquently when investigating the incident of the Challenger; he wrote: "You know the danger of computers, it's called GIGO: garbage in, garbage out" (Feynman and Leighton 2001,

p. 107). Hence, the challenge of ensuring the quality of the information appears to not be in for a technical solution. Instead, institutional mechanisms should be put in place to ensure that reporting institutions and tax authorities are appropriately incentivized to verify the correctness of the information. However, one tangential aspect of the principle of information quality in which DLT could play a significant role is temporality. An element of temporality is the ability to timestamp data effectively. The CRS schema has an element called Timestamp to identify the date and time when the message was compiled. It is expected that this element will be "automatically populated by the host system" (OECD 2017b, p. 235). One of the crucial elements of a DLT architecture is a timestamp server, that is, a DLT "proves that the data must have existed at the time, obviously, in order to get into the hash. Each timestamp includes the previous timestamp in its hash, forming a chain, with each additional timestamp reinforcing the ones before it" (Nakamoto 2008, p. 2). In this instance, a DLT solution appears to be preferable because the timestamp function would be distributed before the information is transmitted so that reliance would be increased on the timestamp element paired with the significant reduction in the possibility of tampering with the data.

The second principle is taxpayer privacy. In this case, a DLT-based approach offers new solutions. A first option is pseudonymizing personal data with a technique similar to how Bitcoin's public addresses are generated. In Bitcoin's case, the public address is a 160-bit hash of the public portion of a public/private ECDSA keypair; a similar process might be implemented concerning identifying information to pseudonymize the data. Then, in case of an audit procedure, the original data would be made available by the reporting institution. Additionally, this process would render much more challenging to identify taxpayers in case of a data breach, so that, the information in this format could be exchanged more safely with entities that do not necessarily have state-of-the-art security. In the context of the CRS, the seed for the generation of pseudonymous identities might be the taxpayer identification number (TIN).

A second option is to use a DLT system as decentralized storage and attribute-based-encryption (ABE) to specify access policy to achieve fine-grained access control over taxpayers' data. In particular, with the adoption of a DLT system, the trusted public-key-generator for the ABE encryption is not needed (Wang et al. 2018). However, this might not be necessary if the participants are known, which I believe to be a necessary feature of the system, more on this in the next section.

The third principle discussed above is data security. In this regard, DLT solutions appear to be particularly robust. All the major incidents involving cryptocurrencies did not involve an attack on the distributed database itself. The incidents affected the various entities that interact with a DLT system, such as exchanges and faulty smart contracts, not the DLT protocol itself. The Bitcoin blockchain, for example, has been running for more than ten years without being compromised despite the tremendous financial incentives to do so. Therefore, it seems fair to conclude that a DLT-based approach would increase data security, at minimum, by implementing hashing techniques in a distributed setting to preserve the integrity of data and prevent manipulation. Moreover, access control to specific fiscal data via a blockchain system could result in increased security. Of course, the data security properties of DLT heavily depends on their design and adversarial settings, topics that lie outside the scope of this work.

The last principles to develop an effective EoI system is traceability. In practice, this means having the ability to trace back the path of the information and to identify the entities involved in the creation, transfer, and manipulation of financial data. In this regard, DLT systems appear well fit as the several traceability use-cases show. More precisely, DLT are being developed to enable entities to precisely track various assets from chickens to diamonds as the ongoing initiatives of Carrefour and Everledger show. Therefore, a DLT-based exchange system could enable tax authorities, reporting entities and, ultimately, taxpayers to access the complete history of the information, a relevant feature for auditing and for safeguarding taxpayers' rights. With respect to other tacking solutions, DTL are arguably more robust as they function in a distributed fashion without a single entity in charge of the entire system.

Moreover, the ability to trace financial data could foster trust among the various entities involved in the exchange process. However, the benefits of a DLT system in the international tax domain might go beyond the effective safeguard of the above principles by enabling new affordances due to the peculiar characteristics of the technology.

For example, a computational layer could be implemented to signal anomalies or to even provide automatic payments thereby enabling real-time collection of tax obligations by implementing smart contracts (Ainsworth and Musaad 2017; Vishnevsky and Chekina 2018).

Moreover, there have been calls for the establishment of a global financial registry (Cockfield 2017a, b). It may seem that a DLT-type system would be the right approach to develop such a system; after all, the core affordance of this class of technologies is a global, shared ledger. While a permissioned-type system could be politically feasible it is unlikely that a permissionless system would be. This raises the philosophical concern that a permissioned system is not a blockchain at all but only a decentralized database. However, one need not relinquish the possibility to use some, but not all, of the affordances brought by blockchain technology in a permissioned setting, as the many initiatives in the permissioned DLT space seem to corroborate, i.e. Corda, and Hyperledger. In this case, privacy concerns could be addressed by limiting access and pseudonymizing personal data. Then, a DLT system would enable tax authorities and reporting entities to establish secure communication without relying on a centralized third party; this characteristic is particularly appealing since a world tax organization does not seem to be politically feasible (Tanzi 2005). An exciting possibility is to design a mechanism to incentivize co-operation and establish revenue-sharing schemes by linking the exchange of information to a digital token (Keen and Ligthart 2006b). The International monetary fund could allocate a fraction of its special drawing rights (SDRs) as the 'currency' for the exchange of information. SDRs are an international reserve asset created by the IMF to supplement member countries' official reserves, at the time of writing the IMF has allocated the equivalent of about 291 billion USD (Williamson 2009). The XDR (ISO 4217 code for SDRs) could be used to secure the network by providing monetary incentives and implement revenue-sharing schemes. Admittedly, this scenario lies a long way in the future, but it is a possibility worth discussing for its potential in enabling a new paradigm in the exchange of financial information and due to Christine Lagarde's positive attitude toward blockchain technology.

On this basis, the next section explores possible designs of a DLT-based system for the EoI. It is envisioned that this first attempt to identify major design choices will lay the groundwork for exploring the adoption of DLT in the international taxation area.

4 Design Principles

Blockchains and distributed ledger architectures come in a surprising variety of designs. The sheer number of technical solutions developed in the newly found field of distributed systems is daunting. For example, recent work identified 18 different families of consensus protocols developed in the context of DLT alone (Feng et al. 2018).

Preliminarily, it is useful to spend a few words on the legal instrument that seems necessary to establish a DLT-based system for international taxation. Multilateralism is fundamental. Distributed ledgers enable multiple distrusting parties to exchange information and coordinate without the need for a central authority. Therefore, a multilateral instrument is crucial to harness the benefits of distributed ledgers. Among the current legal instruments, the Convention on Mutual Administrative Assistance in Tax Matters appears as the best option. The Convention facilitates international co-operation by providing all possible forms of administrative co-operation between states. Article 6 of the Convention may lay the basis upon which a DLT-based system could be implemented, perhaps under the oversight of the multilateral competent authorities. Another legal instrument that could justify the development of a DLT solution is the aforementioned directive on administrative co-operation in force in the EU. However, this instrument is limited to EU member states, and it seems fair to argue that a broader instrument such as the Convention would yield better results. Transitioning from the legal to the technical side, I will spend a few words on a design blueprint of a DLT-based architecture to exchange financial information.

In the following paragraphs, the DLT system is considered as a software connector. It seems that the optimal option is to design a DLT system that connects to legacy systems of tax authorities and reporting entities so that it can provide communication and coordination, and facilitation services among the nodes (Xu et al. 2016). To explore possible designs, I adopt the methodology provided by Xu et al. (ibidem). It consists of seven design decisions, and it allows us to discuss design trade-offs.

The first design decision concerns transaction throughput. Many DLT systems suffer from poor transaction throughput due to their adversarial setting. Fully open systems such as Bitcoin and Ethereum are limited in this respect because any arbitrary party can join the network at any time, and validating nodes are not known (Harz and Boman 2018). It seems unlikely that a DLT system for international taxation would operate in the same fashion. Hence, validating nodes will probably be known. If this is the case, the throughput of the system increases dramatically. For example, systems such as EOS and TRON, where validating nodes are known, achieve transaction throughputs orders of magnitude higher than fully open ones (TRON 2018; Xu et al. 2018). Thus, by adopting a design where validating nodes are known, it is possible to achieve a high enough throughput to reduce concerns regarding scalability.

The second design decision deals with the consensus protocol, i.e., the mechanisms of selecting the data to be included in the distributed ledger (Bano et al. 2017). Since, as mentioned earlier, validating nodes are likely to be known, it is possible to implement well-known consensus algorithms that share this assumption. Algorithms in this set are PAXOS, BFT, Honeybadger, and proof-of-stake (PoS, DPoS) variations. While recommending a specific solution is premature at the moment, we can rule out 'open' consensus algorithms such as proof-of-work or Nakamoto consensus (Cachin and Vukolić 2017). This design choice also eliminates environmental concerns associated with the wasteful energy consumption of open solutions (Krause and Tolaymat 2018; Stoll et al. 2019).

The third design decision regards the data structure. More precisely, the types of data that need to be stored on the distributed ledger. In other words, one needs to decide between storing data on-chain and off-chain, i.e., on the network or the nodes. Two options appear possible when considering the CRS framework. Either reporting entities use the distributed ledger to transfer checksums (or hash pointers) of the XML schema to timestamp it and provide a trail of subsequent transfers, or transactions could be made using the XML attributes so that the transfer of the information occurs directly on the ledger. In the latter case, the attributes of the XML schema will be used to model the transaction structure of DLT system, so that each transfer of the information is a transaction within the system from, for example, a reporting entity to a national tax authority. While the first option is simpler to implement and requires fewer initial investments, the second one is more robust for all the relevant elements of the AEoI are transferred on the distributed ledger.

The fourth design decision appears straightforward. The choice is between a public system and a private one from the management perspective. When considering the CRS, the management should be allocated to the competent authority identified by the multilateral agreement (MCAA), thereby making the system private. More importantly, such an organization would be responsible for the issuance of identity certificates and for ordinary maintenance work to be performed on the ledger. Hence, the system should be private when compared to public options such as most cryptocurrencies; however, it is public in the sense that its management would be carried out by public institutions and/or international organizations. Details in the management of the system should be covered in the MCAA.

The fifth design choice concerns deciding between a single-ledger architecture or a multi-ledger one. The former has the benefits of easier management of the network and its permissions, but it comes with trade-offs in data management because the system would operate in isolation. Additionally, a single ledger does not suffer from integration problems. On the other hand, a multi ledger solution appears harder to manage both on the network and permission sides, yet it allows for more granularity, and different data structures might be implemented across the different ledgers.

Concerning the present use case, it appears that a single ledger solution is more desirable as a starting point. Development and testing would be less complicated and sound management of permissions and of the ledger itself is a crucial element to ensure that the system instantiates the core principles outlined above.

The sixth design choice concerns sources of data outside the ledger. Two options are possible; first, a solution based on an external validation oracle or, second, an internal source of external data that periodically inserts data in the ledger. At the moment, it is unclear if incorporating external data into the system is needed. More precisely, it appears that no external source of data is needed for the function of the system as it is supposed to perform mainly as a communication and coordination connector between other ICT systems. In any case, the MCAA could also issue certificates to entities that would act as trusted oracle if the need to feed external data to the DLT system arises.

The last design option is between permissionless or permissioned architectures. Given the nature of the information shared and the privacy concerns highlighted above, a permissionless system is out of the question. Selected entities should have the permissions to validate and write data to the ledger—i.e., tax authorities. Others, such as reporting entities should be permitted to submit data to be appended on the network (both in the case of hash pointers or transaction modelled based on the CRS XML schema). Similarly, read access should be granted only to tax authorities while participation in the network should also be allowed to reporting entities as well. That is, reporting entities should be able to broadcast transactions to the pool of validators, i.e., the tax authorities, but should not be able to read the entire state of the resulting ledger. This design choice comes out of necessity when considering the nature of the data stored in the ledger and its associated privacy concerns. It is possible to envision how taxpayers could be granted access on the occasion of an audit procedure. This will allow taxpayers to access the entire history of their information stored in the distributed ledger.

Interestingly, recent work on data sharing in the context of cloud infrastructures showed how a layered approach based on programs executed on a distributed ledger could be used to facilitate secure data sharing, particularly among multiple organizations that have distinct authorizations (Wang et al. 2018). This would also allow for incentivizing data sharing by offering rewards. Within the context of the exchange of international financial data, the fundamental value of DLT-based layered data sharing is to enable granular access control that relies on the consensus process and provides traceable validations, an enticing characteristic currently absent. Table 1 summarizes the key design choices discussed above.

5   Conclusion and Future Research Directions

In this contribution, I presented the issues of the information exchange of financial data among tax authorities and evaluated if a DLT approach might be desirable. This research contributes to the growing literature on the possible use cases of DLT in

Table 1 Summary of design choices

Design choice	Recommendation	Rationale
1. Transaction throughput	High (≈1000–10,000 TPS)	To accommodate the flow of financial data
2. Consensus protocol	Avoid PoW protocols	To avoid Sybil attacks and environmental concerns
3. Data structure (hash pointers versus entire transactions)	Indifferent	Both options are possible and desirable, trade-offs apply
4. Management of the network	MCAA	As provided by the relevant international instrument
5. Single or multiple architecture	Single ledger	Multiple ledgers introduce unnecessary design complications
6. Permissionless or permissioned network	Permissioned	Due to privacy and regulatory concerns

the domain of government services (Alexopoulos et al. 2019; Jun 2018; Ølnes and Jansen 2017, 2018; Ølnes et al. 2017; Sup and Erdenebold 2018). The goal was to outline some fundamental design choices in the architecture of a DLT-based system for the cross-border exchange of financial data. Many challenges still need to be addressed, yet the blueprint for an architecture that seems capable of addressing the main principles of the EoI is in place. To sum up, a multilateral legal instrument is of paramount importance to allow multiple states to benefit from a shared information-sharing infrastructure. The Convention appears to be suited for the task. Then, the system would—ideally—be based on a permissioned, private yet publicly owned, single, distributed ledger in which tax authorities act as validators while reporting institutions are only allowed to submit data for validation and where access to data is controlled within the consensus process. It is essential that legal and policy scholars engage at a more technical level to evaluate if existing technologies—such as distributed ledgers—might help in establishing a better international financial system. When discussing DLT systems, one must keep in mind that the goal of an international tax environment is curbing tax evasion and laying the foundation for an international tax system fit the twenty-first century. Several challenges persist, yet distributed ledgers appear an excellent technical solution for their ability to address the problem of coordination by displacing trust with reliance on a technical protocol. The international fiscal landscape is made of multiple distrusting parties that are currently struggling to establish a sound mechanism for co-operation. This situation is strikingly comparable to Bitcoin's starting assumption: no one needs to be trusted, yet the electronic transfer of valuable information should be possible without a centralized third party. As practical advice, it seems fair to argue that the OECD should start examining DLT-based solutions within the context of its Global Forum on Transparency and Exchange of Information for Tax Purposes. A reliable, secure, system to exchange financial information across a multitude of—distrusting—entities would be an essential step in enabling a better global financial system. In this regard, DLT might, finally, show its worth.

References

Ainsworth, R. T., & Alwohaibi, M. (2017). *Blockchain, bitcoin, and VAT in the GCC: The missing trader example.* Boston Univ. School of Law. Law and Economics Research Paper No. 17-05.

Ainsworth, R. T., & Shact, A. (2016). *Blockchain (distributed ledger technology) solves VAT fraud.* Boston Univ. School of Law. Law and Economics Research Paper No. 16-41.

Ainsworth, R. T., & Viitasaari, V. (2017). *Payroll Tax & the Blockchain.* Tax Notes International, pp. 1007–1024.

Ainsworth, R. T., & Musaad, A. (2017). *The first real-time blockchain VAT—GCC solves MTIC fraud.* Boston Univ. School of Law. Law and Economics Research Paper No. 17-23.

Alexopoulos, C., Charalabidis, Y., Androutsopoulou, A., Loutsaris, M. A., & Lachana, Z. (2019). *Benefits and obstacles of blockchain applications in E-government.* Paper presented at the Proceedings of the 52nd Hawaii International Conference on System Sciences.

Bano, S., Sonnino, A., Al-Bassam, M., Azouvi, S., McCorry, P., Meiklejohn, S., & Danezis, G. (2017). *SoK: Consensus in the age of blockchains.* Retrieved April 12, 2019 from https://arxiv.org/pdf/1711.03936.pdf.

Bean, B. W., & Wright, A. L. (2014). The US foreign Account tax compliance act: American legal imperialism. *ILSA Journal of International and Comparative Law, 21,* 333.

Benčić, F. M., & Žarko, I. P. (2018). *Distributed ledger technology: Blockchain compared to directed acyclic graph.* Retrieved January 21, 2019 from https://arxiv.org/pdf/1804.10013.pdf.

Bradbury, D., & O'Reilly, P. (2018). Inclusive fiscal reform: Ensuring fairness and transparency in the international tax system. *International Tax and Public Finance.* https://doi.org/10.1007/s10797-018-9507-2.

Cachin, C., & Vukolić, M. (2017). Blockchains consensus protocols in the wild. In *International Symposium on Distributed Computing* (Vol. 31).

Cockfield, A. J. (2001). Designing tax policy for the digital biosphere: How the internet is changing tax laws. *Connecticut Law Review, 34,* 333.

Cockfield, A. J. (2017a). How countries should share tax information. *Vanderbilt Journal of Transnational Law, 50*(5).

Cockfield, A. J. (2017b). Tax law and technology change. In E. S. K. Y. Roger Brownsword (Ed.), *Oxford handbook of the law and regulation of technology.* Oxford: University of Oxford Press.

Elisa, N., Yang, L., Chao, F., & Cao, Y. (2018). A framework of blockchain-based secure and privacy-preserving E-government system. *Wireless Networks.*

Feng, Q., He, D., Zeadally, S., Khan, M. K., & Kumar, N. (2018). A survey on privacy protection in blockchain system. *Journal of Network and Computer Applications.* https://doi.org/10.1016/j.jnca.2018.10.020.

Feynman, R. P., & Leighton, R. (2001). " *What do you care what other people think?" Further adventures of a curious character.* WW Norton & Company.

Flora, M. G. D. (2017). Protection of the taxpayer in the information exchange procedure. *Intertax, 45*(6), 447–460.

Glaser, F., & Bezzenberger, L. (2015). *Beyond cryptocurrencies-a taxonomy of decentralized consensus systems.* Paper presented at the 23rd European Conference on Information Systems (ECIS), Münster, Germany.

Harz, D., & Boman, M. (2018). The scalability of trustless trust. Retrieved November 8, 2018 from https://arxiv.org/abs/1801.09535.

Iansiti, M., & Lakhani, K. R. (2017). The truth about blockchain. *Harvard Business Review, 95*(1), 118–127.

Johnson, S. R. (2016). The future of American tax administration: Conceptual alternatives and political realities. *Columbia Journal of Tax Law, 7,* 5.

Jun, M. (2018). Blockchain government—A next form of infrastructure for the twenty-first century. *Journal of Open Innovation: Technology, Market, and Complexity, 4*(1), 7. https://doi.org/10.1186/s40852-018-0086-3.

Keen, M. (2008). Tax competition. In S. N. Durlauf & L. E. Blume (Eds.), The new palgrave dictionary of economics (Vols. 1–8, pp. 6516–6523). London, UK: Palgrave Macmillan.

Keen, M., & Ligthart, J. (2006a). Information sharing and international taxation: A primer. *International Tax and Public Finance, 13*(1), 81–110. https://doi.org/10.1007/s10797-006-3090-7.

Keen, M., & Ligthart, J. (2006b). Incentives and information exchange in international taxation. *International Tax and Public Finance, 13*(2–3), 163–180. https://doi.org/10.1007/s10797-006-2316-z.

Krause, M. J., & Tolaymat, T. (2018). Quantification of energy and carbon costs for mining cryptocurrencies. *Nature Sustainability, 1.*

Nakamoto, S. (2008). *Bitcoin: A peer-to-peer electronic cash system.* Retrieved October 13, 2016 from https://bitcoin.org/en/bitcoin-paper.

Narayanan, A., Bonneau, J., Felten, E., Miller, A., & Goldfeder, S. (2016). Bitcoin and cryptocurrency technologies: A comprehensive introduction. Princeton University Press.

OECD. (2017a). *Model Tax Convention on Income and on Capital: Condensed Version 2017.*

OECD. (2017b). *Standard for Automatic Exchange of Financial Account Information in Tax Matters* (2nd ed.).

OECD, & Council of Europe. (2011). *The Multilateral Convention on Mutual Administrative Assistance in Tax Matters.*

Ølnes, S., & Jansen, A. (2017). Blockchain technology as s support infrastructure in e-government. In: M. Janssen et al. (eds.), *Electronic government. EGOV 2017. Lecture Notes in Computer Science* (Vol. 10428). Cham: Springer.

Ølnes, S., & Jansen, A. (2018). *Blockchain technology as infrastructure in public sector: An analytical framework.* Paper presented at the Proceedings of the 19th Annual International Conference on Digital Government Research: Governance in the Data Age.

Ølnes, S., Ubacht, J., & Janssen, M. (2017). Blockchain in government: Benefits and implications of distributed ledger technology for information sharing. *Government Information Quarterly, 34*(3), 355–364. https://doi.org/10.1016/j.giq.2017.09.007.

Panisi, F., Buckley, R. P., & Arner, D. (2019). Blockchain and public companies: A revolution in share ownership transparency, proxy voting and corporate governance? *Stanford Journal of Blockchain Law & Policy.* Retrieved May 26, 2019 from https://stanford-jblp.pubpub.org/pub/blockchain-and-public-companies.

Shahaab, A., Lidgey, B., Hewage, C., & Khan, I. (2019). Applicability and appropriateness of distributed ledgers consensus protocols in public and private sectors: A systematic review. *IEEE Access.*

Stoll, C., Klaaßen, L., & Gallersdörfer, U. (2019). The carbon footprint of bitcoin. *Joule.* https://doi.org/10.1016/j.joule.2019.05.012.

Sup, S. J., & Erdenebold, T. (2018). The use of blockchain technology in e-government domain. In *International Conference on Future Information & Communication Engineering* (Vol. 10, No. 1).

Swan, M. (2015). *Blockchain: Blueprint for a new economy.* O'Reilly Media, Inc.

Tanzi, V. (2005). Globalization, tax system, and the architecture of the global economic system. Retrieved September 29, 2016, from https://publications.iadb.org/publications/english/document/Globalization-Tax-System-and-the-Architecture-of-the-Global-Economic-System.pdf.

Tapscott, D., & Tapscott, A. (2016). *Blockchain revolution: How the technology behind bitcoin is changing money, business, and the world: Penguin.*

TRON. (2018). *TRON advanced decentralized blockchain platform*. TRON Foundation. Retrieved March 5, 2018 from https://tron.network/static/doc/white_paper_v_2_0.pdf.

Vishnevsky, V. P., & Chekina, V. D. (2018). Robot vs. tax inspector or how the fourth industrial revolution will change the tax system: A review of problems and solutions. *Journal of Tax Reform, 4*(1), 6–26.

Wang, S., Zhang, Y., & Zhang, Y. (2018). A blockchain-based framework for data sharing with fine-grained access control in decentralized storage systems. *IEEE Access*.

Williamson, J. (2009). *Understanding special drawing rights* (SDRs). No. PB09–11. Peterson Institute for International Economics: Washington, DC.

Wood, G. (2014). Ethereum: A secure decentralised generalised transaction ledger. *Ethereum project yellow paper, 151*(2014), 1–32.

Xu, B., Luthra, D., Cole, Z., & Blakely, N. (2018). *EOS: An architectural, performance, and economic analysis*. Retrieved June 11, 2019.

Xu, X., Pautasso, C., Zhu, L., Gramoli, V., Ponomarev, A., Tran, A. B., & Chen, S. (2016). *The blockchain as a software connector*. Paper presented at the Software Architecture (WICSA), 2016 13th Working IEEE, 2016.

Yermack, D. (2017). Corporate governance and blockchains. *Review of Finance, 21*(1), 7–31.

Marco Crepaldi is a Ph.D. candidate of the joint doctorate in law, science and technology LAST-JD in co-tutelle with the University of Bologna and Luxembourg University. He graduated in law from the University of Turin and practiced law before turning to academic research. His research interests include blockchains, distributed ledgers, the legitimacy of algorithms, tax law, and space law.

A Blockchain Supported Solution for Compliant Digital Security Offerings

Andrew Le Gear

Abstract Ethereum launched in 2015 ushering a sea change over its predecessors in it's ability to tokenise an asset. This was a technical innovation and an *Initial Coin Offering* (ICO) boom ensued, peaking in 2017. The legal and compliance requirements of tokenisation failed to keep step in these early stages, but were eventually brought to bear after the ICO bubble burst, forcing technological liberalism to confront regulatory realities. The *Digital Security Offering* (DSO)—a name change intended to reflect full compliance—was coined. However, truly executing a fully compliant DSO remained elusive for many. In this chapter we navigate the regulatory landscape for DSOs and construct a compliant blockchain solution, using it to support the DSO capital raise for a product named *Talketh* in December of 2018. The journey discusses the key compliance concerns of *Know-Your-Customer* (KYC), *Anti-Money-Laundering* (AML), Custody, Tokenisation and onward secondary trading as part of a *Distributed Exchange* (DEX).

Keywords Blockchain · Initial public offering · IPO · Security token offering · STO · Digital security offering · DSO · Initial coin offering · ICO · Custody · Primary issuance · Secondary trading · Distributed exchange · DEX · Compliance

1 Introduction

A veritable tsunami of token offerings, exceeding $2.3 billion, washed through the initial coin offering (ICO) market in 2017 signalling the high watermark for this unregulated space (Zetzsche et al. 2018). By early 2018 it is estimated that half of these had already failed. A financial scandal of this scale did not go unnoticed by regulators. In the United States and Switzerland the respective agencies FINRA and FINMA brought existing securities legislation to bare on token offerings. The ICO space would no longer be the refuge from red tape and regulation for businesses

A. Le Gear (✉)
Horizon Globex Ltd, Zug, Switzerland
e-mail: andrew.legear@horizon-globex.ie

© Springer Nature Switzerland AG 2020　　　　　　　　　　　　　　　113
H. Treiblmaier and T. Clohessy (eds.), *Blockchain and Distributed Ledger Technology Use Cases*, Progress in IS, https://doi.org/10.1007/978-3-030-44337-5_6

raising investment that it once was. The *Securities and Exchange Commission* (SEC) officially declared Ether and Bitcoin as currencies, bringing the baggage of existing banking statutes in tow, and enforcement actions and subpoenas began to be served to non-compliant token offerings (Clayton 2018).

Out of necessity, a new breed of compliant token offerings have begun to emerge. Disassociating themselves from past scandals, the interchangable acronyms of DSO (Digital Security Offering) and STO (Security Token Offering) have come into parlance, whose names serve as an acknowledgement that token offerings are in fact subject to securities legislation and must be structured accordingly (Koverko and Housser 2018). This forces the issuer of a DSO or STO to acknowledge explicitly in their token contracts the roles of actors and processes that were gleefully ignored in the now archaically trivial business logic of an ERC-20. The roles of broker, issuer or transfer agent and processes for anti-money laundering (AML), know-your-customer (KYC) and dictated holding periods for tokens are mandated by law and must now be explicitly enforced in smart contracts. These requirements create as much overhead for a DSO or STO as there is experienced in a traditional initial public offering (IPO). Despite this, we quickly realise that there is no better innovation positioned to enforce the roles and procedures of an IPO/DSO/STO than a smart contract enabled blockchain solution.

Described in this chapter is such a platform and shows how the blockchain can be leveraged to support regulated requirements:

- *Notarisation*: Notarisation of the receipt of official documentation.
- *KYC*: The purpose of providing irrefutable proof of identity and source of investment funds.
- *AML*: Anti-money laundering procedures applied to KYC processes.
- *Regulation D 506c and Regulation S*: Non US offerings brought to the US market must be held by US citizens for one year post purchase.
- *Transfer Agents (Custody)*: A legally separate role whose responsibility is to move ownership of tokens between individuals, release securities in the event of an owners death and to enforce special holding periods where buyers or sellers of a token are registered affiliates of the issuing company.
- *Token Types—Utility Tokens versus Security Tokens (Primary Issuance)*: Depending on the categorisation of the token, it's primary function might be to provide a utility (e.g. gaining access to another platform), as opposed to representing an investment and legal ownership of an entity, as is the case with security tokens.
- *Bespoke Exchange (Secondary Trading)*: A means for onward, secondary trading, post-DSO, while also enforcing holding periods for US and non-US citizens.

Also described is a live executed example DSO, detailing the real world usage of an implementation of this platform. We use it to launch the DSO for a blockchain VoIP communications product called "Talketh" represented by a token with the exchange symbol "VOX." We explain the entire experience of executing this DSO including KYC, AML, custody, tokenisation and onward trading, all enabled and fully compliant as part of the blockchain solution platform on Ethereum.

For the issuer and other participating actors, the live example paints a picture of true success in forging compromise between the apparent utopian future of trustless solutions on the blockchain against the immovable regulatory institutions of old. We believe it provides a model for future adoption of blockchain solutions where existing legislation is embraced rather than subverted—disruptive technologies do not necessarily need to flirt with illegality.

2 The Security Lifecycle

First, let us expand upon the blockchain use case we are solving. Figure 1 presents a high-level view of the security lifecycle. Subtleties on a per jurisdiction basis exist as you drill into each of these steps. However, at this level of granularity, issuing a security will follow these steps the world over.

The actors involved include:

- *Issuer*: This the legal owner of the entity for which public ownership is being issued. This is the most accountable role in the process flow. All responsibility for breach of securities law ultimately resides with the issuer.
- *Reviewer*: A licensed professional who assesses KYC submissions. Relevant background checks are performed (AML) on a best effort basis and are approved accordingly to become investors in the primary issuance of the security. The role of the KYC reviewer is discussed further in the section "A Note on KYC Reviewers."
- *Transfer Agent*: The role can go by other names in other jurisdictions. We use the United States terminology here. A transfer agent is a form of "custodian" who, for various legal reasons, is empowered to hold the issued securities on behalf

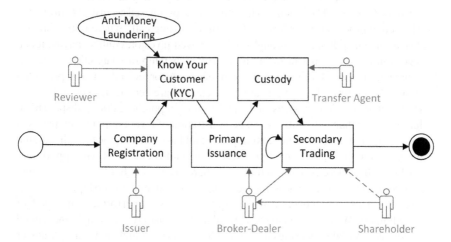

Fig. 1 The security lifecycle

of shareholders and the government. We discuss this role in more detail in the "Custody" section.

- *Broker-Dealer*: A licensed intermediary between the shareholders and all other actors in the process flow. Their role is especially pronounced where the securities are distributed, traded and investors are initially solicited.
- *Shareholders*: The owner of of an issued security. They may have gained ownership as part of the initial DSO, or later through a secondary trading venue.

The various actors then engage in the security lifecycle as follows (Fig. 1):

1. *Company Registration*: The lifecycle begins with a legal entity for which fractional ownership that will ultimately be distributed in the form of securities. The initial ownership, prior to public primary issuance, must be carefully recorded and stored. Where and how it is recorded is known as a "Good Control Location" in regulatory parlance (Ballard 1993). However, the means by which this is achieved is not explicitly stipulated—it must simply be "well known" and described in the company registration documents. The consequence of this is that an issuer may record the ownership of a company on the back of a napkin should they wish to. Obviously this is unwise, however, it is not uncommon to find private company ownership recorded on a single spreadsheet on a company hard drive. While beyond the scope of this chapter, it is worth highlighting yet another valuable blockchain use case opportunity here.

2. *KYC*: At this point, prospective investors are vetted for suitability. Reasonable effort must be employed to prove the identity of the investor. This can include, photographs, identity documents, live interviews and official payment documents from other utilities.

3. *AML*: Closely related to the KYC step, the Anti-money laundering step includes a legally required effort to exclude known criminals, politically exposed individuals and investors from sanctioned countries from the primary issuance.

4. *Primary Issuance*: The official distribution of the purchased securities to investors. The actual process often takes the form of a "closing call" where issuer, broker-dealer and custodian step through each approved investor, confirm payment and record in the good control location the new ownership of shareholder. Note, as emphasised in step 1, this is how the ownership is recorded and not, as is presented in popular culture, through a share certificate. Share certificates certainly exist. However, their role is more as a receipt for proof of purchase during dispute resolution, rather than a definitive legal demonstration of ownership. In fact, physical certificates are becoming increasingly rare and have been replaced with a digital representation for quite some time (Morris and Goldstein 2009). The opportunity for blockchain here is not to replace the share certificate, but to create a public, trusted, good control location for the company register of ownership.

5. *Custody*: This topic covers a wide range of functions performed on behalf of shareholders. We cover this in more detail in the "Custody" section. In the United States, as part of the securities lifecycle, a licensed individual known as a "transfer agent" performs this role. Key responsibilities include:

- Safe storage of physical share certificates.
- Preventing onward distribution of securities for legally required holding periods, post-primary issuance.
- Protecting investors from insider trading by preventing the onward sale of securities by affiliates of the issuing company.
- Reissuing certificates where a share certificate has been lost.
- Implementing court orders where securities must be transferred to the state in the event of a shareholder death or a criminal proceedings.

6. *Secondary Trading*: Finally, shareholders are now able to sell their issued securities onward in a licensed secondary market either directly or via a broker-dealer. We discuss blockchain supported options for this step in the section on "Secondary Trading".

3 The Talketh DSO

It is important to highlight that the blockchain supported solutions for the security lifecycle, that is described in the following sections, is not merely aspirational. It describes the real world implementation of live software and smart contracts, used to realise the Talketh VoIP DSO, which ran from November 2018 to February 2019.

Talketh is an optimised voice over IP (VoIP) smart phone app produced by Horizon Globex Ltd.[1] The app's value proposition was threefold:

- The patented optimised VoIP aspect of the product allowed the use of VoIP on 2G and Edge networks in parts of the world where other VoIP apps were unusable (Dantas et al. 2017).
- Competitive pricing for call minutes over traditional mobile carriers.
- The app could be topped up using cryptocurrency allowing up to 1 billion unbanked individuals access to the VoIP market.

The Talketh DSO was intended as a capital raise to fund expansion into it's intended markets. The DSO came under Swiss financial jurisdiction and was executed in compliance with regulations set out by FINMA (Thompson 2013).

To achieve regulatory compliance, we implemented the following products to execute the Talketh (and other future) DSOs:

- A "Know Your Customer" (KYC) solution called "KYCWare".[2]
- An Anti-Money-Laundering (AML) solution called "AML Cop".[3]
- A custody solution called "CustodyWare".[4]

---

[1] https://horizon-globex.com.

[2] https://kycware.com.

[3] https://amlcop.com.

[4] https://custodyware.com.

- A tokenisation solution called "Tokenetics".[5]

In the following sections we will explore the blockchain use cases employed in realising these solutions and specifically how they applied to the Talketh VoIP DSO.

4 Proposing a Blockchain Supported Solution for the Security Lifecycle

With our use case clearly defined we can now propose a blockchain supported software solution that adds value and trust to the process. Figure 2 summarises this proposal outlining key public blockchain hooks.[6] The following subsections will explore each of the components in detail:

- *KYC App + KYC and AML Web Service*: A white labeled smart phone application intended to be used by a prospective shareholder. The app will glean relevant KYC details, package them and submit them to the server. At the point of upload, the hash of the KYC pack is notarised to the blockchain to facilitate future dispute resolution and also to give the user confidence that the uploaded pack has remained untampered with throughout the process.
- *KYC Reviewer + KYC and AML Web Service*: A web client dashboard (Fig. 5) to be used by an approved KYC Reviewer. The KYC reviewer can review submissions

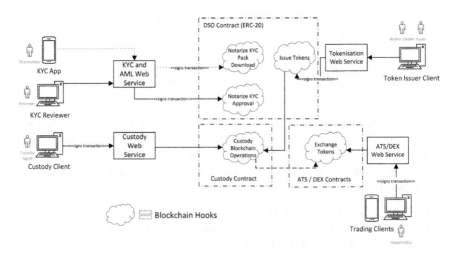

Fig. 2 A blockchain supported software solution for the security lifecycle

---

[5] https://tokenetics.com.

[6] Where a "blockchain hook" refers to an entry point on a smart contract that can be executed by traditional software.

and approve if appropriate. The approval is notarised to the blockchain to provide a verifiable chain of trust in the approval process.

- *Token Issuer Web Client + Tokenisation Web Service*: Once the issuer and broker dealer are satisfied with the suitability and identity of the prospective investor, the DSO is executed—security/utility tokens are minted and distributed to the wallets of shareholders on the blockchain. Depending on the local regulations or the type of shareholder, the tokens are deposited with a transfer agent who will custody the tokens on the shareholders behalf.
- *Custody Web Client + Custody Web Service*: A web front end intended to be used by a regulated transfer agent. Importantly, this solution makes the transfer agent responsible for maintaining their own private key for signing transactions to execute typical transfer agent tasks. This eliminates the potential that someone impersonated the transfer agent as part of the custody process. In the section "Custody" we discuss exactly what these "transfer agent tasks" are.
- *Trading Clients + ATS/DEX Web Service*: Finally, the custodian (transfer agent) releases the tokens to the shareholder for onward secondary trading. This can only be done if specific regulatory conditions are met (see the "Secondary Trading" section). An app and web service are provided to execute the exchange of tokens between shareholders. Shareholders sign transactions to execute this exchange, however centralised oversight is still needed to meet regulatory requirements. While this may be anathema to decentralised blockchain evangelists, it is a necessary step to ensure regulatory compliance. This can neatly be summarised for our system as "Decentralised trading, centralised control."

In the following subsections we will expand upon each of the subprocesses in Fig. 2 to demonstrate how they are implemented.

5 Know Your Customer and Anti-money Laundering

A KYC and AML process is stipulated by financial regulators to prevent criminal activity in the financial markets and to protect investors participating in those markets. The protections referred to may not be initially obvious. Many public offerings, while perfectly legitimate, can be deemed of high risk and not suitable for investors of lesser means. Effectively, the regulator's role here is to prevent individuals from being reckless with their own money, by only allowing individuals above a certain wealth threshold, known as "accredited investors" (Lee 2011), to participate.

Common KYC and AML requirements include:

- Identifying details such as name, address, phone number, photograph.
- Proof of address such as a utility bill.
- Proof of citizenship by way of passport or drivers license.
- Meeting the individual.
- The individual is not politically exposed or has a criminal history.

Fig. 3 Compliant KYC and AML app

• The individual has the financial means to participate in the investment.

Figure 3 shows several screen shots from our solution, implementing a compliant KYC solution, mapping to the "KYC App" from Fig. 2. However, in the context of this chapter we will only focus on how the solution integrates with the blockchain and adds value to a compliant KYC process.

5.1 A Note on KYC Reviewers

The role of reviewer in the KYC process is not simply an actor in a use case. It is an official, regulated role in many jurisdictions. The common structure is shown in Fig. 4. Residing at the top level is the financial regulator of the country. Taking the United States and Switzerland as examples, this maps to the SEC (Seligman 1982) and Swiss *Financial Market Supervisory Authority* (FINMA) (Thompson 2013) respectively. These regulators then in turn fund a non-profit entity to enforce these regulations—in our example this maps to the *Financial Industry Regulator Authority* (FINRA) (Black 2013) in the US and the *Financial Services Standards Association* (VQF) (Müller-Studer 2004) in Switzerland. The role of these authorities is to legally enforce the regulations in that jurisdiction and, importantly, to authorise any professionals who operate in this marketplace. This includes individuals who are authorised to review and approve KYC information, who must acquire a license from the enforcement agency.

5.2 A Compliant, Blockchain Supported KYC Platform

Our compliant blockchain supported solution for KYC and AML has three important blockchain hooks:

1. Ethereum wallets:

   • Token receiving wallet.

Fig. 4 KYC reviewer in a
regulatory context

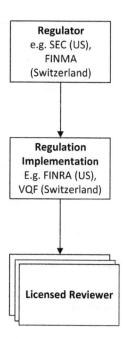

- Payment wallet.

2. Notarisations:

  - Hash of KYC pack upon upload.
  - KYC approval by the KYC reviewer.

Ethereum Wallets

Unlike a traditional KYC process, when operating within a blockchain and security tokenisation space, the opportunity for fraud is rampant (Fleder et al. 2015; Griffin and Shams 2018; Spagnuolo et al. 2014). If the investor wishes to pay in cryptocurrency[7] or has identified a wallet to receive security tokens, then those wallets must be subjected to a level of due diligence. Our solution provides for two blockchain supports to ease the KYC and AML assessment of these wallets (Fig. 5):

1. *Clean Wallet Creation*: Built into the process flow of the KYC app[8] is the option to create a new wallet, purely for the purposes of receiving tokens as part of the offering. A fresh wallet, with no pre-existing transactions, cannot by definition have any fraudulent transactions, thus dramatically easing the review process. Post-DSO, an investor can then move their tokens from this "hot wallet" to more secure "cold storage" in the form of a hardware wallet or printed key in a safe (Wong and Pocock 2018).
2. *Assisted Wallet Forensics*: The *public* wallet addresses, provided as part of the KYC process are uploaded to the server as part of the KYC pack for the reviewer

---

[7]Which, incidentally, is illegal in most jurisdictions as of July 2019.

[8]Visit https://kycware.com for further information.

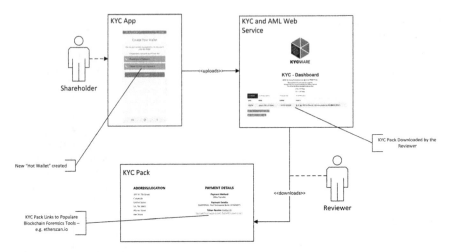

Fig. 5 Blockchain hooks for ethereum wallets

Fig. 6 Hash of KYC pack, post upload

to assess. We can then link the reviewer to popular blockchain forensic tools to aid in an AML assessment of these wallets.

Notarisations

We also leverage the Ethereum blockchain to provide providence at two steps of the KYC process. The KYC App uploads a zip file (the KYC pack) to the server. A hash of this file is provided to the user at the time of upload (shown in Fig. 6). The

KYC reviewer is also aware of this hash, while thirdly, the hash is also stored to the Ethereum smart contract, shown here:

Listing 6.1 Notarisation of Hash

```
function setKycHash(bytes32 sha) public onlyOwner {
    kycHashes.push(sha);
}
```

This is incredibly important where disputes arise, as a single byte change to the KYC Pack file will result in a drastically different hash. Both investor and reviewer can know with confidence that untampered KYC packs are being referenced when resolving disputes.

Finally, when a KYC reviewer is satisfied that a pack has passed KYC and AML checks, he will approve the pack to participate in the DSO. The new state of the KYC review—that it is now approved for the receiving wallet—is notarised to the Ethereum smart contract:

Listing 6.2 Notarisation of Approval

```
function kycApproved(bytes32 sha) public onlyKycProvider {
    kycValidated.push(sha);
}
```

Note the "onlyKycProvider" modifier in this case. This modifier is defined as:

Listing 6.3 Only KYC Provider

```
modifier onlyKycProvider {
    require(msg.sender = regulatorApprovedKycProvider, "Only_the_KYC_Provider_can_call_this_function.");
    _;
}
```

It stipulates that only a specific nominated private key can approve submissions. The KYC provider must sign these transactions and only she possesses the private key of the nominated wallet. This enforces the securities regulations dictated at a blockchain smart contract level.[9]

6 Primary Issuance

Primary issuance refers to the initial creation of securities as part of a public offering (Gray et al. 1997). The security originates from the issuer and was not acquired through a third party, as you would when trading in a marketplace. In a blockchain context, "tokenisation" is a primary issuance where the issued securities are expressed within a smart contract and distributed to wallets owned by shareholders (Chen 2018). The act of tokenising an asset for the purposes of sale as part of a capital raise is a "Digital Securities Offering" (DSO)—The blockchain equivalent of an IPO (Kranz et al. 2019).

---

[9]For reference, a deployed example of this contract is here: https://kovan.etherscan.io/address/ 0x88e6f26a86caf47873e7c84bd43808f895b88b5a#contracts.

The most prevalent approach to creating a security token on the Ethereum blockchain is to implement the ERC-20 standard (Vogelsteller and Buterin 2018). At the time of writing, several other competing standards have been proposed, but none have achieved the same widespread adoption as ERC-20. These other ERC's include ERC-223, ERC-677, ERC-777, ERC-721 and ERC-827.[10] They attempt to solve various problems such as minting, fungibility and token loss, which were all vulnerabilities of the original ERC-20 specification.

The focus of the proposed solution in this chapter centers around compliance. Our approach has been to take a standard ERC-20 implementation and augment it to satisfy regulatory requirements including:

- Transfers can only occur between token holders approved through the KYC process.
- The definition of the DSO being complete, and then restricting transfers to the issuer only until the DSO is complete.
- Burning of tokens to reduce supply.

An example of these requirements deployed to Ethereum mainnet is here:

https://etherscan.io/address/0xbaf8f642e51e4dd275f1a4bdc960dcf14d9094b4# contracts—a contract used to tokenise the "Talketh VoIP" DSO. The specific blockchain hooks corresponding to the above list are:

Listing 6.4 Key ERC-20 Ammendments for Compliant Tokenisation

```
// (1)
    function _transfer(address from, address to, uint256 value) internal returns (bool) {
    require(isAuthorised(to), "Target_of_transfer_has_not_passed_KYC");

...

// (2)
    function icoTransfer(address to, uint256 value) public onlyOwner {
    require(!isIcoComplete, "ICO_is_complete,_use_transfer().");

...

// (3)
    function _burn(address addressToBurn, uint256 value) private returns (bool success)
```

Earlier, the KYC reviewer possessed a separate key for signing transactions when notarising KYC approval. This now becomes more important as it creates a deliberate compliance barrier between the issuer, broker-dealer and regulated approver and, as will become evident in the following section, a divide between the custodian also. This provides clear and compliant separation of roles. To allow a broker-dealer to interact with these hooks as part of the tokenisation flow of a DSO we provide a web client for ease of use (Fig. 7). For this component, the web client is password protected and the private key of the issuer installed on the web server within a secure network, which is used to sign transactions needed to distribute the tokens. The

---

[10]The full list of Ethereum Request for Comment (ERC) is here: https://github.com/ethereum/EIPs/tree/master/EIPS

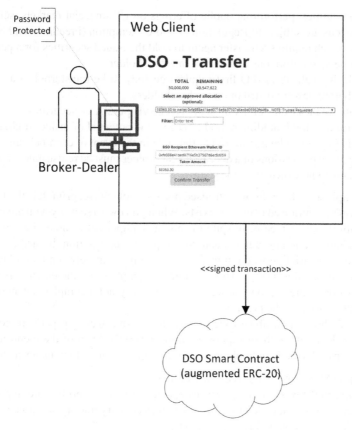

Fig. 7 Compliantly distributing tokens

broker and issuer, as part of the closing call, can then use the web client to distribute the tokens to complete the DSO. Figure 7 describes this flow. One important feature, that will be expanded upon in the next section, is that in certain circumstances, the regulations require that the tokens be transferred directly to a custodian and marked as "held" for shareholder. The web client described automatically handles this scenario, depending on the jurisdiction of the DSO.

7 Custody

Custody in the regulated securities markets is a core concept, and yet is one that, until recently, has been completely overlooked by the utopian, distributed token vision provided by blockchain. As part of the United States primary security issuances market, the role of the custodian is called a "Transfer Agent" (Loader 2013). Important functions performed by a transfer agent include:

- Foreign entities, performing public offerings on US financial markets, selling to US citizens are subject to Regulation D 506-c exemption (Freedman and Nutting 2015), which requires a transfer agent to hold the issued securities for a period of up to one year before onward sale by the shareholder.
- The closing call of an IPO first requires custody to be transferred to a transfer agent before onward distribution to shareholders.
- Affiliates of the issuing entity must deposit newly purchased securities to a transfer agent for a 3 month holding period to negate the potential of insider trading.
- Seized assets must be transferred to the state in the event of criminal suits.
- The security possessions of a deceased shareholder must be redistributed by transfer agents to new owners or the state.

The implication here for decentralised purists is, of course, grim. It is the law that some form of centralised oversight exists. When you own a security, you are not free to do with it as you please. In spite of this, it is important to note, that giving up some decentralisation does not equate to complete centralisation. In fact, earlier we discussed the restriction where transfers could only occur between individuals that had been subjected to KYC—This is another example of an incremental retrenchment towards centralisation—however, it is certainly not a complete abandonment of decentralisation in the process.

Figure 8 shows a dashboard we provide to transfer agents to perform common custody tasks to allow them support compliant DSO's. Each of the menu items is supported by a blockchain hook on a separate smart contract to manage custody:

- *Transfer*: Move tokens between two wallets.
- *Custody*: Pull tokens into custody from a token holder who has pre-approved a transfer.[11] This is intended to be used where secondary trading has already begun and tokens are being returned to custody.
- *Release*: Transfer control of tokens back to a shareholder. This moves tokens from the custody contract to the shareholders wallet.
- *Partial Release*: Same as previous, except only a portion of the tokens are released.
- *Holding Details*: Query the token quantities currently being held on behalf of a shareholder.
- *Add Time*: Increase or decrease the holding period assigned to a shareholder.
- *Set Affiliate Status*: Mark a shareholder as an "affiliate." Thus if they receive tokens they would be subject to a holding period before they could be released.

A complete code listing for the custody smart contract can be found here

https://etherscan.io/address/0xb966bb63027f82fcb8de4f07bc4084c5735d5112# contracts. We noted above, that the "Custody" function was one entry point to custody, post-DSO. The other entry point is part of the initial token distribution and was alluded to at the end of the previous section. We perform this transfer in an uncommon way, worth expanding on. First, tokens are transferred to the address of the custody smart contract. Then "hold()" is executed on the custody smart contract

---

[11]Used the "approve()" and "transferFrom()" operations on the standard ERC-20 interface.

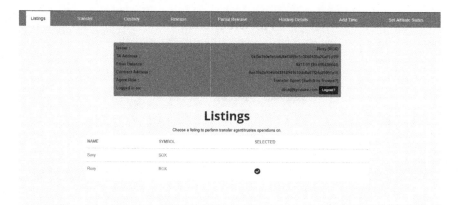

Fig. 8 Compliant custody dashboard for a transfer agent

to place a ledger entry that this custody contract is holding a portion of it's tokens for a specific shareholder. Note, that the transfer was not to the wallet address of the transfer agent, but to the actual smart contract address where the range of operations that can be performed with the tokens is strictly limited to clearly defined roles of a transfer agent. The transfer agents wallet is the only wallet permissioned to execute these functions on the custody smart contract, but equally the transfer agent is prevented from stealing the tokens for himself. Also, the semantic difference here is important—the transfer agent has the tokens in custody, but is never actually an owner of the tokens.

8 Secondary Trading

Technically, by this stage, the DSO is complete. For completeness we will discuss the secondary trading phase, however this topic is vast. A full discussion of blockchain distributed exchanges and secondary trading venues is beyond the scope of this chapter.

We will discuss a single secondary trading venue example, that is narrow in scope, yet compliant within it's jurisdiction. It is a simple DEX for the exchange of Talketh utility tokens and is deployed on the Ethereum Mainnet[12] here

https://etherscan.io/address/0x01e15429fedbc08dec25e127df09b4af17167f5e# contracts

At it's simplest, the DEX is an Ethereum smart contract which records bids and asks from token holders. A "bid" states the maximum that buyer is willing to pay, and the "ask" is the minumum a seller is willing to accept. If there is an overlap

---

[12]The name ascribed to the production network of Ethereum.

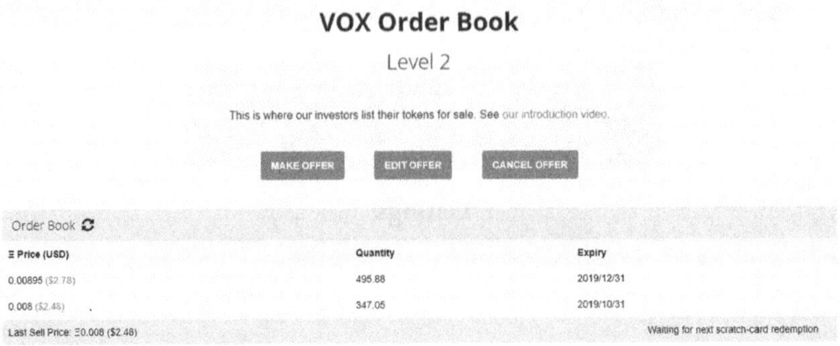

VOX Order Book

Level 2

This is where our investors list their tokens for sale. See our introduction video.

| MAKE OFFER | EDIT OFFER | CANCEL OFFER |

Order Book ⟳

⟂ Price (USD)	Quantity	Expiry
0.00895 ($2.78)	495.88	2019/12/31
0.008 ($2.48)	347.05	2019/10/31
Last Sell Price: Ξ0.008 ($2.48)		Waiting for next scratch-card redemption

Fig. 9 Web client for the DEX

between these two prices a "cross" occurs and tokens are transferred, using the existing "transfer()" on the related ERC-20 an exchange, from seller to buyer. These DEX functions correspond to the following on the smart contract:

Listing 6.5 Bid/Ask and Cross on the DEX Interface

```
// Buy
function multiExecute(address[] sellers, uint256 lastQuantity) public payable returns (uint256 totalVouchers)
// Ask
function offer(uint256 quantity, uint256 price, uint256 expiry) public
// Execute
function execute(address seller, uint256 quantity, uint256 price)
```

Beyond these basic hooks, the DEX contract also offers support for cancels, price floors and ceilings, restricting trading to KYC'd individuals, fees, and specific calls where vouchers are being redeemed (discussed below). Asks can be placed on the DEX and the current order book viewed using a provided web client shown in Fig. 9. As with the other previous services provided, placing asks and cancels can only be achieved by the holder of the private key in order to sign the transactions. The transactions are signed locally and the private key never leaves the device of the user—in this sense it is a true distributed exchange.

The token economics needed to drive the liquidity of such a DEX emerges from the following business drivers:

- The minted tokens are "utility" tokens rather then "security" tokens. That is, their value is a utility that can be redeemed, rather than representing legal ownership of a company.
- In this case, the utility represented is discounted international call minutes.
- Large investors in the Talketh DSO would adopt the role of international wholesalers of call minutes, and thus would purchase the utility token at scale upon launch of the DSO.
- The capital raised as part of the DSO would then be deployed to fund sales and marketing of the platform internationally.
- Next, two mechanisms to provide an exit for the initial utility token purchasers are structured:

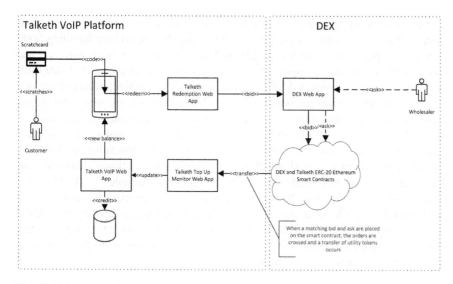

Fig. 10 Using a scratchcard to match an ask placed on the DEX

1. Local re-sellers[13] of call credit for Talketh can purchase minutes from the wholesalers on the DEX for onward distribution, with the wholesalers offering a typical markup on their ask price. Since the utility tokens were originally minted to redeem discounted minutes, the scope for profit margin lies in the difference between the face value of the minutes represented and the original token price.
2. Dealing with blockchain, wallets, signing transactions and acquiring cryptocurrency are quite significant technical barriers to entry for the average individual. As such, the Talketh platform has also rolled out a scratch card system for topping up. Scratch cards can be purchased with local currency and redeemed in the app. Instead of simply purchasing credit at full price, the scratch card redemption is linked to the DEX and will automatically attempt to purchase a discounted utility token from the market. The incentive here is clear: The customer has the opportunity to receive more credit than the apparent face value of the scratchcard, while also providing an exit with a margin for the wholesaler. This redemption mechanism is described in Fig. 10.

8.1 A Note on Blockchain Capacity for High Volume DEX Platforms

The capacity of a blockchain, like Ethereum, to scale is often cited as a looming problem (Gencer et al. 2018). As it currently stands, Ethereum can handle up to

---

[13]For example, the owner of a corner shop.

25 transactions per second (Buterin 2016c). The comparative use case that is often cited is that of the traditional platforms of Visa and Mastercard both handling 5000 transactions per second (Beck et al. 2016). Even choosing the much narrower use case of trading systems (as opposed to global transactions of all sorts), NASDAQ still requires 10 times the reported Ethereum maximum of 15 transactions per second. Arguably, some of these criticisms are unfair. Discounting the upcoming throughput gains promised by Ethereum 2.0 (Buterin 2016a, b), the comparative use cases of Visa, Mastercard and NASDAQ refer to the largest transactional systems of their kind on the planet. While an ambitious and worthy goal for blockchain technology, for which it currently falls short, there are many large traditional platforms that Ethereum currently has ample capacity to disrupt. For example, "OTC Markets" is the public home of over 10,000 listed American companies. By contrast, the NASDAQ has only 3300 listings. Yet, the OTC only requires a capacity of 180,000 trades per day. Ethereum could handle 10 times the volumes of the OTC as it currently stands (Domanski and Heath 2007)—Facts worth considering given the prevalence of counter arguments to this opinion.

9 Conclusion

Over the course of this chapter we have discussed the difficult blockchain use case of security offerings. This difficulty is not so much a technical, but a regulatory and compliance one. Navigating international securities regulation requires expert legal and professional input in lock step with a technical implementation team. Demonstrating with a live execution, in the form of the Talketh DSO, we have accomplished this goal, and produced a reusable implementation of the regulatory business logic, supported by the blockchain at its core. We are already applying this platform to more DSO's and future work will focus on compliant secondary trading in the United States to complement the platform. As a base technology, blockchain is now well positioned to add real value to complicated use cases like compliant security offerings and holds the real potential now to be at the center of one of the worlds most valuable technology genres.

References

Ballard, S. V. V. L. (1993). Memorandum of understanding between the United States. *SEC Docket, 54*(5).

Beck, R., Stenum Czepluch, J., Lollike, N., & Malone, S. (2016). Blockchain—The gateway to trust-free cryptographic transactions.

Black, B. (2013). Punishing bad brokers: Self-regulation and finra sanctions. *Brooklyn Journal of Corporate, Financial & Commercial Law, 8,* 23.

Buterin, V. (2016a). Ethereum 2.0 mauve paper. In *Ethereum developer conference* (Vol. 2).

Buterin, V. (2016b). Ethereum 2.0 mauve paper. In *Ethereum developer conference* (Vol. 2).

Buterin, V. (2016c). Ethereum: Platform review. *Opportunities and Challenges for Private and Consortium Blockchains.*

Chen, Y. (2018). Blockchain tokens and the potential democratization of entrepreneurship and innovation. *Business Horizons, 61*(4), 567–575.

Clayton, J. (2018). Chairman's testimony on virtual currencies: The roles of the sec and cftc. In *Testimony before the committee on banking, housing, and urban affairs, United States senate.*

Dantas, R., Exton, C., & Le Gear, A. (2017). Improving mobile voip quality through bandwidth optimisation.

Domanski, D. & Heath, A. (2007). Financial investors and commodity markets. *BIS Quarterly Review.*

Fleder, M., Kester, M. S., & Pillai, S. (2015). Bitcoin transaction graph analysis. arXiv:1502.01657.

Freedman, D. M., & Nutting, M. R. (2015). The growth of equity crowdfunding. *Value Examiner,* 6–10.

Gencer, A. E., Basu, S., Eyal, I., Van Renesse, R., & Sirer, E. G. (2018). Decentralization in bitcoin and ethereum networks. arXiv:1801.03998.

Gray, S., et al. (1997). Government securities: Primary issuance. Handbooks.

Griffin, J. M., & Shams, A. (2018). Is bitcoin really un-tethered? Available at SSRN 3195066.

Koverko, T., & Housser, C. (2018). *Growth,* 4, 5.

Kranz, J., Nagel, E., & Yoo, Y. (2019). Blockchain token sale. *Business & Information Systems Engineering,* 1–9.

Lee, S.-Y. (2011). Why the accredited investor standard fails the average investor. *Review of Banking and Financial Law, 31,* 987.

Loader, D. (2013). *Clearing, settlement and custody.* Butterworth-Heinemann.

Morris, V. B., & Goldstein, S. Z. (2009). *Guide to clearance & settlement: An introduction to dtcc.* Lightbulb Press, Inc.

Müller-Studer, L. (2004). The function of self-regulating organisations in the swiss money laundering control scheme. *Journal of Money Laundering Control, 7*(1), 69–74.

Seligman, J. (1982). *The transformation of wall street: A history of the securities and exchange commission and modern corporate finance.* Boston: Houghton Mifflin.

Spagnuolo, M., Maggi, F., & Zanero, S. (2014). Bitiodine: Extracting intelligence from the bitcoin network. In International conference on financial cryptography and data security (pp. 457–468). Springer.

Thompson, J. H. (2013). A global comparison of insider trading regulations. *International Journal of Accounting and Financial Reporting, 3*(1), 1.

Vogelsteller, F., & Buterin, V. (2018). Erc-20 token standard, 2015. https://github.com/ethereum/EIPs/tree/master/EIPS, 04–13.

Wong, S., & Pocock, A. (2018). Digital assets and their impact on wealth management. Available at SSRN 3367451.

Zetzsche, D. A., Buckley, R. P., Arner, D. W., & Föhr, L. (2018). The ICO gold rush: It's a scam, it's a bubble, it's a super challenge for regulators.

Author Biographies

Andrew Le Gear received a B.Sc. 1st Class Honours Degree in Computer Systems from the University of Limerick in 2003. This was followed by a research scholarship with the Software Architecture Evolution Group at the same university until December 2006, when he received a Ph.D. in Computer Science entitled "Component Reconn-exion." Andrew is the author of numerous publications in the fields of software maintenance, architecture, analysis and more recently in blockchain analysis and reverse engineering. Since completing his Ph.D., Andrew has also worked as a professional software engineer in several of the worlds most software intense companies including Dell, IBM, QAD, Lehman Brothers, Nomura, and most recently as CTO at Horizon Globex Ltd. Andrew's main academic and professional interests now converge on blockchain technologies and applications.

A Blockchain-Driven Approach to Fulfill the GDPR Recording Requirements

Wolfgang Radinger-Peer and Bernhard Kolm

Abstract On 25th May 2018, the European General Data Protection Regulation (GDPR) came into effect and required transformation into national legislation in all member states of the European Union. GDPR stipulates that businesses may only process personal data on documented instructions. Furthermore, article 33 paragraph 5 states that any personal data breach and its effects have to be documented. As a conclusion, any processing (article 4 paragraph 2) has to be recorded in an appropriate manner. To this end, Blockchain technology presents a suitable approach. Blockchain technology has clear advantages in comparison to classical recording techniques, which can be manipulated and deleted more easily. The use case described in this chapter is the application of Blockchain technology to fulfill the GDPR documentation requirements for a Log Management System (LMS). The purpose is to monitor sensitive data (files or folders) that can be defined via a configuration. To facilitate recording in an appropriate manner, a private and distributed architecture of a Blockchain with a two-level hierarchy is described. In the data block the SuperBlockchain (higher level) contains a SubBlockchain (lower level) which stores the log file information. The SubBlockchain is valid for a specific time span e.g. for one day, which speeds up any search in the log files in the case of an incident.

1 Introduction

At first glance, the GDPR and Blockchain technology follow different goals. On the one hand, the GDPR aims to give the individuals sovereignty over their own data and offers them the opportunity to control which personal data can be stored. On the other hand, Blockchain technology allows for the storing of data in a decentralized, transparent, and immutable fashion. This apparent contradiction has been dubbed

W. Radinger-Peer (✉) · B. Kolm
University of Applied Sciences, FH Campus Wien, Vienna, Austria
e-mail: wolfgang.radinger-peer@edu.fh-campuswien.ac.at

B. Kolm
e-mail: bernhard.kolm@stud.fh-campuswien.ac.at

© Springer Nature Switzerland AG 2020
H. Treiblmaier and T. Clohessy (eds.), *Blockchain and Distributed Ledger Technology Use Cases*, Progress in IS, https://doi.org/10.1007/978-3-030-44337-5_7

the Blockchain-GDPR Paradox (Coelho and Younes 2018; Van Humbeeck 2017). Nevertheless, the broad functionality of Blockchain Technology means it can also be used to fulfill recording requirements defined in the GDPR.

In a classical IT system environment the whole system, or parts thereof, can break down, or users may complain about the accessibility or performance of the system. In such cases, the subsequent analysis is mostly based on log files written by the system during operation. They are important to support any investigation into the cause and/or the originator. In addition to simple technical reasons why these log files may become corrupted, the originator-perhaps a malicious employee or an attacker from the outside-is motivated to delete the log files and to blur any traces of their interference. The parties responsible for an incident in a company's IT system could try to delete or change traces so that the fault is attributed to a different source, i.e. unauthorized access to sensitive data. Log files are therefore key elements for forensic investigation, so their security and stability is indispensable. The manipulation of log files can take many different expressions, but the possibilities to recognize such manipulations also vary greatly. "File verification" mechanisms seek to ensure that a file has not been changed. For example, checksum or hash techniques can be used to verify content, authors or digital ownership. Such services are already offered by Blockchain-based service providers including Proven Open EXcellence (*poex.io*, Araoz and Ordano 2019). This platform proves the existence of a file at a determined moment by saving an SHA-256 hash of the file and timestamp on a Blockchain. Hence, such platforms can assure the existence of a file at a specific point in time. However, "Proof-of-Existence" providers cannot be used for a scalable LMS, as there is no proper search function. A search function is essential in case of an incident to have a possibility to search within the log file. Moreover, the provision of these services by third parties (centralized authority/platform) necessitates trust in the service provider. In this context, a self-managed LMS which is traceable, verifiable, and invariable yields specific benefits.

Blockchain technology has received enormous attention in the last years and seems to be a suitable approach for many problems. Sometimes a classical client-server architecture would also serve as an appropriate solution. This case study for an LMS is classified based on Treiblmaier (2019), and accordingly outlines why the decision for a Blockchain-based solution is appropriate.

Wüst and Gervais (2018) provide a flow chart to determine if Blockchain technology is suitable in a given situation. The first condition is that "data" needs to be stored, which is the case in an LMS, since the Blockchain acts as a distributed database for the generated log data. Blockchain solutions are viable where multiple users or systems need access via a network and can use the Blockchain to store data; in this case the logging information and meta information (e.g. filename, path). If there is only a single user with writing permissions, a traditional database can also fulfill the requirements. In this particular use case, multiple servers and clients serve as potential log event sources and therefore justify a Blockchain-based solution. The final, i.e. perhaps the key argument for the use of Blockchain technology, is that the various participating users cannot be fully trusted.

Holt (2006) describes an approach for the immutability of log files. He uses a Message Authentication Code (MAC) based on a secret "head of the hash chain", which has to be stored in a safe place like "slip of paper locked in a safe" or "separate trusted computer". Every time the file changes or a new file is added, this occurs via a one-way function. In the case of an attack, the aggressor has no possibility to change the log files unnoticed (integrity), or to recover the secrets encoded by the MACs. Only the administrator can "recover" the hash-chain with the original password to check if the logs are unchanged. The drawback of this approach is that files can be deleted, which is not possible using Blockchain technology. Holt (2006, p. 2) defines three elements of Logcrypt which form the foundation of its security:

1. Logs begin in a known state which is recorded in a secure external system.
2. The security of an earlier state can be used to verify the integrity of a later state, assuming the system is secure in both states.
3. Once a secret is used to secure a log entry, it is erased from memory as soon as possible.

The first two points also apply to a Blockchain solution: the Blockchain-based LMS can be seen as an external system, and due to the Blockchain technology the security is system-immanent. While the administrator can check whether log files have been changed or deleted, the problem of this approach is that they cannot be restored in case they have been manipulated. The aim of this work is to design and implement an immutable LMS based on Blockchain technology, which addresses the GDPR recording requirements and also the privacy rights of the individual user. This system stores log data on the Blockchain, receives the log files, calculates the hashes, and stores them immutably.

In the next section, the underlying GDPR framework is discussed to highlight which articles affect the design. This is supplemented with a discussion of the related work concerning Blockchain and GDPR.

2 The GDPR Framework

Two years after it had been formally adopted on 27 April 2016, the GDPR came into force. According to article 3 paragraph 2a and 2b, "Territorial scope", (Council of the European Union 2018c) the GDPR addresses anyone around the world for "*offering of goods or services, irrespective of whether a payment of the data subject is required, to such data subjects in the Union*" or "*the monitoring of their behaviour as far as their behaviour takes place within the Union.*" This applies to any online platform which logs the customers' IP address. Even the IP address is personal data according to recital 30 of the GDPR (Council of the European Union 2018h): "*Natural persons may be associated with online identifiers provided by their devices, applications, tools and protocols, such as internet protocol addresses, cookie identifiers or other identifiers such as radio frequency identification tags.*" In article 28 paragraph 3a the GDPR defines that businesses must process "personal data only on documented instructions from the controller ..."

One of the main motivations for the designed system is compliance with article 33 paragraph 5 of the GDPR, which states that *"The controller shall document any personal data breaches, comprising the facts relating to the personal data breach, its effects and the remedial action taken. That documentation shall enable the supervisory authority to verify compliance with this Article."* To find out what personal data have been breached, it is essential that the log files which document the data breaches are neither deleted nor modified, and are saved in an appropriate way. The GDPR defines several articles concerning preprocessing of data, especially personal data. Those bearing some relation to Blockchain technology or to LMS are discussed next.

Article 5, named "Principles Relating to Processing of Personal Data", defines the six principles for data processing under the responsibility of the data controller (Council of the European Union 2018e):

- Lawfulness, fairness and transparency
- Limitation of processing to legitimate purposes
- Data minimization
- Accuracy
- Limitation on time period of storage
- Integrity and confidentiality.

This article provides a lot of space for interpretations as the GDPR does not define how to implement it. Any approach must be lawful, must ensure the integrity of the data, and must restrict processing to the minimum time necessary according to the purpose for which they are collected. Hence, the log files are saved in an appropriate manner resulting in a state where the files cannot be modified or deleted.

The term controller is defined in GDPR article 4 "Definitions" (Council of the European Union 2018d) paragraph 7 as *"controller: means the natural or legal person, public authority, agency or other body which, alone or jointly with others, determines the purposes and means of the processing of personal data."*

The main inconsistency between GDPR and Blockchain can be found in article 17, called the "Right to be forgotten" (Council of the European Union 2018a). This article grants data subjects the right to have their data erased. Using Blockchain Technology, however, makes it impossible to delete data previously stored on the Blockchain (Lima 2018; Van Humbeeck 2017).

However, this article is not always automatically applied to all people, as paragraph 2 of the same article stipulates the conditions under which this right can be exercised. Therefore, there is no general "right to be forgotten". Rather, the authors describe in Kunde (2017) that *"If the request for deletion threatens the existence of the entire Blockchain because the deletion would make the further operation of the nodes impossible, the balancing of interests have to be performed in favor of the responsible node operators."* Furthermore, Article 17 (3) of the GDPR describes that *"the right to be forgotten is not applicable to the assertion, exercise or defense of rights"*. Special categories of personal data (e.g. sensitive data) pertinent to the right to be forgotten do not apply to log information.

Herian (2018) discusses the discrepancy between GDPR article 17 and Blockchain technology. He states that *"It is important to note that 'erasure' is not an absolute right to be forgotten under the terms of the legislation, however, and if, for example, the data involve defense of a legal claim or have overriding public interest, then a data controller can refuse to comply with the right."* (Herian 2018, p. 13). Further, the approach of encrypting the personal data on the Blockchain and deleting the encryption keys is not enough to fulfill the GDPR requirements. Herian (2018, p. 14) cites (Maxwell and Winston 2017), who describes this issue

> One of the design features of Blockchain architecture is that transaction records cannot be changed or deleted after-the-fact. A subsequent transaction can always annul the first transaction, but the first transaction will remain in the chain. The GDPR recognizes a right to erasure. The broad principle underpinning this right is to enable an individual to request the deletion or removal of personal data where there is no compelling reason for its continued processing. What constitutes 'erasure' is still open to debate. Some data protection authorities have found that irreversible encryption constitutes erasure. In a Blockchain environment, erasure is technically impossible because the system is designed to prevent it.

On the other hand Lima (2018) and Van Humbeeck (2017) provide two approaches for an off-chain data architecture. The aim is to store the personal data of the user (email, phone number, geolocation, computer IP-address etc.) in a traditional database (Van Humbeeck 2017) or in the cloud (Lima 2018). Both approaches store only a hash key of the sensitive data on the Blockchain. If a customer or user applies article 17, the data are deleted in the respective data store and the hash remains on the Blockchain. The off-chain data storage is used for all personal data, while other data can still be stored in the Blockchain to comply with article 17. The approach of also storing personal data in the Blockchain and merely deleting the encryption key in case of a request to delete the data is not an acceptable solution, according to Van Humbeeck (2017): " *...throwing away your encryption keys which encrypts personal data in a Blockchain technology is not acceptable as 'erasure of data' according to GDPR."*

Coelho and Younes (2018) propose an architecture with on-ledger trust and off-ledger data, which is characterized firstly by efficiency in real-world use cases, secondly by compliance with the GDPR, and finally by the Blockchain attributes of Trust and Non-Repudiation. The so-called consortium approach is characterized as efficient because it is not on a public domain and is GDPR compliant according to article 17. They separate data between the Blockchain and off-chain data, and only a generated transaction ID to signify the storage of personal data, which can even be deleted by third-party applications.

In summary of article 17, it can be said that users can request that their data is erased, but that data controllers can decline such requests under specific circumstances, especially *"for compliance with a legal obligation which requires processing by Union or Member State law to which the controller is subject or for the performance of a task carried out in the public interest or in the exercise of official authority vested in the controller"* according to article 17 paragraph 3b.

For example, in the banking sector, official regulations are defined whereby every decision in process has to be logged to be transparent. Most often decisions have to be made in accordance with the four-eyes principle. While log data do not constitute sensitive data from a user's perspective, they are sensitive from the company's point of view. Log information must therefore be kept for documentation purposes and cannot be deleted for compliance reasons, which can be achieved using Blockchain technology. Thus, to conform with the GDPR, this approach stores minimal user information, such as name and (business) IP address.

While in Permissioned Blockchains the compression of any number of blocks into a smaller number of blocks or the insertion of a block into the existing Blockchain (Ateniese et al. 2017) can result in data on the Blockchain being deleted, this is not possible with Permissionless Blockchain, where it is impossible for any node to efficiently delete data.

Another relevant article is GDPR article 25, "Privacy by Design", which defines (Council of the European Union 2018b):

> Taking into account the state of the art, the cost of implementation and the nature, scope, context, and purposes of processing as well as the risks of varying likelihood and severity for rights and freedoms of natural persons posed by the processing, the controller shall, both at the time of the determination of the means for processing and at the time of the processing itself, implement appropriate technical and organizational measures, such as pseudonymisation, which are designed to implement data-protection principles, such as data minimisation, in an effective manner and to integrate the necessary safeguards into the processing in order to meet the requirements of this Regulation and protect the rights of data subjects.

The original resolution of Privacy by Design goes back to the 32nd International Conference of Data Protection and Privacy Commissioners in 2010 (Resolution on Privacy by Design 2010). The Resolution onPrivacy by Design (2010, p. 2) outlines the foundational principles as follows:

- Proactive not Reactive; Preventative not Remedial
- Privacy as the Default
- Privacy Embedded into Design
- Full Functionality: Positive-Sum, not Zero-Sum
- End-to-End Lifecycle Protection
- Visibility and Transparency
- Respect for User Privacy.

Kolain (2018) describe an approach to ensuring that software systems comply with the principle of Privacy by Design. In doing so, they follow data on the Blockchain which is not saved as plain text. Most Blockchain systems do not store names, addresses or emails, and instead store hashes and cryptographic keys. Hence, Blockchain technology is often described as "anonymous", and the processing of anonymous data is not covered by the GDPR.

Privacy by Design describes various possibilities to guarantee data protection rights from the beginning of the system development (Gürses et al. 2011). In recent years various examples of *Privacy enhancing technologies* (PET) have been introduced. They all aim to increase data protection in the digital age, yet they have to be in use for some time in order to demonstrate that they are capable of withstanding attacks. Antignac and LeMtayer (2014) state that *Privacy by Design* is an essential step for the implementation of data protection, but there is still a long way to go before appropriate frameworks are developed for all industry areas.

According to recital 26 of the GDPR, anonymous information is defined as: *"The principles of data protection should therefore not apply to anonymous information, namely information which does not relate to an identified or identifiable natural person or to personal data rendered anonymous in such a manner that the data subject is not or no longer identifiable."* In most companies there is an entity that can determine the identity of a person, for example a database which stores the relation between a key and a person, and offers a service to identify the person using these means. According to Council of the European Union: *"Personal data which have undergone pseudonymisation, which could be attributed to a natural person by the use of additional information should be considered to be information on an identifiable natural person."*

In an LMS storing of names is a must to identify a person. Even if only keys or IDs are stored on the Blockchain, the data protection officer must be able to identify the party the log file originated from.

Article 83 (Council of the European Union 2018f) "General conditions for imposing administrative fines" is one of the most discussed articles, because it describes the penalties that can be imposed due to violations of the GDPR: *"Infringements of the following provisions shall, in accordance with paragraph 2, be subject to administrative fines up to 10.000.000 EUR, or in the case of an undertaking, up to 2% of the total world-wide annual turnover of the preceding financial year, whichever is higher."* Hence, an LMS clearly has to address multiple aims, i.e. to fulfill the GDPR privacy requirements explained in this section, and also meet the GDPR documentation requirements. Table 1 provides an overview of all relevant GDPR articles and recitals.

In this study, a multi-level Blockchain architecture is defined to immutably store log files and other sensitive data transparently on the Blockchain. In line with Treiblmaier (2019), this approach deals with the dual challenges of privacy protection and regulation compliance.

3   The Blockchain Solution

Since the appearance of Blockchain technology, a range of different approaches have been developed in order to achieve consensus across the Blockchain. The fundamental consensus mechanisms ensure that only blocks containing exclusively valid data are added to the Blockchain, with the legitimacy of blocks being validated by every node. The most widely used Blockchain consensus finding protocol, Proof of Work (PoW), requires for full nodes that all nodes in the network process all blocks. This requires miners to furnish a lot of hardware and resources to generate a new block.

Table 1 Overview of relevant GDPR articles

Article	Topic	Description	LMS
Article 3	Territorial scope	GDPR has to be applied if the business is in the EU	Needs to be addressed if the operation is within Europe
Article 4	GDPR—definitions	Controller defines how the data is processed	
Article 5	Principles relating to processing of personal data	Data may only be processed in good faith, for clarity purposes and only as long as necessary	Log files have to be saved in an appropriate manner which prevents modifying or deleting of files
Article 7	Conditions for consent		
Article 17	Right to erasure ('right to be forgotten')	Every customer can request that their data be deleted	Users may request their data to be erased, but data controllers can decline such requests under specific circumstances
Article 25	Data protection by design and by default	The controller takes appropriate technical and organizational measures to ensure that data is processed securely	Privacy by design is used to guarantee data protection rights from the beginning of the system development
Article 28 3a	Processor	Personal data may only be processed in a documented manner	A main reason for the LMS Blockchain design
Article 33 5	Notification of a personal data breach to the supervisory authority	The controller documents violations of the protection of personal data	Personal data breach is reduced by using blockchain technology
Article 83	General conditions for imposing administrative fines	Fines for GDPR violations	LMS systems help to avoid any administrative fines
Recital 26	Not applicable to anonymous data	GDPR does not apply if users can no longer be identified, e.g. by means of pseudonymisation	An aim of LMS is to identify the causer of events; hence, anonymous data cannot be used
Recital 30	Online identifiers for profiling and identification	For example IP addresses are used in combination with other information to uniquely identify a person	LMS is configurable to log various user-specific information, which are needed for tracing needed

(Berentsen and Schär 2018). An alternative for processing all blocks is lightweight nodes, which only process the block headers to verify transactions.

As a result, substantial resources are needed to solve the mathematical problem and create a valid block. Further consensus models like Proof-of-Stake (PoS) have been developed to fulfill the same purpose as PoW: achieving consensus on the Blockchain. In a cryptocurrency system, the validator is designated by the number of cryptocurrencies they possess, which reflects their interest in keeping the system stable. With the possession of a certain amount of cryptocurrencies, the validator is able to validate new blocks in the Blockchain (Schütz and Fertig 2019).

In a business environment, it is difficult to implement a PoW approach because all nodes need to process the full Blockchain and this is resource consuming. Hence, the approach is to design a multi-level Blockchain, consisting of several Blockchains, whereby they differentiate between a *SuperBlockchain* and a *SubBlockchain*. The first is similar to a common Blockchain, yet contains an additional field-the *Final Block*-which is an outcome of the underlying *SubBlockchain* (cf. Pourmajidi and Miranskyy 2018).

The confirmation of a Superblock automatically leads to confirmation of all Sub-blocks, and thereby reduces the number of operations required. Huge amounts of data are typically stored on the Blockchain in LMSs, hence, such a multi-level approach ensures that such systems remain scalable (see Fig. 1).

SubBlockchain: is a unique Blockchain which has its own *Genesis Block* as well as a *Final Block*, which forms the end of a SubBlockchain to indicate that no more blocks can be added. The *Final Block* is then submitted to the SuperBlockchain (Submitting). The Sub-Blockchain is considered "open" and allows blocks to be added up to a maximum number of blocks or for a specific period of time.

Genesis Block: generated as the first block in the SubBlockchain, marking that the SubBlockchain is considered "open". The SubBlockchain has a single *Genesis Block*. The first *Block Hash* in each SubBlockchain is set to 0.

Block Hash: is calculated by referring to the data of block headers by a hash function (e.g. SHA-256). In the block header, the timestamp, the Previous Hash, the hash value, and the data block are saved.

Previous Hash: is the block hash of the previous block (index-1). Consequently, it results in a chaining of the blocks and builds the Blockchain.

Final Block: similar to the *Genesis Block*, except that it indicates the end of the respective SubBlockchain. When this is created, the Sub-Blockchain is marked as "closed" and can no longer produce blocks. The hash is generated by concatenating all the *Block Hashes* of the preceding blocks. The *Final Block* can provide additional information, such as a *timestamp* indicating when the SubBlockchain is valid, to facilitate an efficient search for log files.

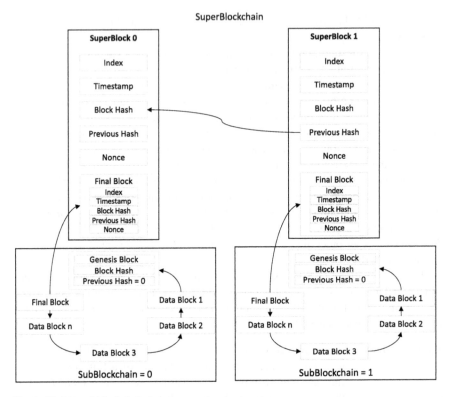

Fig. 1 Multi-level blockchain for a log management system

Superblock: is a normal block, except that all fields are stored in the *Final Block*.

As mentioned, the resources of a company's infrastructure prevent a PoW consensus protocol. Hence, a different consensus-finding protocol has to be used, which allows the data on the Blockchain to remain unchanged. In this approach the SuperBlockchain and the SubBlockchain are generated by different participants in the network (compare Fig. 1). Since the individual log files in the SubBlockchain are calculated and verified, they consume more resources than the SuperBlockchain. Masternodes are defined and made readily available for the calculation of the SubBlockchain. These masternodes generate the individual blocks of the SubBlockchain by means of "randomized block selection". As soon as a *Final Block* has been generated, this block is sent to the other nodes (clients) which generate the SubBlockchain. For generating a Superblock, a node is selected by means of "randomized block selection". The process for the generation of the block is depicted in Fig. 2.

As soon as a client (client 1 to n) produces a log event, the log file is sent into the "LogFilePool", which can be compared with the Mempool in the Bitcoin network (see Fig. 2(1)). This pool collects the log files, which are not yet verified in a block.

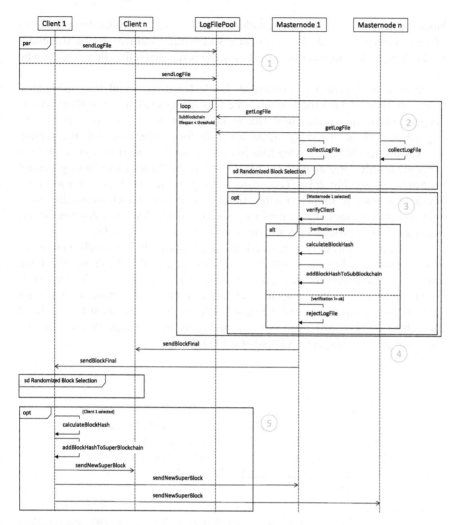

Fig. 2 Sequence diagram for adding a new log file on the blockchain

This part runs in parallel because the clients are independently generating their log information (visualized by the block "par"). From this pool, the masternodes pick the pending log files to verify a new Subblock. Whenever enough log files are collected by the masternodes (e.g. one kilobyte or a certain lifespan is reached), the masternodes determine who will generate the Subblock by randomized block selection (see sequence diagram block "Randomized Block Selection") , which means they "roll the dice". The process will stay in the loop (see sequence diagram block "loop") until the condition *lifespan < threshold* is fulfilled. A masternode can use any random source of seed, e.g. a randomly chosen log file, and create a hash; the masternode with the highest hash will generate the block (see Fig. 2(2)). The sequence diagram block for calculation of the hash is marked as option ("opt") because the second part of the process is only called if the client is successfully verified. After a successful verification, hashes are calculated or the log file is rejected if the client could not be verified.

Once the block-generating masternode is selected, it verifies all pending log files, if they are legal. If a log file is invalid, the files are rejected. It can be illegal if it is not generated by a legitimate user. Due to the fact that all log files are signed by the original user, noone else can generate a log file for another user. This is essential, as every user could generate log files in another user's name if the system did not verify the log files. Just as every log file is verified, the chosen masternode generates the Subblock (see Fig. 2(3)). The masternodes generate Subblocks until a certain threshold is reached. In this case the threshold is one day, which means that every SubBlockchain is marked as "open" for a specific, single day. After this threshold is reached, a new SubBlockchain will be generated by the masternodes.

As soon as the threshold is reached, the last Block in the SubBlockchain (*Final Block*) is submitted to the clients (see Fig. 2(4)). After the clients get the *Final Block*, they also determine through randomized block selection who can generate the Superblock. After the generation of the Superblock, the chosen client sends the new block to all clients and the masternode, so every participant has the latest Blockchain (see Fig. 2(5)). This block is marked as "opt" to show that the selected client will process this part. Example of the log file:

```
{
    "Log_File": {
        "Log_File_Signature": "b1aae4fec35b5a84c2ec90
        6b55b30b5c5a7e338ff905ed92f48f748d12450030",
        "Log_File_Hash": "2a462bd2034780a9f7aba
        a076843b06e8894994352c1c3d86abd467a38d4cc4f",
        "Subject": "Employee1",
        "File":
        {
          "Path": "V:\Very_Secret_Folder\Very_Secret_Document",
          "Option": 1
        }
    }
}
```

The fields in the log file have the following meaning:

Log_File_Signatue: signature of the log file, to ensure that the log file belongs to this node.

Log_File_Hash: the SHA-256 Hash of the log file.

Subject: user who created the event to be logged.

Path: path to the file, which has been generated or changed.

Option: to identify the operation on the file: (0 = file created, 1 = file changed, 2 = file deleted).

For generating a superblock, a node is selected by means of "Randomized Block Selection". The node which is selected for the generation of the block is determined in the following way:

1. The nodes receive *Final Block* from the masternode
2. The last log file they send is hashed using the hash function
3. The node with the highest hash (e.g. 0aacf8 > 00c87) generates the new SuperBlock.

Since log files are accessible on all nodes in the network (at least the hashes of the log files), all nodes can calculate the hashes for block generation and check whether the selected node really has the highest hash. Should a node calculate an incorrect hash, that block will be discarded by the other nodes and block generation will start again.

Limitations depending on the number of clients are attacks to the described LMS. These attacks are especially problematic for small Blockchains with few participants problematic because the likelihood of a party having more than 50% computational increases. An aggressor on the network can cause various attacks on the Blockchain, as soon as he has taken over a certain number of nodes. These malicious nodes try to create a longer Blockchain. Since the healthy nodes try to attach the next node to the longest part of the chain, this can result in a second Blockchain with invalid data.

If two Blockchains exist, a veracious n and a malicious m, which have been split on a specific block, the system is stable as long as the length[1] of Blockchain n is greater than the length of m. If the aggressor owns more than 51% of the nodes and the length of m is greater than the length of n, new blocks will be attached to the malicious chain. Hence, all nodes on the veracious chain starting from the splitting point are interpreted as invalid.

4 Results

The design of the multi-level Blockchain allows for fulfillment of GDPR recording requirements, while ensuring that manipulation of the log files is made impossible. Further, deletion of the log files also becomes impossible because every change of the file is recorded. Due to the Blockchain approach, the file is also distributed across several nodes, which increases security. Asymmetric cryptography via certificates ensures that the sending node is the node which generated the log file: so, sending incorrect log files is impossible as well.

As another result of the multi-level Blockchain, the LMS has the ability to facilitate highly efficient searches. Every SubBlockchain is assigned for a defined time period and open to accept new data only during that time. Of course, the duration of this

---

[1]Length means amount of blocks.

time period can be adapted to individual circumstances: if there is more logging effort, the period can be shorter; if there is less logging effort, the time period can be extended. By defining the period as a single day, the SubBlockchain contains only the logs for this day and thereby allows for efficient searches. Hence, the Blockchain offers advantages in terms of safety against the manipulation and extinguishing of data, and this safety increases further with the number of participating nodes.

5   Conclusion

This case study aims to provide a contribution on how to overcome the Blockchain-GDPR Paradox as described in (Coelho and Younes 2018; Van Humbeeck 2017). Some articles of the GDPR are in contradiction to the core principles of the Blockchain Technology. The GDPR Article 17 (Council of the European Union 2018a) demands the right to forget, while the Blockchain Technology provides its main advantage of immutability if the Blockchain setup is correct. This argument is important for LMS because of the need to offer a solution where a potential attacker cannot change or delete log files or generate false entries to burden others. The presented implementation of an LMS uses a multi-level Blockchain solution. The approach shows a GDPR-conform solution to address the documentation requirements (Council of the European Union 2018d) where any processing has to be logged in a suitable way. This solution allows simple and effective monitoring of files and folders on the operating systems events *create*, *change* and *delete*. It can be deployed easily and is already suitable for small network environments as well as for large networks. The main design criterion was a performate search option which is guaranteed due to the multi-level architecture. It turned out that in environments with a large amount of log messages an additional layer could be considered. The aim of non-repudiation could be achieved with this architecture and the Blockchain Technology. The use of asymmetric cryptography creates the possibility of the user not being able to deny a log file. This ensures that the respective sender of the log file is really responsible for data breaches, as they cannot deny the log file afterward. From the GDPR point of view, LMS contains user sensitive data such as username, name or IP addresses. In this case, the information can also be seen as sensitive data from a company's point of view. Hence, it conforms to the GDPR (Kunde 2017) and allows the use of the Blockchain technology to store log messages in conformance with the GDPR.

References

Antignac, T., & Le Métayer, D. (2014). Privacy by design: From technologies to architectures. In *Annual privacy forum* (pp. 1–17). Springer.
Araoz, M., & Ordano, E. (2019). *Proven Open Excellence*. Retrieved March 15, 2019, from http://poex.io/.

Ateniese, G., Magri, B., Venturi, D., & Andrade, E. (2017). *Redactable blockchain—or—Rewriting history in bitcoin and friends* (pp. 111–126). https://doi.org/10.1109/EuroSP.2017.37.

Berentsen, A., & Schär, F. (2018). *Bitcoin, Blockchain und Kryptoassets: Eine umfassende Einführung.* Norderstedt: BoD.

Coelho, F., & Younes, G. (2018). The GDPR-Blockchain paradox: A work around. In *Conference: 1st workshop on GDPR compliant systems, co-located with 19th ACM international middleware conference*, Rennes, France.

Council of the European Union. (2018a). *Article 17 "GDPR Right to erasure ('right to be forgotten')".* Retrieved from https://gdpr-info.eu/art-17-gdpr/.

Council of the European Union. (2018b). *Article 25 "GDPR Data protection by design and by default".* Retrieved from https://gdpr-info.eu/art-25-gdpr/.

Council of the European Union. (2018c). *Article 3 "GDPR Territorial scope".* Retrieved from https://gdpr-info.eu/art-3-gdpr/.

Council of the European Union. (2018d). *Article 4 "GDPR definitions".* Retrieved from https://gdpr-info.eu/art-4-gdpr/.

Council of the European Union. (2018e). *Article 5 "GDPR principles relating to processing of personal data".* Retrieved from https://gdpr-info.eu/art-5-gdpr/.

Council of the European Union. (2018f). *Article 83 "GDPR general conditions for imposing administrative fines".* Retrieved from https://gdpr-info.eu/art-83-gdpr/.

Council of the European Union. (2018g). *Recital 26 "Not applicable to anonymous data".* Retrieved from https://gdpr-info.eu/recitals/no-26/.

Council of the European Union. (2018h). *Recital 30 "Online identifiers for profiling and identification".* Retrieved from https://gdpr-info.eu/recitals/no-30/.

Gürses, S., Troncoso, C., & Diaz, C. (2011). Engineering privacy by design. *Computers, Privacy & Data Protection, 14*(3), 25.

Herian, R. (2018). Regulating disruption: Blockchain, GDPR, and questions of data sovereignty. *Journal of Internet Law, 22*(2), 1, 8–16. Retrieved from http://oro.open.ac.uk/56264/.

Holt, J. E. (2006). Logcrypt: Forward security and public verification for secure audit logs. In *ACM international conference proceeding series* (Vol. 167, pp. 203–211).

Kolain, M., & Wirth, C. (2018). Privacy by blockchain design: A blockchain-enabled GDPR-compliant approach for handling personal data. https://doi.org/10.18420/blockchain2018_03.

Kunde, E. (2017). Faktenpapier Blockchain und Datenschutz. Bundesverband Informationswirtschaft, Telekommunikation und neue Medien e. V.

Lima, C. (2018). *Blockchain-GDPR privacy by design: How decentralized blockchain internet will comply with GDPR data privacy.* In *IEEE Blockchain.* Retrieved from https://blockchain.ieee.org/images/files/pdf/blockchain-gdpr-privacy-by-design.pdf.

Maxwell, J., & Winston, S. (2017). *A guide to blockchain and data protection.* Hogan Lovells. Retrieved from www.hlengage.com/uploads/downloads/5425GuidetoblockchainV9FORWEB.pdf.

Pourmajidi, W., & Miranskyy, A. V. (2018). Logchain: Blockchain-assisted log storage. CoRR, abs/1805.08868. arXiv: 1805.08868. Retrieved from http://arxiv.org/abs/1805.08868.

Resolution on Privacy by Design. (2010). *32nd international conference of data protection and privacy commissioners*, Jerusalem, Israel. Retrieved from https://edps.europa.eu/sites/edp/files/publication/10-10-27jerusalemresolutiononprivacybydesignen.pdf.

Schütz, A., & Fertig, T. (2019). *Blockchain für Entwickler: Das Handbuch für Software Engineers.* Grundlagen, Programmierung, Anwendung: Mit vielen Praxisbeispielen. Rheinwerk Computing. Rheinwerk Verlag GmbH. Retrieved from https://books.google.at/books?id=q1OWvQEACAAJ.

Treiblmaier, H. (2019). Toward more rigorous Blockchain research: Recommendations for writing Blockchain case studies. *Frontiers in Blockchain, 2*, 3. https://doi.org/10.3389/fbloc.2019.00003.

Van Humbeeck, A. (2017). The blockchain-GDPR paradox. Retrieved from https://medium.com/wearetheledger/the-blockchain-gdpr-paradox-fc51e663d047.

Wüst, K., & Gervais, A. (2018). Do you need a Blockchain? (pp. 45–54). https://doi.org/10.1109/CVCBT.2018.00011.

Author Biographies

Wolfgang Radinger-Peer MBA is an External Lecturer at the University of Applied Science FH Campus Vienna. He received a Ph.D. in Electrical Engineering and Information Technology in 2004 from the Vienna University of Technology. He has more than twenty years of experience as a software developer and consultant and has worked on projects in the banking field. His interests include modern software technologies like Machine Learning and use cases of Blockchain Technology.

Bernhard Kolm has finished his master in IT-Security at the University of Applied Science, FH Campus Vienna in Austria. He received his bachelor's degree in Business and Information System Engineering from the University of Vienna, Austria. For his master's degree, he ventured into IT-Security, writing his master thesis about the implementation of Security Log File Management Systems using Blockchain technology. During his studies, he worked as an IT-Trainer teaching IT-Security and different programming languages to companies in Austria. In 2016, he started working as a consultant for different industrial software companies. Since the industrial sector generates a lot of Log Files, which must be stored securely, he started research on new Log File Management Systems. Due to personal interests in Blockchain Technology, he combined these two fields, finding the Blockchain Technology as a suitable approach for storing Log Files securely.

Wibson: A Case Study of a Decentralized, Privacy-Preserving Data Marketplace

Matias Travizano, Carlos Sarraute, Mateusz Dolata, Aaron M. French, and Horst Treiblmaier

Abstract The Internet offers unprecedented opportunities to collect large amounts of personal data at low cost. Typically, it is not only the data collection process but also their further use which is opaque to the individuals. Blockchain technology promises to return Internet users control over their personal data. In this chapter we present and discuss Wibson, a decentralized data marketplace based on the blockchain that provides a way for individuals to control and monetize their personal information in a trusted environment. By using a token and blockchain-enabled smart contracts Wibson allows data sellers and buyers to interact while allowing them to keep their desired level of anonymity. This chapter is based on qualitative interviews and the thorough analysis of the technical documentation. We describe the underlying rationale and functioning of Wibson and provide suggestions for future research at the intersection of blockchain and privacy.

1 Introduction

In 1999, Scott McNealy, the chairman of SUN Microsystems, told a group of reporters and analysts: "You have zero privacy anyway. Get over it" (Sprenger 1999). Two years later, the start-up Itsmyprofile.com was launched with the intention of providing consumers a platform to sell their private data (Scheeres 2001). Their business

M. Travizano (✉) · C. Sarraute
Wibson, Gibraltar, UK
e-mail: mat@wibson.org

M. Dolata
University of Zurich, Zurich, Switzerland
e-mail: dolata@ifi.uzh.ch

A. M. French
The University of New Mexico, Albuquerque, USA
e-mail: afrench@unm.edu

H. Treiblmaier
Modul University Vienna, Vienna, Austria
e-mail: horst.treiblmaier@modul.ac.at

© Springer Nature Switzerland AG 2020
H. Treiblmaier and T. Clohessy (eds.), *Blockchain and Distributed Ledger Technology Use Cases*, Progress in IS, https://doi.org/10.1007/978-3-030-44337-5_8

model never prevailed, and the site is defunct now. In the years that followed, the online collection of personal data and personalized advertising started to skyrocket and turned into a billion-dollar business. Web beacons and third-party scripts collect detailed information about Internet users and create sophisticated revenue models for sharing profits among all parties involved (Zawadziński 2015), except for the users themselves. The rise of the so-called "personal data economy (PDE)", in which companies purchase data from individuals, and models such as "pay-for-privacy (PFP)", in which consumers even pay to avoid the collection of their data, highlight the monetary value of personal data (Elvy 2017) and the importance of individuals' privacy concerns (Treiblmaier and Pollach 2011). Recently, various start-ups emerged that enable individuals to sell their private data directly to businesses and brokers (Parra-Arnau 2018).

The Internet is a decentralized system by design that links billions of interconnected devices to improve communication, access to information, and economic possibilities for people across the globe. Yet despite its distributed nature, giant technology companies have used the underlying technical protocols to build layers of proprietary applications that capture and control massive amounts of personal data. The top five companies (i.e., Google, Facebook, Apple, Microsoft and Amazon) boast a combined market value of almost $3.5 trillion, which exceeds the entire economy of the United Kingdom (Associated Press 2018). Over the past two decades numerous cases of data breaches have occurred, with hundreds of millions individuals' personal data being compromised. Such events entail serious and costly efforts from the side of the companies to restore their reputation, consumer trust, and repurchase intention (Curtis et al. 2018; Goode et al. 2017). Additionally, data security breaches were shown to negatively affect company performance, which also includes spillover vulnerabilities from rival firms' breaches (Martin et al. 2017).

Under the current system, individuals lack control over how data brokers collect, analyze, protect, and use their personal data. Over the years, different revenue models have emerged evaluating how users can monetize their personal data (Kemppainen et al. 2018). Additionally, governmental bodies and consumer rights organizations, especially in the European Union, are trying to maintain an appropriate balance between transparency, personal data use, and data access. When it comes to personal data, however, regulation authorities are fighting an uphill battle (Inverardi 2019). The prevailing data ecosystem misallocates data's value away from the owner—the individual—and prevents society from effectively tackling many of its biggest challenges. Privacy advocates therefore claim that the time has come for citizens to regain control over their personal data and benefit from the value it creates, which sometimes results in new legislation (Alix 2018). Hence, two research questions evolve:

1. *How can a blockchain-based decentralized marketplace empower Internet users to control their personal data?*
2. *How can a blockchain-based decentralized marketplace empower Internet users to monetize their personal data?*

We answer these questions combining using a case study approach and presenting a practical implementation of a decentralized marketplace for personal data. This chapter is organized as follows. First, we discuss the background problem underlying the current case and previous limitations to addressing this issue. Then, we introduce the notion of a data marketplace that is decentralized and privacy preserving, along with a division in general components of the functionality required by such a marketplace. We then present the construction of the Wibson protocol, which provides a marketplace exhibiting the key properties of a general decentralized Privacy-Preserving Data Marketplace (dPDM). We define the relevant participants, components, data structures, incentives, and mechanism of the protocol. The next section delves into the current Wibson implementation, detailing the decentralized applications. We then develop a framework followed by some implications and a conclusion.

2 Background Problem

Throughout history, organizations have relied on the collection and use of personal data to make business decisions and increase sales. As technology evolves, the ability to capture, track, and analyze data continues to increase providing more opportunities for companies to improve their business and profit. The commercialization of the Internet in the 1990s and growth of social media have captured the attention of consumers regarding the collection and use of their information. This has raised ethical concerns about the ownership of personal data and how it should be used. Various practical and theoretical-based research have been conducted evaluating information privacy and security concerns related to the collection, use, dissemination, and ownership of personal information (Alashoor et al. 2017; Pavlou 2011; Yun et al. 2019). Various groups have researched ideas related to empowering users and giving back control of their own personal data and a few have made attempts to implement these ideas.

The concept of giving users control of their own personal data has received attention by several entities over the past two decades. However, these attempts have several shortcomings limiting full scale adoption by customers and companies in the data marketplace. The biggest challenge is the reliability of the data being generated. When organizations collect, the information generated is based on the customers' actions (i.e. web traffic, product view, purchases, etc.). The attempts to give customers the ability to sell their own data has primarily been based on surveys and user provided data. When using surveys to provide customer information, such as purchase history, companies are relying on customers to provide complete and honest feedback of their purchase history as they remember it. Customers may only share information they are comfortable providing rather than all the details of every transaction that took place. There may even be instances where user perceptions of their shopping habits differ from their actual shopping habits creating incomplete or inaccurate data. There is also the issue of motivation for providing personal information by the users. By offering monetary benefits for filling out surveys to profit from their own information, the focus is on obtaining the benefits rather than providing accurate information. This could cause reliability and accuracy issues when users are motivated to complete the survey but not motivated to ensure the accuracy or completeness of the data. Due to these reasons alone, companies have the advantage in terms of accurate and complete data that is better suited for making decisions. The technological capabilities have not been available for customers to easily maintain this level of reliable data until now. With the introduction of blockchain, the capability for users to access their transactional history of data becomes a reality providing the opportunity to empower users.

Blockchain is a distributed ledger technology defined as a "digital, decentralized and distributed ledger in which transactions are logged and added in chronological order with the goal of creating permanent and tamper-proof records" (Treiblmaier 2018, p. 547). This differs from traditional databases companies often use in eCommerce by creating a public immutable record of customer transactions. In traditional databases, the company controls and maintains the data directly, assuming ownership of all transactions that take place. In these marketplaces, companies can only view the history of transactions that occur at their online store. This creates data marketplaces where companies sell their transaction data to each other and profit from customer information. With blockchain, all transactions that occur across the entire marketplace are kept on the public ledger giving the customer access to their transactional history. Blockchain technology provide customers with the opportunity to access their transactions across all online companies giving them the advantage of richer and more complete data than any single online retailer.

With these new capabilities and access to transactional data by customers, the concept of empowering customers to profit from their own personal data have transitioned from theory to reality. Large-scale solutions to reach this goal are empowered through the implementation of blockchain as the moderator to access and control of externally stored data (Zyskind et al. 2015). A model introducing a dedicated and trusted third party has been introduced to allow for transactional privacy and the use of smart contracts (Kosba et al. 2016). Proposed blockchain solutions addressing privacy have been introduced for a variety of industries such as IoT and smart homes (Dorri et al. 2017b), mobility (Dorri et al. 2017a), and healthcare (Yue et al. 2016). The proposed blockchain solutions offer improvements over current systems while addressing customer control issues related to their personal data and providing a platform where customer can exchange their data for money, tokens, or other benefits. The major limitation of the proposed solutions to date is that they fail to consider the entire marketplace and focus on individual industries instead. To truly empower users with control of their personal data, a solution managing the whole ecosystem is required. The concept of a dPDM provides the ecosystem to make this idea a reality.

3 Methodology

In this paper, we present the case-study findings from an explanatory, single-unit, and single-case design. The unit of analysis were the artifacts that can be created to allow Internet users to control and monetize their personal data. The analysis relies on the description and critical assessments of the artifacts. Construct validity was ensured by using multiple sources of data (i.e., interviews and documents) and having key informants review the draft. Reliability was ensured by keeping a case study protocol and documenting all parts of the research process (Yin 2013). The main sources of information were five interviews that were conducted with the core development team from Wibson as well as a thorough analysis of the technical documentation (Travizano et al. 2018). The interviews lasted between 15 and 20 min respectively and were conducted between March and May 2019. We recorded, transcribed and analyzed them following the standard procedures of qualitative data analysis (Glaser and Strauss 1999). Following the methodological suggestions from Urquhart (2012) and the recommendations from Treiblmaier (2019) on how to design blockchain case studies, we first describe the concept of dPDM and how the proposed solution helps to overcome several pending problems. We then use the interview data to evaluate the proposed solution as well as the general ecosystem and highlight main areas for future research.

4 Decentralized, Privacy-Preserving Data Marketplaces

In this section we describe the operating principles of a dPDM in a stepwise manner (Travizano et al. 2018). We first define a *Data Marketplace (DM)* as a platform for the trade of information that provides the following:

- infrastructure where sellers offer their personal information in exchange for something of value from buyers;
- data evaluation and valuation mechanisms;
- incentives for all market participants to act honestly; and
- incentives for all participants to ensure data quality, including an enforcement mechanism to guard against low-quality data.

More specifically, a *decentralized Data Marketplace (dDM)* is a DM such that:

- there is no central authority to actively regulate market participants;
- there is no central data repository; individuals maintain full control of their personal information at all times; and
- in place of a central funds repository, participants maintain control of their own funds in a distributed manner.

Finally, a *decentralized Privacy-Preserving Data Marketplace (dPDM)* is a *dDM* which allows users to sell personal information, while providing them the following privacy guarantees:

- anonymity, such that the identity of the Sellers and Buyers is not revealed without their consent. In particular, the identity of the Data Seller is not revealed to the Data Buyer without the consent of the Data Seller;
- transparency over data usage: The Data Seller has visibility on how his Data is used by the Buyer; and
- control over data usage: The Data Seller can modify the rights over its Data at any moment in time.

We divide the functionality required by a *dPDM* into a set of components, which we describe briefly in this section. In a later section we will provide more details on how these components are implemented in the Wibson protocol. Initially a *Decentralized Auditable Data Storage* is needed, in which *Data Sellers* store their own data encrypted and available off-chain (e.g., in a client-side storage, or a cached distributed system like IPFS, Interplanetary File System, Protocol Labs 2019), preventing unauthorized users from accessing it. The blockchain stores hashes of the data, but not the data itself, allowing later proof-of-existence. When required by the protocol, the *Sellers* must provide their data for audits to a trusted mutually agreed third party. The *Querying System* is a communication system used by the Data Buyer to request data from the Data Seller. The *Data Pricing Mechanism* assigns data prices and transacts data operations. The *Data Payment System* transfers tokens securely and efficiently between market participants. Finally, the *Incentive System* provides mechanisms and incentives to verify the trustworthiness of data and incentivizes honest marketplace behavior.

5 The Wibson Case

Wibson is an open protocol which combines blockchain, cryptography and market design. The latter refers to the way in which buyers and sellers interact with the help of notaries and the incentives that they receive. According to the CEO, there were basically two reasons for building a blockchain solution:

> First, it is an enabler for our core principles [...] transparency, control, anonymity and fairness. Blockchain was the best technology that enabled us to implement the core principles. Second, it is also consensus. Over time this should turn into a user-friendly technology. Users should decide on their own future, they should have control over the destiny of the network. This is something that we really value.

The Wibson application allows access to the underlying protocol. Given the open source nature of the project, the protocol is open for everyone to develop their own applications. The goal is to level the playing field between data consumers (i.e., companies, organizations) and data owners (i.e., individuals). Wibson creates a blockchain-based, decentralized data marketplace that provides the infrastructure for individuals to securely and anonymously sell personal information that is validated for accuracy.

As an engineering manager states:

> Most of the value of personal data today is exploited by a handful of companies. Wibson is a way to distribute the value that comes out of data. We want to put people in control of their own data.

Wibson is built up on a set of the aforementioned core principles, as well as individuals' ultimate control over the use of their personal information. In the Wibson marketplace, individuals will be able to participate in a decentralized data market that provides both financial incentives and control over personal information, without sacrificing privacy. In this section, we describe the main components of the marketplace and the protocol.

5.1 Marketplace Participants

The protocol specifies three types of market participants: *Data Sellers (Seller)*, *Data Buyers (Buyer)*, and *Notaries*. The *Seller* owns personal data and therefore has the right to sell them. We denote the set of Sellers as $S = \{S_1, ..., S_m\}$. A *Buyer* is defined as any entity which wants to purchase data. We denote the set of Buyers as $B = \{B_1, ..., B_n\}$. Furthermore, we introduce the role of *Notary* as a verification entity to verify participants' information when required, verify data quality and trustworthiness when required, and arbitrate in case of conflict between Data Sellers and Data Buyers. We denote the set of Notaries as $N = \{N_1, ..., N_p\}$. To qualify, the *Notary* must have access to *ground truth* information with respect to the data being exchanged in the marketplace. In other words, the Notary will be an entity which possesses information on the Data Sellers and is able to verify that information. All *Notaries* need to have public identities and a verifiable off-chain reputation. The marketplace is *decentralized* since any participant which fulfills the basic requirements can enter the marketplace as Data Seller, Data Buyer or Notary. No central authority exists which controls participation in the market, or grants/denies permission to act in the market. This is a clear contrast with most common marketplaces that are controlled by a central authority.

5.2 Wibson Components and Functioning

The market provides a *Decentralized and Auditable Data Storage System*, where personal data is stored on the client side, and the blockchain provides references to the data, but not the data themselves. Each Seller hosts its own data, which is encrypted, on their devices, such as mobile phones or personal computers. Data transfers from Sellers to Buyers are performed off-chain. The blockchain stores hashes of the Sellers' Data, which serve as references to the full data set for validation purposes. The unencrypted data can be required by the Notary in case of an audit. Wibson also implements an *Augmented Chain* that joins data stored off-chain plus and the references (i.e., hashes of the data) on-chain. This Augmented Chain contains all the data of the system, and is always accessible to the Notary in case of an audit. If the Seller fails to provide his/her data to the Notary, in case of a conflict or in case of being audited, the Notary may arbitrate against the Seller.

Potential Buyers communicate their data requirements on-chain by placing Data Orders on the blockchain. The Buyer publishes on the blockchain the price offered for each Data Order. After screening the Data Responses, the Buyer publishes on the blockchain the selected Sellers, the price paid, and the hashes of the data. The initial implementation of the payment system uses Ethereum smart-contracts (Buterin 2014; Wood 2014) and an ERC20 token (Vogelsteller and Buterin 2015) implemented with the Zeppelin Standard Token.

A reward system provides mechanisms and incentives to certify participants, verify that data is trustworthy, and incentivize honest marketplace participant behavior. In the on-chain incentive system Notaries audit transactions by signing them on the blockchain. The result of these Notary audits is added as a transaction on the blockchain and used to reward or penalize market participants. Additionally, an off-chain verification is performed by Notaries based on their existing proprietary information. Notaries earn tokens by verifying participant's information, validating data, resolving conflicts, or from selected audits. In order to allow participants to interact with the system, Wibson provides *Decentralized Applications* (dApps) (i.e., applications that run on a P2P network of computers rather than on a single computer) for Data Sellers, Data Buyers, and Notaries.

5.3 Wibson Protocol

The *Data Ontology* is a publicly available document that formalizes naming, definition, structure, and relationships (Gruber 1993) pertaining to the marketplace's data and can be used as a reference to generate Audiences and Data Requests. It defines a "dictionary" for buyers and sellers to ensure that they use identical data fields. It is comprised of a comprehensive variable list that defines available *Data Entities* as well as *Data Query Models* for each variable type, and *Audience Query Models* to filter available Data Sellers. Each particular implementation must define variables for each category. Given the publicly available Data Ontology, a Data Buyer requests a particular Data Entity (e.g., browsing history) with additional parameters defined in the Data Query Model (e.g., two days of browsing history) from an audience defined in the Audience Query Model (e.g., men who reside in Spain).

In order to participate in the Wibson protocol, a Data Seller S is required to own a Master Ethereum address to send and receive payments (Wood 2014), public/private keys for signing transactions and encrypting data as well as Audience attributes.

Similarly, a Data Buyer B is required to have an Ethereum address to send and receive payment, public/private keys for signing transactions and encrypting data, an off-chain address (e.g., URL or IP address) to receive Data Responses and an off-chain address to receive Data. Participation requirements for a Notary are an Ethereum address to send and receive payments, public/private keys for signing transactions and encrypting data, and an off-chain address to receive Data. Furthermore, Notary N must reveal his/her public identity by publishing the Ethereum address and public key in a publicly verifiable place.

Data Orders placed on-chain by Data Buyers include the following information: (i) audience, (ii) data requested, (iii) Data Buyer's public key, (iv) address to upload Data Seller's responses and data via HTTPS post, (v) price per response, (vi) list of Notaries and their fees, terms of service and signature in agreement, (vii) minimum audit budget, and (viii) terms and conditions of data use. *Audience* is a filter of potential sellers for the Data Order, written in terms of the Audience Query Model defined in a publicly published data ontology (e.g., Gender = Women, Age ≥ 40, Income $\geq$ \$200,000, Current Residency = Spain). *Data Requested* is a list of Data Entities with certain parameters as defined in the Data Query Model. It can, for instance, include a request for credit card transactions over the last seven days or the web browsing history over the last thirty days. A Data Buyer can also create a Data Order with an empty Data Requested field in order to estimate how many Data Sellers match certain criteria. In this case, the Data Buyer obtains the information about how many Data Sellers fit the specified criteria. The Data Buyer pays each Data Seller for disclosing the information that fulfills the criteria.

The address to upload the Data Seller's Responses and Data U_B (i.e., the public address of buyer B) is a public address (e.g., public URL) from which the Buyer can receive data. Furthermore, the Buyers specify Notaries who are eligible to audit transactions, based on the match between Data Requested and Notary's verification capabilities. The protocol forces Data Buyers to set a minimum mandatory cost (m_a), which is deployed as a minimum budget assigned for audits conducted by selected which could be executed not only in completed orders, but also in uncompleted ones. This prevents Data Buyers from creating massive amounts of queries without cost.

The *Data Response* is sent off-chain by the Sellers to the Buyers and includes the following information: (i) address to receive payment, (ii) hash of data, (iii) selected Notary who is included in a Notary list and has signed the transaction, (iv) the data order to which it belongs, (v) the price of that data order, and (vi) a signature to add a transaction to the blockchain. The *Payment Address E_i* is an Ethereum wallet address to receive the payment from the Data Buyer. The Hash of Data $\langle H(D_i) \rangle$ is written on the blockchain to guarantee the immutability of the unencrypted Data. H is based on the hash function SHA-256 (Lilly 2004). The Data Seller has to decide which Notary N_{i*} should audit the transaction. The Notary should be included in the list of Notaries L (of the Data Order) and should have signed the transaction ($N_{i*} \in L^*$). Finally, a signature (sig_{Si}) is needed to add a transaction on the blockchain and to authenticate Data Seller S_i.

5.4   Flow of Operations

Figure 1 shows the regular mechanisms and flows of operations of the Wibson protocol. The process comprises ten steps:

1. Data Buyer creates a Data Order query $DO = \langle A, R, PK_B, U_B, m_a, tc \rangle$ and sends it to all Notaries he wants to include, in order to obtain their fees, terms of service for the Date Order and their signatures over all this information in agreement with the conditions described by the Data Buyer. The Date Order includes:

    - audience A;
    - data requested R;
    - the Data Buyer's public key PK_B;
    - public URL to upload Data Seller's responses and encrypted data via HTTPS post U_B;
    - minimum audit budget m_a; and
    - terms and conditions of data use t_c.

2. Data Buyer places the Data Order on the smart contract adding also the list of Notaries with their fees, terms of services and signatures $L = \{N_{k1}, ..., N_{ks}\}$. The tokens (corresponding to minimum audit budget m_a) leave the Data Buyer's control.

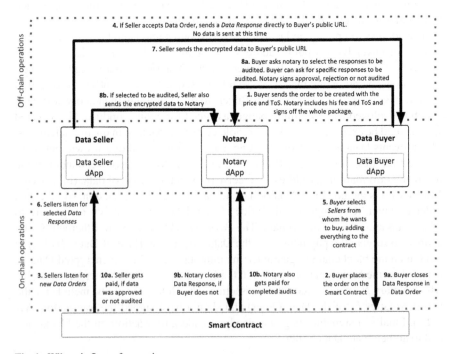

Fig. 1 Wibson's flow of operations

3. Data Sellers monitor Data Orders and look for opportunities which:

    - match Data Order's audience A;
    - agree on data requested R;
    - accept suggested Notary (only one);
    - accept Data Order's price p; and
    - accept terms and conditions of data use.

4. Data Sellers may send Data Response to Data Buyer's public URL (off-chain). The Data Response consists of seven items: $DR = \langle E_i, DO, p, \sigma_i, H(\sigma_i||D_i), N_{i*}, tc, sig_{Si} \rangle$:

    - address E_i to receive the payments;
    - the Data Order's address DO;
    - the price p of the Data Order (for which the Sellers are willing to sell the requested data);
    - the hash of unencrypted data D_i computed using SHA-256 $\langle H(D_i) \rangle$ (Lilly 2004);
    - the selected Notary $N_{i*} \in L*$ who is included in the list of Notaries $L*$ who have signed the transaction;
    - link to the accepted terms and conditions of data use; and
    - Data Seller's signature over all of the above sig_{Si} (to add the transaction in the blockchain).

      No Data Seller data is sent at this point.

5. Data Buyer selects the set of Data Sellers T from whom he wants to buy and adds them to the Data Order contract. Tokens to pay Data Sellers leave the Data Buyer's control at this point (the selection happens on-chain in the transaction). The Data Buyer also pays for an eventual audit, if the minimum budget for audit was already surpassed. In the case that Data Buyer B does not select any Data Seller (and thus does not complete the purchase): if the Data Order was selected for audit, the Notaries $N_k \in L$ share the payment of the minimum audit budget (without any further action required from the Notaries).

6. Data Sellers listen for selected Data Responses.

7. Data Sellers $S_i \in T$ who have their offer approved upload the data file (encrypted with the public key of the Data Buyer PK_B) to the requested address U_B.

8. Once the Data Buyer receives the personal information, the next step is to close the transaction and transfer the tokens accordingly. In order to close a Data Response over a Data Order, the Data Buyer must check with the Notary if the data must be notarized or not. Then the Notary will hand over the Data Buyer a signed certificate specifying one of the following scenarios:

    - The Data will not be notarized;
    - The Data was notarized and is valid; and
    - The Data was notarized and is invalid.

      Unless the Data Buyer specifically asks the Notary to audit a Data Seller, it is up to the Notary to decide who will be notarized or not.

9. With the Notary's signed certificate, the Data Buyer closes the given Data Response (a.k.a. Data Transaction). The contract will verify this certificate and transfer the money to the Data Seller in scenarios (a) and (b), or to the Data Buyer in scenario (c). For all this to happen, the Data Buyer or the Notary must call the 'close Data Response' method over the smart contract.

10. Finally, the contract calls the transfer method to send the tokens to the Data Seller or to the Data Buyers account. The Notary also gets paid. If the Data Buyer decides to stop receiving new Data Responses, he may close permanently the Data Order contract.

5.5 Real World Applications

We illustrate the market roles with two examples, namely credit card transactions and location data. In the former the Data Seller is a client of a Bank, who offers on the market (anonymized) credit card transactions. The Data Buyer can be any entity requiring transactional data, for example, to train its machine learning models. In this scenario, the Bank is the ideal Notary since it can verify that the Data Seller is actually a client of the Bank. This can be done by requiring the Data Seller to provide information for authentication. In case of conflict, the bank can verify whether the data on credit card transactions sent by the Data Seller to the Data Buyer is valid and trustworthy. This can be easily accomplished by comparing the client's credit card transactions with the Bank's own records.

In the case of location data, the Data Seller is a client of a telecommunications company (Telco), which offers on the market anonymized records with the requested information. Again, the Data Buyer can be any entity requiring location data, for example, to train its machine learning models. In this case a Telco is the ideal Notary since it can verify that the Data Seller is actually a client of the Telco. This can be done by requiring the Data Seller to provide authentication information. In case of conflict, the Telco can act as a Notary and verify whether the location information sent by the Data Seller to the Data Buyer is valid and trustworthy, which simply requires a comparison with the Telco's own records of the client's location during the use of mobile phone services.

5.6 Implementation of the Wibson Data Marketplace

There are three decentralized applications to operate on Wibson, one for each type of participant, which enable them to follow the entire protocol previously described. With the first decentralized app, the *Data Seller dApp*, the Data Seller may perform on-chain operations, such as listening to new *Data Orders* placed on the blockchain, accepting Data Orders with a new signed Data Response, or checking if a *Data*

Response was approved, namely selected to be bought. After the transaction has been carried out, the Data Seller receives the payment through the dApp and can keep track of the token balance in the wallet. Furthermore, there is a range of off-chain operations the dApp offers to the Data Seller. They may locally store the data, as well as integrate and link it with external data sources including social networks or other devices. Finally, the Data Sellers uses the dApp to send the data or *Data Responses* to the Data Buyer's public URL if they want to sell.

With the second decentralized app, the *Data Buyer dApp*, the Data Buyer may perform on-chain operations, such as placing new *Data Orders* on the blockchain (including the specification of the intended audience and further information), adding the wanted Data Responses to the contract and signing transactions. The Data Buyer uses the dApp to pay the Seller for the data and the Notary for the audit, and keeps track of the token balance in the wallet. Concerning off-chain operations, the dApp provides an API, which the Data Buyer may expose publicly to receive *Data Responses* or the data itself. It further provides functionality to keep track and show status for every *Data Order* placed and all *Data Responses* received.

The third decentralized app, the *Notary dApp*, allows the Notary to perform on-chain operations such as agreeing to act as Notary when requested by Data Buyer, signing transactions, and keeping track of the status of every transaction in which they are involved. The Notary uses the dApp to receive the fee for every audit done and to keep track of the token balance in the wallet. In terms of off-chain operations, the dApp notifies the Notary when a challenge was requested by the Data Buyer or the Data Seller, provide functions to validate the information and to sign the audit results. Notaries have a public profile with public "seller acceptance rules". If a Data Seller chooses to use a certain Notary, he is accepting implicitly that he is eligible to be notarized. If this is not the case, the Notary may automatically judge against him. For example, if a Data Seller is selling bank data and choosing a bank as a notary, he must confirm that he is a customer of that specific bank. This ensures that the Notary is able to judge the quality of a seller's data.

6 Emerging Topics

To evaluate the technical functionality of the platform and its potential value contribution for individuals, data was collected from five interviews consisting of two researchers, an engineering manager, the Chief Technology Officer and the VP of engineering of Wibson. The interviews were transcribed and the data was analyzed following the basic tenets of qualitative research (Urquhart 2012). Four major topics were identified pertaining to the project: technological ecosystem, market structures, behavioral change, and environmental uncertainty.

6.1 Technological Ecosystem

The blockchain technological ecosystem is still in a state of development, which does not only pertain to the Wibson protocol, but also to the underlying Ethereum blockchain. Since most of Wibson's transactions will be one to many (i.e., one buyer and many sellers) as opposed to the commonly used one-to-one transactions on a blockchain, new solutions need to be developed that allow for an increase in scale. A Wibson Engineering Manager states:

> We did a lot of research on how to scale up. We analyzed Plasma, state channels, and different things. We ended up writing smart contracts that allow you to carry out massive payments in one transaction using an ERC token. We developed that ourselves.

Another pending topic is the need for resources caused by a decentralized solution. Typical blockchain consensus mechanisms were not applicable. Proof-of-work or proof-of-space were impossible due to technical limitations, while proof-of-stake would be problematic because of potential centralization risks. Innovative solutions need to be found to accommodate to the fact that the applications are intended to primarily run on mobile phones. According to a Wibson researcher:

> To generate the proof, you need a lot of resources. Our users run the applications on mobile phones, which means that they do not have a lot of processing power. So, we focus on some specific protocols for our problem set, we were able to develop some zero knowledge proofs [...] without requiring this exorbitant hardware power.

Furthermore, the cost per transaction needs to be reduced, which was already improved with the launch of a new protocol version. As one researcher explains:

> When we have millions of users, we have high gas [i.e., internal pricing for running a transaction in Ethereum] costs. The seller does not have to pay the gas. He does not have to pay anything to enter the marketplace. The buyer pays for the gas and obviously for the data and the notary for validating the data.

6.2 Market Structures

Decentralization calls for new market structures. In traditional markets, personal data was gained free of charge by large companies by tracking and tracing their own customers or web site visitors and either used by themselves or sold to third parties. By enabling private individuals to market their own data, they are enabled to get into direct contact with the final data users, which may be, for example, an advertising company. In this model, intermediaries become obsolete. According to a Wibson researcher:

> The advantage of the Blockchain is that the marketplace is completely decentralized and there is no central role for Wibson or any of the other players. Anybody can enter as seller, buyer, or as a notary.

However, a critical success factor is the involvement of various market players with complementary interests concerning the data. Consequently, trading data via Wibson should be attractive to as many potential stakeholders as possible: one-time and repetitive data sellers, one-time and repetitive data buyers, potential future users, etc. This should be achieved through the variety of exchange options and potential applications of the Wibson token. As a Wibson researcher remarked:

> You can trade the Wibson token for other tokens or get fiat currency out of it at some exchange. At some point it might make sense to include merchants trading for it. […] With a token you are free to do whatever you like and trade it elsewhere.

6.3 Behavioral Change

From a social and economic perspective, widespread adoption depends on new types of behavior. Customers need to understand the value of their personal data (Kugler 2018), the extent to which they are able to control their use, and how they are able to do that. The CEO of Wibson highlighted the broader social context of personal data control:

> You can look at data ownership as a human right. We believe in the social value of data ownership. When companies use our personal data, what we are giving to them is the ability to control us. There are deep implications for democracy and freedom.

The creators of Wibson are driven by the vision of democratizing the ability to control an individual's own data and to promote knowledge about the management of personal data. They see the distribution of value generated from data as their declared goal. A Wibson researcher puts it that way:

> Most of the value of personal data today is exploited by a handful of companies. Wibson is a way to distribute the value that comes out of data. In today's world [individuals] are trading privacy for services. Those services are not free, they pay with the privacy. Wibson makes more honest and gives more control to the end user. Furthermore, they will get some awareness about their personal data.

Even though the solution has great disruptive potential, the Wibson creators are well aware of the fact, that this requires broad masses of users to join the platform. A Wibson researcher acknowledges that user adoption requires more than just a working solution and that the way Wibson works may not be self-explanatory to a standard user:

> Wibson researcher: The Issue of user adoption has to do with user experience, but also how we can get a gradual adoption. Users need to be aware how the blockchain works.

Accordingly, the Engineering Manager sees the proof-of-scalability as the next turning point for his organization:

Engineering Manager: Initially we focused on optimization. Now we need to prove that we can scale. We need the number of people who are willing to sell data to make it interesting for buyers. The second version is able to reduce the gas costs by three orders of magnitude. A thousand times less than before.

Since the Wibson project started, the situation on the market for selling and buying personal data has changed. Wibson CTO is well aware that competition will become increasingly harder, but hopes that the distinctive features of Wibson will help the company get established on the market:

Wibson CTO: When we started, there were not many competitors, but as time progresses others are coming into play. However, still there is no single project that is the clear winner in the space. It is still very early. There are other solutions, but I have not seen one yet where one of the players is a notary and this is something that distinguishes us from the other projects.

Summarizing, several interviewees highlighted that a change in individuals' awareness regarding the actual amount of data collected and used from companies is needed. This corresponds to previous academic research that identified the so-called privacy paradox, namely a situation in which consumers voice concerns about their ability to control personal data while simultaneously freely providing them online (Norberg et al. 2007). The question arises to what extent the availability of a privacy-preserving technology will change customers' actual behavior so that it is more in line with their stated preferences.

6.4   Environmental Uncertainty

External factors exist that represent major challenges. First and foremost, the market for blockchain-based privacy solutions is new and clear structures need to emerge. According to the VP of Engineering:

Right now in this stage there is no one in a dominant position. This is a very new field and everyone is trying different approaches. There is no clear way to do this. What we are creating is a market. We have an application, of course, and we hope that this will be the first successful use case for this market.

New challenges arise when operating cross-borders. This especially pertains to country-specific jurisdiction regarding the treatment of personal data, regulatory and compliance issues, and various laws related to operating in different geographical regions. As the VP of Engineering states:

[…] For example, the law in Europe and the law in California. Empowering the individual in the use of data is a huge topic. There is a huge public awareness, but this needs to transform into action. This is happening. GDPR [i.e.: General Data Protection Regulation] in Europe is an opportunity for us. Companies need to change their processes and they need tools to do that. Not only the technological tools. It is an ecosystem that also includes awareness and Wibson may empower them. Wibson is GDPR compliant since the users are in control.

Furthermore, the combination of sophisticated data analytics methods might create new ways to leverage the data but also poses new risks. On the one hand, the availability of personal data is necessary to extend the potential of AI through training and adaptation, such that providing easier access to it may accelerate developments of new and better AI solutions. On the other hand, understanding and controlling AI requires new approaches to data handling. The CEO of Wibson explained:

> I really believe that when you look at the economy in the future, AI systems will be the tools to increment the GDP the most and they will be fueled by personal data. Data and AI are closely related, and I am very concerned about the future of AI but I also recognize that it is very difficult to control it. It is as difficult as controlling ideas. The way to start thinking about how we can regulate AI is the way to start thinking about how we can regulate data. The role of data becomes critical.

Overall, the development of Wibson occurs at a time in which several external factors remain uncertain: competitors come and go, law regulations are missing or are unsystematic, and the future developments are hard to predict. However, the requirement to guarantee privacy and the need to scale the solution seem most urgent to the Wibson team. The CEO frames it as follows:

> Wibson CEO: There are a lot of science fiction problems. This is beyond the horizon that we are looking at. But there are other concerns, more related to privacy and how you can really encode a privacy preserving blockchain. I am looking at it from Wibson's perspective. What is most important for us is privacy and scalability. If Ethereum will deploy better technologies in the future, it will be cool for us.

7 Implications

Wibson is an underlying open source protocol that enables the deployment of a wide variety of applications. The proposed solution allows individuals to regain control over their personal data and, in case they want to do so, to monetize them. For academics, new research topics emerge.

7.1 Practical Implications

Data marketplaces have been around for several decades. Historically, they have been dominated by large collectors of data without any active participation from consumers. In recent years, this market has substantially grown and new techniques such as machine learning and artificial intelligence will further increase organizations' appetite for personal data. The deployment of blockchain not only enables individuals to control their desired level of privacy but also to monetize their personal data in case they want to do so. By providing data in an aggregated form, according to the specifications of the data buyers, companies' ever-growing need for information can be fulfilled without forfeiting individuals' need for privacy. This also allows to combine behavioral data that spans industries and user activities to avoid an isolated view of historical transactions previously provided by individual retailers. Simultaneously, this will lead to new market structures and potentially to the elimination of data intermediaries. In turn, this could potentially lead to severe consequences for organizations whose business model is mainly based on the collection, aggregation and sale of personal data.

7.2   Theoretical Implications

There are numerous theoretical implications that can be identified through the creation of a new industry such as dPDM being implemented on emerging technology such as blockchain. Digital disruption is a significant implication from this technology as data markets transition from organizational control to consumer control. This adds an additional layer in the business-to-consumer (B2C) relationship where customers not only purchase goods and services from companies but also gain the ability to sell their data in return. This reciprocated relation not only influences the dynamic of B2C transactions but also has significant behavioral considerations in terms of adoption, use, trust, privacy, and security. Previously, trust and security were required on behalf of the company for transactions to take place but with the new dynamic of consumer provided data, additional responsibility is put on the consumer to build trust in the data that they are able to provide. The long history of research evaluating purchase intention, trust, privacy and security from a business-to-consumer perspective needs to be revisited and evaluated from a reciprocated relationship with an evaluation of constructs looking at the consumer-to-business (C2B) relationship.

8   Discussion and Conclusion

In this paper we discuss the Wibson decentralized marketplace which aims to restore individuals' ownership over their personal information. The current research is based on two main research questions, namely (1) how a blockchain-based decentralized marketplace can empower Internet users to control their personal data and (2) how a blockchain-based decentralized marketplace can empower Internet users to monetize their personal data.

The Wibson platform strives to achieves those two goals by giving corporate marketers and advertisers access to verified data and creating an explicit consumer consent mechanism that accounts for new privacy regulations. Based on the principles of transparency, anonymity, fairness and control, a dPDM will gain individuals' trust and business confidence needed to develop a data exchange ecosystem which is beneficial for both Data Sellers and Data Buyers. This can fundamentally change the way marketers collect and use personal information. Wibson gives marketers access to data types and individual characteristics that were in many cases previously unavailable, even if they were working through the biggest advertising platforms.

In this paper we describe the basic functioning of the Wibson platform. First, it identifies and defines roles necessary for trading data in blockchain. Second, it describes components and functions necessary to enable the interaction between the involved parties. Third, it defines the protocol that describes who takes what action and how. Fourth, it proposes a flow to specify the order of actions. In sum, it characterizes the foundation blocks of a marketplace, a sphere for commercial exchange of commodities. While the previous literature has studied aspects of privacy in blockchain and suggested the use of this technology to put the control over the data back to the individual (Kosba et al. 2016; Zawadziński 2015), Wibson strives to go a step further by outlining the mechanisms and entities necessary for a marketplace to emerge.

In this paper we present the findings from a case study embedded into the current economic system of sharing and using personal data. Limitations exist pertaining to external validity which are aggravated because of different country-specific jurisdictions. Future research is needed to assess the economic viability of the underlying business model and the acceptance from the side of the consumers. Furthermore, not only the Wibson protocol is constantly being improved but also the underlying blockchain technology is under development. Future research needs to document this progress and its potential implications on businesses and society.

Acknowledgements The authors thank Daniel Fernandez, Cristian Adamo, Ariel Futoransky, Gustavo Ajzenman and Martin Manelli for their work on the implementation of the Wibson platform.

References

Alashoor, T., Han, S., & Joseph, R. C. (2017). Familiarity with big data, privacy concerns, and self-disclosure accuracy in social networking websites: An APCO model. *Communications of the Association for Information Systems, 41*, 62–96.

Alix, L. (2018). California passes nation's first statewide consumer privacy law. *American banker* (183:126), p. 1.

Associated Press. (2018). Apple, Amazon, Facebook, Alphabet, and Microsoft are collectively worth more than the entire economy of the United Kingdom. *Inc.Com*, April 27. https://www.inc.com/associated-press/mindblowing-facts-tech-industry-money-amazon-apple-microsoft-facebook-alphabet.html. Accessed 24 May 2019.

Buterin, V. (2014). Ethereum: A next-generation smart contract and decentralized application platform. *Ethereum white paper*. https://github.com/ethereum/wiki/wiki/White-Paper. Accessed 30 May 2019.

Curtis, S. R., Carre, J. R., & Jones, D. N. (2018). Consumer security behaviors and trust following a data breach. *Managerial Auditing Journal, 33*(4), 425–435.

Dorri, A., Steger, M., Kanhere, S. S., & Jurdak, R. (2017a). BlockChain: A distributed solution to automotive security and privacy. *IEEE Communications Magazine, 55*(12), 119–125

Dorri, A., Kanhere, S. S., Jurdak, R., & Gauravaram, P. (2017b). Blockchain for IoT security and privacy: The case study of a smart home. In *2017 IEEE International Conference on Pervasive Computing and Communications Workshops*, March, pp. 618–623.

Elvy, S. -A. (2017). Paying for privacy and the personal data economy. *Columbia Law Review,* *117*(6), 1369–1459.

Glaser, B. G., & Strauss, A. L. (1999). *Discovery of grounded theory: Strategies for qualitative research.* New Brunswick: Taylor & Francis Inc.

Goode, S., Hoehle, H., Venkatesh, V., & Brown, S. A. (2017). User compensation as a data breach recovery action: An investigation of the Sony playstation network breach. *MIS Quarterly, 41*(3), 703–A16.

Gruber, T. R. (1993). A translation approach to portable ontology specifications. *Knowledge Acquisition, 5*(2), 199–220.

Inverardi, P. (2019). The European perspective on responsible computing. *Communications of the ACM, 62*(4), 64–69.

Kemppainen, L., Koivumäki, T., Pikkarainen, M., & Poikola, A. (2018). Emerging revenue models for personal data platform operators: When individuals are in control of their data. *Journal of Business Models, 6*(3), 79–105.

Kosba, A., Miller, A., Shi, E., Wen, Z., & Papamanthou, C. (2016). Hawk: The blockchain model of cryptography and privacy-preserving smart contracts. In 2016 IEEE Symposium on Security and Privacy (SP), May, pp. 839–858.

Kugler, L. (2018). The war over the value of personal data. *Communications of the ACM, 61*(2), 17–19.

Lilly, G. M. (2004). *Device for and Method of One-Way Cryptographic Hashing.* US Patents.

Martin, K. D., Borah, A., & Palmatier, R. W. (2017). Data privacy: Effects on customer and firm performance. *Journal of Marketing, 81*(1), 36–58.

Norberg, P. A., Horne, D. R., & Horne, D. A. (2007). The privacy paradox: Personal information disclosure intentions versus behaviors. *Journal of Consumer Affairs, 41*(1), 100–126.

Parra-Arnau, J. (2018). Optimized, direct sale of privacy in personal data marketplaces. *Information Sciences, 424,* 354–384.

Pavlou, P. A. (2011). State of the information privacy literature: Where are we now and where should we go? *MIS Quarterly, 35*(4), 977–988.

Protocol Labs. (2019). *The IPFS project.* https://ipfs.io/. Accessed 25 Jan 2018.

Scheeres, J. (2001). My shoe size? It'll cost you. *Wired.* https://www.wired.com/2001/06/my-shoe-size-itll-cost-you/. Accessed 12 May 2019.

Sprenger, P. (1999). Sun on privacy: 'Get over it.' *Wired.* https://www.wired.com/1999/01/sun-on-privacy-get-over-it/. Accessed 10 April 2019.

Travizano, M., Minnoni, M., Ajzenman, G., Sarraute, C., & Della Penna, N. (2018). Wibson: A decentralized marketplace empowering individuals to safely monetize their personal data. *White paper.* https://wibson.org/#app. Accessed 5 June 2019.

Treiblmaier, H. (2018). The impact of the blockchain on the supply chain: A theory-based research framework and a call for action. *Supply Chain Management: An International Journal, 23*(6), 545–559.

Treiblmaier, H. (2019). Toward more rigorous blockchain research: Recommendations for writing blockchain case studies. *Frontiers in Blockchain, 2*(3), 1–15.

Treiblmaier, H., & Pollach, I. (2011). The influence of privacy concerns on perceptions of web personalisation. *International Journal of Web Science, 1*(1/2), 3–20.

Urquhart, C. (2012). *Grounded theory for qualitative research: A practical guide.* SAGE Publications Ltd., London, Los Angeles.

Vogelsteller, F., & Buterin, V. (2015). ERC-20 token standard. *Eip-20-Token-Standard.Md.* https://github.com/ethereum/EIPs/blob/master/EIPS/eip-20-token-standard.md. Accessed 23 June 2019.

Wood, G. (2014). Ethereum: A secure decentralised generalised transaction ledger. *Ethereum project yellow paper,* Vol. 151. https://gavwood.com/paper.pdf. Accessed 5 June 2019.

Yin, R. K. (2013). *Case study research* (5th ed.). Los Angeles: Sage Publications.

Yue, X., Wang, H., Jin, D., Li, M., & Jiang, W. (2016). Healthcare data gateways: Found healthcare intelligence on blockchain with novel privacy risk control. *Journal of Medical Systems, 40*(10), 218.

Yun, H., Lee, G., & Kim, D. J. (2019). A chronological review of empirical research on personal information privacy concerns: An analysis of contexts and research constructs. *Information & Management, 56*(4), 570–601.

Zawadziński, M. (2015). The truth about online privacy: How your data is collected, shared, and sold—clearcode blog. *Clearcode—Enterprise-grade software development.* https://clearcode.cc/blog/online-privacy-user-data/. Accessed 24 May 2019.

Zyskind, G., Nathan, O., & Pentland, A. (2015). Decentralizing privacy: Using blockchain to protect personal data. In *2015 IEEE Security and Privacy Workshops*, pp. 180–184.

Matias Travizano is an executive with a focus on turning scientific breakthroughs into high-impact companies. Mat is the founder & CEO of Grandata, a San Francisco-based technology company with the mission of building a privacy-preserving data monetization platform. Mat serves as a Director for several technology companies and is also an investor in technology companies. Throughout his career, Mat has published articles in renowned publications, from Wired, and Forbes, to prestigious scientific journals like Nature.

Carlos Sarraute is director of Research at Grandata and Wibson, in Buenos Aires, Argentina. He studied Mathematics at the University of Buenos Aires (UBA) and received his Ph.D. in Informatics Engineering from Instituto Tecnológico de Buenos Aires (ITBA). Inb his thesis he developed methodologies to perform Automated Planning of Computer Network Attacks, research that combined innovative Information Security and Artificial Intelligence techniques. He has worked as specialized researcher in cryptography, information security and vulnerability research for 12 years; and he presented his work at hacking and security conferences around the world. Carlos currently is director of research at Grandata, where he works in understanding and predicting Human Dynamics, by analyzing big data coming from mobile phone companies and the banking industry, along with other sources of data and metadata. He also leads the research efforts at Wibson on providing data privacy in a blockchain-based decentralized data marketplace. Carlos participates in scientific collaborations with MIT, City College of New York, INRIA Paris, ENS Lyon, and UBA among others. He has presented his work in data science and social network analysis conferences, such as ASONAM, KDD, and NetMob. He has published in several journals including Nature Communications.

Mateusz Dolata is a senior research assistant in information management at the University of Zurich, Switzerland, where he received a Ph.D. in 2018 based on his work regarding the digital transformation of service encounters. In his research, he focuses on issues generated by introducing recent technological developments, like blockchain or conversational agents, into professional collaborative settings. He applies a multidisciplinary perspective shaped by his background in computational linguistics, philosophy, and applied computer science. His research has appeared in journals and was presented on conferences such as *Computer Supported Cooperative Work (Journal)i-com: Journal of Interactive MediaFinancial Innovation,Proceedings of ACM on Human-Computer InteractionInternational Conference on Information SystemsEuropean Conference on Information SystemsACM Conference on Computer-Supported Cooperative Work and Social Computing*, or *Hawaii International Conference on System*. He has served as associate editor and on the program committees of those and other scientific outlets.

Aaron M. French is an associate professor of management information systems in the College of Business at the University of New Mexico. He received his Ph.D. in Business Information Systems at Mississippi State University. Dr. French is active in software development and the evaluation emerging technologies. His research has been published in the *Journal of Information Technology, Information & Management, Decision Support Systems, Behaviour & Information Technology, Journal of Computer Information Systems, Communications of the Association for Information Systems,* and *Pacific Asian Journal of the Association of Information Systems.* His research interests include social networking, cross-cultural studies and emerging technologies such as blockchain, 5G, and artificial intelligence.

Business Process Transformation in Natural Resources Development Using Blockchain: Indigenous Entrepreneurship, Trustless Technology, and Rebuilding Trust

Ushnish Sengupta and Henry Kim

Abstract Worldwide, there are many Indigenous (the convention in literature for capitalizing "Indigenous" in referring to people is used in this document). communities who distrust the Natural Resources industry due to historical economic, environmental, social, and cultural practices. These communities also often distrust National and Sub-National governments that regulate these industries. At the same time, long-term support and a license to operate from local Indigenous communities has become a critical and necessary requirement for Natural Resource Development. Blockchain constitutes an emerging technology that can be applied to mitigate trust issues, in contexts where there is distrust between decentralized stakeholders. In this chapter, we posit that those business processes that require participation by Indigenous communities, Natural Resources companies, and different levels of governments who lack trust in each other can be performed more effectively using blockchain technologies. The research method included interviews with the Natural Resource industry and Indigenous entrepreneurship subject matter experts, and a case study using an enterprise analysis tool, the Business Model Canvas. Ultimately, our research indicates that governance level control by Indigenous communities over the development and operation of blockchain platforms can be pivotal in rebuilding trust between stakeholders in Natural Resources development. In our findings, control of development and operation by Indigenous communities does not necessarily mean hands on end to end solution deployment, but involves continuous and genuine input into the requirements and direction of blockchain technology development. In the evolving response to the long-term issues of distrust between stakeholders involved in Natural Resource projects, this paper also describes the potential for long-term Smart Contracts, a blockchain technology enabled solution that continues to demonstrate promising applications. Long-term Smart Contract implementation, which can span multiple decades similar to long-term legal contracts, provide an additional layer of assurance that agreements made by all stakeholders involved will be honored through an additional mechanism of software code.

U. Sengupta (✉) · H. Kim
Schulich School of Business, York University, 4700 Keele Street, Toronto, ON M3J 1P3, Canada
e-mail: ushnish@schulich.yorku.ca

H. Kim
e-mail: hkim@schulich.yorku.ca

H. Treiblmaier and T. Clohessy (eds.), *Blockchain and Distributed Ledger Technology Use Cases*, Progress in IS, https://doi.org/10.1007/978-3-030-44337-5_9

Keywords Blockchain · Smart contract · Indigenous · Natural resources · Corporate Social Responsibility

1 Introduction

Worldwide, there are many Indigenous communities who live in an interdependent relationship with land. The same land is the source of income for Natural Resource extraction industries. The Indigenous communities often distrust the Natural Resources industry, who may be viewed as opportunistic and exploitative. This distrust also stems from history and legacy practices by the industry (Keeling and Sandlos 2015). These communities also often distrust National (e.g. Federal) and Sub-National (e.g. Provincial) governments due to treaty promises broken in the past (Mercredi and Turpel 1993). Blockchain constitutes an emerging technology that is intentionally designed for contexts like this where there is distrust between decentralized stakeholders. Bitcoin for example, the most publicly known use of a blockchain, works on the basis of each actor being able to verify transactions on a distributed ledger, obviating the need for people using the network to have ongoing trust based relationships (Vigna and Casey 2018). The inherent features of blockchain technology: Permanent/immutable transactions (Vigna and Casey 2018; Treiblmaier 2019); Transparency and visibility of each transaction (Tapscott and Tapscott 2016); Distributed database without centralized authority (Kim and Laskowski 2018); Smart Contracts/Programmatically Executable Transactions (Kim and Laskowski 2017), enable a set of solutions to contentious problems of trust in Natural Resource development.

In the context of projects that involve historical and current power imbalances, such as projects involving Indigenous and non-Indigenous stakeholders, the power based influence of different stakeholders in a project result in differential outcomes for each stakeholder in the project. In this particular case of blockchain technology development, formalized organizational leadership by Indigenous individuals and communities is one process among others for addressing the existing power imbalance dynamic. Therefore it is not only sufficient for blockchain technology itself being inherently trustless, but increasing and achieving a high level of trust among inherently distrusting stakeholders involves trust in the governance process of new projects. We make the case that Indigenous entrepreneurs leading the development and operation of blockchain platforms associated with Natural Resource development projects, can embed appropriate values, and maintain requisite control over the direction and outcomes of technology development.

As blockchain adoption evolves beyond Bitcoin and cryptocurrencies, it is becoming apparent that blockchains meant for use solely by permissioned but decentralized stakeholders benefit greatly from having "sponsors" rather than intermediaries. For example, in the case of a blockchain to ensure food traceability, a dominant ecosystem/supply chain stakeholder like Walmart and an infrastructure provider like IBM serve as sponsors, though clearly not as intermediaries (Kamath 2018; Redman 2019).

Walmart uses its dominant position to incentivize companies along a supply chain to comply with an edict to participate in blockchain-based traceability. IBM uses its technological know-how to help build out, and ultimately, operate, the requisite blockchain infrastructure. Therefore the "sponsor" organization who provides the initial capital, the technology provider that provides technological expertise, and the governing body that determines the direction and requirements for technology can be different entities. In the context of blockchain applications for Natural Resource development, Indigenous communities can provide meaningful input into the direction and requirements for application development through a governing body, but that does not necessarily mean providing the technological expertise for hands on end to end solution deployment, or being the sponsor i.e. the initial or major provider of financial capital.

In this chapter, we posit that those business processes that require participation by Indigenous communities, Natural Resource companies, and different levels of governments who lack trust in each other can be performed more effectively using blockchain technologies. Moreover, we make the case that the Indigenous communities benefit the most if Indigenous entrepreneurs serve in governance roles to provide continuous and meaningful input into development of blockchain platforms. We have specifically identified Indigenous entrepreneurs as the leaders required for initiating blockchain projects as it is entrepreneurs who lead and develop new products and services. The identity of entrepreneurs is critical as entrepreneurs set the initial direction of projects and organizations based on their own values. If Indigenous community values are to be genuinely included in blockchain projects, it is Indigenous entrepreneurs who necessarily need to initiate the process of identification of needs, devise solutions and setup governance structures. Otherwise, despite applying novel technology, the same historical power dynamics would likely re-emerge with Natural Resources companies and governments, mitigating much of the trust benefits possible from blockchain use.

The research questions addressed in this chapter are:

1. What are the issues of trust in the Natural Resource industry that can be addressed by blockchain based solutions?
2. What is the potential for Indigenous Entrepreneurship combined with blockchain technology in addressing the identified issues of trust in the Natural Resource industry?
3. What are the business models that enable sustainable development and operation of blockchain technology projects involving a broad range of stakeholders in the Natural Resource industry?

In the next sections, we discuss more in-depth, the Duty to Consult and Accommodate Indigenous Communities, Indigenous Entrepreneurship, and blockchain technologies. To ensure that some of the potentially abstract concepts are understood in a concrete context, we then provide a case study of a consortium currently in the process of development, Indigenous Blockchain Resource Development (IBRD). Following that, we provide a detailed business-level analysis of IBRD using the enterprise analysis tool, the Business Model Canvas (BMC). In our conclusion, we distill our analysis to identify implications for research.

2 Duty to Consult and Accommodate Indigenous Communities

The Duty to Consult and Accommodate Indigenous Communities is an important concept in understanding the required interactions between Indigenous and non-Indigenous communities, yet it is a relatively unknown concept among developers of blockchain technology projects. The Duty to Consult and Accommodate Indigenous Communities is a fundamental component required for building trust between Indigenous and non-Indigenous communities in Natural Resource projects, and is the foundation for the development of a blockchain based applications. When the consultation process has been completed, the resulting agreement can be considered to be a multi-party contract, where blockchain technology provides the mechanisms for a transparent record of each contract related transaction, and associated smart contracts can distribute related payments. This section describes the Duty to Consult and Accommodate Indigenous Communities at different levels of governance, from the United Nations to international bodies such as the OECD, to national governments and Indigenous communities, all of which provide the foundation for developing contextual blockchain technology solutions.

The United Nations Declaration on the Rights of Indigenous Peoples (UNDRIP) uses the following working definition of Indigenous people, used in this paper: "Indigenous communities, peoples and nations are those which, having a historical continuity with pre-invasion and pre-colonial societies that developed on their territories, consider themselves distinct from other sectors of the societies now prevailing on those territories, or parts of them. They form at present non-dominant sectors of society and are determined to preserve, develop and transmit to future generations their ancestral territories, and their ethnic identity, as the basis of their continued existence as peoples, in accordance with their own cultural patterns, social institutions and legal system." (United Nations Department of Economic and Social Affairs 2014, p. 50).

The World Bank estimates there are 370 million Indigenous people worldwide, in over 90 countries, approximately 5% of the global population (The World Bank 2018). Indigenous peoples are referred to in the literature as Native Americans in the USA, Aboriginal, Metis and Inuit in Canada, and Aboriginals in Australia. Indigenous entrepreneurs, therefore are entrepreneurs who belong to Indigenous communities. As described by Dana (2015), Indigenous entrepreneurship is an under-researched field. Peredo and McLean (2013) also describe Indigenous Entrepreneurship as being distinct from other types of entrepreneurship.

International agreements such as the UNDRIP provide a point of reference from which the duty to consult Indigenous peoples can be understood. UNDRIP Article 32 refers to Indigenous people's rights related to resource development:

1. "Indigenous peoples have the right to determine and develop priorities and strategies for the development or use of their lands or territories and other resources.
2. States shall consult and cooperate in good faith with the indigenous peoples concerned through their own representative institutions in order to obtain their free and informed consent prior to the approval of any project affecting their lands or territories and other resources, particularly in connection with the development, utilization or exploitation of mineral, water or other resources." United Nations General Assembly (2007, p. 18).

Therefore the UNDRIP both affirms the rights of Indigenous peoples regarding use of land and resources, and simultaneously requires states (national governments) to consult with Indigenous peoples for mineral, water and other resource development. It is useful to note that four countries that originally voted against UNDRIP, Canada, USA, Australia and New Zealand, have now become signatories to the declaration. In Canada, the relationship between Indigenous and non-Indigenous communities continues to evolve over a long-term time scale spanning over multiple centuries. The evolution of the duty to consult Indigenous communities is simply one chapter in this long-term process. In Canada, Natural Resources development is carried out primarily by private sector firms and not government entities. Therefore the duty to consult involves three types of entities: Indigenous communities, private sector Natural Resource companies, and different levels of government. The government of Canada currently describes the duty to consult in relationship with the Natural Resources industry as follows:

"While the duty to consult is an obligation that rests with the Crown, the Government of Canada will, where appropriate, expect industry proponents to carry out significant procedural aspects of consultation on a proposed project. The Government of Canada will also rely on the impact avoidance, mitigation, offset and compensation measures carried out by industry, where appropriate, for accommodation purposes." Indigenous and Northern Affairs Canada (2015, https://www.aadnc-aandc.gc.ca/eng/1430509727738/1430509820338).

Therefore the Canadian government explicitly delegates to the private sector "proponent" or private sector firm, the process of consultation with Indigenous communities for the purpose of Natural Resource development. The Canadian government also explicitly places the responsibility of accommodation "measures" and costs resulting from the consultation to the "proponent" or private sector firm. In Canada therefore, the process of consultation and the majority of financial costs of accommodation are borne by private sector Natural Resource firms, who proportionately receive the greatest financial benefit for the project.

There are frequent objections from Natural Resource firms that the processes involved in the duty to consult are not clearly defined. As a response, the international Organization of Economic Cooperation and Development (OECD) has consultatively developed a 118 page document on *Due Diligence Guidance for Meaningful Stakeholder Engagement in the Extractive Sector* (OECD 2017). This document consulted an advisory group including the governments of Canada and Norway, International Council on Mining and Metals, Prospectors and Developers Association of Canada, Mining Association of Canada, and a number Non-Governmental Organizations (NGOs) and Indigenous communities. Furthermore, larger Indigenous communities such as Nishnawbe Aski Nation in Northern Ontario in Canada, that have the scale and capacity to develop their own recommendations for consultations independent of government, have similarly developed consultation procedure documents (Nishnawbe Aski Nation 2007). Therefore for technology solution developers looking for process guidance, detailed descriptions of the process for the Duty to Consult and Accommodate Indigenous Communities exists from different types of governance bodies, from the UN to Indigenous communities. The ultimate process required for a specific project is determined through negotiation and then can be modeled in a blockchain based solution. A blockchain based solution has the potential for providing an additional layer of trust, to a process that has traditionally had an endemic level of mistrust.

In the next section we describe in detail Indigenous entrepreneurship, focusing on the identity of entrepreneurs and governance structures for blockchain technology based development in the Natural Resource industry project context. We argue that in concert with the Duty to Consult, Indigenous entrepreneurship and Indigenous governance, are essential components for building trust in the development and operation of blockchain based technology projects in the Natural Resource industry project context.

3 Literature Review

The Indigenous identity of entrepreneurs is important to the worldview, community values and project requirements that are different from the requirements of other stakeholders. Dana (2015) describes Indigenous entrepreneurship as an emerging global field of research. Peredo and McLean (2013) list differences between the motivations and growth intentions for Indigenous entrepreneurs and non-Indigenous entrepreneurs. For instance, Indigenous entrepreneurs tend to have a more communitarian orientation. Therefore, a blockchain platform developed by a consortium of Indigenous and non-Indigenous organizations may be more desirable than disparate platforms. A consortium led by Indigenous entrepreneurs will engender a higher level of trust from Indigenous communities at the initial stages, which can be foundational for building greater long-term trust among all stakeholders. If the early and genuine involvement of Indigenous entrepreneurs demonstrates the desired long-term benefits of lower friction and fewer disputes for Natural Resource projects, there will be greater buy in to the consortium approach from a broader range of stakeholders. Light and Dana (2013) explain suppression of Indigenous entrepreneurship when the social capital of a dominant non-Indigenous group becomes manifest, providing further support that a solution developed by a limited coalition of non-Indigenous organizations is not desirable. Significantly, Peredo and Anderson (2006) describe Indigenous entrepreneurship as a process of changing the power dynamics between Indigenous and non-Indigenous communities, providing support for the aim of rebuilding trust through recognizing power dynamics. Leadership by Indigenous entrepreneurs in technology projects in the Natural Resources sector is therefore part of the longer-term process of changing power dynamics in favour of Indigenous communities (O'Faircheallaigh 2013).

As described by Dana (2015), Indigenous Entrepreneurship is an under-researched field, and there are few peer reviewed articles describing Indigenous entrepreneurship in Information and Communications Technology (ICT). The limited peer reviewed literature on Indigenous entrepreneurship in ICT is a result of both under research and the under-representation of Indigenous individuals in ICT professions. The grey literature provides some insight into Indigenous entrepreneurship in ICT. Specifically in Canada, the Canadian Council for Aboriginal Business (2016) reports that Indigenous entrepreneurship has been growing at a faster rate than entrepreneurship in the overall population between the years 2000–2015. The same report also indicates a similar proportion of Indigenous entrepreneurs involved in primary or Natural Resource industries as non-indigenous entrepreneurs. While there is an existing supply of Indigenous entrepreneurs in Natural Resource sector, there is an under-representation of Indigenous entrepreneurs in the ICT sector. To gain a better understanding of Indigenous Entrepreneurship in technology, we define entrepreneurship broadly to include Indigenous technology projects with economic, social, environmental or cultural objectives. The following are some international examples of Indigenous entrepreneurs utilizing technology to achieve economic, social, environmental or cultural goals. In an application of new technology to support traditional activities, Udén (2008) describes the use of Information and Communications Technology (ICT) for traditional reindeer herding activities by Indigenous Sami women entrepreneurs in Sweden. Indigenous applications of technology includes the implementation of renewable energy projects in Bolivia (Pansera 2012). Mills et al. (2016) describe multimodal ICT use in Indigenous community led education in Australia. Virtanen (2015) describes the use of social media by Indigenous communities in Southwestern Amazonia to maintain social relationships and to organize politically. ICT has been used for cultural revitalization through digital recreation of important cultural practices and artefacts in New Zealand (Ngata et al. 2012). Galla (2016) describes the positive benefits of the use of ICT for Indigenous language revitalization and education in multiple countries, based on an international survey.

In Canada, Indigenous entrepreneurs have developed internet access services owned by local communities in Ontario (Kakekaspan et al. 2014), and in Quebec (McMahon and Mangiok 2014). Under the broader definition of entrepreneurship involving Indigenous technology projects with economic, social, environmental or cultural objectives, Romero (2017) describes the use of ICT by Indigenous women who are independent animation film developers. Digital storytelling is also an emerging narrative method for preserving and promoting Indigenous oral wisdom (Cunsolo et al. 2013). Roth and Audette-Longo (2018) discuss the use of digital media and transformation in Canadian Indigenous communities, and how there have been more positive effects when projects have been co-developed with Indigenous communities. Lameman and Lewis (2011) describe an Indigenous digital game development enterprise partnering with a Canadian post secondary institution to teach Indigenous youth how to develop digital games. A study involving multiple games indicates the perspective used in the development of games by Indigenous entrepreneurs, is significantly different from non-Indigenous game developers (Madsen 2017). Winter and Boudreau (2018) discuss Indigenous entrepreneurs shaping digital infrastructure by engaging with digital media and digital culture. If we take a broader view of Indigenous technology entrepreneurship to include renewable energy projects, Karanasios and Parker (2018, p. 178) describe the differences between "utility sustainability perspectives" and "community sustainability perspectives" and how the different levels of involvement by Indigenous communities in the governance of renewable energy projects. Therefore in bringing a different perspective to technology projects, Indigenous entrepreneurs are able to shape the direction of the project, often to achieve economic, social, environmental and cultural goals that include continuity of Indigenous culture.

An important note here is that Indigenous entrepreneurs do not have to be the hands on developers or implementers in ICT projects, or even the majority of the project team to lead projects. Indigenous entrepreneurs have to be in a leadership position to guide the direction of the project. Lameman and Lewis (2011), for example, discuss how Indigenous educators partnered with a Canadian post secondary institution but guided the direction of the project. Madsden (2017) discusses the development of a game by a non-Indigenous organization, utilizing an Indigenous story, shaped by more than 40 Indigenous elders during development. Indigenous leadership in an ICT project can therefore guide the development and direction of the project, using Indigenous values and philosophies, to achieve outcomes relevant for Indigenous communities.

The intersection between Indigenous entrepreneurship and blockchain technology has been limited due to a number of factors, including both the newness of blockchain technology, and more importantly the under-representation of potential Indigenous entrepreneurs in ICT professions in countries with Indigenous sub-populations such as Canada (The Information and Communications Technology Council 2017; Pogue and Olawoye 2018; Vu et al. 2019). The literature review shows that there has been one unsuccessful attempt at developing an Indigenous Cryptocurrency, Mazzacoin, in the United States (Tekobbe and McKnight 2016). The purpose of Mazzacoin was to enable a more independent local economy that would provide the community with more control over local economic, social and cultural development. At the same time, with knowledge of this cryptocurrency failure, Canadian scholars argue that an Indigenous cryptocurrency may be viable in Canada (Alcantara and Dick 2017). Internationally, Indigenous communities have started using blockchain for e-identity (IDGO Team 2018). Another application of blockchain is tracking climate data by Northern Indigenous communities in Canada (Scott 2018), who are more acutely affected by climate change. There is one blockchain project related to energy royalties and Indigenous communities in Canada, but it is not led by Indigenous entrepreneurs (GuildOne 2018). Therefore, there is a lack of Indigenous entrepreneur led blockchain technology projects in the Natural Resource sector. Given that Indigenous communities are expected to experience many of the potential costs and benefits of Natural Resource development, Indigenous leadership shaping technology solution development in the Natural Resource sector is essential for ensuring the benefits of the technology accrue to a broad set of stakeholders. For example, Canada is the global centre for mining, with the majority of mining companies in the world being listed on the Toronto Stock Exchange (Mining Association of Canada 2018). Simultaneously, Canada is also going through the implementation of the recommendations of a formal truth and reconciliation process with Indigenous communities (Truth and Reconciliation Commission of Canada 2015). The combination of the following factors makes Canada a generative locale for developing and operating ICT projects in the Natural Resource sector led by Indigenous entrepreneurs, (1) an ongoing reconciliation process with Indigenous communities; (2) a recognition by the private sector Natural Resource industry of the necessity of genuine Indigenous partnerships, and (3) a recognition in the technology sector of the underrepresentation of Indigenous professionals; (4) increasing evidence that Blockchain technology can address the lack of trust that currently exists. The next section describes the features of Blockchain technology that enable an appropriate solution to be developed to resolve the listed issues. The issues related to Indigenous entrepreneurship from the literature review are summarized in Table 1.

4 Blockchain and the Trust Process

The following features of blockchain provide a solution space for rebuilding trust in the current environment in the Natural Resources sector, which has different stakeholders, common and overlapping interests, but a lack of trust: Permanent/Immutable transactions; Transparency and visibility of each transaction; Distributed database without centralized authority; Smart Contracts/Programmatically Executable Transactions.

4.1 Permanent/Immutable Transactions

Blockchain provides a permanent or more accurately "immutable" record of transactions (Vigna and Casey 2018). Indigenous communities in Canada have experienced a long history of broken treaty promises, where contractual treaty clauses were not honoured at all, or followed by letter but not in spirit. Therefore a *permanent or immutable* record of transactions that have been completed, which is an integral feature of blockchains, will increase trust in the process of contract completion, and over the long-term increase trust between Indigenous communities and other stakeholders the Natural Resource sector.

Table 1 Summary of issues from literature review

Issue	Finding	Implication
Indigenous entrepreneurship is an under researched area	Indigenous entrepreneurship is more communitarian than non-Indigenous entrepreneurship (Peredo and McLean 2013) In Canada, Indigenous entrepreneurship growing at a faster rate than non-Indigenous entrepreneurship (Canadian Council for Aboriginal Business 2016)	Involve Indigenous entrepreneurs from the start of technology development projects when the direction is determined
Interaction between Indigenous and non-Indigenous entrepreneurs	Indigenous entrepreneurship can be suppressed by dominant groups (Light and Dana 2013) Indigenous entrepreneurship changes the power dynamics between Indigenous and non-Indigenous communities (Peredo and Anderson 2006)	Recognizing that project governance structures are about balancing power dynamics, Ensure the governance of technology projects involves genuine and meaningful roles for Indigenous entrepreneurs
Indigenous entrepreneurship in ICT	Indigenous entrepreneurship in ICT is used for different purposes such as cultural revitalization (Ngata et al. 2012; Galla 2016; Romero 2017; Roth and Audette-Longo 2018) Under-representation of potential Indigenous entrepreneurs in ICT professions in countries with Indigenous sub-populations such as Canada (The Information and Communications Technology Council 2017; Pogue and Olawoye 2018; Vu et al. 2019)	Recognize the importance of culture and other factors that are important to potential ICT entrepreneurs, and support the development of these elements as well as the Indigenous entrepreneurs as part of the technology development project
Indigenous cryptocurrency projects	One unsuccessful attempt at developing an Indigenous Cryptocurrency, Mazzacoin, in the United States (Tekobbe and McKnight 2016) Canadian scholars argue that an Indigenous cryptocurrency may be viable in Canada (Alcantara and Dick 2017)	Potential for cryptocurrency solution, although not incorporated into this case study
Indigenous blockchain projects	Indigenous communities have used blockchain for e-identity (IDGO Team 2018), and tracking climate data by Northern Indigenous communities in Canada (Scott 2018)	Potential for different applications of blockchain technology for different purposes by Indigenous communities

A "permissioned" blockchain implementation is appropriate in this context, where each entity has specific permissions to add transactions to the blockchain. This blockchain implementation is not accessible to "everyone" such as the Bitcoin blockchain. Each completed transaction is therefore visible and verifiable by all stakeholders with viewing permission, but changeable only by stakeholders with additional permissions for changes in the form of additional transactions.

4.2 Transparency and Visibility of Each Transaction

Blockchain provides a transparent list of all transactions completed in the form of a "triple entry" ledger where the results of all transactions are visible and verifiable by all relevant stakeholders (Tapscott and Tapscott 2016). In the context of the experience of Indigenous communities in Canada, where the obligations in treaties were not completed at all, or completed by letter but not in spirit, a "triple entry" ledger enabled by blockchain, where every transaction is verifiable by all stakeholders, provides the potential for an additional layer of trust. In some cases there were different interpretations of treaty clauses, or different methods of recording agreements, e.g. written and oral, leading to different understandings. Therefore a *transparent* record of transactions that have been completed will increase trust in the process of contract clause completion, and over the long-term increase trust between Indigenous communities and other stakeholders in the Natural Resource sector.

A "private" blockchain implementation is appropriate in this context, where relevant entities are invited and can view all transactions. Since many transactions will be based on commercial contracts, this blockchain implementation is not visible to "everyone" to protect business contract confidentiality requirements. Each completed transaction is therefore visible and verifiable by all *permissioned* stakeholders, and each stakeholder's record of the list of transactions, the blockchain, is exactly identical to every other permissioned stakeholder's record of transactions.

4.3 Distributed Database Without Centralized Authority

Blockchain maintains the record of completed transactions in the form of a distributed database that is not controlled by a central authority (Kim and Laskowski 2018). The issue of distributed and decentralized control is important to Indigenous communities in Canada, where centralized control policies by governments, whether they were well-intentioned or not, have had long-term negative consequences on Indigenous communities. Therefore a *decentralized database* ensures that control over the record of transactions is not placed with a central authority, such as a government, or a single Natural Resource firm. A decentralized database, which is an integral feature of blockchain, is likely to increase trust in the process of contract completion, and over the long-term increase trust between Indigenous communities and other stakeholders in the Natural Resource sector.

As opposed to public blockchains such as Bitcoin that can have millions of nodes (Lielacher 2019), this permissioned, private blockchain initially has dozens and ultimately hundreds of nodes, where each node is operated by a permissioned organization or individual with appropriate identity credentials. The ledger or database of transactions is identically maintained across each permissioned node. A node can be as simple as a single device such as a desktop computer, or a highly secure, partitioned, cloud-based storage solution that most permissioned stakeholders have implemented.

4.4 Smart Contracts/Programmatically Executable Transactions

Smart contracts can theoretically exist independently of blockchains (Kim and Laskowski 2017). In this instance the combination of Smart Contracts with the particular implementation of blockchain as described in this section provides a powerful impetus for creating trust at the beginning of the process. Smart Contracts increase trust by coding contracts, or agreed on future actions and payments into programmatically executable applications. Smart Contracts do not replace legal contracts, but provide a high level of assurance that transactions will be automatically initiated when certain concrete conditions are met. Furthermore, Smart Contracts ensure that the value of the contract is stored through a legally binding mechanism (e.g. escrow, or insurance) so that each party to the contract cannot renege on the contract, when the predetermined conditions have been met. Specifically in the context of Indigenous community relations, where there has been a history of broken promises, and unfulfilled treaties, a technology enabled solution that guarantees both future execution of clauses, and release of value, is essential in creating the higher level of trust required for Indigenous communities to sign on to new agreements and contracts.

To be codified in a software application, Smart Contract clauses need to be agreed to by parties to the contract in advance, similar to legal clauses, and are visible and verifiable by all permissioned stakeholders. In this particular case, the majority of legal clauses in a legal contract between Natural Resource industry proponents and Indigenous communities can have corresponding smart contracts attached to them. The greater the proportion of legal clauses that can be turned into Smart Contracts, the higher the level of ex ante trust between stakeholders that the contract clause will be executed reliably. The technical term for a legal contract with a matching and equivalent Smart Contract is a Ricardian Contract (Clack et al. 2016). Smart contracts can execute workflow in connected software applications. The entry conditions for smart contracts can be initiated by authorized human actions, other Smart Contracts, or other software applications.

In this particular application Smart Contracts can be used to ensure royalty payments to Indigenous communities which are scheduled and tied to production, release funds for local employment, and building local infrastructure, and environmental protection or remediation. Royalty payments to Indigenous communities as a part of Natural Resource development project have become an international norm (Manson and Mbenga 2003; Scudder et al. 2019; Qiolevu and Lim 2019). In many projects, agreements between the local Indigenous community and the Natural Resource project proponent strategically involve employment and training for local Indigenous community members (McCreary et al. 2016). In other cases, agreements between Indigenous communities and Natural Resource project stakeholders include clauses for the provision of infrastructure such as roads and utility services or environmental protection and remediation requirements. Each of these requirements can be coded into Smart Contracts, providing an additional layer of assurance that contracts will be fulfilled in addition to, and not as a replacement for conventional contract process. This chapter therefore introduces the concept of long-term Smart Contracts lasting years and decades similar to long-term conventional contracts, whereas the focus of research has currently been on short-term Smart Contracts (Pinna et al. 2019). We believe the requirements for long-term Smart Contracts are an important research gap to be addressed if Smart Contracts are to become as prevalent as conventional contracts.

5 Methodology

The methodology for this project included literature reviews, case study interviews and qualitative analysis. The literature reviews provided the background for identifying the issues in the interactions between Indigenous and non-Indigenous communities in the context of Natural resource industry, where blockchain technology can provide potential solutions. Interviews of three subject matter experts were conducted to determine important aspects of possible solutions and the current direction of a project in development. Since the project is in early stages of development, confidentiality was important for interviewees, and has been maintained by changing the name of the project and not attributing any direct quotations to any interviewees. The qualitative analysis focused on framing the description of the project by utilizing a familiar entrepreneurship framework, the Business Model Canvas. Two versions of the Business Model Canvas were developed to demonstrate the iterative nature of the analysis process.

6 Organization Case Study: IBRD

The following case study provides a description of an organization illustrating the concepts described in this chapter. The case study describes an organization in an early development stage, formed by Indigenous entrepreneurs and non-Indigenous junior miners who determined that the appropriate organizational form for implementation of software projects in the Natural Resource sector is a formally incorporated organization. The Indigenous and junior miners were primarily involved in mining precious metals such as Gold. In this chapter the pseudonym IBRD is used to protect proprietary details of the corporation.

The consortium also recognized that it was not only blockchain technology, but also the membership of the group which leads development of the technology that generates a high level of trust. Being connected to both Natural Resource and Technology sectors, the consortium had a heightened awareness of the ongoing issues of under-representation of Indigenous communities in the technology sector (The Information and Communications Technology Council 2017; Pogue and Olawoye 2018; Vu et al. 2019). Additionally, the consortium had a substantial understanding of the value systems embedded in information technology development. In the Artificial Intelligence domain for example, Li (2018) describes how there are no software development projects that are independent of values of the developers, and that the direction of software development is significantly determined by the values of the developers. To ensure Indigenous values are represented in IBRD and its projects, the consortium of Indigenous entrepreneurs and junior miners therefore intentionally and explicitly formalized Indigenous leadership in the corporation through the articles of incorporation. Indigenous leadership does not preclude non-Indigenous individuals or companies from being a significant part of the corporation. Indigenous leadership was formalized within IBRD by requiring that the majority of board members are Indigenous. Governance systems explicitly mandating Indigenous leadership ensures the development of blockchain technology is guided by Indigenous values and principles, to benefit Indigenous communities and simultaneously benefit other stakeholders.

The Indigenous leadership of IBRD centers Indigenous interests in an industry that is increasingly dependent on resources from Indigenous community owned land, and therefore increasingly dependent on positive relationships with Indigenous communities. IBRD promotes Indigenous approaches to Natural Resource development, which for example involves developing respectful relationships with host communities at an early stage in the Natural Resource project lifecycle. Over the long-term horizon, Indigenous approaches to Natural Resources development are more holistic in ensuring that development of a Natural Resource delivers multifaceted community benefits and outcomes. A holistic Indigenous approach avoids the negative outcomes of the 'Resource Curse', which leaves Natural Resource based communities more impoverished due to ongoing social and environmental costs after the completion of a Natural Resource development project (Gamu et al. 2015). While the Natural Resource industry and project management profession moves towards triple bottom line considerations (Silvius and Schipper 2014), a holistic Indigenous approach involves an additional dimension, culture, for quadruple bottom line outcomes (economic, social, environmental, and cultural) (Scrimgeour and Iremonger 2004; Walters and Takamura 2015; Dalziel et al. 2006; Sengupta et al. 2015). In a multicultural environment for Natural Resource Development, such as the countries where Indigenous and non-Indigenous cultures are present, the cultural bottom line is often unrecognized by individuals and organizations based in the dominant culture, since the dominant culture is ubiquitous, and Indigenous culture is not adequately understood (O'Faircheallaigh 2008). Indigenous authors have argued that the suppression of Indigenous culture is often related to the broader project of disconnecting Indigenous communities from their land for the purpose of resource extraction (Preston 2017; Hall 2013; Howlett et al. 2011). The combination of Indigenous leadership and application of Indigenous approaches has resulted in a higher level of trust between IBRD and Indigenous communities in Canada compared to other industry consortiums, where both membership and approaches are different. Linking back to Indigenous entrepreneurship, Indigenous leadership in IBRD contributes to the process of changing the power dynamics between Indigenous and non-Indigenous communities. Additionally, Indigenous community partnership approaches deployed by the Indigenous leadership at IBRD contributes to the implementation of the United Nations Declaration on the Rights of Indigenous Peoples (UNDRIP), as well as facilitating Duty to Consult requirements. In summary, Indigenous leadership in IBRD ensures Indigenous interests and approaches are central to the strategy and operations of the organization.

6.1 The Opportunity for IBRD

The Canadian Chamber of Commerce (CCoC), an organization representing the private sector in Canada, has released a position paper reframing the duty for consultation with Indigenous Communities from being primarily and expense to being a valuable investment (Canadian Chamber of Commerce 2017). Investing the requisite effort and resources into the outcomes of the duty to consult can potentially reduce the costs of some long-term risks. Risks from unresolved issues with Indigenous communities and Natural Resource projects include stoppages, cancellations, risk premiums for insurance and future liabilities (Conde 2017). Large global consulting firms such as Deloitte have also identified the area of improving trust with stakeholders as an opportunity: "As the mining industry's value proposition is increasingly called into question, mining companies are beginning to see that they cannot succeed into the future unless they change the way they operate. This is about more than enhancing efficiencies. It's about re-establishing trust with stakeholders and collaborating to devise better responses." Glenn Ives, Americas Mining Leader, Deloitte Canada (Deloitte 2018, p. 3).

Another big four global consulting company, KPMG, interviewed Mining Executives to identify risks (KPMG 2018). Among the top ten risks identified by mining executives in 2018 are:

- Permitting Risk
- Community Relations and Social License to Operate
- Environmental Risk.

Therefore a broad base of business leaders, global consulting firms, and mining executives independently identify improving trust in stakeholder relationships as an important and immediate issue to be resolved by the industry. IBRD provides an entrepreneurial solution for the recognized issues in duty to consult, stakeholder relations and community relations. The business model and associated technology aspects of the solution are described in the next section, through an analysis of the business.

7 Analysis of the IBRD Blockchain Solution

The organization IBRD is analyzed using the Business Model Canvas (BMC), developed by Osterwalder et al. (2010). The BMC has become a prevalent tool for teaching entrepreneurship (Türko 2016). The BMC has been used for analyzing growing industries such as renewable energy (Horváth and Szabó 2018), stable industries such as airlines (Urban et al. 2018), and the Natural Resource sector (Kajanus et al. 2018). The BMC is a useful tool for explaining a business model through a short one page summary of the business.

The BMC uses the following elements for analyzing a business model:

1. Customer Segments
2. Value Propositions
3. Channels
4. Customer Relationships
5. Revenue Streams
6. Key Resources
7. Key Activities
8. Key Partnerships
9. Cost Structure.

The Business Model Canvas is used in an iterative process until a viable business model is developed. For the purpose of illustration, an example of the current status quo of the Natural Resource industry business model is presented in the framework of a Business Model Canvas, including risks in Fig. 1. The final iterated canvas presented in Fig. 3 at the end of this chapter demonstrates how the identified risks can be highlighted effectively and resolved through iterating a business model on paper before implementing it in operation.

7.1 IBRD Customer Segments

There are three primary customer segments for IBRD:

1. Natural Resource companies

Business Model Canvas – IBRD

KEY PARTNERS	KEY ACTIVITIES	VALUE PROPOSITIONS	CUSTOMER RELATIONSHIPS	CUSTOMER SEGMENTS
Separate technology investments by individual Natural Resource companies: -Cloud solution providers -Internet Service providers -Outsourced services *Risk of each individual system is not necessarily compatible with systems used or developed by other companies*	Separate technology investments by individual Natural Resource companies: -Investment in ICT infrastructure -Maintenance of applications -Enhancement of applications *Risk of each individual system is not necessarily compatible with systems used or developed by other companies* *Risk of high levels of investment in technology required for each individual company*	Provide lowest cost product to customer by reducing total economic cost of production through minimizing and externalizing expenses for local community requirements *-Risks of delays and stoppages* *-Low reliability of cost and time estimates* *-Limited social license to operate*	-Fulfillment of contracts -Delivery of products with specified quantity, quality, price and schedule requirements *Risks to supply chain reliability for customers* *Demand from end consumers for end products made from socially and environmentally responsible supply chains*	Product Buyers
		Minimum cost expenditures for addressing Indigenous community interests. View of Duty to Consult only as a cost and not an investment *-Risks lack of trust in delivery of benefits for Indigenous community* *- Risks ability of Natural Resource projects to address long-term community needs*	Short term expenditures rather than long-term investments. *Limited development of ICT and other long-term infrastructure for community*	Indigenous communities
		-Transactional relationship with government. -Minimum interaction with government with the intention of minimizing costs *-Risks in ensuring all stakeholder requirements have been met for permits* *-Increased need for enforcement of corrective actions and punitive regulations* *-Uncertainty on the completion of duty to consult with Indigenous communities*	Short term expenditures rather than long-term investments. *Risks of adversarial relationship with government* *Delays in permit and regulatory approvals*	Government departments

KEY RESOURCES	CHANNELS
-Workflow applications -Database Infrastructure -Hardware/Cloud Infrastructure	**CHANNELS** -Relationship building -Tendered contracts -Commodity markets

COST STRUCTURE	REVENUE STREAMS
-System development costs -Maintenance of required systems -Costs for outsourced services -Marketing costs -Administration costs -Financial costs	-Product contracts -Commodity markets

Fig. 1 The current state or status quo business model canvas

2. Indigenous communities
3. Government departments.

In this case there is no overlap among customer segments, customers belonging to one customer segment are not also part of another customer segment. The critical task for IBRD is to maintain a delicate balance between the three customer segments: Natural Resource companies, Indigenous communities and Government departments are required to all participate in each project. When the requirements of one of these key customer segments is not adequately met, a number of project risks may be realized, including delays, stoppages, and outright cancellation of the project. Each project therefore requires at least one Natural Resource company who is normally the proponent, at least one Indigenous community, who is affected by the project, and at least one government department, whose approvals are on the critical path for the project.

7.2   IBRD Value Propositions

The value proposition is central to developing a business, and therefore it has a central position and role in the BMC (Osterwalder et al. 2014). Value propositions are based on solving customers problems. In the case of IBRD, the value propositions are different for each customer segment, although related to each other. IBRDs value propositions for each customer segment is based on increasing trust.

The primary value proposition in utilizing the IBRD solution for Natural Resource companies is the reduction of risks of delays and stoppages for Natural Resource projects. Natural Resource projects involving Indigenous land incur a number of risks of delays and stoppages, when there is a lack of trust between the proponent company and the affected Indigenous community. Utilizing a blockchain based IBRD solution that engenders increased trust, there will be fewer risks of delays and project stoppages related to the relationship with the affected Indigenous community. Increased reliability of cost and time estimates provide the possibility of increased external investment and lower cost of acquiring capital for further investment into company projects. Over a longer-term horizon, the industry gains an increased social license to operate. With a proven solution for increased trust, different companies can operate projects though a more positive relationship with the same Indigenous community over a longer period of time.

The primary value proposition in utilizing the IBRD solution for affected Indigenous communities is greater trust in the delivery of economic, social, environmental and cultural benefits for the community, from partnerships that involve local Natural Resources. The IBRD blockchain based solution fundamentally addresses issues that have resulted in the breakdown of trust between Indigenous organizations and Natural Resource projects, due to noncompliance to agreements and non-delivery of commitments. The IBRD solution ensures transparent verification of completion of transactions, as well as robust financial provision for planned future expenses and commitments. For example, the costs of an anticipated environmental cleanup will be put aside in an escrow related mechanism, ensuring that the Indigenous community is not saddled with additional costs. The longer-term value proposition for Indigenous communities is an increased ability to use Natural Resource projects to address long-term community needs. Long-term community needs that can be supported by Natural Resource projects include quadruple bottom line elements: employment and human Natural Resource, physical infrastructure development, social equity and cultural project development and implementation.

The primary value proposition in utilizing the IBRD solution for government departments is the increased ability to ensure all stakeholder requirements have been met for Natural Resource projects. The IBRD solution provides transparently verifiable transaction records as well as provision for future anticipated costs that are in conformance with the applicable government department regulations. Governments at different levels (federal, provincial, municipal, and band council) have different requirements. Additionally, different departments within the same level of government have different regulatory requirements. With a more transparent and predictable solution for Natural Resource projects, there is a decreased need for enforcement of corrective actions and punitive regulations. Over the long-term horizon, the different levels of government will fulfil the duty to consult with Indigenous communities.

The understanding of value proposition for each different customer segment is essential for IBRD. Each segment has different but overlapping value propositions, pain and gain points. Natural Resource development companies are primarily interested in economic benefits and risks. Indigenous communities are interested in quadruple bottom line economic, social, environmental and cultural benefits and risks. Government departments are interested in ensuring regulatory and policy requirements are met. Addressing the different value propositions for different customer segments requires developing quantitative and qualitative Key Performance Indicators (KPIs) that can be used to measure achievement of the different value propositions.

7.3   IBRD Channels

Channels involve methods of communication with current and potential customers, including distribution of products and services. The IBRD blockchain based solution will be distributed in the form of Software as a Service (SAAS). Therefore a cloud based implementation is envisioned. Blockchain implementations require a distributed database infrastructure, where each physical computer connected to the network is a potential node. As a private, permissioned blockchain application, the IBRD application uses a Proof of Authority (PoA) mechanism to validate nodes with the appropriate permissions. The different stakeholders, including Natural Resource companies, Indigenous communities, and government departments will select their own cloud service providers to maintain independence and distributed database requirements. In remote settings where many Natural Resource projects are implemented, the issue of availability of network and cloud services are part of the critical infrastructure to be considered, and not assumed to be available as we do in large urban settings.

7.4 IBRD Customer Relationships

In the case of the IBRD solution, maintaining relationships with all three customer segments: Natural Resource companies; Indigenous communities; and government departments, is essential. Any one customer segment not actively participating in the process can lead to project failure. IBRD has established relationships with stakeholders from all three customer segments, and maintains relationships with them. Ongoing maintenance of relationships will require fulfilment of promised features, protection of security of customer data, and protection of privacy in the majority of projects where proprietary information is involved. Whereas many B2B software application customer relationships are based on low touch interactions, IBRD customer relationship models require high touch interactions, including relationship building activities, such as in person attendance at important Indigenous community events, and sponsorship of strategic community activities. In the past, Natural Resource organizations have often tried to build goodwill and the social license to operate in Indigenous communities years prior to large projects by sponsoring for example sports and recreation activities. IBRD has been strategic in customer relationship building activities, and has included ICT infrastructure building projects in remote communities, including increasing satellite and local network capacity, and local human resource capacity in maintaining ICT infrastructure through investment in training programs.

One of the implications for IBRD is understanding the minimal technology requirements for ensuring implementation of distributed databases across different customer segments. Particular attention needs to be paid to remote and Indigenous communities, where existing technology and network bandwidth infrastructure may not deliver equivalent performance to other customer segments. In addition to ensuring equivalency of performance, long-term operation and maintenance of ICT infrastructure in remote and Indigenous communities requires innovative technology and human resource solutions.

7.5 IBRD Revenue Streams

There are a number of different possible revenue streams, including membership, licensing, cost per transaction, or fixed price for multiple transactions. The central revenue stream for IBRD is a cost per transaction paid by each stakeholder, in this case primarily Natural Resource companies. The cost per transaction model matches the cost structure for IBRD, which has to pay a cost per transaction for utilizing the underlying Ethereum Blockchain. Members of the corporation pay an additional annual fee based on the size of organization. Licensing options are being considered, but have not been implemented. As the Natural Resource sector is a global sector, and Indigenous communities are by definition local, licensing the technology to local Indigenous entrepreneurs in each national jurisdiction enables these entrepreneurs to build customized solutions for their jurisdiction on a proven platform.

There are five types of transactions that are eligible for charging a cost for transaction. Each Natural Resource project will contain one or more contracts between the different stakeholders, for example between a Natural Resource company and an Indigenous community. Each contract is a legal contract, simultaneously implemented as a Smart Contract in IBRDs blockchain based application. An important feature of smart contracts, or previously described programmatically executable transactions, is that their execution is automated. Therefore if the entry condition is met, the related actions for the contract are executed. Each contract between stakeholders in a Natural Resource development project has a number of clauses. In the implementation of the relevant clauses into smart contracts, each relevant clause can be conceptually defined as IF THEN statements. Transactions are used by IBRD to collect revenue per transaction:

1. Creation a of a contract clause
   The clauses can pertain to short-term (exploration) or long-term (environmental cleanup). Each contract contains multiple clauses.
2. Confirmation of contract clause by each stakeholder
   The simple existence of a clause does not imply agreement. A separate "transaction" is required to ensure all stakeholders agree to the clause, as it will be automatically executed as soon as conditions are met.
3. Triggering of a condition of a contract clause
   Each contract clause will have entry conditions, in coding terms, entry conditions can be expressed as a series of IF statements.
4. Completion of all requirements of a contract clause
   Each contract clause will have completion or exit conditions, in coding terms, exit conditions can be expressed as a series of THEN statements.
5. Completion of a sub-contract or the main contract i.e. completion of all clauses of the contract.
   In the implementation of smart contracts, it is beneficial if a complete legal contract can be divided into subcontracts, so that subcontracts can be completed independently of each other, as well as have conditions that connect them together.

Modification of clauses by all stakeholders are a permissible activity, and will follow modifications in legal contracts. A transaction recording the mutually agreed upon and modified clause is simply a special case of a new clause transaction, and is treated as such.

A conceptual diagram summarizing key portions of the Smart Contract process is provided in Fig. 2.

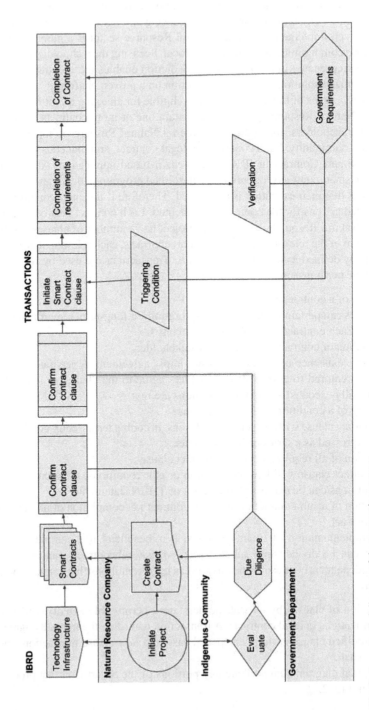

Fig. 2 A conceptual diagram of the transaction process

7.6 IBRD Key Resources

The main product and service for IBRD is a software application, therefore the software application is the key resource. The ability to deploy the blockchain application in a distributed database format entails a number of secondary resources. Each stakeholder who has a validated permission to enter transactions from a node will need to maintain their own database infrastructure, in most cases hosted on cloud-based solutions. The Smart Contract Management System, although part of the same seamless application for most end users, is an important subsystem and therefore a key resource. The Smart Contract Management System will interface with organization specific workflow systems to implement the requirements of each clause. The entire software and hardware "stack" required to maintain the blockchain, Smart Contract Management System, and related business Workflow applications forms a set of key resources. Finally the development of ICT systems is dependent on human resources and therefore human resources are a key resource. Loss of architects, developers and other key human resources to competitors will affect the business.

The implications for IBRD are to appropriately plan for the long-term operation and maintenance of technology and related human resources required for the blockchain application. Issues of technology obsolescence, and human resource succession planning that receive little attention in short-term projects require increased attention in longer term projects. IBRD's plans for maintaining currency of technology and key human resources must be adequate and transparent enough for customer segments entering long-term projects to have the required confidence and trust in IBRDs ability to deliver long-term support.

7.7 IBRD Key Activities

Setting up Information technology infrastructure for stakeholders is a key activity. As previously mentioned, ICT infrastructure such as high-speed networks, cannot be taken for granted in remote locations or Indigenous communities. An investment in ICT infrastructure, which is appropriate for the local environment, is therefore a key activity. Once the initial blockchain application has been developed, there is a requirement for continued maintenance. Maintenance includes the blockchain application, related Smart Contract management system, and related Business Workflow applications. Maintenance in this context is not only about mitigating potential failure risks, but also enhancing features as required by stakeholders. The final key activity is continual expansion of all customer segments to increase the benefit of network effects. The Natural Resource industry can benefit from synergies of development by using the same organization IBRD for different projects. For example, the community ICT infrastructure setup for one project will benefit subsequent projects, and therefore costs can be amortized or shared over multiple projects.

7.8 IBRD Key Partnerships

Key Partnerships for IBRD include the outsourced services required to maintain the different blockchain, Smart Contract Management System, and related business Workflow applications. As previously described, these software applications operate on software and hardware stacks, which are typically outsourced and not maintained in house. Therefore suppliers of services required to maintain the underlying software and hardware stacks are key partners. Other outsourced essential services required for information technology infrastructure, such as Internet Service providers are key providers. As previously mentioned, in remote settings where many Natural Resource projects are implemented, the issue of availability of network and cloud services are part of the critical infrastructure to be considered, and not assumed to be available as in large urban settings.

7.9 IBRD Cost Structure

The cost structure for IBRD has six essential components:

1. Amortization of initial development costs
2. Maintenance of required systems
3. Costs for outsourced services
4. Marketing costs
5. Administration costs
6. Financial costs.

The most initial cost is the cost of development of the application, which is amortized over a long-term horizon. Maintenance of software and hardware systems for continued operation is the next most significant cost. Since the application is deployed on cloud based and networked infrastructure, the cost of outsourced services will be significant. Marketing costs are required to maintain and expand the customer base. Administration costs including human resource costs are a required investment for long-term operations. Financial costs include the costs of capital for long-term investments.

In summary, IBRD demonstrates the implementation of the main principles described in this chapter, such as the duty to consult, and Indigenous entrepreneurship. The governance of the organization and the long-term relationships with different customer segments are as valuable as the innovative features of blockchain technology. In essence the innovative features of blockchain technology in combination with a different way of doing business in the Natural Resources sector strategically positions IBRD to be a leader in the sector.

A summary of the analysis of IBRD using the BMC format is provided in Fig. 3.

Business Model Canvas – IBRD

KEY PARTNERS	KEY ACTIVITIES	VALUE PROPOSITIONS	CUSTOMER RELATIONSHIPS	CUSTOMER SEGMENTS
-Cloud solution providers -Internet Service providers -Outsourced services (applies to all customer segments)	-Investment in ICT infrastructure -Maintenance of applications -Enhancement of applications (applies to all customer segments)	-Reduction of risks of delays and stoppages -Increased reliability of cost and time estimates -Increased social license to operate	-Fulfilment of promised features -Protection of security of customer data -Protection of privacy	Natural Resource companies
		-Greater trust in delivery of economic, social, environmental and cultural benefits for the community -Increased ability to use Natural Resource projects to address long-term community needs	Development of ICT infrastructure	Indigenous communities
		-Increased ability to ensure all stakeholder requirements have been met -Decreased need for enforcement of corrective actions and punitive regulations -Fulfil the duty to consult with Indigenous communities	Approvals Licenses	Government departments
	KEY RESOURCES -Smart Contract applications -Workflow applications -Blockchain Platform -Database Infrastructure -Hardware/Cloud Infrastructure		**CHANNELS** -Relationship building -Software As A Service (SAAS)	

COST STRUCTURE	REVENUE STREAMS
-Amortization of initial development costs -Maintenance of required systems -Costs for outsourced services -Marketing costs -Administration costs -Financial costs	-Membership -Cost per transaction -Fixed price for multiple transactions -Licensing

Fig. 3 IBRD business model canvas

8 Conclusion

This chapter describes the basis for an implementation of a blockchain based solution for projects in the Natural Resource Sector, where the majority of project involve Indigenous communities. The chapter summarizes both the technology implementation as well as the governance and business model that is required for the solution to rebuild trust in a sector where there is a lack of trust between key stakeholders. The solution is made concrete through describing an organization in development, IBRD. IBRD strives to achieve a solution to the persistent problem of trust in Natural Resources projects in three ways. First, Indigenous leadership of the organization enables application of Indigenous values and philosophies including quadruple bottom line outcomes, that creates trust with Indigenous communities. Second, IBRD takes advantage of new developments in blockchain technology and is inherently built on principles of building trust, therefore adding a technology based layer of trust to its solution. Third, the organizational structure of IBRD ensures that the revenues cover costs and enable ongoing investment into further technology development. Since the innovative technology solution is licensable, Indigenous entrepreneurs in other jurisdictions can license and then customize an appropriate organizational and software application model that is localized for their context. A standardized solution may not be inappropriate for different local contexts. In summary, a blockchain based implementation provides a solution for a complex problem in the Natural Resources industry, by combining Indigenous leadership, with technology innovation, and business model.

Future Research A number of areas of future theoretical research have been identified from this practical project. First, organizational forms that enable genuine multi-stakeholder participation need to be explored further. Second, the potential solutions for developing long-term Smart Contracts need to be understood in terms of multi-decade maintenance of software, hardware and governance processes for changes. Third, the business models that enable consortiums to sustainably distribute costs and revenues of blockchain technology projects over the long-term horizon need to be understood, as many blockchain projects will only be sustainable through consortium based business models.

References

Alcantara, C., & Dick, C. (2017). Decolonization in a digital age: Cryptocurrencies and indigenous self-determination in Canada. *Canadian Journal of Law & Society/La Revue Canadienne Droit et Société, 32*(1), 19–35.

Canadian Chamber of Commerce. (2017). Seizing six opportunities for more clarity in the duty to consult and accommodate process. Retrieved August 30, 2019 from: https://www.chamber.ca/media/blog/160914-seizing-six-opportunities-for-more-clarity-in-the-duty-to-consult-and-accommodate-process/.

Canadian Council for Aboriginal Business. (2016). Promise and prosperity: The 2016 aboriginal business survey. Retrieved August 30, 2019 from: https://www.ccab.com/research/ccab-research-series/promise-and-prosperity https://www.ccab.comwp-contentuploads201610ccab-pp-report-sq-pdf/

Clack, C. D., Bakshi, V. A., & Braine, L. (2016). Smart contract templates: Foundations, design landscape and research directions. arXiv preprint arXiv:1608.00771.

Conde, M. (2017). Resistance to mining. A review. *Ecological Economics, 132*, 80–90.

Cunsolo W. A., Harper, S. L., & Edge, V. L. (2013). 'My Word': Storytelling and digital media lab, & Rigolet Inuit community government. Storytelling in a digital age: digital storytelling as an emerging narrative method for preserving and promoting indigenous oral wisdom. *Qualitative Research, 13*(2), 127–147.

Dalziel, P., Matunga, H., & Saunders, C. (2006). Cultural well-being and local government: Lessons from New Zealand. *The Australasian Journal of Regional Studies, 12*(3), 267.

Dana, L. P. (2015). Indigenous entrepreneurship: an emerging field of research. *International Journal of Business and Globalisation, 14*(2), 158–169.

Deloitte. (2018). Tracking the trends 2018 The top 10 issues shaping mining in the year ahead. Retrieved August 30, 2019 from: https://www2.deloitte.com/content/dam/Deloitte/ca/Documents/energy-resources/ca-en-ER-TTT2018_Jan_18_FINAL_Web_AODA.PDF.

Galla, C. K. (2016). Indigenous language revitalization, promotion, and education: Function of digital technology. *Computer Assisted Language Learning, 29*(7), 1137–1151.

Gamu, J., Le Billon, P., & Spiegel, S. (2015). Extractive industries and poverty: A review of recent findings and linkage mechanisms. *The Extractive Industries and Society, 2*(1), 162–176.

GuildOne. (2018). GuildOne introduces thunderbird consensus—Indigenous rights, truth and reconciliation on blockchain. Retrieved August 30, 2019 from: https://guild1.co/2018/06/14/guildone-introduces-thunderbird-consensus-indigenous-rights-truth-reconciliation-on-blockchain/

Hall, R. (2013). Diamond mining in Canada's Northwest territories: A colonial continuity. *Antipode, 45*(2), 376–393.

Horváth, D., & Szabó, R. Z. (2018). Evolution of photovoltaic business models: Overcoming the main barriers of distributed energy deployment. *Renewable and Sustainable Energy Reviews, 90*, 623–635.

Howlett, C., Seini, M., McCallum, D., & Osborne, N. (2011). Neoliberalism, mineral development and indigenous people: A framework for analysis. *Australian Geographer, 42*(3), 309–323.

IDGO Team. (2018). Orchid Island makes history by introducing indigenous e-Identity—The quintessence of blockchain in indigenous communities. Retrieved August 30, 2019 from: https://medium.com/idgo/orchid-island-makes-history-by-introducing-indigenous-e-identity-44d708ee6cf0.

Indigenous and Northern Affairs Canada. (2015). Consultation and accommodation advice for proponents. Retrieved August 30, 2019 from: https://www.aadnc-aandc.gc.ca/eng/1430509727738/1430509820338.

Kajanus, M., Leban, V., Glavonjić, P., Krč, J., Nedeljković, J., Nonić, D., ... Wilhelmsson, E. (2018). What can we learn from business models in the European forest sector: Exploring the key elements of new business model designs. *Forest Policy and Economics*.

Kakekaspan, M., O'Donnell, S., Beaton, B., Walmark, B., & Gibson, K. (2014). The first mile approach to community services in fort Severn first nation. *The Journal of Community Informatics, 10*(2).

Kamath, R. (2018). Food traceability on blockchain: Walmart's pork and mango pilots with IBM. *The JBBA, 1*(1), 3712.

Karanasios, K., & Parker, P. (2018). Tracking the transition to renewable electricity in remote indigenous communities in Canada. *Energy policy, 118*, 169–181.

Keeling, A., & Sandlos, J. (2015). *Mining and communities in Northern Canada: History, politics, and memory*.

Kim, H., & Laskowski, M. (2017, July). A perspective on blockchain smart contracts: Reducing uncertainty and complexity in value exchange. In *2017 26th International Conference on Computer Communication and Networks (ICCCN)* (pp. 1–6). IEEE.

Kim, H. M., & Laskowski, M. (2018). Toward an ontology-driven blockchain design for supply-chain provenance. *Intelligent Systems in Accounting, Finance and Management, 25*(1), 18–27.

KPMG. (2018). Canadian mining executives identify top risks for 2018. Retrieved August 30, 2019 from: https://home.kpmg.com/ca/en/home/media/press-releases/2018/03/canadian-mining-executives-identify-top-risks-for-2018.html.

Lameman, B. A., & Lewis, J. E. (2011). Skins: Designing games with first nations youth. *Journal of Game Design and Development Education, 1,* 54–63.

Li, F. (2018, March 08). How to make A.I. That's good for people. *The New York Times* Retrieved August 30, 2019 from: https://www.nytimes.com/2018/03/07/opinion/artificial-intelligence-human.html.

Lielacher, A. (2019). How many people use bitcoin in 2019? Bitcoin Market Journal. Retrieved October 14, 2019 from: https://www.bitcoinmarketjournal.com/how-many-people-use-bitcoin/.

Light, I., & Dana, L. P. (2013). Boundaries of social capital in entrepreneurship. *Entrepreneurship Theory and Practice, 37*(3), 603–624.

Madsen, D. L. (2017). The mechanics of survivance in indigenously-determined video-games: Invaders and never alone. *Transmotion, 3*(2), 79–110.

Manson, A., & Mbenga, B. (2003). The richest tribe in Africa': Platinum-mining and the Bafokeng in South Africa's North West Province, 1965–1999. *Journal of Southern African Studies, 29*(1), 25–47.

McCreary, T., Mills, S., & St-Amand, A. (2016). Lands and resources for jobs: How Aboriginal peoples strategically use environmental assessments to advance community employment aims. *Canadian Public Policy, 42*(2), 212–223.

McMahon, R., & Mangiok, T. (2014). From the first mile to outer space: Tamaani satellite internet in northern Quebec. *The Journal of Community Informatics, 10*(2), 81–100.

Mercredi, O., & Turpel, M. E. (1993). *In the rapids: Navigating the future of First Nations.* Toronto, ON, Canada: Penguin Group.

Mills, K. A., Davis-Warra, J., Sewell, M., & Anderson, M. (2016). Indigenous ways with literacies: Transgenerational, multimodal, placed, and collective. *Language and Education, 30*(1), 1–21.

Mining Association of Canada. (2018). Annual report 2017. Retrieved August 30, 2019 from: https://mining.ca/documents/mac-annual-report-2017/.

Ngata, W., Ngata-Gibson, H., & Salmond, A. (2012). Te Ataakura: Digital taonga and cultural innovation. *Journal of Material Culture, 17*(3), 229–244.

Nishnawbe Aski Nation. (2007). *A handbook on consultation in natural resource development* (3rd ed.). Retrieved August 30, 2019 from: https://www.nan.on.ca/DutytoConsult.

O'Faircheallaigh, C. (2008). Negotiating cultural heritage? Aboriginal–mining company agreements in Australia. *Development and Change, 39*(1), 25–51.

O'Faircheallaigh, C. (2013). Extractive industries and Indigenous peoples: A changing dynamic? *Journal of Rural Studies, 30,* 20–30.

OECD. (2017), OECD due diligence guidance for meaningful stakeholder engagement in the extractive sector. Paris: OECD Publishing. https://doi.org/10.1787/9789264252462-en. Retrieved August 30, 2019 from: https://www.oecd.org/publications/oecd-due-diligence-guidance-for-meaningful-stakeholder-engagement-in-the-extractive-sector-9789264252462-en.htm.

Osterwalder, A., Pigneur, Y., Bernarda, G., & Smith, A. (2014). *Value proposition design: How to create products and services customers want.* Hoboken, NJ, USA: Wiley Inc.

Osterwalder, A., Pigneur, Y., In Clark, T., & Smith, A. (2010). *Business model generation: A handbook for visionaries, game changers, and challengers.* Hoboken, NJ, USA: Wiley Inc.

Pansera, M. (2012). Renewable energy for rural areas of Bolivia. *Renewable and Sustainable Energy Reviews, 16*(9), 6694–6704.

Peredo, A. M., & Anderson, R. B. (2006). Indigenous entrepreneurship research: themes and variations. In C. S. Galbraith & C. H. Stiles, (Eds.), *Developmental entrepreneurship: Adversity, risk, and isolation* (pp. 253–273). Elsevier.

Peredo, A. M., & McLean, M. (2013). Indigenous development and the cultural captivity of entrepreneurship. *Business and Society, 52*(4), 592–620.

Pinna, A., Ibba, S., Baralla, G., Tonelli, R., & Marchesi, M. (2019). A massive analysis of ethereum smart contracts empirical study and code metrics. *IEEE Access, 7,* 78194–78213.

Pogue, M., & Olawoye, L. (2018). Tech for all: Breaking barriers in toronto's innovation community. MaRS. Retrieved August 30, 2019 from: https://marsdd.com/media-centre/mars-releases-tech-for-all-breaking-barriers-in-torontos-innovation-community/.

Preston, J. (2017). Racial extractivism and white settler colonialism: An examination of the Canadian tar sands mega-projects. *Cultural Studies, 31*(2–3), 353–375.

Qiolevu, V. S., & Lim, S. (2019). Stakeholder participation and advocacy coalitions for making sustainable fiji mineral royalty policy. *Sustainability, 11*(3), 797.

Redman, R. (2019, June 13). Walmart joins FDA blockchain pilot for prescription drugs. *Supermarket News.* Retrieved August 30, 2019 from: https://www.supermarketnews.com/health-wellness/walmart-joins-fda-blockchain-pilot-prescription-drugs.

Romero, C. (2017). Toward an indigenous feminine animation aesthetic. *Studies in American Indian Literatures, 29*(1), 56–87.

Roth, L., & Audette-Longo, P. H. (2018). Co-movement revisited: Reflections on four decades of media transformation in Canadian Indigenous communities. *Development in Practice, 28*(3), 414–421.

Scott, M. (2018, March 24). A Canadian Indigenous Community's Ambitious Blockchain Trek. *Cryptonews.* Retrieved August 30, 2019 from: https://cryptonews.com/exclusives/a-canadian-indigenous-community-s-ambitious-blockchain-trek-1454.htm.

Scrimgeour, F., & Iremonger, C. (2004). *Maori sustainable economic development in New Zealand: Indigenous practices for the quadruple bottom line.* Hamilton, New Zealand: University of Waikato.

Scudder, M. G., Baynes, J., & Herbohn, J. (2019). Timber royalty reform to improve the livelihoods of forest resource owners in Papua New Guinea. *Forest Policy and Economics, 100,* 113–119.

Sengupta, U., Vieta, M., & McMurtry, J. J. (2015). Indigenous communities and social enterprise in Canada: Incorporating culture as an essential ingredient of entrepreneurship. *Canadian Journal of Nonprofit and Social Economy Research, 6*(1).

Silvius, A. J., & Schipper, R. P. (2014). Sustainability in project management: A literature review and impact analysis. *Social Business, 4*(1), 63–96.

Tapscott, D., & Tapscott, A. (2016). *Blockchain revolution: How the technology behind bitcoin is changing money, business, and the world.* Toronto, ON, Canada: Portfolio.

The Information and Communications Technology Council. (2017). Digital economy talent supply: Indigenous Peoples of Canada. Retrieved August 30, 2019 from: https://www.ictc-ctic.ca/wp-content/uploads/2017/06/Indigenous_Supply_ICTC_FINAL_ENG.pdf.

The World Bank. (2018). Indigenous peoples. Retrieved August 30, 2019 from: https://www.worldbank.org/en/topic/indigenouspeoples.

Tekobbe, C., & McKnight, J. C. (2016). Indigenous cryptocurrency: Affective capitalism and rhetorics of sovereignty. *First Monday, 21*(10).

Treiblmaier, H. (2019). Toward more rigorous blockchain research: Recommendations for writing blockchain case studies. *Frontiers in Blockchain, 2,* Article 3, 1–15. https://doi.org/10.3389/fbloc.2019.00003.

Truth and Reconciliation Commission of Canada. (2015). Truth and reconciliation commission of Canada: Calls to action. Retrieved August 30, 2019 from: https://nctr.ca/reports.php.

Türko, E. S. (2016). Business plan vs business model canvas in entrepreneurship trainings: A comparison of students' perceptions. *Asian Social Science, 12*(10), 55.

Udén, M. (2008). Indigenous women as entrepreneurs in global front line innovation systems. *Journal of Enterprising Communities: People and Places in the Global Economy, 2*(3), 225–239.

United Nations Department of Economic and Social Affairs. (2014). Study of the problem of discrimination against Indigenous populations: Final report submitted by the Special Rapporteur, Mr. José Martínez Cobo. Third Part. Chapter XXI–XXII. Conclusions, proposals and recommendations. UN document number: E/CN.4 Sub.2/1983/21/Add.8/. Retrieved Oct 14, 2019 from: https://www.un.org/development/desa/indigenouspeoples/publications/2014/09/martinez-cobo-study/.

United Nations General Assembly. (2007). United Nations declaration on the rights of indigenous peoples. Retrieved from: https://www.un.org/development/desa/indigenouspeoples/declaration-on-the-rights-of-indigenous-peoples.html.

Urban, M., Klemm, M., Ploetner, K. O., & Hornung, M. (2018). Airline categorisation by applying the business model canvas and clustering algorithms. *Journal of Air Transport Management*.

Vigna, P., & Casey, M. J. (2018). *The truth machine: The blockchain and the future of everything*. New York, NY, USA: St. Martin's Press.

Virtanen, P. K. (2015). Indigenous social media practices in Southwestern Amazonia. AlterNative: An international. *Journal of Indigenous Peoples, 11*(4), 350–362.

Vu, V., Lamb, C., & Zafar, A. (2019) Who are Canada's tech workers? Brookfield Institute for Innovation + Entrepreneurship. Retrieved August 30, 2019 from: https://brookfieldinstitute.ca/report/who-are-canadas-tech-workers/.

Walters, F., & Takamura, J. (2015). The decolonized quadruple bottom line: A framework for developing indigenous innovation. *Wicazo sa review, 30*(2), 77–99.

Winter, J., & Boudreau, J. (2018). Supporting self-determined indigenous innovations: Rethinking the digital divide in Canada. *Technology Innovation Management Review, 8*(2).

Ushnish Sengupta holds degrees in Industrial Engineering (BASc) and Business Administration and (MBA) from the University of Toronto. He is the author of a number of peer reviewed published articles on Indigenous organizations. He has taught courses at the undergraduate and graduate levels in post-secondary institutions and at community based organizations. In addition to his academic experience, he has worked in various private sector and public sector organizations including Atomic Energy of Canada Limited, Cedara Software Corp, Canadian Broadcasting Corporation, Centre for Addiction, and Mental Health, OntarioMD, Ontario Telemedicine Network, and eHealth Ontario. Ushnish has worked in different roles including Project Manager and Product Manager and is currently project manager at the Blockchain Lab at York University.

Henry Kim is an associate professor at the Schulich School of Business, York University in Toronto, and is the Director for blockchain.lab at Schulich. As one of the leading blockchain scholars in Canada, he has authored more than 20 publications on blockchain topics and over 60 overall. Prof. Kim is engaged in blockchain research projects with Toronto and Region Conservation Authority (on electricity micro-grid), the Canadian blockchain startup Aion (on AI-based consensus mechanism), Ontario Ministry of Agriculture and Rural Affairs (on food traceability), Don Tapscott's Blockchain Research Institute (on commercial insurance) and many others. He is the co-organizer for the Fields Institute Seminar Series on Blockchain and the 2020 IEEE Conference on Blockchain and Cryptocurrencies and speaks and consults broadly on Digital Transformation. He also serves as a Senior Research Fellow for two start-ups: Novera, a Canadian decentralized finance enabler, and Insolar, a Swiss blockchain platform provider. Prof. Kim has a Ph.D. in Industrial Engineering from University of Toronto and a Master's from University of Michigan.

Smart City Applications on the Blockchain: Development of a Multi-layer Taxonomy

Esther Nagel and Johann Kranz

Abstract Blockchain Technology (BT) has become widely recognized beyond the financial sector. Various other fields of application for the ground-breaking innovation are discussed by researchers and practitioners alike. One such field is the smart city. Driven by startups, projects aimed at alleviating negative effects of urbanization build on the properties of BT to improve quality of life, administrative processes, and environmental sustainability. Yet, due to the entrepreneurial dynamics and abundant fields of application for BT in smart cities, an integrated and boundary-spanning analysis is lacking. This study aims at developing a multi-layer taxonomy that illustrates how BT is used in different smart city business models. For this purpose, we identified a sample of 80 startups which offer applications for smart cities and examined their business models. The paper explores business model configurations and technological characteristics of blockchain-based smart city applications. We identify BT startup archetypes in several domains: sharing economy, privacy and security, and internet of things (IoT). The paper will be useful for researchers, practitioners, and regulators interested in gaining novel insights about how startups leverage BT to create and capture value.

Keywords Blockchain · Smart city · Taxonomy · Business model

1 Introduction

Blockchain technology (BT) has the potential of changing how our cities work and how we live in them. The blockchain, an innovation with general purpose character, represents a new form of a database technology with the novelty of being fully

Note: An earlier version of this paper was presented at the European Conference on Information Systems (ECIS) 2019.

E. Nagel (✉) · J. Kranz
Ludwig Maximilian University of Munich, Munich, Germany
e-mail: nagel@bwl.lmu.de

J. Kranz
e-mail: kranz@bwl.lmu.de

distributed with a consensus mechanism that replaces a central point of control (Beck et al. 2016). Prior to BT, an intermediary was needed to control, maintain, and oversee databases and networks. Due to new consensus mechanisms, a blockchain enables every network member to contribute to the network and work as a control instance (Davidson et al. 2016). With first use cases in finance and banking, the technology is triggering game-changing applications in further sectors. Because of their decentralized nature and potential for automation, smart cities are an important field of application for BT. The initiative "Smart Dubai", for instance, aims at creating urban solutions based on BT by 2020 (Rizzo 2017).

With the world's population expected to exceed 9 billion people by the year 2050 and more than half of the population living in cities, urban areas are facing the challenge of managing rapid growth in a sustainable way. In smart cities, information and communication technologies (ICTs) are used to address the challenges inherent to a growing population in urbanities. These challenges occur in areas such as pollution, resource shortages, governance, or transportation. The main idea behind smart cities is to connect people, institutions and infrastructures in order to use resources more sustainably and efficiently (Harrisson and Donnelly 2011). Smart cities aim at reshaping all areas of life within cities including traffic handling, water and waste management, energy consumption, or smart living (Chourabi et al. 2012).

Given the high relevance of BT for applications beyond finance such as smart cities (Swan 2015), the literature on concrete blockchain use cases is surprisingly scarce. Moreover, prior literature has focused primarily on technological features of BT, but neglected the economic and societal implications of using BT. Prior taxonomies have examined BT in the fields of governance and architecture (Glaser 2017; Xu et al. 2017), fintech (Beinke et al. 2018), entrepreneurial finance (Chanson et al. 2018; Fridgen et al. 2018; Kazan et al. 2015; Kranz et al. 2019), and general applications (Labazova et al. 2019). The objective of our study is to provide insights on the economic and technological characteristics of blockchain-based smart city applications to develop a taxonomy which enables researchers and practitioners to understand, evaluate, and structure blockchain-based smart city innovations. Therefore, we analyzed business models and technological features smart city applications. Our economic and technological perspective allows to assess how the pieces of a business (Magretta 2002) and a technology fit together to create, deliver, and capture value.

To achieve this goal, we analyzed in-depth how startups in the smart city context build upon BT to increase the efficiency, sustainability, and quality of life in urban agglomerations. Therefore, we consider solutions for the smart city core areas energy, transportation, building, health, and government (Komninos et al. 2013; Washburn et al. 2009). We focus on startup firms since radical and disruptive innovations frequently emerge from these new market entrants rather than incumbents (Chesbrough 2006; Weiblen and Chesbrough 2015). Based on our analysis, we identify three primary archetypes of BT startups, i.e., sharing economy, privacy and security, and the Internet of Things (IoT). These archetypes leverage BT's primary benefits, such as automation via smart contracts, auditability, and security by design to render value to users.

The remainder of this article is structured as follows: First, we elaborate on the study's background. Next, we explain our research design. In the following section, we present the results and identified archetypes. The chapter concludes with a discussion of the results, limitations, and opportunities for further research.

2 Background

2.1 Blockchain Technology

At its core, BT is a distributed database that is curated by several participants in a P2P network. Changes to the database are initiated using public key cryptography and updated following a consensus mechanism. The history and current structure of the database are rendered immutable by hash functions in a chain of blocks (Beck et al. 2016). BT offers an innovative solution to the Byzantine Generals' Problem as it allows two anonymous parties to securely exchange information over an unreliable network without relying on an intermediary (Zheng et al. 2016). Beside the consensus mechanism, the chosen permission model is an important distinctive feature of a blockchain. The permission model defines which nodes may read and validate transactions on a blockchain (see Table 1).

Since Nakamoto's original idea of using BT for the cryptocurrency Bitcoin (Nakamoto 2008), BT has gained broader applicability beyond cryptocurrencies and applications in the financial sector owing mainly to two extensions. First, BT can be used to store so-called smart contracts as source code which are automatically executed without human interference once prespecified events occur. Similar to the exchange of Bitcoins, which also follows a simple and highly standardized set of rules, sophisticated smart contracts have the potential to automate many types of transactional contracts such as spot market purchases or machine-to-machine transactions (Sikorski et al. 2017). To facilitate token issuance and smart contracts, Blockchain protocols like Ethereum and Hyperledger include sophisticated scripting languages to model complex interactions for different kinds of native (i.e., embedded in the blockchain) and tokenized (i.e., asset value fragmented into crypto tokens) assets. Second, this issuance of asset-backed tokens (referred to as tokenization) is

Table 1 Blockchain typology (Beck et al. 2018)

Access to transactions	Access to transaction validation	
	Permissioned	Permissionless
Public	All nodes can read and submit transactions. Only authorized nodes can validate transactions	All nodes can read, submit, and validate transactions
Private	Only authorized nodes can read, submit, and validate transactions	Not applicable

enabled by BT and the overlying smart contracts. BT can thus store and transmit transactions to include further asset classes, such as intangible or fungible assets (e.g. patents, electricity), or rights associated with an asset (e.g. digital media). In addition to financial transactions, experts particularly expect a rise of identity-related, property, and communication-based transactions (Hileman 2016). The possibility to tie different kinds of information to a transaction not only broadens the application scope of BT but makes it a highly versatile medium for general information processing.

2.2 Smart Cities

Under current predictions, 70% of the world's population will live in cities by 2050 (United Nations 2016). The increasing trend towards urbanization creates various problems as cities are a major cause of environmental degradation. Cities further raise novel societal and institutional challenges (Kramers et al. 2014; Lövehagen and Bondesson 2013). These issues call for innovative solutions that enable cities to organize in novel, "smarter" ways to ensure an adequate infrastructure, environment, and life quality of citizens (Chourabi et al. 2012).

In this context, the term "smart city" was introduced in the 1990s (Cocchia 2014). Due to the newness and boundary-spanning nature of the concept, a consistent definition has not yet been established (Komninos et al. 2013; Ojo et al. 2014). After reviewing 46 definitions in different domains, Nam and Pardo (2011) differentiate between three core perspectives on smart cities: institutional, human, and technology. The institutional perspective encompasses policy reworks, changes in government structures and the creation of smart communities as vehicles for sustainable urban transformation (Moss Kanter and Litow 2009), while the human perspective emphasizes investments in innovativeness and learning (Boulton et al. 2011; Glaeser and Berry 2006). The technological perspective focuses on how ICTs can be leveraged to make cities work smarter (Kramers et al. 2014). The latter perspective on smart cities forms an essential building block of the emerging Green IS research stream (Melville 2010; Watson et al. 2010).

As the boundary-spanning nature and importance of ICTs are key characteristics of smart cities, this study follows Washburn et al. (2009, p. 2) who define smart cities as "the use of smart computing technologies to make the critical infrastructure components and services of a city—which include city administration, education, healthcare, public safety, real estate, transportation, and utilities—more intelligent, interconnected, and efficient." ICT-enabled systems and infrastructures create value through savings in time, emissions and energy, and through positive externalities via the stimulation of the economy, innovation, and citizen engagement (Manville et al. 2014). In practice, smart cities apply ICTs in a range of interoperating (hybrid) layers, from physical infrastructure and integration layers like smart grids, sensor technology, and cloud services to pure service applications (Granath and Axelsson 2014;

Clohessy et al. 2014). Several studies have pointed towards the substantial opportunities of BT for smart cities arising from improved data reliability and resilience, faster and more efficient operation, and smart-contract-based automation. However, these studies have a narrow focus on particular technological solutions to smart city challenges in fields such as security (Biswas and Muthukkumarasamy 2017), vehicular networks (Sharma et al. 2017), energy (Pieroni et al. 2018), and digital identity (Rivera et al. 2017). We aim to contribute a more comprehensive perspective.

Prior research has studied the features and particularities of business models in smart cities. Timmers (1998, p. 4) defines a business model as "an architecture of the products, services, and information flows", recognizing stakeholders, business value, and revenue streams as key components of an organization's operations. Kuk and Janssen (2011) explore how organizations enhance existing services or launch new ones in a smart city context. Other studies have focused on the business model impact of specific technologies, such as mobile telecommunication (Walravens 2015), smart grid solutions (Lee et al. 2010), and big data analytics (Hashem et al. 2016). Smart cities are described as a fertile breeding ground for innovative business models given the interconnection of product streams and information streams as well as fast growing markets (Anthopoulos et al. 2016).

3 Methodology

We developed a taxonomy of blockchain-based smart city business models offered by startups following the guidelines of Nickerson et al. (2013). Taxonomies are schemes that allow for the grouping of objects. They offer a structured approach to describe and classify existing or future objects of interest, thereby providing order in complex areas (Nickerson et al. 2013). Especially in the case of novel phenomena—such as the use of BT in the smart city context—taxonomies provide valuable insights as they help understand, analyze, and structure extant domain knowledge (Nickerson et al. 2013) and generate more solid concepts upon which future research can build (von Krogh et al. 2012). Particularly in the fast-changing domain of information systems (IS), classifying objects into taxonomies is a useful and important research method (Son and Kim 2008; Williams et al. 2008).

3.1 Data Collection

First, we gathered data on startup firms that offer blockchain-based smart city innovations. Startups are known for developing novel, high-risk, and cutting-edge ideas and are likely to be first movers regarding innovative technologies (Chesbrough 2006; Freeman and Engel 2007; Weiblen and Chesbrough 2015). Therefore, blockchain taxonomies have put a focus on the analysis of startups (Eickhoff et al. 2017; Gimpel et al. 2017). Accordingly, we focus on startups to analyze how blockchain can be used for achieving smart city objectives. Our data collection included global startups in different investment stages—from seed to series A.

We collected the data using databases of technology startups, curated by Crunch-Base (www.crunchbase.com) (last update: June 30, 2018), AngelList (www.angel.co) (last update: June 30, 2018), and Outlier Ventures (www.outlierventures.io) (last update: March 10, 2019). CrunchBase provides various information on more than 500,000 general-purpose startup ventures while AngelList allows to filter for Blockchain startups, covering 1245 startups. Third, Outlier Ventures provides a blockchain startup tracker that comprises 1350 startups.

In the CrunchBase database, the search term "blockchain" yielded 482 startups. We first eliminated duplicates and startups that do not offer solutions for the smart city core areas of administration, education, healthcare, public safety, real estate, transportation, or utilities (Washburn et al. 2009). From the initial set of startups (n = 3077), 438 startups remained in the sample. Second, we excluded startups that focus on general blockchain infrastructure including the hardware and fabric layer upon which the application layer builds (Glaser 2017). The resulting sample consisted of 163 startups. Third, we considered only startups for our analysis that were active at the time of our search and for which sufficient information for classification was publicly available (e.g. websites, press releases). In several instances, we additionally reached out to startups to gather additional information. This procedure resulted in a final sample of 80 startups (see Appendix 1), of which some operate in more than one smart city area.

3.2 Taxonomy Development

To develop our taxonomy, we follow the methodological guidelines provided by Nickerson et al. (2013) as depicted in Fig. 1. In the first step, a meta characteristic is determined. A meta characteristic is "the most comprehensive characteristic that will serve as the basis for the choice of characteristics in the taxonomy" (Nickerson et al. 2013, p. 343). When determining the meta characteristic, the taxonomy's purpose and the interests of its future user group has to be considered. Therefore, our study's meta

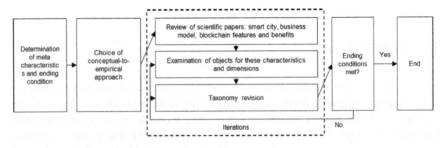

Fig. 1 Taxonomy development based on Nickerson et al. (2013)

characteristic is defined as the application of BT in smart city areas. This definition complies with the purpose of our taxonomy, namely to identify the potential uses of blockchain in smart cities encompassing both business- and technology-related attributes.

In the second step, objective and subjective ending conditions need to be determined. The eventual taxonomy is composed of layers that combine related dimensions and their modes of occurrence, called characteristics. As the compilation of dimensions and corresponding characteristics occurs iteratively, the researcher must define conditions that will indicate the completeness of the taxonomy beforehand. Objective ending conditions include the uniqueness of each characteristic and dimension, and that at least one object falls into the category of each characteristic and dimension included in the taxonomy (Nickerson et al. 2013).

The subjective ending conditions require the taxonomy to be concise, robust, extendible, and explanatory. Although we avoided redundancies in our choice of characteristics, the taxonomy's application on our sample revealed that in some instances several characteristics can be applied. However, this outcome does not violate the taxonomy properties as the alternative would be an inflated set of characteristics (Püschel et al. 2016). We checked the ending conditions before finishing the iterations.

As a third step, Nickerson et al. (2013) recommend choosing either a conceptual-to-empirical or an empirical-to-conceptual approach for each iteration of the taxonomy development procedure. In the conceptual-to-empirical approach, the researcher determines the taxonomy's dimensions using "his/her knowledge of existing foundations, experience, and judgment to deduce what he/she thinks will be relevant dimensions" (Nickerson et al. 2013, p. 346). The researcher then tests the relevance of the chosen dimensions and characteristics by examining objects. If no object can be grouped into these dimensions and characteristics, they should be eliminated. By contrast, in the empirical-to-conceptual approach, the researcher starts with examining actual objects. The researcher identifies a subset of objects to be classified and then groups the objects according to common dimensions with discriminating characteristics. Both approaches are highly iterative, meaning that dimensions and characteristics are constantly added, deleted, merged, or split.

For this study, we chose a conceptual-to-empirical approach during the first iteration. During this iteration, we defined the taxonomy dimensions based on various approaches to smart city areas, business models, and BT properties in order to determine characteristics of structural difference in the subsequent iterations. We performed several empirical-to-conceptual iterations on the basis of our sampled startups until we were not able to identify any further characteristics. In the following iterations, characteristics for the dimensions were therefore continuously added, edited and consolidated. After each round, we revised the taxonomy through an expert panel (3 researchers, 3 practitioners) to assure the validity of the taxonomy and the subsequent derivation of archetypes. As a result, we were able to classify all startups and meet the ending conditions as proposed by Nickerson et al. (2013).

4   Results

Our final taxonomy consists of three layers (see Appendix 1). In the first layer, smart city application area, we identified five smart city areas in which startups operate. The business model layer comprises four dimensions along the sub-layers value proposition, value delivery, and value capture. The blockchain application layer comprises dimensions that refer to technological attributes of the startups' solutions.

4.1   Smart City Application Area

We assigned each startup in our sample to one or more smart city application area and, more specifically, to a role within this area (Table 2). Overall, we find the highest number of startups in the government (n = 21) and energy domains (n = 20), followed by building (n = 16), health (n = 15), and transportation (n = 10).

Energy: Our sample includes energy blockchain startups in five categories. A core aim of the smart city concept is that energy is produced and consumed as efficiently and sustainably as possible. Blockchain startups address these goals in several ways. First, blockchain is used to enable peer-to-peer transactions between consumers and the tracking of energy units, especially those generated by renewables. Startups such as LO3 and GridSingularity offer blockchain-based peer-to-peer energy distribution which allows prosumers to convert their energy surplus into energy tokens that they can price themselves and sell locally to other consumers. Another way of using blockchain for energy efficiency is to generate energy coins that reimburse leases for solar systems given to private persons or businesses in developing countries via crowdfunding platforms (e.g. SunExchange). We further identified startups that use blockchain to act as transaction platforms for energy stakeholders including traditional corporate suppliers (e.g. OmegaGrid), as well as startups that support solutions for carbon asset management (e.g. Energy Blockchain Lab) or scientific research (e.g. ElectricChain).

Transportation: In the area of transportation, we identified five categories. The startup Oaken Innovations enhances automotive sensor capabilities by integrating blockchain-enabled nodes, which can automatically pay tolls for usage of roads or

Table 2 Smart city application areas of blockchain startups

Smart city application area	**Energy**	Platform for P2P transactions	Crowdfunding platform	Corporate energy transactions	Carbon asset management	Research
	Transportation	Tolls	Ride sharing	Parking	PEV charging	Container logistics
	Building	Energy consumption	Property transactions		Funding	Building access authorization
	Health	Patient records	Research data provision	Pharmaceutical authenticity verification	Digital nudging	Emergency alerts
	Government	Registry services	Voting	Citizen dialogue	Donation tracking	Digital citizenship

bridges. In addition, applications based on BT may soon fully decentralize peer-to-peer car sharing models (Pick and Dreher 2015). In our sample, the startups Arcade City, Chasyr, and La'Zooz are launching P2P ride sharing services that operate on a trustless basis, making rent-seeking intermediaries like Uber or Lyft obsolete. Users can access ride offers through the platform and trade in proprietary tokens. In the field of transportation, blockchain startups further address issues of device identity and payment in parking (e.g. Parq), container logistics (e.g. T-Mining), and solutions for plug-in electronic vehicle (PEV) charging (e.g. Slock.it). Powertree's approach addresses private persons who are willing to make their house's grid available for passing PEV users for a fee that is paid via smart contracts.

Building: Several startups address issues related to buildings' energy consumption. To overcome privacy concerns regarding metering and to optimize energy consumption (Kranz et al. 2010), BT is used to store the data anonymously and securely. The startup Ubirch offers sensors that connect to a digital platform which allows users to track consumption and reduce their energy costs using blockchain for encryption. Similarly, Silvertown sources data regarding temperature, humidity and noise levels, air quality and motion from smart beacons to assist housing associations and managers of large properties with metering. Manual readings become obsolete and blockchain ensures data integrity and privacy of tenants.

Another area tackled by startups are smooth and secure real estate transactions. Startups use BT to verify users' identities, making mediators like realtors obsolete while ensuring cheaper, faster and more reliable transactions. BT is further used as a crowdfunding and tokenized ownership solution by the startups to enable buyers to take out loans from private or business investors through smart contracts. Another application area of BT is to verify persons who try to access buildings (e.g., Slock.it).

Health: Blockchain may emerge as a key enabler of e-health solutions that improve the quality and accessibility of diagnosis and treatment in smart cities. We identified various solutions that enable stakeholders including patients, payers, health apps, and hospitals to combine health data on the blockchain via secured APIs. Further, some startups provide the option to make the data accessible to scientists, leading to a crowdsourced approach to medical research. Beside initiatives in the fields of diagnosis and treatment, blockchain is also used to authenticate pharmaceutical supply chains to mitigate the risk of pharmaceutical counterfeits (e.g. Blockpharma). Due to its fraud-resistant technology, startups use blockchain to register pharmaceutical fabrications throughout the supply chain all the way to the end consumer. BT is further used for digital nudging by providing reliable token systems that reward persons for healthy behaviors. HealthCoin, for instance, offers a blockchain-based diabetes prevention application which allows insurers or employers to reward health conscious lifestyles based on biomarker indications. The startup DAERS offers a decentralized autonomous emergency reporting system which stores vital signs and

GPS location information on the blockchain. This information can be accessed by authorized international organizations or rescue units in case of emergency.

Government: Blockchain technologies may contribute to more user-friendly public services, improved transparency, and the elimination of corruption (OECD 2017). We identified five categories of blockchain startups in the government application area. A number of startups in our sample offer registry services, e.g. for taxes, property titles, or other documentation. Especially regarding land titles, many startups are emerging, such as BitLand Global in Ghana. In countries that are troubled by unstable governments, a weak rule of law or political disputes, blockchains offer a reliable way of storing land titles. Beside registry services, smart city applications use blockchain for voting and citizen dialogue. Regarding e-voting, the advantages of blockchain technologies stem from its authentication abilities and the possibility to store votes securely and make elections more transparent. To enhance citizen dialogue, the anonymity and disintermediation enabled by BT is used for citizen engagement. For instance, the startup MiVote enables citizens to submit a vote for upcoming parliamentary elections, thereby giving politicians and the media the ability to get an accurate picture of popular opinions. Another area in which BT can contribute to smarter governments relates to the tracking of donation funds. As blockchain tokens or currencies can be traced easily, startups enable donors to track their donations. Finally—and perhaps most radically—blockchain startups provide solutions for digital citizenships. The concept of digital identity is currently being introduced in Estonia (Rivera et al. 2017). The startups BitNation and Borderless are offering digital citizenship, even including self-determined constitutions.

4.2 Business Model

A business model describes how a firm creates, delivers and captures value (Osterwalder and Pigneur 2010; Teece 2010). As the very nature of smart cities is to overcome industry boundaries and to link various infrastructures and stakeholders (Mulligan and Olsson 2013), the business model concept provides a useful framework for analyzing how blockchain enables ecosystem-based value creation in smart cities (Table 3). BT's effects on business models has recently gained attention. Studies envision that BT integration may alter or even disrupt the logic of value proposition and value capture throughout industries in the near future (Holotiuk et al. 2017; Iansiti and Lakhani 2017).

Value proposition: The second part of the business model layer examines in which ways the offers of blockchain startups create unique value for their customers, i.e., helping customers to perform a particular job better than alternative offerings (Johnson et al. 2008).

One major benefit offered by blockchain startups is the reduction of transaction costs which result from uncertainty or unforeseen contingencies and from writing and enforcing contracts (Tirole 1999). We distinguish between three core benefits

Table 3 Business models of smart city blockchain startups

Business model	Value proposition	Primary blockchain benefit	Security by design	Auditability	Smart contracts	Dis-intermediation	User verification	Micro transactions	Data reconciliation speed	Tokenization	Anonymity
	Value delivery	Customer type	Consumers		Prosumers		Businesses			Governments	
		Product composition	Cyber-physical				Purely digital				
	Value capture	Revenue model	Free		Freemium		Fee-based		Subscription		Upfront payment

of BT with regard to transaction cost reduction (security by design, auditability, and smart contracts). Blockchains are secure by design as the decentralized ledger renders entries tamper-proof (Zyskind and Nathan 2015). Especially startups in government registry services, voting, and building access solutions benefit from this feature. Auditability refers to the transparency stemming from BT's affordance to review past entries and a token's history (Davidson et al. 2016; Orsini et al. 2016). We find that auditability is primarily exploited by startups in the areas of donation tracking, pharmaceutical authentication, voting, and logistics. Smart contracts reduce transaction costs because expenses related to writing and enforcing contracts are significantly lowered (Kiviat 2015). Smart contracts are particularly effective regarding lowering transaction costs when transactions are highly standardized and occur frequently as in the energy sector (e.g., SunExchange, LO3) or when they occur between parties otherwise unknown to each other as in ride sharing or real estate funding.

Further blockchain-specific benefits are disintermediation (which in some instances is a consequence of lower transaction costs), user verification, micro transactions, data reconciliation speed, tokenization, and anonymity. Disintermediation is especially prevalent in peer-to-peer business models that render previous mediator platforms obsolete. User verification plays a main role in voting and registry startups as user identification is critical in these domains. Further, BT facilitates micro transactions which are often used in the energy and transportation areas. Speed in data reconciliation is another blockchain-specific benefit arising from our analysis. For instance, energy startups can provide accurate and close to real-time data on consumption and generation. Tokenization refers to the possibility of issuing cryptographic tokens on the blockchain, to be incorporated in the business model. Finally, we elicit that business models profit from the anonymity BT grants which is a core asset in citizen dialogue, medical research or automated energy metering.

Value delivery: Value delivery describes the apparatus an organization sets up to deliver value (Teece 2010). Our taxonomy shows how startups use BT to deliver value targeting customer types and product composition.

The dimension customer type captures to whom a firm markets its product. Digital technologies have led to a shift towards direct company-customer interaction throughout industries (Wikström 1996). BT in particular has facilitated niche products targeting small, technology-minded communities (Malović 2014). We find that the startups in our sample also cater to both businesses and end customers. Startups further address individual professionals such as doctors or environmental scientists. BT is often related to disintermediation. Blockchain systems promote P2P transactions and enable novel prosumer markets. We find P2P startups specifically in the smart city areas energy and transportation. Energy P2P-platforms such as Sonnen enable to purchase green electricity from peers without using existing electricity grids. Moreover, governments are addressed by blockchain-based smart city startups. For example, Bitfury is working on a registry of land titles for the Republic of Georgia (Underwood 2016). In addition, voting providers like Voatz are collaborating with municipalities and federal government units. In addition, governments are involved in blockchain-based healthcare business models to settle processing claims and ensure smooth healthcare transactions.

Another important dimension emerging from our analysis is whether an offer is composed of physical and software components (cyber-physical) or is purely digital, hence intangible. With increasing levels of digitization, an increasing number of physical products is equipped with software (e.g., sensors or actuators) that allows for new value-added services such as monitoring and control. Blockchain-based applications can occur in digital or cyber-physical forms. Most startups of our sample provide digital solutions. In these instances, BT itself provides sufficient value and acts independently of physical assets. However, we also identify several startups that process data from physical objects, often provided by the startup itself. For example, Oaken Innovations recently turned a Tesla into a smart vehicle that automatically pays via the cryptocurrency Ether at toll gates. Further, startups in the 'building' application area are launching cyber-physical systems that convey verification or usage data by using blockchain technologies.

Value capture: The last dimension of the business model layer concerns the type of value capture mechanism, which is a main aspect of an organization's business model (Osterwalder et al. 2005). It describes how an organization extracts value from its operations, enabling sustainable operations. We find that smart city blockchain startups have found various ways to capture value. Voting and citizen dialogue startups tend to operate on a free or freemium basis. The startups that enable transactions in real estate, energy and transportation predominantly use a fee-based approach. Subscription models are prevalent in government registry and healthcare solutions. Business models for cyber-physical products combine upfront payments for hardware with subscription or fee-based payments during utilization.

5 Blockchain Application

In the third layer of our taxonomy, we consider how startups apply BT from a technical perspective. We refer to the technical setup in two sub-layers, the permission model and protocol provider (Table 4).

Permission model: System centralization is concerned with "the extent to which a network is evenly distributed or nuclear in terms of ownership and administration" (Walsh et al. 2016, p. 3). The question of centralization addresses two kinds of permission restrictions: permission to read and to write (Walsh et al. 2016; Xu et al. 2017).

On a public blockchain, there are no restrictions on reading blockchain data, while only predefined users can read the records on a private blockchain. The advantages of using a public blockchain are better information transparency and auditability, while performance and information privacy are sacrificed (Xu et al. 2017). We find that most of the startups in our sample rely on public blockchains, therefore satisfying the desire for transparency and auditability. Especially voting startups emphasize their added value from being publicly accessible, thus rebuilding trust in election results. These arguments are also valid for applying public blockchains in the application areas donation tracking, energy, and transportation. We find private blockchains in areas where data privacy is critical, such as in healthcare and government registry services that involve identity solutions.

In terms of permission restrictions related to writing, the eligible processors can either be predefined (permissioned blockchain) or unrestricted (permissionless blockchain). Services with a single provider in regulated industries, such as governments or courts, are examples of permissioned technologies (Xu et al. 2017). The choice of scope in regard to permissioned verifiers is bound to tradeoffs in terms of transaction processing rate, cost, censorship resistance, reversibility, finality, and flexibility (Xu et al. 2017). In the startups of our sample we find a tendency for permissionless networks (74%). Permissionless verification is combined with the independence of random processors, for example in voting and citizen dialogue startups or energy data transaction platforms. We find permissioned networks in cases in which verification processes are executed in controlled environments to guarantee formality of the entries, e.g., in registry, health, and property transactions.

Protocol provider: Blockchain applications run on a specific protocol which forms the foundation for its functionalities (Morabito 2017). We found startups building upon the Bitcoin blockchain in all smart city areas, except transportation. However,

Table 4 Blockchain application of smart city blockchain startups

Blockchain application	Permission model	Reading	Public			Private	
		Writing	Permissionless			Permissioned	
		Protocol provider	Bitcoin	Ethereum	Hyperledger	Bitshares	Other/proprietary

the by far most commonly used protocol is the public Ethereum blockchain. Startups from all smart city areas in our sample build upon Ethereum. Moreover, smart city blockchain startups frequently build upon the Hyperledger and Bitshares platforms. Hyperledger is an initiative led by the Linux Foundation in cooperation with companies like IBM, Airbus and Samsung to explore the possibilities of private blockchains (Morabito 2017). Our sample shows that startups in the areas energy and health tend to use Hyperledger. Bitshares, on the other hand, is a trade-centric platform that is mainly used to exchange securities and financial instruments like derivative contracts. Moreover, some startups of our sample use proprietary platforms or specialized computing platforms such as Multichain, Expanse, and Tierion.

6 Evaluation and Archetypes

From our in-depth analysis to develop a taxonomy, three archetypes of blockchain-based business models in the smart city emerged (Table 5). An archetype is a knowledge model which represents commonalities between entities found through prior classification. The determination of archetypes guides theory-led design and supports sense-making in research by emphasizing primary differences among entity types (Püschel et al. 2016; Fernández-Breis et al. 2006). Each of our archetype has a different focus and is linked to specific characteristics assessed in our taxonomy. While these archetypes represent prototypical combinations, we emphasize that the

Table 5 Archetypes of smart city blockchain startups

Business model	Sharing economy	Privacy and security	Internet of things
Description	• Startups providing sharing economy offerings, e.g. in contracting, billing, and fulfillment • Applications allow transactions between consumers and/or prosumers at lower transaction costs, following rules set by smart contracts	• Startups leverage BT's distributed architecture to record and store immutable entries • Ensuring data access only to authorized persons	• Cyber-physical objects store data on a blockchain or record transactions • BT application lower risks such as fraud or man-in-the-middle attacks
Main smart city application areas	• Energy • Transportation	• Government • Health	• Transportation • Building • Energy
Primary blockchain benefit	• Disintermediation • Smart contracts	• Security by design • User verification	• Micro transactions • Smart contracts

archetypes are not mutually exclusive. Emerging blockchain startups tend to combine archetypes in order to assort a unique value proposition and gain a competitive advantage.

6.1 Sharing Economy

The first archetype emerging from our analysis is *sharing economy* which is defined as "collaborative consumption made by the activities of sharing, exchanging, and rental of resources without owning the goods" (Lessig 2008, p. 143). In this archetype blockchain allows to increase the efficiency of sharing economies at the process level in which "consumers, providers and intermediaries are connected by different types of process categories" (Puschmann and Alt 2016, p. 96), particularly contracting, billing, and fulfillment. As such, agents will be able to act autonomously and, even more, they will coordinate complying with pre-defined rules. Therefore, blockchain-based sharing economy systems can operate at close-to-zero transaction costs. Startups that follow the archetype sharing economy will commonly fulfill the following main characteristics in our developed taxonomy (see Table 6). The dimension customer type concerns private consumers and/or prosumers that meet on a two- or more-sided market. Since the elimination of intermediaries is a central characteristic of BT-enabled business models in the sharing economy, disintermediation and smart contracts are primary blockchain benefits pertaining to this archetype. The majority of startups belonging to this archetype also incorporates decentralization in their technical setup. As such, these startups typically choose public and permissionless

Table 6 Sharing economy archetype properties. Note. Gray shading shows typical patterns per dimension

Smart city application area			Energy		Transportation		Building	Health		Government	
Business model	Value proposition	Primary blockchain benefit	Security by design	Auditability	Smart contracts	Micro transactions	Disintermediation	User verification	Data reconciliation speed	Tokenization	Anonymity
	Value delivery	Customer type	Consumers		Prosumers		Businesses			Governments	
		Product composition	Cyber-physical				Purely digital				
	Value capture	Revenue model	Free		Freemium		Fee-based	Subscription		Upfront payment	
Blockchain application	Permission model	Reading	Public				Private				
		Writing	Permissionless				Permissioned				
	Protocol provider		Bitcoin		Ethereum		Hyperledger	Bitshares		Other/proprietary	

blockchains. We find startups that use blockchain technology for sharing economy business models mainly in the smart city areas energy and transportation.

6.2 Privacy and Security

We found that many startups in the smart city domain leverage BT's potential to provide privacy- and security-affording products and services. Blockchain technology is secure by design as it provides a distributed ledger of transactions. Thus, BT can be regarded as being designed to be secure from the outset. In comparison to centralized systems, blockchain's distributed architecture has no single point of failure, increasing trust in the system and data security as its functioning does not depend on a single intermediary or a restricted number of participants (Nofer et al. 2017).

In the following, we describe the characteristics of our taxonomy that indicate that startups match with the privacy and security archetype (see Table 7). Startups that belong to this archetype are specialized in the secure storage of entries. Therefore, they rely on the security by design and user verification properties as main blockchain benefits. Further, most archetypal startups follow a centralized network approach with a private reading mechanism and a pre-determined set of processors (permissioned writing). We observed that startups offer privacy and security solutions primarily in the smart city application areas health and government.

Table 7 Privacy and security archetype properties

Smart city application area			Energy		Transportation		Building	Health		Government	
Business model	Value proposition	Primary blockchain benefit	Security by design	Auditability	Smart contracts	Micro transactions	Disintermediation	User verification	Data reconciliation speed	Tokenization	Anonymity
	Value delivery	Customer type	Consumers		Prosumers			Businesses		Governments	
		Product composition	Cyber-physical				Purely digital				
	Value capture	Revenue model	Free		Freemium		Fee-based		Subscription	Upfront payment	
Blockchain application	Permission model	Reading	Public				Private				
		Writing	Permissionless				Permissioned				
		Protocol provider	Bitcoin		Ethereum		Hyperledger	Bitshares		Other/proprietary	

6.3 Internet of Things

Startups belonging to the Internet of Things (IOT) archetype connect the physical to the digital world equipping physical objects with sensor and communication technology to integrate them via the internet (Yoo 2010; Yoo et al. 2012). As these cyber-physical objects need to communicate securely and to transact value in general or money in particular, blockchain technology seems to be a natural fit (Christidis and Devetsikiotis 2016). In an IoT environment, cyber-physical objects with the appropriate hardware can become part of a blockchain-enabled system. This enables sending and receiving small amounts of money such as a few cents—or even amounts in the sub-cent range—between objects without risks of man-in-the-middle attacks and always with a proof that a specific transaction in question has been initiated by a specific device, thus ruling out fraud.

Typical characteristics for the IoT archetype (see Table 8) include micro transactions, smart contracts, and often a high data entry frequency as IoT systems maintain constant contact with their associated ledger. This relation persists in cyber-physical product compositions. Startups in the IoT archetype typically utilize smart contracts to facilitate instantaneous transactions on multi-sided markets. In the smart city context, IoT startups are typically found in the areas transportation, building, and energy.

Table 8 Internet of Things archetype properties

Smart city application area		Energy		Transportation		Building	Health		Government	
Business model — Value proposition	Primary blockchain benefit	Security by design	Auditability	Smart contracts	Micro transactions	Disintermediation	User verification	Data reconciliation speed	Tokenization	Anonymity
Value delivery	Customer type	Consumers			Prosumers		Businesses			Governments	
	Product composition	Cyber-physical					Purely digital				
Value capture	Revenue model	Free		Freemium		Fee-based		Subscription		Upfront payment	
Blockchain application — Permission model	Reading	Public					Private				
	Writing	Permissionless					Permissioned				
Protocol provider		Bitcoin		Ethereum		Hyperledger		Bitshares		Other/proprietary	

7 Conclusion

This study aimed at providing insights on the intersection of two increasingly important research topics—blockchain technology and smart cities. For this purpose, we developed a taxonomy that points out the manifold ways in which blockchain technology can be applied in the smart city context. The taxonomy further shows how blockchain technology enables and impacts business models and which technological setup are used. Based on the results of our in-depth analysis, we inferred three archetypes that represent prominent solution approaches.

Our contribution to the literature is twofold. First, we investigate an emerging phenomenon on which research is scarce. In the spirit of a "phenomenon-based research strategy" (von Krogh et al. 2012), we explored a new phenomenon by describing and classifying blockchain-based smart city applications. Our multi-layer taxonomy reflects the variety of the analyzed sample. We identified three BT-based business models archetypes (sharing economy, privacy and security, and IoT) and delineate how startups in different smart city application areas typically make use of BT. Thus, our study provides structure in a complex domain and can serve as a basis for further theorizing (von Krogh et al. 2012). Second, we contribute to research on IT-enabled and digital business models (Veit et al. 2014) as we scrutinize how a digital innovation such as BT can be used to transform consumer behavior and society. Particularly, we provide insights on how blockchain shapes the delivery, creation, and capture of economic value.

Overall, we find that smart cities can greatly benefit from the unique advantages of blockchain technologies. Given that the majority of current (and future) mega cities is located in developing countries where unstable governments and unreliable utility infrastructure are prevalent (Kennedy et al. 2014), the decentralization that blockchain offers in respect to secure data storage and new ways of utility management could improve the life quality of millions. Equally, city dwellers and governments in developed nations make use of blockchain-enabled IoT, security, and sharing economy solutions. At a time when trust in government institutions and corporate intermediaries runs low (Gallup 2016; Mayer 2013) blockchain technology can reestablish trust, and contribute to more independent and active citizenship, especially—but not limited to—countries with weak institutions and unstable regimes.

However, the usage of blockchain technologies in smart cities may also lead to new challenges, for example with respect to governance. It remains an open question how blockchain technology will be predominantly deployed and governed in a smart city environment. Similar to Bitcoin, which simultaneously facilitates community-based P2P payments and centrally governed digital currencies (e.g. U.S. Federal Reserve Fedcoin; McElroy 2017), BT applications in smart cities may originate from community-based P2P focused initiatives (e.g. Transactive Grid P2P energy sharing; Cardwell 2017) or from broader government or private sector initiatives (e.g. city-wide blockchain pilots from the Smart Dubai Office, Rizzo 2016; Wanxiang engagement in smart city blockchain application development, Rizzo 2017).

Both modes of deployment and governance may ultimately prove to be highly compatible. While P2P initiatives facilitate spontaneous, local and dynamic markets for economic, social or political activities (conceptually captured by the idea of catallaxies; Davidson et al. 2016; Hayek 1960; Lubin 2016), the system-wide integration of single activities on a city, country or even global level will be necessary to realize larger efficiency gains and overarching goals (e.g. reduction of carbon emissions). Technically this may lead to a mesh of blockchains (e.g. energy and mobility blockchains) and will require solutions facilitating blockchain interoperability (e.g. Polkadot, Cosmos Network or Interledger). On a technological level, scalability is another challenge to the dissemination and efficiency of blockchain solutions in smart cities. Rigid infrastructures and costly mining processes restrict the usefulness of blockchains on a greater scale. For instance, annual carbon emissions of the Bitcoin blockchain are comparable to those of cities like Hamburg and Las Vegas (Stoll et al. 2019). Yet, newly developed ledger technologies–most recently IOTA with the so-called tangle–aim to mitigate these problems (Cachin and Vukolić 2017). To which extent such new technologies can be established remains to be seen.

Finally, we need to point to a couple of limitations which should be addressed by future research. The process of taxonomy development in general presents the quest for a useful rather than optimal solution (Nickerson et al. 2013). Thus, we encourage researchers to build on, extend, or adapt our results. For example, including blockchain-based smart city applications of established companies or further startups are potential avenues for future research. Moreover, many of the examined startups can offer their products or services to customers irrespective of population density. Thus, the startups in our sample are not necessarily focusing on urban environments, but on providing a solution for an urgent urban need or performing a useful activity in the smart city context. As Nickerson et al. (2013) state, a useful taxonomy is extendable. Dimensions and characteristics may be added as the studied field grows or assumes new shapes. This attribute seems especially valuable in our context as many of the examined startups are in early stages. Business and technological characteristics will be subject to dynamic change.

Appendix 1: Sample Structure

Smart city application area	Startups (country)
Energy	• Bankymoon (ZA) • Dajie/Prosume (UK) • ElectricChain (AD) • Jump Software (USA) • Sunride (GER) • Electron (USA) • Energy Blockchain Lab (CHN) • Grid Singularity (AUT) • LO3 (USA) • MyBit (CHE) • TerraLedger/Voltmarkets (USA) • Smappee (USA) • Solether (n/a) • Batan (UK) • Omega Grid (USA) • Sonnen (USA) • SunExchange (ZA) • Wattcoin (USA) • Consensys (USA) • SolarChange (ISR)
Transportation	• Arcade City (USA) • T-Mining (BEL) • Chasyr (USA) • Oaken Innovation (USA) • Parq (NL) • Powertree (USA) • La'Zooz (ISR) • Slock.it (DEU) • Cloudpark (USA) • Parkgene.io (GRC)
Building	• Ubirch (DEU) • HomeSidekick (USA) • Propy (USA) • Smappee (USA) • Silvertown (UK) • Slock.it (DEU) • Ubiquity (USA) • Blocksquare (SVN) • Tapclose (USA) • Flip (USA) • BrikShares (IT) • Propify/Coicio (USA) • Cleverent (USA) • REIDAO (SGP) • REX (USA) • Realblocks (USA)
Health	• Blockpharma (FR) • BurstIQ (USA) • Hashed Health (USA) • Patientory (USA) • Health Chain (UK) • SimplyVital Health (USA) • Open Health Network (USA) • Healthcombix (USA) • PointNurse (USA) • Betternot.rest (BRA) • GEM (USA) • Health Wizz (USA) • Healthcoin (USA) • DAERS (CH)
Government	• Advocate (USA) • BitFury (USA) • Bitland Global (GH) • Follow My Vote (USA) • Neocapita (AUT) • PlaceAVote (USA) • Socioneers (NL) • Voatz (USA) • Disberse (UK) • Helperbit (IT) • Authenteq (DE) • MiVote (AUS) • Crowdesto (UK) • Start Network (UK) • Bitnation (n/a) • Democracy Earth (n/a) • VoteHQ (CAN) • Borderless (n/a) • Procivis (CH) • BitGive Foundation (USA) • Votem (USA)

(n/a) expresses startups that do not provide a registered office

Appendix 2: Classification Results

Smart city application area						
Energy (24%)	P2P transaction platform (32%) [10%]	Crowdfunding platform (24%) [8%]	Corporate energy transactions (32%) [10%]	Carbon asset management (8%) [2%]	Research (4%) [1%]	
Transportation (12%)	Tolls (9%) [1%]	Ride sharing (27%) [4%]	Parking (36%) [5%]	PEV charging (18%) [2%]	Container logistics (9%) [1%]	
Building (20%)	Energy consumption (18%) [4%]	Property transactions (47%) [10%]	Funding (29%) [6%]	Building access authorization (6%) [1%]		
Health (18%)	Patient records (50%) [13%]	Research data provision (23%) [6%]	Pharmaceutical authenticity verification (9%) [2%]	Digital nudging (14%) [4%]	Emergency alerts (5%) [1%]	
Government (26%)	Registry services (22%) [6%]	Voting (26%) [7%]	Citizen dialogue (17%) [5%]	Donation tracking (22%) [6%]	Digital citizenship (13%) [4%]	

Business model

Value proposition — **Primary blockchain benefit**	Security by design (15%) [40%] · Auditability (17%) [45%] · Smart contracts (18%) [50%] · Micro transactions (10%) [27%] · Disintermediation (13%) [37%] · User verification (7%) [18%] · Data reconciliation speed (10%) [27%] · Tokenization (6%) [17%] · Anonymity (4%) [12%]	
Value delivery — **Customer type**	Consumers (37%) [61%] · Prosumers (13%) [22%] · Businesses (35%) [57%] · Governments (14%) [23%]	
Value delivery — **Product composition**	Cyber-physical (32%)	Purely digital (68%)
Value capture — **Revenue model**	Free (20%) [22%] · Freemium (2%) [2%] · Fee-based (33%) [35%] · Subscription (34%) [37%] · Upfront payment (10%) [11%]	

Blockchain application

Permission model — **Reading**	Public (82%)	Private (18%)
Permission model — **Writing**	Permissionless (74%)	Permissioned (26%)
Protocol provider	Bitcoin (11%) · Ethereum (59%) · Hyperledger (5%) · Bitshares (2%) · Other/proprietary (23%)	

(…): relative ratio, […]: absolute ratio

The absolute ratio is the number of occurrences per characteristic related to the number of startups in the sample.
To ensure comparability for non-exclusive dimensions, we in those cases additionally calculated the relative ratio, which relates the number of occurrences per characteristic to the total number of occurrences per dimension.

References

Anthopoulos, L., Fitsilis, P., & Ziozias, C. (2016). What is the source of smart city value? A business model analysis. *International Journal of Electronic Government Research, 12*(2), 56–76.

Beck, R., Czepluch, J. S., Lollike, N., & Malone, S. (2016). Blockchain–The gateway to trust-free cryptographic transactions. In *Proceedings of the 24th Conference on Information Systems (ECIS)*, Istanbul, Turkey.

Beck, R., Müller-Bloch, C., & King, J. L. (2018). Governance in the blockchain economy: A framework and research agenda. *Journal of the Association for Information Systems*, 1020–1034. https://doi.org/10.17705/1jais.00518

Beinke, J. H., Nguyen, D., & Teuteberg, F. (2018). Towards a business model taxonomy of startups in the finance sector using blockchain. In *Proceedings of the 39th International Conference on Information Systems (ICIS)*, San Francisco, CA, USA.

Biswas, K., & Muthukkumarasamy, V. (2017). Securing smart cities using blockchain technology. In *Proceedings of the 18th IEEE International Conference on High Performance Computing and Communications*, Sydney, Australia.

Boulton, A., Brunn, S. D., & Devriendt, L. (2011). 18 Cyberinfrastructures and 'smart' world cities: Physical, human and soft infrastructures. In P. Taylor, B. Derudder, M. Hoyler, & F. Witlox (Eds.), *International Handbook of Globalization and World Cities* (pp. 198–208). Cheltenham, UK: Edward Elgar.

Cachin, C., & Vukolić, M. (2017). Blockchains consensus protocols in the wild. In *Proceedings of the 31st International Symposium on Distributed Computing*, Vienna, Austria.

Cardwell, D. (2017, March). Solar Experiment Lets Neighbors Trade Energy Among Themselves. Retrieved September 22, 2018 from https://www.nytimes.com/2017/03/13/business/energy-environment/brooklyn-solar-grid-energy-trading.html.

Chanson, M., Risius, M., & Wortmann, F. (2018). Initial Coin Offerings (ICOs): An introduction to the novel funding mechanism based on blockchain technology. In *Proceedings of the 24th Americas Conference on Information Systems (AMCIS)*, New Orleans, LA, USA.

Chesbrough, H. (2006). Open innovation: A new paradigm for understanding industrial innovation. In H. Chesbrough, W. Vanhaverbeke, & J. West (Eds.), *Open innovation: Researching a new paradigm* (pp. 0–19). Oxford, UK: Oxford University Press.

Chourabi, H., Nam, T., Walker, S., Gil-Garcia, J. R., Mellouli, S., Nahon, K.,… Scholl, H. J. (2012). Understanding smart cities: An integrative framework. In *Proceedings of the 45th Hawaii International Conference on System Sciences (HICSS)*, Manoa, HI, USA.

Christidis, K., & Devetsikiotis, M. (2016). Blockchains and smart contracts for the internet of things. *IEEE Access, 4,* 2292–2303.

Clohessy, T., Acton, T., & Morgan, L. (2014). Smart city as a service (SCaaS): A future roadmap for e-government smart city cloud computing initiatives. In *Proceedings of the IEEE/ACM 7th International Conference on Utility and Cloud Computing*, London, UK, pp. 836–841.

Cocchia, A. (2014). Smart and digital city: A systematic literature review. In R. P. Dameri & C. Rosenthal-Sabroux (Eds.), *Smart city* (pp. 13–43). Berlin, Germany: Springer.

Davidson, S., De Filippi, P., & Potts, J. (2016, March). Economics of Blockchain. Retrieved September 30, 2018 from https://ssrn.com/abstract=2744751.

Eickhoff, M., Muntermann, J., & Weinrich, T. (2017). What do FinTechs actually do? A taxonomy of FinTech business models. In *Proceedings of the 38th International Conference on Information Systems (ICIS)*, Seoul, South Korea.

Fernández-Breis, J.T., Vivancos-Vicente, P.J., Menárguez-Tortosa, M., Moner, D., Maldonado, J.A., Valencia-García, R., & Miranda-Mena, T.G. (2006). Using semantic technologies to promote interoperability between electronic healthcare records' information models. In *Proceedings of the 2006 International Conference of the IEEE Engineering in Medicine and Biology Society*, New York, NY, USA, pp. 2614–2617.

Freeman, J., & Engel, J. S. (2007). Models of innovation: Startups and Mature Corporations. *California Management Review, 50*(1), 94–119.

Fridgen, G., Regner, F., Schweizer, A., & Urbach, N. (2018). Don't slip on the ICO—A taxonomy for a Blockchain-enabled form of crowdfunding. In *Proceedings of the 26th European Conference on Information Systems (ECIS)*, Portsmouth, United Kingdom.

Gallup. (2016, June). Americans' Confidence in Institutions Stays Low. Retrieved September 15, 2018 from https://www.gallup.com/poll/192581/americans-confidence-institutions-stays-low.aspx.

Gimpel, H., Rau, D., & Röglinger, M. J. E. M. (2017). Understanding FinTech start-ups—A taxonomy of consumer-oriented service offerings. *Electronic Markets, 28*(3), 1–20.

Glaeser, E. L., & Berry, C. R. (2006). Why are smart places getting smarter. *Taubman Center Policy Briefs* 2.

Glaser, F. (2017). Pervasive decentralisation of digital infrastructures: A framework for blockchain enabled system and use case analysis. In *Proceedings of the 50th Hawaii International Conference on System Sciences (HICSS)*, Manoa, HI, USA.

Granath, M., & Axelsson, K. (2014). Stakeholders' views on ICT and sustainable development in an urban development project. In *Proceedings of the European Conference on Information Systems (ECIS)*, Tel Aviv, Israel.

Harrison, C., & Donnelly, I. A. (2011). A theory of smart cities. In *Proceedings of the 55th Annual Meeting of the ISSS*, Hull, UK.

Hashem, I. A. T., Chang, V., Anuar, N. B., Adewole, K., Yaqoob, I., Gani, A., ... Chiroma, H. (2016). The role of big data in smart city. *International Journal of Information Management, 36*(5), 748–758.

Hayek, F. Av. (1960). *The constitution of liberty*. Chicago, IL, USA: University of Chicago Press.

Hileman, G. (2016, January). State of Bitcoin and Blockchain 2016: Blockchain hits Critical Mass. Retrieved October 10, 2018 from https://www.coindesk.com/state-of-bitcoin-blockchain-2016/.

Holotiuk, F., Pisani, F., & Moormann, J. (2017). The impact of blockchain technology on business models in the payments industry. In *Proceedings of the 13th International Conference on Wirtschaftsinformatik*, St. Gallen, Switzerland.

Iansiti, M., & Lakhani, K. R. (2017). The truth about blockchain. *Harvard Business Review, 95*(1), 118–127.

Johnson, M. W., Christensen, C. M., & Kagermann, H. (2008). Reinventing your business model. *Harvard Business Review, 86*(12), 57–68.

Kazan, E., Tan, C.-W., & Lim, E. T. (2015). Value creation in cryptocurrency networks: Towards a taxonomy of digital business models for bitcoin companies. In *Proceedings of the 19th Pacific Asia Conference on Information Systems (PACIS)*, Singapore.

Kennedy, C., Stewart, I. D., Ibrahim, N., Facchini, A., & Mele, R. (2014). Developing a multi-layered indicator set for urban metabolism studies in megacities. *Ecological Indicators, 47*, 7–15.

Kiviat, T. I. (2015). "Smart" Contract Markets: Trading Derivatives Contracts on the Blockchain. Retrieved September 29, 2018 from https://www.academia.edu/10766594/_Smart_Contract_Markets_Trading_Derivatives_on_the_Blockchain.

Komninos, N., Pallot, M., & Schaffers, H. (2013). Special issue on smart cities and the future internet in Europe. *Journal of the Knowledge Economy, 4*(2), 119–134.

Kramers, A., Höjer, M., Lövehagen, N., & Wangel, J. (2014). Smart sustainable cities—Exploring ICT solutions for reduced energy use in cities. *Environmental Modelling and Software, 56*, 52–62.

Kranz, J., Gallenkamp, J., & Picot, A. (2010). Power control to the people? Private consumers' acceptance of smart meters. In *Proceedings of the 18th European Conference on Information Systems (ECIS)*, Pretoria, South Africa.

Kranz, J, Nagel, E., Sandner, P., & Hopf, S. (2019). Blockchain token sale. In *Business and information systems engineering* (pp. 1–9). Retrieved May 25, 2019 from https://link.springer.com/article/10.1007/s12599-019-00598-z#citeas.

Kuk, G., & Janssen, M. (2011). The business models and information architectures of smart cities. *Journal of Urban Technology, 18*(2), 39–52.

Labazova, O., Dehling, T., & Sunyaev, A. (2019). From hype to reality: A taxonomy of blockchain applications. In *Proceedings of the 52nd Hawaii International Conference on System Sciences (HICSS)*, Manoa, HI, USA.

Lee, J., Jung, D. K., Kim, Y., Lee, Y. W., & Kim, Y. M. (2010). Smart grid solutions, services, and business models focused on telco. In *Proceedings of the 2010 IEEE/IFIP Network Operations and Management Symposium Workshops*, Osaka, Japan, pp. 323–326.

Lessig, L. (2008). *Remix: Making art and commerce thrive in the hybrid economy*. New York, NY, USA: The Penguin Press.

Lövehagen, N., & Bondesson, A. (2013). Evaluating sustainability of using ICT solutions in smart cities–Methodology requirements. In *Proceedings of the International Conference on Information and Communication Technologies for Sustainability*, Zurich, Switzerland.

Lubin, J. (2016). Towards a dynamic economic, social and political mesh. In *Proceedings of Devcon1 Developer Conference*, Las Vegas, NV, USA.

Magretta, J. (2002). Why business models matter. *Harvard Business Review, 80*(5), 3–8.

Malović, M. (2014). Demystifying bitcoin: Sleight of hand or major global currency alternative? *Economic Analysis, 47*(1–2), 32–41.

Manville, C., Cochrane, G., Cave, J., Millard, J., Pederson, J. K., Thaarup, R. K., … Kotterink, B. (2014). Mapping Smart Cities in the EU. Retrieved September 18, 2018 from https://www.rand.org/pubs/external_publications/EP50486.html.

Mayer, C. (2013). *Firm commitment: Why the corporation is failing us and how to restore trust in it.* Oxford, UK: Oxford University Press.

McElroy, W. (2017, January). Fedcoin: The U.S. Will Issue E-Currency That You Will Use. Retrieved September 11, 2018 from https://news.bitcoin.com/fedcoin-u-s-issue-e-currency/.

Melville, N. P. (2010). Information systems innovation for environmental sustainability. *MIS Quarterly, 34*(1), 1–21.

Morabito, V. (2017). *Business innovation through blockchain: The B3 perspective.* Berlin, Germany: Springer.

Moss Kanter, R., & Litow, S. S. (2009). Informed and interconnected: A manifesto for smarter cities. Harvard Business School General Management Unit Working Paper 09-14. Retrieved October 22, 2018 from https://papers.ssrn.com/sol3/papers.cfm?abstract_id=1420236.

Mulligan, C. E., & Olsson, M. (2013). Architectural implications of smart city business models: An evolutionary perspective. *IEEE Communications Magazine, 51*(6), 80–85.

Nakamoto, S. (2008). Bitcoin: A Peer-to-Peer Electronic Cash System. Retrieved September 15, 2018 from https://bitcoin.org/bitcoin.pdf.

Nam, T., & Pardo, T. A. (2011). Conceptualizing smart city with dimensions of technology, people, and institutions. In *Proceedings of the 12th Annual International Digital Government Research Conference: Digital Government Innovation in Challenging Times*, College Park, MD, USA.

Nickerson, R. C., Varshney, U., & Muntermann, J. (2013). A method for taxonomy development and its application in information systems. *European Journal of Information Systems, 22*(3), 336–359.

Nofer, M., Gomber, P., Hinz, O., & Schiereck, D. (2017). Blockchain. *Business and Information Systems Engineering, 59*(3), 183–187.

OECD. (2017). Does Technology Against Corruption Always Lead to Benefit? The Potential Risks and Challenges of the Blockchain Technology. Retrieved September 30, 2018 from https://www.oecd.org/cleangovbiz/Integrity-Forum-2017-Kim-Kang-blockchain-technology.pdf.

Ojo, A., Curry, E., & Janowski, T. (2014). Designing next generation smart city initiatives–harnessing findings and lessons from a study of ten smart city programs. In *Proceedings of the European Conference on Information Systems (ECIS)*, Tel Aviv, Israel.

Orsini, L., Wei, Y., & Lubin, J. (2016). Use of blockchain based distributed consensus control. *Google Patents.* Retrieved September 20, 2018 from https://patents.google.com/patent/US20170103468A1/en.

Osterwalder, A., & Pigneur, Y. (2010). *Business model generation: A handbook for visionaries, game changers, and challengers.* Hokoben, NJ, USA: Wiley.

Osterwalder, A., Pigneur, Y., & Tucci, C. L. (2005). Clarifying business models: Origins, present, and future of the concept. *Communications of the Association for Information Systems, 16*(1), 1–25.

Pick, F., & Dreher, J. (2015, May). Sustaining hierarchy–Uber isn't sharing. *Kings Review 5.* Retrieved October 20, 2018 from https://www.researchgate.net/profile/Julia_Dreher/publication/275889451_Sustaining_Hierarchy_-_Uber_isn't_sharing/links/5552753908ae980ca606afbb.pdf.

Pieroni, A., Scarpato, N., Di Nunzio, L., Fallucchi, F., & Raso, M. (2018). Smarter city: Smart energy grid based on blockchain technology. *International Journal on Advanced Science, Engineering and Information Technology, 8*(1), 298–306.

Püschel, L., Röglinger, M., & Schlott, H. (2016). What's in a smart thing? Development of a multi-layer taxonomy. In *Proceedings of the 37th International Conference on Information Systems (ICIS)*, Dublin, Ireland.

Puschmann, T., & Alt, R. (2016). Sharing economy. *Business and Information Systems Engineering, 58*(1), 93–99.

Rivera, R., Robledo, J. G., Larios, V. M., & Avalos, J. M. (2017). How digital identity on blockchain can contribute in a smart city environment. In *Proceedings of the 2017 International Smart Cities Conference (ISC2)*, Ho Chi Minh City, Vietnam.

Rizzo, P. (2016, September). Blockchain to Drive Wanxiang's $30 Billion Smart Cities Initiative. Retrieved September 25, 2018 from https://www.coindesk.com/blockchain-smart-cities-china-wanxiang/.

Rizzo, P. (2017, March 14). Dubai Government Taps IBM for City-Wide Blockchain Pilot Push. Retrieved September 10, 2018 from https://www.coindesk.com/dubai-government-ibm-city-blockchain-pilot/.

Sharma, P. K., Moon, S. Y., & Park, J. H. (2017). Block-VN: A distributed blockchain based vehicular network architecture in smart city. *Journal of Information Processing Systems, 13*(1), 184–195.

Sikorski, J. J., Haughton, J., & Kraft, M. (2017). Blockchain technology in the chemical industry: Machine-to-machine electricity market. *Applied Energy, 195,* 234–246.

Son, J. -Y., & Kim, S. S. (2008). Internet users' information privacy-protective responses: A taxonomy and a nomological model. *MIS Quarterly, 32*(3), 503–529.

Stoll, C., Klaaßen, L., & Gallersdörfer, U. (2019). The carbon footprint of bitcoin. MIT CEEPR Working Paper Series 2018-018. Retrieved November 1, 2019 from https://ceepr.mit.edu/files/papers/2018-018.pdf.

Swan, M. (2015). *Blockchain: Blueprint for a new economy.* Sebastopol, CA: O'Reilly Media Inc.

Teece, D. J. (2010). Business models, business strategy and innovation. *Long Range Planning, 43*(2), 172–194.

Timmers, P. (1998). Business models for electronic markets. *Electronic Markets, 8*(2), 3–8.

Tirole, J. (1999). Incomplete contracts: where do we stand? *Econometrica, 67*(4), 741–781.

Underwood, S. (2016). Blockchain beyond bitcoin. *Communications of the ACM, 59*(11), 15–17.

United Nations. (2016). The World's Cities in 2016. Retrieved September 15, 2018 from https://www.un.org/en/development/desa/population/publications/pdf/urbanization/the_worlds_cities_in_2016_data_booklet.pdf.

Veit, D., Clemons, E., Benlian, A., Buxmann, P., Hess, T., Kundisch, D., … Spann, M. (2014). Business models. *Business and Information Systems Engineering, 6*(1), 45–53.

von Krogh, G., Rossi-Lamastra, C., & Haefliger, S. (2012). Phenomenon-based research in management and organisation science: When is it rigorous and does it matter? *Long Range Planning, 45*(4), 277–298.

Walravens, N. (2015). Qualitative indicators for smart city business models: The case of mobile services and applications. *Telecommunications Policy, 39*(3–4), 218–240.

Walsh, C., OReilly, P., Gleasure, R., Feller, J., Li, S., & Cristoforo, J. (2016). New kid on the block: A strategic archetypes approach to understanding the blockchain. In *Proceedings of the 37th International Conference on Information Systems (ICIS)*, Dublin, Ireland.

Washburn, D., Sindhu, U., Balaouras, S., Dines, R. A., Hayes, N., & Nelson, L. E. (2009). Helping CIOs Understand "smart city" initiatives. *Growth, 17*(2), 1–17.

Watson, R. T., Boudreau, M. -C., & Chen, A. J. (2010). Information systems and environmentally sustainable development: Energy informatics and new directions for the IS community. *MIS Quarterly, 34*(1), 23–38.

Weiblen, T., & Chesbrough, H. W. (2015). Engaging with startups to enhance corporate innovation. *California Management Review, 57*(2), 66–90.

Wikström, S. (1996). Value creation by company-consumer interaction. *Journal of Marketing Management, 12*(5), 359–374.

Williams, K., Chatterjee, S., & Rossi, M. (2008). Design of emerging digital services: A taxonomy. *European Journal of Information Systems, 17*(5), 505–517.

Xu, X., Weber, I., Staples, M., Zhu, L., Bosch, J., Bass, L., ... Rimba, P. (2017). A taxonomy of blockchain-based systems for architecture design. In *Proceedings of the 2017 IEEE International Conference on Software Architecture (ICSA)*, Gothenburg, Sweden.

Yoo, Y. (2010). Computing in everyday life: A call for research on experiential computing. *MIS Quarterly, 34*(2), 213–231.

Yoo, Y., Boland, R. J., Jr., Lyytinen, K., & Majchrzak, A. (2012). Organizing for innovation in the digitized world. *Organization Science, 23*(5), 1398–1408.

Zheng, Z., Xie, S., Dai, H. -N., & Wang, H. (2016). Blockchain Challenges and opportunities: A survey. *International Journal of Web and Grid Services, 14*(4), 352–375.

Zyskind, G., & Nathan, O. (2015). Decentralizing privacy: Using blockchain to protect personal data. In *Proceedings of the 36th IEEE Symposium on Security and Privacy Workshops*, San Jose, CA, USA, pp. 180–184.

Esther Nagel is a research associate and doctoral candidate at the Professorship for Internet Business and Internet Services at the LMU Munich School of Management. She received a Master's degree from the University of St. Gallen and studied abroad at Luiss in Rome and Keio University in Tokyo. Her research interests include the platform economy, blockchain applications, and token sales. She has published her research in *Business and Information Systems Engineering* and the *Proceedings of the European Conference on Information Systems*.

Johann Kranz is professor and director of the Professorship for Internet Business and Internet Services at the LMU Munich School of Management, Germany. He was a visiting scholar at Columbia University (New York City, USA), Syracuse University (New York, USA), and Waseda University (Tokyo, Japan). His primary research interests include blockchain, sustainability, digital innovation and transformation, and digital platform economics. Among others, his research has been published in *Information Systems JournalJournal of Service ResearchElectronic Markets*, and *Energy Policy*.

A Case Study of Blockchain-Induced Digital Transformation in the Public Sector

Horst Treiblmaier and Christian Sillaber

Abstract Public administration has long faced the challenge of addressing a steadily growing workload with limited resources. Blockchain and related technologies promise manifold applications which might alleviate this tension, but adoption may be hampered by the dearth of academic literature documenting existing use cases and the lessons learned from them. This case study examines a public administration use case which was initiated by the state government of South Tyrol in Northern Italy in cooperation with the firm SAP. Many important lessons have been learned in pursuit of the main project goal of streamlining the complex administrative processes surrounding the business of building and modifying cell towers. Exploiting the full potential of blockchain necessitates a complete rethinking of public management, yet holds the potential for a leaner and more service-oriented administration that reestablishes citizen trust in public institutions. However, several disadvantages also emerged, which highlight specific limitations of blockchain technologies. In this paper we apply a single case study approach and derive several best practices based on the analysis of qualitative interviews and rich project documentation.

Keywords Blockchain · Distributed ledger technology · Digital transformation · Public sector · Public administration · Governance · Transparency · Efficiency · Trust

1 Introduction

Lack of transparency, excessive bureaucracy, and even cases of corruption, have created a downward spiral of citizen trust in public administration (Dubnick 1996; Persson et al. 2017). Many countries have sought to arrest this trend by increasing the supervision of public officials: in some places to such an extent that many processes

H. Treiblmaier (✉)
Modul University Vienna, Vienna, Austria
e-mail: horst.treiblmaier@modul.ac.at

C. Sillaber
University of Innsbruck, Innsbruck, Austria
e-mail: research@christiansillaber.com

© Springer Nature Switzerland AG 2020
H. Treiblmaier and T. Clohessy (eds.), *Blockchain and Distributed Ledger Technology Use Cases*, Progress in IS, https://doi.org/10.1007/978-3-030-44337-5_11

have been rendered ineffective and personal liability has become a pressing topic for state officials. This situation presents an opportunity to explore new governance and administrative structures which can increase efficiency and improve public account-ability mechanisms. In the Netherlands, for example, the Dutch urban regeneration has yielded a substantial shift in governance principles over the past three decades, which reflects the changing relationships between public and private sector actors in urban governance (Tasan-Kok et al. 2019).

The rise of blockchain technologies has created high expectations regarding trans-formations across business and government. Previous authors have exemplified its disruptive potential in industry sectors as diverse as tourism, energy, finance and public governance (Treiblmaier and Beck 2019a, b). Simultaneously, several authors warn against unrealistic expectations and suggest the carefully scrutiny of each poten-tial use case to identify how blockchain technology actually solves the pending problem, which implies acknowledgement of blockchain's limitations and the new challenges presented (Treiblmaier 2019), and advocate the open documentation of any constraining effects (Hald and Kinra 2019). Such a critical assessment should not be restricted to economic implications, but also needs to include related topics such as legal compliance (Posadas 2018) and problems related to scaling, power consumption, and trust, which are especially relevant for public blockchains (Waldo 2019).

As yet, blockchain's impact on public governance and administration has eluded thorough assessment in the academic literature. The majority of the existing litera-ture focuses on corporate governance and predicts potential gains in efficiency and effectiveness (e.g., lower costs, greater liquidity, more accurate record keeping, trans-parency of ownership) (Yermack 2017) and is often conceptual in nature (Voshmgir 2017). Extending previous research, in this paper we discuss the implementation of a blockchain-based solution in a public institution. In order to increase the overall efficiency and to be able to provide better services to citizens, the state government of South Tyrol decided to exploit the potential of blockchain to achieve the goals of increasing trust in public services, creating transparent and efficient applications, and streamlining governance processes. We report the findings from the KIS ("Kom-munikation, Infrastruktur, Software") project and illustrate how a blockchain-based solution has been implemented to streamline processes related to the building and modification of cell towers. This paper is structured as follows: We initially dis-cuss the role of blockchain technology for public governance in general, followed by a brief presentation of the companies involved and their respective roles in this project. Next, we introduce a guiding research question, four sub-questions, and our methodological approach. We then present the results, which are based on numerous qualitative in-depth interviews and the analysis of various artifacts such as thorough project documentations. Finally, we derive various practices and implications for future research.

2 Blockchain Technology and the Public Sector

According to Treiblmaier (2018, p. 547), blockchain can be defined as a "digital, decentralized and distributed ledger in which transactions are logged and added in chronological order with the goal of creating permanent and tamperproof records". Due to its widespread popularity, it has become common practice to also use the term blockchain when discussing alternative data structures that do not exhibit a sequence of blocks chained together by shared data, and which therefore might be more appropriately denoted as Distributed Ledger Technology (DLT) or so-called "trustless" systems. In this paper we follow this convention and use the term blockchain inclusively.

Previous research has identified various potentials for blockchain technology to impact governance, and indicated a need to depart radically from existing notions of governance (Beck et al. 2018; Voshmgir 2017). However, previous research has also acknowledged new threats associated with blockchain adoption, such as the introduction of new market risks and a loss of anonymity. Furthermore, the immutability of records poses a major problem in public blockchains, as does the risk of hacking in private ones (Magnier and Barban 2018).

A detailed categorization of potential benefits and promises of blockchain technologies for governments can be found in Ølnes et al. (2017). The authors enumerate numerous benefits and promises across the categories of strategic, economic, organizational, informational, and technological concerns, including: increased transparency, avoidance of fraud and manipulation, reduced corruption, increased trust, better auditability, reduced costs, increased resilience, higher data quality, resilience and security. Sullivan and Burger (2019) examine the legal and technical implications of blockchain technologies to authenticate and verify identity for e-Government services and transactions. They conclude that "digital identity on blockchains […] is revolutionizing the delivery of e-government" (p. 256). In light of existing conceptual research that postulates a huge transformative potential of blockchain, we present our guiding research question: *How can blockchain be used to enable transformations in the public sector?* In order to answer this question we apply a case study approach. This generic research question will later be refined into four sub-questions, as reported in the following sections.

3 Methodology

In order to answer the question of how blockchain technology can enable transformations in the public sector, we sought to elicit rich evidence consisting mainly of expert interviews enhanced by a thorough analysis of the complete project documentation. Between June and December 2018 we conducted eight interviews with five key informants from the South Tyrol Informatik AG (SIAG) and the firm SAP to

Table 1 Interview partners

Code	Position within the company
MGMT1	Chief Digital Officer
MGMT2	Service Manager, Project Lead
IT-DEV	IT Solution Architect
SAP1	SAP, Chief Innovation Officer Public Services
SAP2	SAP SE Future City and Blockchain

identify the practices and processes associated with blockchain-based transformation. All of the informants played leading roles in the project. The interviews each lasted between 45 and 120 min. Three follow-up interviews were later conducted to clarify open questions. The participants were interviewed either in person or on the phone, and all interviews were recorded by the authors and subsequently transcribed. Table 1 shows the roles of the interviewees and their relevant qualifications. The project documentation analysed included, for example, various unified modeling language (UML) diagrams, which helped us to better understand the underlying processes and their implementation.

The transcribed interviews and process documentation were processed in three stages following the common procedures of qualitative research (Urquhart 2012). First, we extracted artifacts, activities and requirements that were mentioned as relevant to the transformation process. Second, we created groups of related statements and identified relevant core topics and, third, we combined those topics into theoretical ideas at a higher level of abstraction. Following the case study classification from Yin (2013), this project can be classified as a single case exhibiting holistic (i.e., single unit of analysis) design. We followed an explorative approach and strived to understand the procedures and artifacts being used in the case and their respective impacts. Through the combination of data from different sources (i.e., interviews, artifacts) we were able to validate our findings.

4   Public Administration and Blockchain Technology: The KIS Project

The KIS project was carried out as a cooperation between SIAG and SAP. SIAG is the IT service provider for the governmental and administrative bodies of the independent province of Bolzano in northern Italy. SIAG provides numerous IT Services ranging from implementing a variety of IT applications (such as email and web hosting) to processing workflows for approximately 4500 employees and administrative workers. Over the past 35 years, SIAG has developed and implemented around 1000 service workflows for public services. The provided services are crucial for half a million citizens and log an excess of two million activities per day, ranging from driving license application management to approval processes for buildings. These workflows are provided through a variety of in-house and out-house systems that have grown over time. SAP SE is a multinational software corporation headquartered in Germany and serving more than 430,000 customers in over 180 countries (SAP Global Corporate Affairs 2019). In 2018 SAP officially launched the SAP cloud platform blockchain service which enables customers and developers to build blockchain extensions for existing applications, to integrate DLT features in the blockchain ecosystem and to embed blockchain technology into SAP Leonardo (i.e., a digital innovation system) offerings (Gross 2017).

4.1 Pending Problems

As is the case in many countries, public administration in Italy struggles to offer citizens high-quality services within reasonable periods of time. This is further complicated by complex legacy business processes and legislation. In Italy the level of citizens' trust in public administration has declined over the decades. In 2015, 93% of all Italians declared that they do not trust their own parliament (Merelli 2015). A recent academic study showed that in spite of the reforms driven by the New Public Management (NPM) approach, the public administration in Italy still follows a bureaucratic model. Interestingly, public servants are highly motivated despite having to carry out highly standardized activities. Altogether, several public administrations are perceived by their employees as being anarchistic (Tomo 2019). Our interview partners indicated that other pending problems include the strict supervision by auditors and the fact that even small errors may lead to personal liabilities.

Demand is increasing from both inside the SIAG as well as from politicians and citizens to simplify processes, unify the underlying technologies and improve inter-agency efficiency. Furthermore, due to several regulatory changes, demand for end-to-end workflows has considerably increased in recent years. This especially pertains to processes in which citizens are directly involved and should receive access to workflow execution data, such as the state of the request and name of the administrative entity currently working on the file. For example, the specific workflow to receive approval for building a new cell tower involves three agencies that need to coordinate the paperwork between them. These are the phone company, the owner of the land where the mast is to be built as well as all owners of neighboring properties. Another problem is that digitalization also creates additional work. For example, from a legal perspective only a digital document is valid for the public administration in Italy. Paper documents, after being digitized and certified, can therefore be destroyed. This process is labor-intensive and complex.

4.2   Project Goals

In a first step SIAG and SAP conducted a proof-of-concept (PoC) with the goal to specifically investigate four questions pertaining to the overall potential of blockchain technology:

- Q1: Is it possible to use Blockchain-as-a-Service (BaaS) in the cloud?

Hosting blockchain-based solutions in a cloud environment opens up new opportunities for service providers to offer their customers cloud-based solutions to develop, host and use blockchain functions, applications and smart contracts.

- Q2: How can a public Blockchain solution be integrated with legacy systems?

Public administration often depends on complex legacy systems that have grown over years. It is therefore crucial to carefully investigate the extent to which these systems can be replaced by novel technologies and which parts of the old system must be incorporated into the new solution.

- Q3: What kind of Blockchain-related security aspects need to be taken into account?

Blockchain technology promises immutable and secure data records. The overall security of the system therefore depends on the number of nodes that are responsible for validating data records and adding transactions to the chain.

- Q4: Can a Blockchain-based solution improve the efficiency of workflows?

Workflows in the public administration follow specific rules that are determined by legislation. Characteristics of blockchain that are especially promising to simplify existing processes include the visibility of shared data among various stakeholders as well as the deployment of smart contracts to facilitate decision automation.

The assessment of the PoC yielded positive results pertaining to all of the four questions and led to the decision to put a specific process into production, namely the building and modification of cell towers. Blockchain technology offers new opportunities, but also has limitations and might create new challenges. Existing workflows must therefore be critically investigated and potentially revised prior to deployment. In this special case the envisioned solution was not fully decentralized, since it was controlled by SIAG and SAP, but had the purpose of testing the feasibility of certain blockchain features. KIS was triggered by the need to streamline public administration, and used the VUCA (volatility, uncertainty, complexity, ambiguity) framework (Saleh and Watson 2017) to analyze the current situation and to develop a new strategy to cope with environmental changes. The decision to implement a blockchain-based solution for the building and modification of cell towers can be attributed to its capacity for efficient and transparent processes.

Roughly 600 applications concerning the building or modification of cell towers are submitted each year. The goal of KIS was to model this process end-to-end, starting with the initial application and ending with communicating the decision to the applicant. The process starts in the community which is affected by the cell tower. An environmental impact assessment is then performed in the provincial administration. The outcome of this assessment goes back to the community, where the building community makes the final decision. Additional pressure is put on administration by an Italian rule stating that if the public administration does not respond within 30 days, the construction project is approved. Both the community and the provincial administration want to keep their authority and in order to do so must ensure a fast processing time.

The proposed solution has to function in a cloud and integrate existing legacy systems. Additionally, the idea is to develop an implementation that can serve as a reference for future SAP implementations. The project was designed in three stages. In stage 1, a partnership with SAP was initiated to create a Proof of Concept (PoC), as was already described above. This PoC included the transfer of an analog document into the digital world: a workflow that previously included four laborious steps. Blockchain helped to reduce this into a one-step process, thereby significantly reducing the amount of time needed for completion. Furthermore, data security was improved. In stage 2, which included the development of a technology stack, the government realized that it does not make much sense to digitize discrete parts of a process, and instead recognized that an end-to-end process view is required to achieve successful digital transformation. This also necessitates active participation of all stakeholders involved. One explicit goal in this stage was to transfer the whole process into the cloud. Still, the total impact of digital transformation was not fully understood and various needs for process adaptation emerged. In stage 3, the broad rollout of the technology, the lessons learned are used to create blockchain-supported processes in various sectors of public governance. These processes will be implemented end-to-end and will fully capitalize on the benefits of digital transformation. Based on the lessons learned from the previous phases, design thinking will be used as an analysis instrument and Scrum for realization.

4.3 Results

Figure 1 shows SAP's cloud hosted BaaS, consisting of three layers, namely the infrastructure-as-a-service (IaaS) platform layer, the cloud platform foundry layer and the cloud platform environment. While the former two represent the (largely) customer independent runtime environment for blockchain, the latter implements the specific functionality to run and operate the customer's blockchain. Two immediate observations pertaining to Q1 (*Is it possible to use BaaS in the cloud?*) can be made. First, there is a separation between the workflow-specific implementation of blockchain and the foundry as well as the platform layers, and, second, while the workflow is executed within the SAP environment, the critical data (i.e., sensitive documents) never enter the blockchain: only references are stored. Both factors enable a quick integration into the blockchain but also ensure that both the environment (i.e., SAP's infrastructure) as well as the technology used within this infrastructure can be

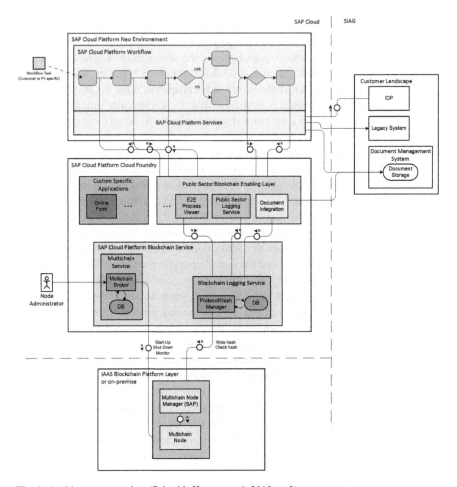

Fig. 1 Architecture overview (Schmidt-Karaca et al. 2018, p. 9)

exchanged without too much friction. Similarly, legacy data is kept on premises in SIAG systems and can be referenced from within the workflow engine (Q2). Aside from general security and privacy considerations that have to be taken into account with any cloud-based workflow solution, it is clear from the design of the reference implementation that none of the security properties typically associated with blockchains currently manifests, as both SAP and SIAG fully control the data and workflows. However, SIAG reported that they intend to operate the node in their own data center, in addition to SAP's plan to operate a full node in the near future that might help identify data manipulation (Q3). Performance wise, the layered approach of SAP's centralized blockchain hosting reportedly allows for the quick addition and removal of resources if performance becomes an issue (Q4).

Figure 2 show the end-to-end process for managing the cell phone tower approval process. There are three involved parties (cf. swim lanes): citizens, municipalities,

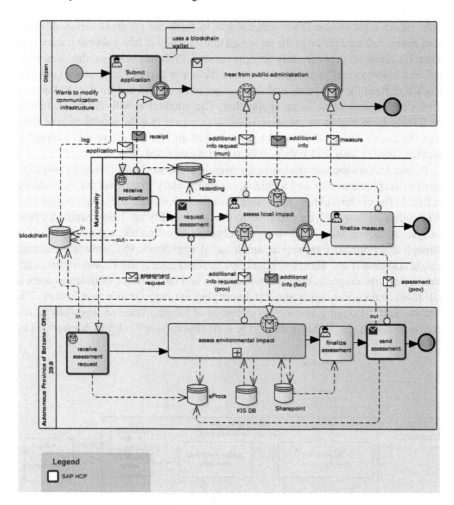

Fig. 2 End to end process to be implemented (Schmidt-Karaca et al. 2018, p. 10)

and the state (i.e., the province of Bolzano). The process model shows how the process works, the data silos involved, and which data is entered and read from the blockchain. The process starts with a citizen submitting an application to modify the communication infrastructure. The application is then submitted to the municipality and assessed for its local impact. The municipality then sends an assessment request to the province of Bolzano. The province assesses the application's environmental impact and sends the assessment result back to the municipality. The municipality then finalizes its assessment and communicates the measure to the applicant. As shown in the process model, the most important functionality of the blockchain is similar to a notarized timestamp server, where selected important events, such as the start and end of subprocesses, are logged to the blockchain for transparency.

This allows citizens and other stakeholders to track the progress across different authorities. Advantages lie in the increased transparency of being able to track where a specific application is currently being processed. Prior this solution, the "hear from public administration" activity as shown in the upper part of Fig. 2 was a complete black box from the perspective of the average citizen, who had no way to know or access the current status of an application. The interaction with the blockchain is performed from within the SIAG system. This means that the workflow tool itself logs the aforementioned activities to the blockchain. For the future it is planned to provide citizens with read-only access to the timestamped data.

Figure 3 shows the technical view for an end-to-end workflow involving two independent corporate bodies and a citizen, complementary to the process view shown in Fig. 2. The citizen submits the online form through the municipality's online tool. While all workflow activities specific to the municipality are being handled within its system, requests to the province of Bolzano's infrastructure are operationalized through a service API as well as email-based workflows. PEC (posta elettronica certificata) emails are digitally signed and certified emails. As shown on the right-hand side of the diagram, both the municipality and the province of Bolzano operate full blockchain nodes, replicating and verifying the entire transaction history. The "Public Sector Logging Service" is in charge of logging selected workflow activities (timestamps) to the blockchain. The E2E Blockchain Workflow Viewer can be

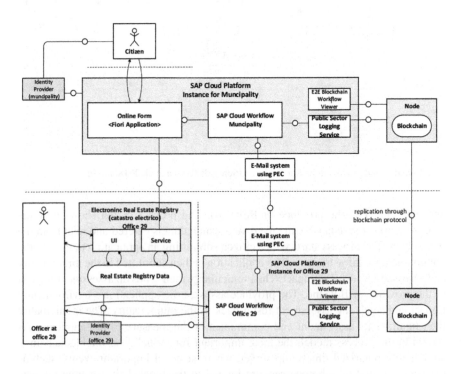

Fig. 3 Architecture components (Schmidt-Karaca et al. 2018, p. 17)

used—on the municipality's and province's side—to access the log data and view the workflow through the lens of its activities logged to the blockchain. Log data obtained from the blockchain can be used to track and monitor the performance of individuals across different workflow activities in order to improve the overall efficiency and transparency. Also, the increased transparency might deter abuse and manipulation.

4.4 Best Practices and Critical Evaluation

Based on the results gained from the interviews and the analysis of the project documentation, we identified five best practices for applying blockchain concepts to mission-critical public administration services. These practices are especially relevant for public organizations that are in the early stages of trying out blockchain solutions:

Practice 1: Invest in the Purposeful Evaluation of Blockchain-Based Transformations Although Blockchain technology is still in an early stage, KIS faced a diversity of different types of solutions for the public sector, and can be considered a pioneering project in this area. One SAP employee stated *"We had for the first time a client in the public sector who was actively seeking for an innovative blockchain solution"*. It is therefore not surprising that many of the available frameworks that guide businesses toward blockchain technology start with a critical evaluation of whether or not blockchain is the right solution in the first place (Pedersen et al. 2019). It is crucial for both the industry and software companies to gain experience in such analyses. What is needed is a careful evaluation of blockchain's potentials and how they can actually contribute value to the company. As a senior manager puts it: *"Simply implementing a blockchain does more harm than good. We want to pick the parts that fit our needs - even if some blockchain purists would not like that"*. Blockchain is not a single solution but rather a stack of various platforms and technologies, and care has to be taken to pick the right solution: *We explored Ethereum, but ended up with Multichain. It turned out to be the most suitable solution for our innovation scenario. Multichain had the best fit with our use case.* In KIS the process of building and modifying cell towers was analyzed after a successful PoC. Although showing significant potential, the project became too expensive given only 600 cases a year. This led to a modification of the original project goal to have everything in the cloud. As one informant put it: *Either the services in the cloud were not ready or we did not fully understand digital transformation.* It turned out to be the latter. Decisions have to be automated, which leads to different processes, and data drive processes which render previous process definitions redundant.

Practice 2: Identify a Critical Workflow that Can Serve as an Example to Test Both Technical and Legal Assumptions
Organizations need to identify workflows that are important for them as well as possessing appropriate characteristics for deployment on the blockchain. In the case

of KIS it was characteristics such as the visibility of the process for citizens, time pressure and traceability which made cell tower development an ideal use case. On respondent stated: *"With every new technology, you need to know how to use it. So we selected a workflow that required us to thoroughly think about technical, legal and performance requirements and whether they can be met"*. Splitting processes into parts is usually not a good idea and leads to extra effort. Sometimes streamlining the organization implies that the process itself has to be modified. In KIS it turned out that the delegation of authority had to change. A relatively simple procedure such as the approval of cell towers was split between two entities, which complicated the authorization process. Streamlining therefore necessitated consideration of the whole process and all stakeholders involved, as one SIAG representative put it: *In the digital transformation you cannot digitalize sub-processes. You always need to look at a process end-to-end.* The transformation of digital workflows therefore starts with the identification of environmental conditions which might hinder a successful technological implementation and a comprehensive understanding of how the process works as a whole. In the public administration, the application of blockchain makes particular sense where processes crossing different authorities (a) are end-to-end and (b) need a single point of truth.

Practice 3: Accommodate the Goals of All Internal and External Stakeholders
The hype surrounding blockchain generated a "peak of inflated expectations" regarding what the technology could actually achieve, according to the Gartner hype cycle (Kietzmann and Archer-Brown 2019), and led to its application in use cases wherein it could provide little value, resulting in a "trough of disillusionment". Previous experience has therefore enabled a more realistic assessment of the technology and its capabilities to address stakeholders' issues. One interview partner described the incremental moderation of initially polarized perceptions: *"There was quite some skepticism. In October 2016 when we started there was a very positive momentum but also a lot of negative sentiment. By now the expectations are more reasonable"*. Another project partner highlighted the importance of having clearly defined goals: *"You need to know what you are trying to accomplish with a blockchain [...] You have to think beyond cost and the hype and consider what your stakeholders really need"*. Additionally, stakeholders must be open for changes to new ways of thinking in order to exploit what the technology can achieve and to accommodate its limitations: *"You need to have an environment that is also willing to change and to absorb new ways of doing things, especially in the public sector"*. Digital transformation turns out to be far more comprehensive than just modifying selected processes, and therefore demands that all stakeholders collaboratively reexamine the core processes and their respective roles in them. Accommodating the goals of all involved parties finally led to a highly positive project assessment: *"The project was an outstanding success. Innovation for me is creativity plus implementation"*. The application of smart contracts not only yielded an increase in process efficiency but also led to the exemption of state employees from personal liability. Together with improved transparency for citizens, this serves as an example of how blockchain technology can provide new services to stakeholders.

Practice 4: Leverage Existing Technology and Ecosystems

In the case of KIS, a complex legacy system needed to be incorporated into the new structure. Similarly, the input and output of the main process were clearly defined. The technical lead explained: *"We went for the solution implementing [blockchain concepts] from the service provider already providing a majority of services that we rely on. So we can use what we already have and [for example] keep sensitive documents in the database we already use and only move critical parts to the blockchain"*. This led to the decision to adopt a private blockchain which integrates legacy systems. A major part of this process included the analysis of how the integration can be done: *"We had to figure out what is feasible, what is legally allowed"*. Given the scope of KIS and the fact that this was a governmental project, it turned out that permissioned blockchains were easier to implement in comparison to permissionless solutions, which imply numerous attack vectors. The success of the project owed much to the simultaneous consideration of different contingency factors, or, as a senior manager put it: *"[The] trinity of design thinking: Feasible from a technical point of view, viable from a business point of view and it should have a great usability"*. Summarizing, it turned out that it is difficult to completely renovate an existing system which has been in existence for several years and which is fully functioning. KIS is therefore a project which illustrates that blockchain features can be incorporated into existing applications and how the functionality of legacy systems can be enriched by blockchain technology.

Practice 5: Think About Conflict Resolution

Environmental changes, which also include technological change, are often at odds with the logics that were imprinted into organizations in the past (Waeger and Weber 2019). This is not something which is specific to blockchain technology, however, and resistance to organizational change has been well-studied over the past decades (Schulz-Knappe et al. 2019). In the case of KIS, for example, the application of smart contracts led to a (perceived) power shift due to the automatization of a previously manually conducted process. Fortunately, this tension was mitigated by the fact that in the public sector commissions are only allowed to apply rules someone else has come up with. Nevertheless, the phenomena exemplifies what might be the most important criterion for a successful blockchain implementation, as insisted by a senior manager: *"You need to have an organization that is ready for change"*.

5   Discussion and Conclusion

Governments around the world have realized the need to deploy information technology to provide better service to their citizens. In Denmark, for example, the Danish Agency for Digitization was established in 2011 to assume responsibility for the government's digitization policies. The OECD published a working paper in which they included brief descriptions of eight blockchain case studies in the public sector from seven different countries (i.e., Ghana, United Arab Emirates, United States,

Singapore, Sweden, Denmark, Mexico) (Berryhill et al. 2018). The authors of the paper highlight that, in spite of the complexity of the technology, "policy-makers must grasp the technology and its implications, as this trend is already deeply transformative" (p. 9). Previous research also shows that the adoption of such services by citizens depends on a wide variety of factors including hardware and Internet availability, convenience and the supply of non-electronic alternatives (Van de Walle et al. 2018). Blockchain technology offers several characteristics such as immutability, transparency, programmability, decentralization, consensus and distributed trust that can potentially help to streamline processes in the public administration (Treiblmaier 2019). Academia has long postulated that such positive transformations are possible (Voshmgir 2017), but empirical research in that area remains scarce.

In this chapter we discuss the case of KIS, a cooperation between SIAG and SAP in South Tyrol. The application of blockchain technology to provide more efficient and transparent services to citizens turned out to be an interesting testbed. We raised the guiding question of how blockchain technology can be used to enable transformation in the public sector and four sub-questions related to BaaS in the cloud, the integration of blockchain with legacy systems, relevant security aspects, and the design of efficient workflows. The findings from the initial PoC showed that a blockchain solution can be outsourced into the cloud and integrated with a legacy system. Additionally, the transparency for citizens was increased. As far as the potential of blockchain in general is concerned, many important lessons were learned along the way, which we summarize into seven best practices in this paper. In order to fully exploit the potentials of blockchain, organizations need to carefully evaluate the envisaged transformation, identify critical workflows, leverage existing technologies and ecosystems, strive to achieve compliance continuously and consider conflict resolution and data portability. One important finding was that blockchain technology is especially useful to create a single point of truth for business processes that span various administrative units. This case study therefore illustrates that blockchain has the potential to trigger transformation in the public sector. The results from KIS have shown that BaaS and an integration with legacy systems can be achieved, as well as how security aspects can be considered and transparent workflows can be designed.

Blockchain has great potential, but effective implementation requires a careful evaluation of every use case to fit the use case to the technology. Academia is called upon to carefully assess existing use cases and to identify best practices across various industries. Furthermore, rigorous academic research can help to better understand the requirements of successful blockchain adoption and use as well as the influence of various contingency factors on the success of blockchain projects.

6   Limitations and Further Research

Blockchain technology is still under constant development. Numerous variations of public and private blockchains have emerged in recent years with varying scopes of application. In the case of KIS a cloud-based solution that was enhanced by blockchain technology was created. The findings of the project have clearly highlighted the potentials but also shortcomings of blockchain. Numerous obstacles needed to be overcome and valuable lessons were learned for the future. In a nutshell, blockchain technology is a complex technology with huge potential but it is not a silver bullet that can be generically applied to every use case. This case study was conducted in a public administration environment based on specific legislation and care has to be taken when generalizing the results across industries and geographical boundaries. Most importantly, the case includes a private, permissioned blockchain where the validating entities are known. Future research is needed to generalize the findings to other use cases, including in the private sector, as well as to find measures to quantify the benefits which blockchains can generate. Blockchain technology has indicated a huge potential to streamline public processes and to make them more efficient, but it is only by embedding it as yet another useful tool in the bigger concept of digital transformation that the potential of the technology can be fully exploited.

Acknowledgements The authors want to thank all project partners for the open dialogue and the sharing of project-relevant information. Special thanks go to the official project coordinator Stefan Gasslitter, Digital Transformation Leader (Bolzano Area, Italy) and Chief Digital Officer, as well as his team, in particular Matteo Negrello and Michela Cicchetti. From SAP we especially want to thank Heinrich Pfriemer, Chief Innovation Officer Public Services and Holger Tallowitz, Director of Industry Business Unit Public Services.

Appendix

We conducted eight interviews using open-ended questions between July 2018 and December 2018. Three of the interviews were conducted on the premises of SIAG and three via telephone. In two cases it was necessary to follow up via e-mail to clarify pending issues. All the questions below were only used as guidelines.

- What was your role in the Blockchain project?
- What were the goals of the project?
- To what extent did you reach your goals?
- What Blockchain solution did you implement? Why?
- Positive effects of the Blockchain solution
- Negative effects of the Blockchain solution
- Lessons learned from the project
- Based on your experience, what potential does the Blockchain have? What are its limitations?

References

Beck, R., Müller-Bloch, C., & King, J. L. (2018). Governance in the blockchain economy: A framework and research agenda. *Journal of the Association for Information Systems, 19*(10), 1020–1034. https://doi.org/10.17705/1jais.00518.

Berryhill, J., Bourgery, T., & Hanson, A. (2018). *Blockchains Unchained: Blockchain Technology and its Use in the Public Sector.* Retrieved from https://www.oecd-ilibrary.org/governance/blockchains-unchained_3c32c429-en.

Dubnick, M. J. (1996). Challenges to American public administration: Complexity, bureaucratization, and the culture of distrust. *International Journal of Public Administration, 19*(9), 1481–1508. https://doi.org/10.1080/01900699608525155

Gross, L. (2017). *Unveiling Blockchain's Potential Together: SAP Launches SAP Cloud Platform Blockchain Service.* Retrieved June 21, 2019, from SAP News Center website: https://news.sap.com/2017/05/sapphire-now-sap-cloud-platform-blockchain-service/.

Hald, K. S., & Kinra, A. (2019). How the blockchain enables and constrains supply chain performance. *International Journal of Physical Distribution & Logistics Management, 49*(4), 376–397. https://doi.org/10.1108/IJPDLM-02-2019-0063

Kietzmann, J., & Archer-Brown, C. (2019). From hype to reality: Blockchain grows up. *Business Horizons, 62*(3), 269–271. https://doi.org/10.1016/j.bushor.2019.01.001

Magnier, V., & Barban, P. (2018). The potential impact of blockchains on corporate governance: A survey on shareholders' rights in the digital era. *InterEULawEast: Journal for International & European Law, Economics & Market Integrations, 5*(2), 189–226. https://doi.org/10.22598/iele.2018.5.2.7.

Merelli, A. (2015). *93% of Italians don't trust their parliament—And they are right.* Retrieved June 21, 2019, from Quartz website: https://qz.com/328300/93-of-italians-dont-trust-their-parliament-and-they-are-right/.

Ølnes, S., Ubacht, J., & Janssen, M. (2017). Blockchain in government: Benefits and implications of distributed ledger technology for information sharing. *Government Information Quarterly, 34*(3), 355–364. https://doi.org/10.1016/j.giq.2017.09.007

Pedersen, A., Risius, M., & Beck, R. (2019). Blockchain decision path: When to use blockchains? Which blockchains do you mean? *MIS Quarterly Executive, 18*(2), 1–17.

Persson, T., Parker, C. F., & Widmalm, S. (2017). Social trust, impartial administration and public confidence in EU Crisis Management Institutions. *Public Administration, 95*(1), 97–114. https://doi.org/10.1111/padm.12295

Posadas, D. V., Jr. (2018). The internet of things: The GDPR and the blockchain may be incompatible. *Journal of Internet Law, 21*(11), 1–29.

Saleh, A., & Watson, R. (2017). Business excellence in a volatile, uncertain, complex and ambiguous environment (BEVUCA). *TQM Journal, 29*(5), 705–724. https://doi.org/10.1108/TQM-12-2016-0109

SAP Global Corporate Affairs. (2019). *SAP Corporate Fact Sheet.* Retrieved from https://www.sap.com/documents/2017/04/4666ecdd-b67c-0010-82c7-eda71af511fa.html.

Schmidt-Karaca, M., Srikumar, S., Lange, S., Tegno, P., Krompholz, A., Oberhofer, P., et al. (2018). *Architecture concept: End-to-end workflow with blockchain logging* (pp. 1–44) [SAP Document]. SAP.

Schulz-Knappe, C., Koch, T., & Beckert, J. (2019). The importance of communicating change: Identifying predictors for support and resistance toward organizational change processes. *Corporate Communications: An International Journal, 24*(4), 670–685. https://doi.org/10.1108/CCIJ-04-2019-0039

Sullivan, C., & Burger, E. (2019). Blockchain, digital identity, E-government. In H. Treiblmaier & R. Beck (Eds.), *Business transformation through blockchain* (Vol. 2, pp. 233–258). https://doi.org/10.1007/978-3-319-99058-3_9.

Tasan-Kok, T., van den Hurk, M., Özogul, S., & Bittencourt, S. (2019). Changing public account-ability mechanisms in the governance of Dutch urban regeneration. *European Planning Studies, 27*(6), 1107–1128. https://doi.org/10.1080/09654313.2019.1598017

Tomo, A. (2019). Bureaucracy, post-bureaucracy, or anarchy? Evidence from the Italian Public Administration. *International Journal of Public Administration, 42*(6), 482–496. https://doi.org/10.1080/01900692.2018.1485045

Treiblmaier, H. (2018). The impact of the blockchain on the supply chain: A theory-based research framework and a call for action. *Supply Chain Management: An International Journal, 23*(6), 545–559.

Treiblmaier, H. (2019). Toward more rigorous blockchain research: Recommendations for writing blockchain case studies. *Frontiers in Blockchain, 2*(3), 1–15. https://doi.org/10.3389/fbloc.2019.00003

Treiblmaier, H., & Beck, R. (Eds.). (2019a). *Business transformation through blockchain* (Vol. I). Cham, Switzerland: Palgrave Macmillan.

Treiblmaier, H., & Beck, R. (Eds.). (2019b). *Business transformation through blockchain* (Vol. 2). Cham, Switzerland: Palgrave Macmillan.

Urquhart, C. (2012). *Grounded theory for qualitative research: A practical guide*. Los Angeles, CA; London: SAGE Publications Ltd.

Van de Walle, S., Zeibote, Z., Stacenko, S., Muravska, T., & Migchelbrink, K. (2018). Explaining non-adoption of electronic government services by citizens: A study among non-users of public e-services in Latvia. *Information Polity: The International Journal of Government & Democracy in the Information Age, 23*(4), 399–409. https://doi.org/10.3233/IP-170069

Voshmgir, S. (2017). Disrupting governance with blockchains and smart contracts. *Strategic Change, 26*(5), 499–509. https://doi.org/10.1002/jsc.2150

Waeger, D., & Weber, K. (2019). Institutional complexity and organizational change: An open polity perspective. *Academy of Management Review, 44*(2), 336–359. https://doi.org/10.5465/amr.2014.0405

Waldo, J. (2019). A Hitchhiker's guide to the blockchain universe. *Communications of the ACM, 62*(3), 38–42. https://doi.org/10.1145/3303868

Yermack, D. (2017). Corporate governance and blockchains. *Review of Finance, 21*(1), 7–31. https://doi.org/10.1093/rof/rfw074

Yin, R. K. (2013). *Case study research* (5th ed.). Los Angeles: Sage Publications.

Horst Treiblmaier is a professor in international management at Modul University Vienna, Austria. He received a Ph.D. in Management Information Systems in 2001 from the Vienna University of Economics and Business in Austria and worked as a Visiting Professor at Purdue University, University of California, Los Angeles (UCLA), University of British Columbia (UBC), and the University of Technology in Sydney (UTS). He has more than fifteen years of experience as a researcher and consultant and has worked on projects with Microsoft, Google, and the United Nations Industrial Development Organization (UNIDO). His research interests include the economic and business implications of Blockchain, cryptoeconomics, methodological and epistemological problems of social science research and gamification. Currently he serves on the board of the "City of Blockchain", an association promoting blockchain and cryptographic technologies. His research has appeared in journals such as Information Systems Journal, Structural Equation Modeling, The DATA BASE for Advances in Information Systems, Communications of the Association for Information Systems, Information & Management, Journal of Electronic Commerce Research, Journal of Global Information Management, Schmalenbach Business Review, Supply Chain Management: An International Journal, International Journal of Logistics Management, and Wirtschaftsinformatik (Business & Information Systems Engineering).

Christian Sillaber is a senior fellow at the Zicklin Center at Wharton at the University of Pennsylvania. He holds a Ph.D. in computer science and a law degree. Current research projects focus on compliance and governance in decentralized cryptocurrencies, privacy management and enforcement in virtual currency ecosystems and the role of technology in regulatory compliance. He is a co-organizer of the Wharton Cryptogovernance Workshop and the Reg@Tech workshop series at Wharton.

Analyzing the Potential of DLT-based Applications in Smart Factories

Dominik Roeck, Felix Schöneseiffen, Michael Greger, and Erik Hofmann

Abstract While companies struggle to implement Smart Factory initiatives, the emergence of decentralized Distributed Ledger Technology (DLT) promises to support Smart Factories. However, little is known about the extent to which DLT can support Smart Factory initiatives. Thus, this paper examines whether DLT is a useful addition to the Smart Factory concept in the context of Industry 4.0. The focus of the research lies on practical challenges that manufacturing companies are confronted with when creating Smart Factories and integrating them into their value chain. These challenges were worked out with the help of a literature review and interviews, which were conducted with employees of one of the most renowned industrial automation and digitization companies (undisclosed for confidentiality). Based on this, two DLT concepts were developed and discussed with the experts regarding their respective opportunities, risks, and feasibility. The DLT-based Audit Trail is intended to solve the challenge of creating a detailed, consistent and traceable overview of production processes, while the Crypto-based Agent Logic solves the challenge of setting priorities for orders in a fully automated production process. The results show that DLT integration in the context of the Smart Factory concept is to be regarded as useful and should be driven forward by further research.

Keywords Distributed ledger technology · Supply chain · Manufacturing · Smart factory · Use cases · Blockchain

D. Roeck (✉) · M. Greger · E. Hofmann
Institute of Supply Chain Management, University of St.Gallen, St. Gallen, Switzerland
e-mail: dominik.roeck@unisg.ch

M. Greger
e-mail: michael.greger@student.unisg.ch

E. Hofmann
e-mail: erik.hofmann@unisg.ch

F. Schöneseiffen
Roland Berger, Munich, Germany
e-mail: felix.schoeneseiffen@hsgalumni.ch

© Springer Nature Switzerland AG 2020
H. Treiblmaier and T. Clohessy (eds.), *Blockchain and Distributed Ledger Technology Use Cases*, Progress in IS, https://doi.org/10.1007/978-3-030-44337-5_12

245

1 Introduction

The megatrend of *individualization* is increasingly changing the industrial environment (Heß 2008, p. 18). Nourished by consumers' strive for uniqueness and differentiation, a comeback of the individualized product can be observed (Ewinger et al. 2016, pp. 8–12). While mass production was used across most industries in the twentieth century, a contrary trend can be seen in production in recent years based on the changing customer demand. In order to meet demand requirements, manufacturing companies are trying to switch to individual mass production (lot size one). Thereby, one of the main challenges is to produce customer-specific products on a large scale in a cost-efficient manner.

Industry 4.0,[1] as the fourth industrial revolution, is intended to address this challenge by not only linking the physical and the digital world but also connecting IT systems both within and across organizational boundaries (Kagermann 2013, p. 5). The idea of Industry 4.0 is to create interlinked *Smart Factories* with autonomous processes in which operating units adapt autonomously to new conditions. Thereby, the production of smaller lot sizes can still be achieved in a cost-effective way, despite the increasing complexity of customer demand, shorter product lifecycles and ongoing demand fluctuation (Degenhart 2018, pp. 6–8).

However, the industry has not yet been able to implement the Smart Factory concept across the board because it still faces a large number of challenges (Rossmann et al. 2017, p. 15). Apart from a lack of coordination, leadership commitment, and investment, companies lack a vision and future business cases from a strategic perspective in order to implement Smart Factories successfully (p. 15). In addition, companies find it difficult to identify and prioritize opportunities, miss a roadmap and suffer from a lack of maturity in production automation processes from an implementation perspective (p. 15). This paper is intended to address most of these challenges by generating new implementation ideas based on Distributed Ledger Technology (DLT). DLTs are proclaimed to be a promising technology to support the idea of Smart Factories. The objective is to test their integration within the Smart Factory concept based on expert interviews. A particular focus lies on process improvements within Smart Factories to enable mass customization.

In order to fulfill the objective of this research, the authors build on existing literature on Smart Factory and DLT from the field of Operations Management. In addition, seven interviews with experts from a leading industrial machine manufacturer will be integrated. All interviewees are experts on the topic of Smart Factories and their integration into the value chain of their customers. In this way, this paper is intended to make a significant contribution to an area that has only been researched to a limited extent so far.

---

[1] The term Industry 4.0 was coined by the German Federal Ministry of Education and Research (BMBF), which supports medium-sized companies in various funding programs to actually dare the change to Industry 4.0, the digitization of production (Bundesministerium für Bildung und Forschung 2017).

The following chapter synthesizes the literature review with insights of the interviews with industry experts. Afterwards, the methodology describes the development of DLT-based use cases geared to today's challenges, on which manufacturing companies can base possible pilot projects in the future. Consequently, these DLT-based use cases will be presented. Finally, the paper is rounded off by a summary and an outlook.

2 Literature Review

In the following section, the challenge of customization with decreasing lot sizes in production will be described in order to illustrate the need for value creation networks consisting of decentralized, modular Smart Factories. Afterwards, the Smart Factory concept will be presented and the central interfaces for integration into the supply chain will be determined. In addition, the challenges of the Smart Factory concept will be elaborated, for which literature findings will be supplemented with insights of several expert interviews. Finally, the learnings from selected DLT-based initiatives will be presented, which should be considered when eventually implementing the DLT-based ideas of this paper.

2.1 The Current Challenge in Manufacturing—Customization

To this day, manufacturing companies have been seeking to achieve economic advantages primarily through the standardization of business and production processes. Due to high fixed costs and low variable costs, economies of scale have played a major role in industrial manufacturing so far. However, nowaday's customers are striving for individuality and uniqueness, which requires a product mix with smaller quantities and higher diversity, as opposed to standardized mass production (Reger 2018).

This raises the question of how to efficiently produce customized goods. The greater the variety of products and processes, the more complex the business processes and organizations (Schäfermeyer et al. 2012, p. 263). Thus, the goal is to achieve efficient production of *"lot size one"*, or in other words, the individual mass production (Reger 2018). The lot size is the "quantity of a product type or assembly that is manufactured in a production level as a closed item (lot) without interruption by the production of other products or assemblies" (Voigt 2018). Consequently, to enable the production of individualized products at a large scale the production process must be flexible (Kagermann et al. 2013, p. 19f.). In this way, it is possible to meet any customer requirements without having to deviate from mass production and efficiency (Wende and Kiradjiev 2014, p. 206).

2.2 The Solution—Decentralized, Modular, Autonomous Smart Factories

In the context of Industry 4.0, supply chain networks consist of digitally interlinked *Smart Factories*. The efficient production of small lot sizes can only be achieved with the help of connecting different companies in the value chains. Thereby, fully connecting and adapting production both within and across companies represents a big leap forward in manufacturing. In a network of Smart Factories, production processes will run autonomously, and operating units will learn from production data obtained in order to adapt independently to new challenges and conditions (Lasi et al. 2014, p. 240; Radziwon et al. 2014, pp. 1187–1188; Roddeck 2017, p. 676). For this purpose, the factories will use decentralized information and communication structures (Lucke et al. 2008, p. 115). If, for example, a machine in a factory were to fail, automated notification to the digitally connected "sibling factory" would initiate an increase in production and thus compensate for the loss incurred. The result is a more efficient and agile system that offers less production downtime and greater flexibility for companies compared to today's factories (Burke et al. 2018, p. 2).

However, the Smart Factory concept has not yet been implemented across the board in today's industrial environment (Rossmann et al. 2017, p. 15). Even disruptive companies such as Tesla, which have the self-conception to go new ways in the production of goods and have factories that come closest to the definition of Smart Factories, do a role backwards and replace already installed robots by humans (Aiello 2018). To identify and cover all of the challenges, which companies face when implementing Smart Factories, we did not only analyze the findings of the study already mentioned in the introduction (by Rossmann et al. 2017; a summary will be provided in the methodology in Table 1), but also took advantage of the experts' experience. According to them, the following *challenges* of Smart Factories can be observed on an intraorganizational level:

Table 1 Summary of identified challenges

Challenges according to Rossmann et al. (2017)	Challenges according to industry experts
• Lack of clear business case • Lack of a vision • Lack of maturity in lean shop floor automation processes • Challenges in identification and prioritization of opportunities • Lack of a roadmap	• Lack of M2M communication • Retrofitting of existing machines • Lack of standardized interfaces between manufacturing systems • Lack of mutual trust across manufacturing companies of the same supply chain network

- There is still a lack of close cooperation between the various system integrators (I2[2]), even though the Machine-to-Machine (M2M) communication protocol OPC UA is currently emerging as an international standard (Imtiaz and Jasperneite 2013, pp. 501–504). This is necessary in order to implement the connection on the production level more quickly.
- Retrofitting or integrating older production machines is still a major challenge (I2; I3). A company rarely builds a completely new factory (greenfield factory), but instead often integrates new manufacturing systems into an existing factory (brownfield project). Older plants often do not have the necessary communication interfaces to enable M2M communication. Retrofitting older machines is still associated with high costs, which most medium-sized companies cannot afford.
- There are still no standardized interfaces between the manufacturing systems. This incompatibility in communication leads to data silos of the individual machine manufacturers and makes integration across hierarchies extremely difficult. If the production management wants to access the data and to control the production robot, it has to connect to the robot through a connectivity tool of the respective system integrator first. A higher-level system that enables to control all systems centrally is lacking (I1). Such a system would not only enable data-driven decisions by the management by creating transparency across plants (Schuh et al. 2015, pp. 13–14) but also enable the higher hierarchical levels to control the plants centrally. If, for example, an important customer (key account) places a large order, the management team can prioritize the respective production order (I2).

On an interorganizational level, a lack of mutual trust is the main challenge according to the experts. Mutual trust is one of the most important parameters for success in value creation networks, as in all forms of corporate cooperation (Scherle et al. 2016, pp. 252–253). Manufacturing companies are reluctant to send internal production data to external cloud services. They fear a loss of data sovereignty and data security (I1). Furthermore, companies show a limited willingness to share information with suppliers and customers. On the supply side, organizations fear the risk of losing know-how to the supplier (I2). On the demand side, they fear production issues become known to customers and lead to a lower perceived quality (I1). In addition, businesses do not want to create dependencies on third parties, such as cloud infrastructure providers that operate as data monopoly in the supply chain.

2.3   Lessons Learned from Existing DLT-based Solutions

At the same time, the emergence of DLT has fueled high hopes that the technology can also contribute to other fields beyond finance. When looking at the described Smart

---

[2]"I2" stands for the second expert interview, see Table 2 in methodology for more details.

Factory challenges, DLT seems to be able to tackle all challenges mentioned above—except for the retrofitting of machines, which is a hardware challenge. Assuming that the same DLT infrastructure (on the protocol layer) is used in all Smart Factories of a supply chain network, both the M2M communication and connectivity issues within companies as well as the trust issue between companies can be solved thanks to the attributes of DLT systems[3] (enable a network of independent participants to find consensus on transactions, leading to persistent data records, which are tamper-proof and accessible (at least for network participants). Nevertheless, there are several points, which have to be kept in mind when the implementation of DLT-based projects is planned:

- The limited *speed of transactions within public networks*, which results from transaction validations and network consensus mechanism. The speed determines the communication capability between machines and thus the efficiency of an entire supply chain network. While transaction intermediaries such as Visa claim to be able to perform 24,000 transactions per second (Tps), Bitcoin currently achieves an average of only 7 Tps, Ethereum 15 Tps and IOTA 50 Tps (estimation by O'Neal 2019). Even if there are rumors that Visa's actual performance is 1700 Tps (Sedgwick 2018) and IOTA claims to have the capabilities to perform 1500 Tps (O'Neal 2019), the limited performance of DLT networks has to be considered when DLT-based supply chain projects are planned. One solution could be to use so-called "Layer 2" protocols, which are currently being examined by the Lightning Network.[4]
- The costs incurred through increased *electricity consumption within public networks*, which still outweigh the savings made through the automation of processes. These electricity costs are highly influenced by the respective consensus mechanism approach, which is why more efficient mechanisms, such as Proof-of-Stake (PoS), should be considered.
- A decision regarding the *type of DLT network*—either permission-less or permissioned—has to be made. Often, permissioned (private) ledgers are preferred by companies due to privacy concerns and control over the network. Nevertheless, private ledgers inherently contradict the decentralization aim of DLT. In addition, privacy preservation measures can also be utilized on public ledgers (Morris, as cited in Chandler 2019).

---

[3] According to Rauchs et al. (2018, p. 24), a DLT system can be defined as *"[…] a system of electronic records that enables a network of independent participants to establish a consensus around the authoritative ordering of cryptographically-validated ('signed') transactions. These records are made persistent by replicating the data across multiple nodes, and tamper-evident by linking them by cryptographic hashes. The shared result of the reconciliation/consensus process - the 'ledger' - serves as the authoritative version for these records"*.

[4] See https://lightning.network for further information.

3 Methodology

To solve the problems when setting up a decentralized, modular Smart Factory (see Table 1), DLT-based application scenarios will now be developed. The applied methodology can clearly be assigned to design-oriented research (*Design Science Research*) (cf. Simon 1996). The ultimate goal is to solve a problem (design concept of a Smart Factory) that has not been dealt with sufficiently yet.

For the development of the use cases, the process design of Takeda et al. (1990) shall be used (see Fig. 1). They divide the research design into five steps of the "design cycle": Awareness of the problem, suggestion, development, evaluation, and conclusion. In the beginning, a *problem awareness* must be established (Takeda et al. 1990, p. 43).

In the context of this paper, the problem, as explained in the previous chapter, is the cost-efficient production of products tailored to individual customer needs. Smart factories enable manufacturing companies to gain competitive advantages and promise that they remain competitive in the future. However, according to the findings of a survey by Rossmann et al. (2017) with 580 manufacturing companies participating, as well as personally conducted interviews with automation and supply chain experts in this study, the industry faces various challenges when it comes to Smart Factory initiatives (see Table 1). Thus, a scientific problem awareness was generated and necessary information about the described challenges was collected

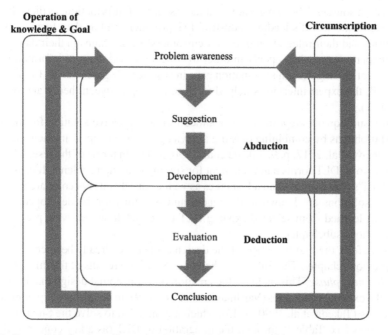

Fig. 1 Research design (own illustration, based on Takeda et al. 1990, p. 45)

Table 2 Table of expert interviews conducted

Interview ID	Date	Function
1st round: focus on Smart Factory challenges		
I1	2018, July 03	Project Leader Inhouse Consulting (Operations)
I2	2018, July 04	Member of Senior Management—Industry 4.0 Division
I3	2018, July 13	Project Leader Inhouse Consulting (Operations)
2nd round: focus on DLT use cases		
I4	2018, September 07	Member of Senior Management—Industry 4.0 Division
I5	2018, September 07	Project Leader Inhouse Consulting (Operations)
I6	2018, September 13	Member of Senior Management—Industry 4.0 Division
I7	2018, September 13	Project Leader Inhouse Consulting (Operations)

from both sources. The experts are a valuable source of information, as they all work for one of the world's leading industrial IoT providers and as they focus on smart factories and their integration into their customers' value chains in their daily work. The experts were asked openly in order to collect a broad mass of information and to prevent closing certain information gaps in advance (Bogner et al. 2014, p. 2324). Overall, the expert interviews helped to close the gap between theory and practice (Table 2).

The subsequent *suggestion phase* aimed to find a creative solution for the identified problems by combining existing knowledge (key concepts) and new elements (Vaishnavi et al. 2017, p. 9; Takeda et al. 1990, p. 43). In terms of the research focus of this work, DLT forms a new element for solving existing problems. It is assumed that DLT's functionality and advantages as well as disadvantages compared to existing IT solutions are known to the reader and will thus not be developed further. Lessons learned from selected existing DLT use cases, however, were presented in the previous subchapter.

Therefore, the first two steps of the design cycle have already been completed in the previous chapter. The following chapter contains the results of the third step, the *development phase*. This includes the creation of a conceptual design that is aligned with the existing challenges (Vaishnavi et al. 2017, p. 9). In detail, the chapter presents use cases (Takeda et al. 1990, p. 43), which are intended to solve the Smart Factory challenges (see Table 1) through the integration of DLT (as a key concept). Based on the previous chapter, an epistemologically and theoretically guided construction mode is to be pursued. Thereby a general solution was specified by the application of DLT in the context of Smart Factories.

Subsequently, in the *evaluation phase*, the fourth step of the design cycle, the developed application examples will be examined with regard to predefined criteria highlighted in the context of problem awareness (Vaishnavi et al. 2017, p. 9). The economic implications of the proposed use cases will be determined on a theoretical basis. In addition, the individual opportunities and risks are evaluated with the help of further explorative expert interviews and discussed with regard to their feasibility.

Finally, the *conclusion* summarizes the results of the work in the last chapter and shows which of the use cases could be adopted and which have to be modified (Takeda et al. 1990, p. 43). Design science research can contribute to different types of knowledge (Gregor and Hevner 2013). Derived from the knowlegde contribution framework, this work falls into the category improvement, which develops new, creative solutions for existing problems (Gregor and Hevner 2013, pp. 345–346). Manufacturing companies should be able to build on the concepts of the developed use cases with regard to future pilot projects and the responsible persons should be able to get an idea of the business implications so that they can better assess the practicability of these concepts. The conclusion represents the end of the investigation cycle and can be used to build a basis for further research (Vaishnavi et al. 2017, p. 10). The paper is supposed to serve as a basis for further research in the field of DLT in an industrial context. Possible research approaches are therefore also proposed in the last chapter.

4 Use Cases

In the following, two elaborated DLT-based use cases are presented, which can help in the implementation of the Smart Factory concept.

4.1 DLT-based Audit Trail

To obtain a detailed, consistent and traceable overview of production processes, manufacturing companies use audit trails. These record sensor data from production, thus enabling production management to identify process improvements or monitor product quality (Schiefer et al. 2003, pp. 1–2). On this basis, production management can make a reliable statement about individual components, product modifications or production conditions before they ship a product to the end customer (Jovanovic 2014). As learned from the interviews with the industry experts (see Table 1), a key challenge of manufacturers is the lack of M2M and system communication. The interfaces often lack standardization; thus data is often not completely aggregated from the outset (I1). This limits data-driven decisions and has a negative impact on the production level (Li et al. 2009, p. 5019).

DLT can address this challenge: a *DLT-based audit trail* can automatically record audit-compliant production data. Based on the Smart Factory concept of Fujitsu, a DLT-based network can be used as a higher-level IT system that maps the entire production process and bundles the data of various system integrators. This audit trail can, on the one hand, support the production management in controlling the production process and thus enable internal quality assurance, but on the other hand, it can also be passed on to third parties (insurance companies, certification agencies, auditors, etc.). Third parties must be able to trace the production process for their individual services in a forgery-proof manner. For this, data stored in a distributed ledger is encrypted by the private key and stored with a time stamp. From a retrospective, it can be determined which party was involved in the production process with the help of the corresponding timestamp and action specifications. Once stored within the DLT-based network, the data is traceable and can no longer be modified due to cryptographic encryption.

Within an *illustrative example* in the context of a Smart Factory, each manufacturing unit (MU) within the Smart Factory represents a "node" at the production level, i.e. a communication point between production and the distributed ledger (see Fig. 2). The nodes transmit and store product-specific (size, origin, color, temperature, clamping time, torque, etc.) and process-specific information (production flow, system integrators involved, etc.) in the DLT network.

At the start of the production process, the goal of production is set based on predefined production and process parameters (e.g. dimensions, surface quality, etc.). Subsequently, required parts are registered, their quality is checked, and finally, all corresponding information is stored in the DLT network. If the delivered parts meet the quality standards, they are marked and stored in the central warehouse of the Smart Factory. At this point, the sensors installed in the warehouse monitor the local

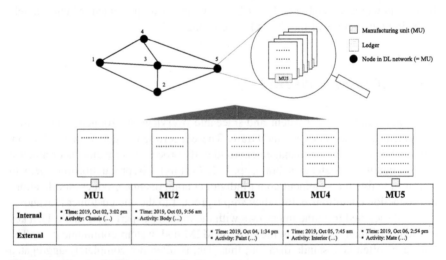

Fig. 2 Use Case 1—DLT-based Audit Trail

conditions, such as humidity or temperature, and transmit this information to the DLT network, linked to the corresponding component. This enables both the production management and the production robots, to monitor the quality of the individual parts and to check them before installation. In case of deviations from the defined quality standards, the identified part can be removed from the process at an early stage. If a part is required by a manufacturing unit during the production process, the assigned transportation vehicle transports it to the respective manufacturing unit. This process is also recorded and shared within the network. By this, each network participant can see where the component is located in the factory. Before the manufacturing unit receives the component, it compares the recorded data of the component with specified quality criteria and carries out a target/actual comparison. In this way, the manufacturing unit ensures that it is an original part and that there is no damage to it. In addition to quality control, the respective production robot can compare the stored product information with product-specific production criteria—for example, specific tightening torques of screws—and adapt the production process accordingly. In the next step, the manufacturing unit installs the respective individual part. Within the manufacturing units, a large number of sensors record the production process—for example, temperatures during welding, torque during the fastening of screws or the time during which the object is clamped—and transmit it via the communication interface to the DLT network. In this way, the production conditions can be recorded holistically and viewed by the production management. Once the production step has been completed, the product is returned to a transportation vehicle, which transports it to the next manufacturing unit. Until completion, the product passes through various manufacturing units in which the process described above is repeated. As a result, periodic quality controls are implemented before each manufacturing unit along the manufacturing process. If the predefined criteria are not met, a notification is sent to the production management so that they can intervene at an early stage. Before the products are handed over to the end customer, final quality control is carried out. In the case of individualized products, this quality control must be based on specific process steps and cannot check standard product properties. The production data recorded in the DLT Audit Trail can be compared with the predefined product and process criteria. In this way, the entire range of customization can be checked without significant additional effort. The quality controls can be mapped within smart contracts to further automate the process. The delivery conditions agreed before the start of production can be compared with the data of the DLT audit trail. If these match during the final quality control, the smart contract programmed on the DLT network can automatically initiate the product shipment to the end customer and trigger both the dispatch of the invoice as well as the payment from the end customer to the manufacturer.

This use case is based on the following *assumptions*:

- The quality of a product, the production conditions and system integrators involved in production can be recorded by sensors in a tamper-proof manner.
- A communication interface can transmit the data acquired by sensors to the DLT network.

- The data recorded within the distributed ledger can be accessed in real-time and there are no time delays due to transaction validation or consensus mechanisms.
- The production management is interested in transparent production conditions, periodic quality controls, and automated goods issue.
- The manufacturer and the customer have agreed on uniform production conditions and quality criteria before the start of production and have recorded these in Smart Contracts.
- No variable quality aspects are included in the supply contracts.

A DLT-based audit trail provides several *advantages,* such as a transparent picture of the production (available capacities and capacity utilization) of the manufacturing company. This allows the company to make data-driven production decisions that improve the company's efficiency in production (Tao et al. 2018). For instance, the real-time transparency created for production would enable reliable quality assurance during the production process by allowing production management to adjust in real-time. The DLT-based network allows the manufacturing robots to access all product characteristics and compare them with the delivery conditions. Through the continuous target-performance comparison within a manufacturing unit, the robots can send a warning notification via a dashboard to the production management, which can intervene in the process and minimize damage in the case of deviation. Thus, costs due to production errors can be minimized and output increased.

In addition, a DLT-based audit trail enables automated production coordination. As with Fujitsu's Smart Factory concept, in addition to process data, all product and component-specific information are stored on the distribute ledger. This would give the manufacturing robot access to product details necessary for further processing of the products. Similar to the industrial M2M communication protocol OPC UA, machine, production, and product data would be described in a readable way for machines (OPC Foundation 2018). Since each manufacturing unit has an overview of production through its individual copy of the production data, each station can react individually to previous production steps and possible special features. Thus, the DLT network in a decentralized production logic can enable the manufacturing robot to have its own autonomous control.

Furthermore, since each manufacturing unit has an identical record of the data set and acts on this basis, the DLT guarantees a single source of truth for manufacturing. If, for example, the production management queries the current production status, it is ensured that a uniform result is generated, and that the data do not contradict each other due to a large number of interfaces (I1). This data integrity is particularly important for modular production designs without uniform product flow or logistics paths.

Furthermore, manufacturing companies can rely on audit-proof data, which is why the experts see no risks about data security in the case of a DLT-based audit trail (I4; I5; I6; I7). This can be highly relevant for third parties such as insurance companies. Audit-proof data would minimize the effort of insurance companies and thus reduce the costs that can be passed on to policyholders through a lower insurance premium.

Lower premiums would, in turn, lead to lower overhead costs for policyholders and to an improved cost structure (Plinke 2000, p. 677).

Moreover, it has to be noted that the stored machine and system data can be used to derive information about the condition of the systems, the wear and tear of the robots as well as the supply levels of oil or other raw materials. Condition monitoring by recording and aggregating device-specific data is a prerequisite for advanced methods such as predictive maintenance, in which proactive maintenance work is carried out to reduce downtimes (March and Scudder 2017). Since status information of specific manufacturing units can be spread throughout the manufacturing network, the manufacturing process of products can be improved further by adjusting the order of manufacturing units involved for example. Additionally, if minimum filling levels are reached, refilling processes can be initiated automatically via smart contracts. This prevents unnecessary downtime of the production robots due to missing operating materials and thus increases production efficiency (Liu et al. 2012, pp. 1–3).

Last but not least, the feasibility is definitely an advantage. Overall, the experts expect the probability of implementation of such a DLT-based audit trail to exceed 50 percent, since there are no fundamental technological obstacles that would impede implementation (I4; I5).

However, the experts also see the following *challenges*. First, a suitable DLT infrastructure must be found (I6). The well-known infrastructures Ethereum and IOTA are unsuitable because they cannot process the necessary amounts of data in real-time (I6). A large number of data generated by second-specific sensors cannot be processed by well-known DLT protocols in real-time. Since only the use of large, well-known DLT protocols with large developer communities makes sense for large manufacturing companies (I4), an intelligent solution consisting of cloud and DLT can be the solution (I6). Large amounts of data would be stored in a proprietary cloud and the generated hash values aggregated in a DLT network. In this way, the data can be stored, guaranteed to be counterfeit-proof and still made accessible in real-time.

Second, the *costs* must be taken into account, which consist of implementation costs, regular maintenance work and the power consumption of the DLT network. These costs can, for example, be divided between the manufacturers and system integrators depending on the individual cost savings (I4; I5; I6; I7).

Third, there would be a potential for conflict about data sovereignty (I5; I6; I7). Currently, large automobile manufacturers do not allow the release of company-internal production data and do not store them in external cloud applications, because the data must remain on-premise (in-house). Since data is shared between the nodes of various intra- and interorganizational Smart Factories, data would also be stored externally from a single company's perspective.

Fourth, data sharing is a concern for two experts (I5; I6). For example, data often cannot or should not be shared in detail with customers today because no production process runs ideally and details about minor quality problems can lead to a negative image of the manufacturer. Furthermore, machine data is not even shared with machine manufacturers today. Thus, intelligent data management with individual read accesses would have to be implemented in the DLT-based Audit

Trail, which would allow the manufacturing company to release only certain data for specific organizations (I6).

4.2 Crypto-Based Agent Logic

The background of this DLT use case is the challenge within the Smart Factory to set priorities for orders in the production process. Customer orders are normally assigned different priorities within the production process, depending on the relevance of the customer to the manufacturing company (I2). For example, the most valuable customers gain priority in the manufacturing process through human intervention using key account management (Woodburn and McDonald 2012, pp. 8–10; I2). Individual support of key accounts is of enormous importance for a company because active customer management has a positive effect on overall profitability (Woodburn and McDonald 2012, pp. 4–5). Accordingly, autonomous, intelligent factories address this capability in the future.

A possible solution would be the implementation of a *crypto-based agent logic* (see Fig. 3) in which the product (agent) can buy its own production from the manufacturing robot with the help of a cryptocurrency. In addition to the robots that carry out production steps, priorities in the production process have a price tag, which can consequently be purchased by the agent. This idea was derived from two pilot projects. On the one hand, the ElaadNL[5] project, in which electric cars automatically pay for electricity purchased on the basis of IOTA, and on the other hand the Fujitsu[6] pilot project, in which robots pay each other for services in the factory. In this way, the agents (products) can make decisions autonomously and would have the ability to coordinate their own production based on their needs (e.g. time criticality) (Nebel

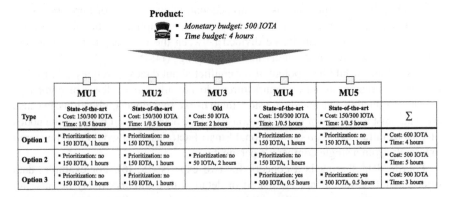

Fig. 3 Use case 2—crypto-based agent logic (including production flow example)

---

[5]See https://www.elaad.nl for further information.

[6]See https://www.youtube.com/watch?v=J-mrQdqVg2I for further information.

et al. 2017, p. 13). Thereby, a DLT-based cryptocurrency is used as a coordination medium that opens up possibilities for the agent to act. On the basis of this, the agent can calculate its individual production costs. Accordingly, the agent can also estimate the number of tokens (cryptocurrency) that are required in order to be preferred by production robots and thus achieve the desired time-saving in production. An individually assigned e-wallet would serve as a billing basis, which stores the manufacturing costs (incl. tokens) required for production. The costs for such a DLT network are settled by the plant operator or the machine operator (I4; I5; I6; I7). However, these costs can be directly passed on to the end customer with the help of a surcharge for fulfilling an ad-hoc production request immediately for instance (I7). Alternatively, they can also indirectly be outweighed by increased customer satisfaction, which has a positive effect on the company's sales development (I7).

In the following DLT application example, the concept is illustrated using a greatly simplified automotive production. The manufacturing costs are a virtual allocation rate, and the IOTA protocol was selected as an example of the infrastructure. At the beginning of the production process, the agent is informed exemplarily that a car must be produced within four hours at the production price of 500 IOTA. On the basis of this order, the agent asks the manufacturing unit for available capacities and the respective usage costs. The agent aggregates these answers and develops time- and cost-optimized production flow options, as shown in Fig. 3. In this example, the agent is given the choice of prioritizing the time/production target parameter or the cost parameter based on the responses received from the manufacturing unit. The agent has the possibility to guide the product through four state-of-the-art, fast and expensive manufacturing units and finish the car according to the production target within four hours. However, instead of 500 IOTA, he would have to spend 600 IOTA and thus exceed the target manufacturing costs. Alternatively, the agent can use three expensive manufacturing units as well as one cheap unit and pay 500 IOTA for production, but the car would not be done within four hours. As a third option, the agent can complete the car in three hours but would have to pay 900 IOTA to use the four state-of-the-art manufacturing units and two of them in prioritized mode. In this case, the agent has to decide whether he wants to make the route through the production plant in a time-driven or cost-driven manner. This example shows the interface between the manufacturing perspective and the overall business perspective, as the agent can control the factory on a cost or time-driven basis, depending on the customer order and profile.

This use case is based on the following *assumptions*:

- The production is based on autonomous, decentralized Smart Factories.
- There are two types of manufacturing units: an expensive and a low-cost cell, which represent different numbers of production process steps and are priced at different levels for the agent.
- An expensive manufacturing unit maps more joining processes and thus has a higher cycle time, but nevertheless shortens the production time compared to low-cost manufacturing unit, since fewer production stages and logistics processes are required.

- The processing costs of a cell can be adequately determined by the manufacturing unit using the cryptocurrency, depending on the cost of machine wear, the capital tied up by the types of robots installed and the raw materials required.
- External parameters influencing manufacturing costs can be included by manufacturing units.
- The agent can pay the production unit for the services received with the specified IOTA value and can use the individual "e-wallet" for this.
- The agent can select the production cells individually and map the production of the car using different production units.
- The agent only has to consider two parameters regarding production planning, namely (a) the production time and (b) the costs.
- The use of different units has a direct and measurable impact on the parameters (a) and (b).
- The agent is given a production target (e.g. a car per hour) and a cost rate (e.g. 500 IOTA).
- No time delays arise from transaction validation/consensus mechanisms in the DLT network.

The concept offers two major *advantages*. On the one hand, the crypto-based agent logic creates a high level of transparency with regard to product-specific manufacturing costs. A transparent overview of the manufacturing costs enables simpler control of the costs for the producer (Bendul and Apostu 2017, pp. 1–3). In corporate planning, target values for manufacturing costs are defined, which can be compared with the actual manufacturing costs of the products recorded in the e-wallets. Among other things, this can help to identify inefficiencies (throughput times, utilization of machines, etc.) and initiate the necessary corrective measures to optimize production and increase the overall profitability of the company. In extreme cases, pay-per-use pricing models of manufacturers can even be implemented transparently in this way. Here a scenario would be conceivable in which all production robots of a shop floor operate on a pay-per-use basis and their manufacturers are paid depending on use— per activity of the robot. In such a case, it is very important to generate a forgery-proof and traceable usage history. Furthermore, from the manufacturer's point of view, it is attractive to be paid directly via a cryptocurrency once the service has been rendered. This would enable a constant and use-dependent cash flow.

On the other hand, in the previous example, it was easy to see that the agent can be guided through the factory both cost-driven and time-driven by parameter settings. This flexibility within production can become an enormous competitive advantage in the future due to ever more complex customer inquiries, shorter product life cycles and thus the increasing demand for higher variety in production (I4). It also enables new, flexible pricing options that can be offered to the manufacturing company's customers. Manufacturers have different types of customers with different needs in terms of the two primary parameters manufacturing cost and production time. For example, customer A follows a just-in-time concept, while customer B orders on stock (Fandel and Francois 1993, pp. 23–24). The former requires priorities in the production process and is prepared to incur higher costs. On the other hand, the stock-ordering customer is more interested in reducing the cost and is willing to prioritize the process and extend his own delivery time. By integrating the DLT concept, the manufacturer would be able to accurately determine the production time, allowing them to respond to complementary customer needs. In our example, Customer A's agent can use IOTA to purchase prioritization within the factory by setting appropriate targets. This additional effort can be transparently mapped via the individually assigned e-wallet. For customer B, the agent would be instructed to prioritize the manufacturing cost parameter and to use the cheaper cells. The result of this planning would be an increased cost price for customer A in favor of a shortened production time and a discounted price for customer B due to extended delivery time. This would be a modification of dynamic pricing, which increases a company's sales if adequately designed and adapted to the customer (Chen and Jasin 2018, pp. 22–23).

However, the security risk and the costly implementation of the concept are clear *disadvantages*. If an agent can be exploited by third parties, there would be an enormous security risk which can lead to considerable damage (I6). For example, an external party can manipulate an agent to block machines or carry out targeted distributed denial-of-service (DDOS) attacks.

The evaluation of the implementation probabilities of a crypto-based agent logic is characterized by a high degree of uncertainty—the number of underlying assumptions shows the visionary nature of this use case. Therefore, a distinction has to be made between the two components of the agent-based planning model and the crypto-based payment model. The integration of the DLT in the form of cryptocurrency can be accomplished with relatively little effort since it is only a matter of changed payment flows in pay-per-use models (I6).

On the other hand, the implementation of the agent-based planning model for production involves significantly higher implementation costs for manufacturing companies (I6). This is a holistic and structural change in the production logic, which is time-consuming and resource-intensive. In addition, there might be a lack of willingness to fully automate a factory and thus replace people in production (I5). For this reason, fundamental societal questions, such as the role of the human being in the factory, must first be answered.

5 Conclusion

The purpose of this paper was to examine whether manufacturing companies face challenges in creating smart factories (and integrating them into the value chain) that can be solved or mitigated by integrating DLT. On the basis of the literature research on the Smart Factory concept, as well as the existing challenges in practice and the central attributes of DLT, two use cases were developed: the DLT-based audit trail and the crypto-based agent logic.

From a process perspective, the application scenarios tailored to the Smart Factory challenges offer operational added value compared to the status quo. The *DLT-based audit trail* creates transparency in production. In addition, by tracking the entire production process and digitally replicating the manufacturing level, quality controls can be automated, robot-specific re-orders can be better coordinated, and revision-proof production data can be transferred to third parties such as insurance companies. These attributes imply cost savings for the manufacturer. Furthermore, the *Crypto-based agent logic* creates a new decentralized production logic. The product acts as an agent that is aware of its own manufacturing history, its current state and alternative paths to the target state and thus coordinates its own production. Along with the production flow, the agent pays for the services received using an individual, crypto-based e-wallet and thereby transparently maps the production costs. In an autonomously operating Smart Factory, priorities or other process adaptations can be controlled via higher agent budgets. The integration of the DLT in a pay-per-use scenario is of interest here, in which the robots are loaned and billed according to use. In this use case, the user of the robot would have an interest in changing the recorded usage data in his favor in order to reduce his usage costs. This manipulation can be prevented by recording in a DLT network. In addition, constant payment flows to the robot manufacturer are made possible, since an automatic, crypto-based cash flow would occur for the use of the robot—after completion of the manufacturing step. The integration of DLT thus implies optimization of the pay-per-use business model and can be used as a coordination medium in agent-based manufacturing. The possibility of dynamic pricing on the sales side holds additional sales potential.

With regard to the *research focus*, the developed use cases support the concept of the Smart Factory and solve strategic as well as practical Smart Factory challenges (see Table 1) in different ways. While both cases provide an idea of potential future business cases, the DLT-based Audit Trail addresses the challenge of system interfaces by creating a consistent, transparent ledger and optimizing coordination at the production level as well as the company-internal hierarchical integration. While the Crypto-based Agent Logic serves as a vision for the automation of shop floor processes, it supports the manufacturer in the decentralization aimed for within the framework of Industry 4.0 and, in this context, enables more flexibility in the production process. The above arguments lead to the conclusion that integration makes sense in the context of the Smart Factory concept and triggers further research, on topics such as the retrofitting of existing machines. An integration of the DLT can facilitate the creation of a Smart Factory integrated into the value creation network and support manufacturing companies in the Industry 4.0 in producing efficiently despite decreasing lot sizes, high product variety, and volatile demand. It has to be noted that the use cases were presented at a conceptual level based on the knowledge of the experts. In order to make a holistic statement on their operational added value and influence on the Smart Factory processes, these would have to be further elaborated and quantified. Above all, the *assumptions* underlying the use cases must be validated. With Crypto-based Agent Logic, for example, it would be necessary to discuss which variables have to be included in the pricing of the individual manufacturing units, according to which rules the agent can negotiate the price with the manufacturing units, and how to ensure that every order is implemented—and that certain customers do not fall off the grid due to priorities granted to others. In addition, a comprehensive *technical analysis* is required. It is necessary to evaluate the potential DLT protocol that suits best for the and what the individual opportunities and risks are. The various market positions of the customers and industries in which they operate have to be taken into account across all use cases. It is obvious that the integration of DLT, depending on the industry and market position of the applying company, will lead to different levels of efficiency gains. On this basis, the resulting costs and operational benefits for a *business case* would have to be quantified. In addition, the use cases have to be tested with regard to possible brownfield adaptations. In very few cases a completely new factory is built, which is why the possibility of integration into existing factories is another relevant research approach.

References

Aiello, C. (2018, April 13). Elon Musk admits humans are sometimes superior to robots, in a tweet about Tesla delays. *CNBC*. Retrieved from https://www.cnbc.com/2018/04/13/elon-musk-admits-humans-are-sometimes-superior-to-robots.html.

Bendul, J., & Apostu, V. (2017). An accuracy investigation of product cost estimation in automotive die manufacturing. *International Journal of Business Administration, 8*(7), 1–15. https://doi.org/10.5430/ijba.v8n7p1.

Bogner, A., Littig, B., & Menz, W. (2014). *Interviews mit Experten: eine praxisorientierte Einführung*. Wiesbaden: Springer-Verlag. Retrieved from https://link.springer.com/content/pdf/10.1007%2F978-3-531-19416-5.pdf.

Bundesministerium für Bildung und Forschung [BMBF]. (2017, August). Industrie 4.0. Innovationen für die Produktion von morgen [brochure]. Retrieved from https://www.bmbf.de/pub/Industrie_4.0.pdf.

Burke, R., Mussomeli, A., Laaper, S., Hartigan, M., & Sniderman, B. (2018). *The Smart Factory: Responsive, adaptive, connected manufacturing* (Series on Industry 4.0, digital manufacturing enterprises, and digital supply chain networks). Deloitte University Press. Retrieved from https://www2.deloitte.com/content/dam/insights/us/articles/4051_The-smart-factory/DUP_The-smart-factory.pdf.

Chandler, S. (2019, August 02). What is the difference between blockchain and DLT. *COIN TELEGRAPH*. Retrieved from https://cointelegraph.com/news/what-is-the-difference-between-blockchain-and-dlt.

Chen, Y., & Jasin, S. (2018). *Power of Dynamic Pricing in Revenue Management with Strategic (Forward-Looking)Customers*. Retrieved from https://papers.ssrn.com/sol3/papers.cfm?abstract_id=3197959.

Degenhart, E. (2018, July 27). Schlagkräftiger ja, Zerschlagen nein. *Handelsblatt*, S. 6.

Ewinger, D., Ternès, A., Koerbel, J., & Towers, I. (Ed.). (2016). Individualisierung der Gesellschaft. In *Arbeitswelt im Zeitalter der Individualisierung: Multigrafie und Multi-Option der Generation Y* (pp. 5–12). Wiesbaden: Springer Gabler. Retrieved from https://www.springer.com/cda/content/document/cda_downloaddocument/9783658127527-c1.pdf?SGWID=0-0-45-1557570-p179994931.

Fandel, G., & Francois, P. (1993). Just-in-Time-Produktion und-Beschaffung Funktionsweise, Einsatzvoraussetzungen und Grenzen. In H. Albach (Ed.), *Industrielles management* (pp. 23–36). Wiesbaden: Springer Gabler. Retrieved from https://link.springer.com/chapter/10.1007/978-3-663-02130-8_2.

Gregor, S., & Hevner, A. (2013). Positioning and presenting design science research for maximum impact. *MIS Quarterly, 37*(2), 337–355. Retrieved from https://pdfs.semanticscholar.org/82a8/6371976aaf181a477745148eab07bb9ed143.pdf.

Heß, W. (2008). Ein Blick in die Zukunft – acht Megatrends, die Wirtschaft und Gesellschaft verändern (Working Paper No. 103). *Allianz Dresdner Economic Research*. Retrieved from https://www.allianz.com/v_1339508238000/media/current/de/images/ein_blick_in_die_zukunft_acht_megatrends.pdf.

Imtiaz, J. & Jasperneite, J. (2013). Scalability of OPC-UA down to the chip level enables "Internet of Things". *Industrial Informatics (INDIN), 11*, 500–505. Retrieved from https://www.researchgate.net/profile/Juergen_Jasperneite/publication/261161659_Scalability_of_OPCUA_down_to_the_chip_level_enables_Internet_of_Things/links/004635367a8832bdf1000000/Scalability-of-OPC-UA-down-to-the-chip-level-enables-Internet-of-Things.pdf.

Jovanovic, S. (2014). *The Importance of Audit Trails and Device History Records* [Video]. Retrieved from https://www.youtube.com/watch?v=MK-rETo2Q_s.

Kagermann, H., Wahlster, W., & Helbig, J. (2013). *Umsetzungsempfehlungen für das Zukunftsprojekt Industrie 4.0*. Bundesministerium für Bildung und Forschung: Abschlussbericht des Arbeitskreises Industrie 4.0. Retrieved from https://www.bmbf.de/files/Umsetzungsempfehlungen_Industrie4_0.pdf.

Lasi, H., Fettke, P., Kemper, H.-G., Feld, T., & Hoffmann, M. (2014). Industrie 4.0. *Wirtschaftsinformatik, 56*(4), 261–264. https://doi.org/10.1007/s11576-014-0424-4.

Li, L., Chang, Q., & Ni, J. (2009). Data driven bottleneck detection of manufacturing systems. *International Journal of Production Research, 47*(18), 5019–5036. https://doi.org/10.1080/00207540701881860.

Liu, J., Chang, Q., Xiao, G., & Biller, S. (2012). The costs of downtime incidents in serial multistage manufacturing systems. *Journal of Manufacturing Science and Engineering, 134*(2), 134–144. Retrieved from https://manufacturingscience.asmedigitalcollection.asme.org/article.aspx?articleID=1461053.

Lucke, D., Constantinescu, C., & Westkämper, E. (2008). Smart factory—A step towards the next generation of manufacturing. In M. Mitsuishi, K. Ueda & F. Kimura (Ed.), *Manufacturing systems and technologies for the new frontier* (pp. 115–118). London: Springer. Retrieved from https://doi.org/10.1007/978-1-84800-267-8_23.

March, S. T., & Scudder, G. D. (2017). Predictive maintenance: strategic use of IT in manufacturing organizations. *Information Systems Frontiers*, 1–15. https://doi.org/10.1007/s10796-017-9749-z.

Nebel, B., Lindner, F., & Engesser, T. (2017). *Multi-agent systems*. Albert Ludwig Universität Freiburg, Lehrstuhl für Informatik, Lecture 1. Retrieved from https://gki.informatik.uni-freiburg.de/teaching/ss17/multiagent-systems/lecture01.pdf.

O'Neal, S. (2019, January 22). Who scales it best? Inside blockchains' ongoing transactions-per-second race. *COINTELEGRAPH*. Retrieved from https://cointelegraph.com/news/who-scales-it-best-inside-blockchains-ongoing-transactions-per-second-race.

OPC Foundation. (2018). What is OPC UA? Retrieved from https://opcfoundation.org/.

Plinke, W. (2000). Einführung in die industrielle Kosten-und Leistungsrechnung. In M. Kleinaltenkamp & W. Plinke (Eds.),*Technischer vertrieb* (pp. 615–689). Berlin: Springer. Retrieved from https://doi.org/10.1007/978-3-642-57165-7_8.

Radziwon, A., Bilberg, A., Bogers, M., & Madsen, E. S. (2014). The smart factory: Exploring adaptive and flexible manufacturing solutions. *Procedia Engineering, 69*, 1184–1190. Retrieved from https://doi.org/10.1016/j.proeng.2014.03.108.

Rauchs, M., Glidden, A., Gordon, B., Pieters, G. C., Recanatini, M., Rostand, F., Zhang, B. Z., et al. (2018). *Distributed ledger technology systems: A conceptual framework*. Retrieved from https://www.jbs.cam.ac.uk/fileadmin/user_upload/research/centres/alternative-finance/downloads/2018-10-26-conceptualising-dlt-systems.pdf.

Reger, J. (2018). Losgröße 1 in Serie produzieren. *Maschinenmarkt, 13*, 42–45. Retrieved from https://www.wiso-net.de/document/MAMA__453028120.

Roddeck, W. (2017). Sensoren und Aktoren. In A. Böge & W. Böge (Ed.), *Handbuch Maschinenbau* (pp. 675–700). Retrieved from https://link.springer.com/chapter/10.1007/978-3-658-12529-5_37.

Rossmann, M., Khadikar, A., Le Franc, P., Perea, L. Schneider-Maul, R., Buvat, J. & Ghosh, A. (2017). Smart Factories: How can manufacturers realize the potential of digital industrial revolution. *Capgemini*. Retrieved from https://www.capgemini.com/wp-content/uploads/2017/07/smart_factories-how_can_manufacturers_realize_the_potential_of_digital_industrial_revolution.pdf.

Schäfermeyer, M., Rosenkranz, C., & Holten, R. (2012). The impact of business process complexity on business process standardization. *Business & Information Systems Engineering, 4*, 261–270. https://doi.org/10.1007/s12599-012-0224-6.

Scherle, N., Boven, C., & Stangel-Meseke, M. (2016). Scheitern in internationalen Unternehmenskooperationen. In S. Kunert (Ed.), *Failure management: Ursachen und Folgen des Scheiterns* (pp. 249–270). Berling: Springer Gabler. Retrieved from https://link.springer.com/chapter/10.1007/978-3-662-47357-3_15.

Schiefer, J., Jeng, J. J., & Bruckner, R. M. (2003). *Real-time workflow audit data integration into data warehouse systems*. Retrieved from https://thoas2.isis.tuwien.ac.at/~js/download/ecis2003.pdf.

Schuh, G., Reuter, C., Hauptvogel, A., & Dölle, C. (2015). Hypotheses for a theory of production in the context of Industrie 4.0. In C. Brecher (Ed.), *Advances in Production Technology* (pp. 11–23). Springer Open. Retrieved from https://link.springer.com/content/pdf/10.1007%2F978-3-319-12304-2_2.pdf.

Sedgwick, K. (2018, April 20). No, Visa Doesn't Handle 24,000 TPS and Neither Does Your Pet Blockchain. *Bitcoin.com*. Retrieved from https://news.bitcoin.com/no-visa-doesnt-handle-24000-tps-and-neither-does-your-pet-blockchain/.

Simon, H. A. (1996). *The sciences of the artificial*. Massachusetts: MIT Press.

Takeda, H., Veerkamp, P., Tomiyama, T., & Yoshikawa, H. (1990). Modeling design processes. *AI Magazine, 11*(4), 37–48. https://doi.org/10.1609/aimag.v11i4.855.

Tao, F., Qi, Q., Liu, A. & Kusiak, A. (2018). Data-driven smart manufacturing. *Journal of Manufacturing Systems*. Retrieved from https://doi.org/10.1016/j.jmsy.2018.01.006.

Vaishnavi, V., Kuechler, W., & Petter, S. (2017). *Design science research in information systems*. Retrieved from https://www.desrist.org/design-research-in-information-systems/.

Voigt, K.-I. (2018). Losgröße definition. In *Gabler Wirtschaftslexikon*. Retrieved from https://wirtschaftslexikon.gabler.de/definition/losgroesse-40747/version-264125.

Wende, J., & Kiradjiev, P. (2014). An implementation of batch size 1 using the principles of Industrie 4.0. *Elektrotechnik und Informationstechnik, 131*(7), 202–206. https://doi.org/10.1007/s00502-014-0222-0.

Woodburn, D., & McDonald, M. (2012). *Key Account Management: The Definite Guide* (3rd ed.). Chichester: Wiley. Retrieved from https://onlinelibrary.wiley.com/doi/pdf/10.1002/9781119207252.ch1.

Dominik Roeck is Ph.D. candidate and research associate at the Institute of Supply Chain Management at the University of St.Gallen Switzerland. Mr. Roeck holds a M.Sc. and a B.Sc. in Industrial Engineering and Management both from the Karlsruhe Institute of Technology (KIT), Germany. His research interest is focused on supply chain transparency, technology adoption and distributed ledger technology in supply chain management and operations management. His research is published in various journals such as the *Journal of Business Logistics*, and the *International Journal of Production Research*.

Felix Schöneseiffen is a consultant in Roland Berger Corporate Performance team. He holds a B.A. in Business Administration and M.A. in Business Management from the University of St.Gallen, Switzerland. Mr. Schoeneseiffen is especially interested in the optimization of business processes through the use of new technologies.

Michael Greger is research assistant at the Institute of Supply Chain Management at the University of St.Gallen, Switzerland and student at the University of St.Gallen. Mr. Greger holds a B.A. in Business Administration from the University of St.Gallen. His research interest focuses on distributed ledger technology in supply chain management.

Erik Hofmann is director of the Institute of Supply Chain Management as well as a Senior Lecturer at the University of St.Gallen, Switzerland. Dr. Hofmann holds a Ph.D. from the Technical University of Darmstadt, Germany. Prior, he studied Industrial Engineering and Management at the Technical University of Darmstadt. His primary research focuses on purchasing, supply chain finance and industry 4.0. He has published in several operations management journals such as the *Journal of Business Logistics, International Journal of Physical Distribution and Logistics Management, International Journal of Production Economics, International Journal of Logistics Management, Journal of Purchasing and Supply Management, International Journal of Production Research, Computers in Industry*. He is also co-author of several awarded books like "Performance Measurement and Incentive Systems in Purchasing" or "Financing the End-to-End Supply Chain".

Next Generation Home Sharing: Disrupting Platform Organizations with Blockchain Technology and the Internet of Things?

Patrick Schneck, Andranik Tumasjan, and Isabell M. Welpe

Abstract During the last decade, the sharing economy has given birth to a number of market mediators, which have grown to become the world's most valuable companies. Centralized sharing platforms like Uber, Didi Chuxing, and Airbnb have transformed several traditional industries. However, with the rise of the blockchain technology, some voices predict that these platform companies will soon be at risk of being disrupted themselves. In this chapter, we address the question of whether blockchain technology has given birth to a new breed of sharing economy platforms that can challenge the incumbents' business models. We identify five different stages of the application of blockchain technology in emerging home sharing startups. We use a stage model to explain the differences among various types of platforms, from which we derive the impact of their differences on potential market success. However, in the home sharing sector, simply copying Airbnb's business model and rebuilding it with blockchain technology is not sufficient for any of the emerging startups to overcome the prevalent barriers to entry. Hence, we use our results to illustrate whether and under what conditions blockchain-based startups might be able to "change the game" in the home sharing economy. Our results indicate that most blockchain-based home sharing startups will likely not be able to truly challenge the incumbent platforms. Nevertheless, by analyzing the different ways of blockchain implementation in the home sharing sectors, we identify several critical factors that may increase the chance to prosper for emerging blockchain home sharing networks.

1 The Sharing Economy: Home of Disruptors

Sharing was not a new phenomenon when the term "sharing economy" grew out of the open-source community. Sharing a ride with a neighbor or letting an acquaintance

P. Schneck (✉) · I. M. Welpe
Technical University of Munich, Munich, Germany
e-mail: patrick.schneck@capgemini.com

A. Tumasjan
Johannes Gutenberg University of Mainz, Mainz, Germany
e-mail: antumasj@uni-mainz.de

© Springer Nature Switzerland AG 2020
H. Treiblmaier and T. Clohessy (eds.), *Blockchain and Distributed Ledger Technology Use Cases*, Progress in IS, https://doi.org/10.1007/978-3-030-44337-5_13

267

stay over in a spare bedroom was far from being a revolutionary concept when ventures like Uber and Airbnb first began to attract public attention. The concept has become increasingly popular over the last decade as a label for "a new class of digitally-enabled exchange [...] across a wide variety of industries" (Sundararajan 2017, p. 9). Nevertheless, the sharing economy gave birth to billion-dollar startups, which have managed to successfully attack the extant business models of traditional industries, such as the hotel and taxi industries. While there have been widespread disputes about whether the sharing economy[1] has anything to do with sharing at all, the term is commonly used as an umbrella term with a range of meanings, often used to describe economic activity involving online transactions mediated by platforms (Taeihagh 2017).

The most successful of these platforms operate in the field of transportation and travel. For instance, as of 2019, Uber operates in more than 650 cities in 83 countries and generated a total revenue of $11.3 billion in 2018 (Zaveri and Bosa 2019). Meanwhile, Airbnb is active in more than 100,000 cities, with 7 million listings and an average of 2,000,000 stays per night (Airbnb Newsroom 2020). Both companies are heavily backed by venture capital and rank first (Uber, $69 billion) and third (Airbnb, $31 billion), respectively, on the list of the world's most valuable startups.

In the following sections of this chapter, we first explain how the concept of collaborative consumption has brought not only economic welfare, but also—in its current manifestation—may put users of sharing platforms at disadvantage. We then give a brief overview of the potential of blockchain technology to mitigate these downsides by enabling a "true" peer-to-peer sharing economy. Subsequently, we present the current landscape of blockchain-based home sharing startups, which stems from one of our previous analyses (Schneck et al. 2018) to answer the question whether or not any of these startups are capable of challenging the incumbent platforms and their business models. We do so by analyzing the different stages of "blockchainification" of the home sharing industry in which the startups operate to determine which types of platforms are most likely to change the way we engage in collaborative consumption. Based on the different ways of real-world blockchain implementation, we derive recommendations for startups to increase their chances of prospering in a highly competitive market.

Our research focuses specifically on the home sharing industry to avoid industry-specific effects interfering with our results. Furthermore, certain characteristics of the home sharing market make it an especially difficult market to enter for any new players. In many sharing markets, one can witness two types of platforms competing: global versus regional players. For example, in the ride-hailing industry in many cities it is a head-to-head race between global and regional players (e.g., ShareNow) (Schellong et al. 2019). However, the market characteristics of home sharing are

---

[1]Throughout this paper, we use the term 'sharing economy' for platform business models that arguably may not have much to do with 'sharing' in the actual sense of the word. However, we find it more useful to think of 'shared value creation' in this context rather than debating the semantics of the word "sharing".

somewhat different in this regard. Since tourism per se and, thus, home sharing platforms function on a global scale, local players can hardly compete with a global player like Airbnb. Thus, the "digitization" of this industry has led to the formation of large quasi-monopolies (especially Airbnb and Priceline) extracting consumer-rent. Based on this reasoning, this market is especially suitable to examine our research question on whether and how powerful incumbents can be overtaken by new technology-fueled challengers. This is primarily because of to the aforementioned specifics of the home sharing industry and because the home sharing industry is an early adopter of the technology with a small number of active platforms that are already blockchain-based.

1.1 The Light and Shadow of Centralized Sharing Platforms

The large players of the sharing economy have been remarkably successful in terms of user attraction. While still not profitable, Uber and Airbnb built a user base of, in sum, over 290 million users across the globe (Mazareanu 2019; Much Needed 2019). Their success is based on the gain in convenience and high usability they offer to their customer base, which has helped them to attract billions of loyal users, especially among digital natives (Bothun et al. 2015).

However, the market wins of these platforms are also fostered by economic phenomena called the 'network effect' and the 'positive feedback effect'. These effects strengthen large players in the market, thus forming natural monopolies. As one would expect, the trend toward increasingly powerful monopolies in the sharing economy has been a source of intense criticism toward companies like Uber and Airbnb, with resulting disadvantages including fixation of high prices, restriction of choice for customers, lack of transparency and reduction of economic welfare (Frenken and Schor 2017). Positive network effects increase the value of a product or marketplace for all users as its usage by other users grows (Shapiro and Varian 1999). Today, this effect is primarily known from social media platforms like Facebook and YouTube. Social networks grow through the so-called 'direct' or 'same-sided' network effect, where an increase of usage of the platform leads to a direct increase in value for the users (Belvaux 2011). In contrast, platform-mediated markets are mainly characterized by 'indirect' or 'cross-sided' network effects. Where there are two distinct groups of users on a platform, each group may exhibit a preference regarding the number of users in their own group (Brosseau and Penard 2007). Indirect network effects play a key role in the staggering success of Airbnb and its relatives.

Network effects lead to "winner-takes-all" markets, because the value of a platform increases with every guest and/or host joining the network (positive feedback loop), and the new users further contribute to the platform's utility and variety. Hence, the largest networks are the most attractive ones, which creates a lock-in effect on both sides of the market (Balaram et al. 2017). For a company in the sharing economy to be able to offer any value at all, it must reach "critical mass"—a minimum number of guests and hosts committed to contributing to the network.

The services offered by sharing economy platforms enable the functioning of peer-to-peer markets: Airbnb matches the supply and demand of underutilized assets (homes) on its marketplaces, settles transactions, offers insurance policies for hosts, provides customer service, and settles disputes between users. These steps help building trust among people who do not know each other through review and reputation mechanisms (Ert et al. 2015). Another, often underestimated, factor used to build trust among users is the platform's brand (Piovesan 2018). Millions of successfully performed peer-to-peer transactions have created widespread trust in the integrity of Airbnb and other well-known intermediaries. This "trusted-brand advantage" is difficult, if not impossible for new market entrants to replicate, which further contributes to the monopolistic character of the sharing economy.

Naturally, these quasi-monopolies and large oligopolies can fix prices and charge high service fees without significant consequences. Fees of the most common platforms range from 6–25% (HomeAway 2017; Ridester.com 2019b). While fees of up to 25% already seem high, the aforementioned oligopolies and monopolies can arbitrarily raise the fees even more without major consequences. Regularly changing fee structures and commissions, which are individually calculated for each transaction based on non-transparent factors, make the pricing schemes of many sharing economy platforms obscurely complex.

2 Blockchain Ushers in the Era of Disintermediation

The previous section showed that Airbnb's and Uber's success and market dominance may have negative implications for the public's perception of the sharing economy as a whole. A negative connotation of something that is inherently an economically and socially desirable concept (the collaborative consumption of otherwise underutilized assets), opens a potential void in the market. Such a void can possibly be filled by a different form of sharing economy network, one that is designed purely to connect the supply and demand side directly in a trustless and secure manner, and one that extracts much less or even no value from the transactions performed within the network. While it can be argued that, as blockchain solutions gain market share, some of these platforms will implement a transaction-based revenue model, at this point, most startups (e.g., Locktrip, Wehome) still advertise a 0% commission.

Considering who the main value contributors are, the amount of commission monopolistic sharing economy platforms extract and transfer to their shareholders may seem unjustifiably high. This raises the question of what would happen if society cloud reap the benefits of collaborative consumption without the downsides (e.g., expensive services, lack of regulation) brought about by centralized market mediators. With the rise of blockchain technology, many experts forecast exactly that—they predict that industry transforming companies like Airbnb may soon be on the verge of disruption themselves (Kollmann et al. 2019; Sundararajan 2017; Tapscott and Tapscott 2016). Blockchain technology may provide the necessary technological infrastructure for frictionless, direct, peer-to-peer exchange of assets without the need for a trusted intermediary (Filippi 2017; Friedlmaier et al. 2018; Tapscott and Tapscott 2016). While some more skeptical voices propose the opposite, arguing that "some established players will be able to use this opportunity (the emergence of blockchain technology) to scale their operations further" (Catalini 2017), numerous projects have emerged to strengthen the claims of those who forsee a decentralized sharing economy resulting from blockchain technology.

With blockchain technology, the digital identities of users can be stored on a distributed ledger, transactions can be settled via smart contracts, and the reputation of the users can automatically be incorporated into these self-executing contracts. By eliminating intermediaries, blockchain technology may constitute the backend for a fairer sharing economy by distributing the value created through the platform more equally among its contributors (Dutra et al. 2018). Platform-native blockchain tokens may function as the preferred means of payment and simultaneously represent a share in the value of the application (Hülsemann and Tumasjan 2019; Oliviera and Zalovokina 2018). According to Mougayar (2016, p. 51), "the blockchain will enable us to do our jobs and be compensated inside new circular economies that have their own currency units and their own work units." Advancing this idea, blockchain technology could also enable new forms of ownership and thereby realize high levels of disintermediation of the sharing economy. Blockchain supercharges cooperatives by enabling "people to translate their willingness to work together into a set of reliable accounting—of rights, assets, deeds, contributions, uses—that displaces some of what a company like Uber does" (Benkler 2015).

In a prior analysis of N = 74 blockchain-based sharing economy startups, we find that home sharing intermediaries are confronted with a considerable number of new competitors that utilize blockchain technology to create a more decentralized sharing economy with substantially lower commission fees (Schneck et al. 2018). Figure 1 shows a non-exhaustive overview of blockchain-based sharing economy startups we have identified and allocated to different categories (Schneck et al. 2018). The startups

Fig. 1 Blockchain startups in the sharing economy (Schneck et al. 2018)

highlighted (category: *Space*) are direct competitors to Airbnb and OneFineStay as well as hotel booking platforms like Priceline's booking.combooking.com.

Our analysis shows that simply rebuilding existing business models with blockchain technology may not be sufficient for the emerging startups to surmount the barriers to entry of the sharing economy based on strong network effects. Blockchain-based startups may only have a chance to change the game if they offer significant customer benefits over traditional intermediaries while maintaining the same level of convenience and user-friendliness (i.e., usability) customers have grown accustomed to. In an analysis of blockchain technology adoption in the sharing economy, Tumasjan and Beutel (2019, p. 104) state that "users place a high value on convenience and accessibility when they anticipate the effort and performance"[2] of blockchain-based sharing economy business models. Increasing the perceived usefulness of new home sharing networks may require combining blockchain with other technologies such as the Internet of Things. Doing so, will allow startups to exceed or at least match user experience and usability on par with existing players. In our following analysis, we examine the different stages of the 'blockchainification' of the home sharing market using real-world examples of ambitious startups, which have no lesser goals than to "disintermediate the current 'sharing economy' platforms and thereby push billion-dollar corporations like [...] Airbnb out of the market" (Tapscott and Tapscott 2016, p. 32).

3   The "Blockchainification" of the Home Sharing Industry

To identify the potential of blockchain technology for the home sharing industry, we use our above mentioned data set of blockchain-based sharing economy startups from prior research (Schneck et al. 2018). The data set was created between July and December 2017. We added to the database all startups that use blockchain technology to some extent and fall into one of the categories of the Collaborative Economy Honeycomb (Owyang 2016). We then extracted all startups that operate in the home sharing sector as well as sharing networks, in which "home sharing" is one out of several possible use cases. The extracted startups were grouped according to six characteristics of a home sharing platform, which we specify in the next section.

Overall, we identified five different stages of 'blockchainification' of the sharing economy. Our research shows that besides the standard centralized home sharing platform (stage 1), there exist three additional types of blockchain-enabled platforms: Crypto Home sharing, Home sharing DAO, and Home sharing DAO + IoT. The fifth stage ("BlockBnB") is a hypothetical scenario that we construct in this article for the sake of illustrating potential future applications. We define the different stages of blockchain-based home sharing startups along the two dimensions 'autonomy'

---

[2]Performance expectancy and effort expectancy are two (of four) factors affecting technology adoption in the model conceived by Tumasjan and Beutel (2019). Both factors are borrowed from the UTAUT model Venkatesh (2013).

and 'automation'. Automation was selected as the first dimension as it refers to the degree to which smart contracts are applied to automate processes (Macrinici et al. 2018) that otherwise would require a trusted third party. Autonomy refers to the degree of managerial influence required to run the network and thus marks the second defining dimension. Both, autonomy and automation are contributing factors through which blockchain technology could potentially mitigate the downsides of the current manifestation of sharing economy platforms (Swan 2015).

The business models of existing blockchain-based sharing economy startups are mostly similar. Most platforms use blockchain technology with the goal to disintermediate the sharing economy and have similar value propositions, namely, an Airbnb-like marketplace for short-term apartment rentals at a significantly lower price point (i.e., lower commission fees). However, there are many differences in the way blockchain technology is used. This became apparent in our analysis of the whitepapers, roadmaps and platform prototypes of our N = 74 startup sample. Some platforms pursue a "radical" approach where blockchain is used to store all data and to automate close to 100% of the operational processes including transaction settlement, customer reviews, reputation, identity and arbitrage. Other platforms pursue a "moderate" approach that still relies on common IT infrastructure (e.g., public cloud databases) and applies blockchain only for selected use cases.

3.1 Five Stages of 'Blockchainification'

For the sake of illustration, let us regard the current home sharing economy as a monopolistic and highly centralized market, and the "ideal" future state of the home sharing economy as a fully decentralized marketplace. On this continuum, we observe that startups working toward this "ideal" future are operating at different stages between the current and the "ideal" future state. These stages represent the different ways in which startups and (potentially) incumbents apply blockchain to automate internal processes and increase the autonomy as well as the degree of decentralization of the underlying platform. The stages range from traditional platforms without blockchain components and conventional organizational structures to so called Decentralized Autonomous Organizations (DAOs) (Swan 2015) that harness IoT in combination with blockchain to create a truly decentralized peer-to-peer platform requiring nearly zero manual processes, intermediation or human interaction. We use six different characteristics of a home sharing platform to differentiate these "blockchainification" stages:

1. **Automation**: Using blockchain technology, many business processes can be streamlined and automated by using smart contracts. Naturally, home sharing platforms are digital business models and thus already rely on a high degree of process automation. However, with smart contracts, self-executing agreements (e.g., return of the deposit held in escrow) can be automatically triggered by events recorded on the blockchain (e.g., expiry of the cryptographic access code).

2. **Autonomy**: The degree of autonomy of a home sharing platform refers to the degree of managerial influence required to run the organization. The most advanced form of blockchain-based autonomous organizations is that of DAOs. Autonomous, blockchain-based business entities—without human managerial influence—can act as independent legal entities and enter contracts with other organizations if legal in the respective country (Swan 2015).

The levels of automation and autonomy directly affect other dimensions of the business model, such as internal transaction costs and commission fees, the organizational structures, the level of human interaction required to facilitate the exchange, and the arbitration methods. Thus, depending on the blockchainification stage of a home sharing platform, the described dimensions differ considerably, which in turn influences the user experience and user value.

3. **Human interaction** refers to the level of human contact necessary to facilitate the trade. In today's sharing economy, human interaction can be virtual or physical. Virtual interaction is typically required to coordinate arrival and checkout times and special requests. Physical interaction between the host and the guest is often still necessary during check-in and checkout (e.g., for the exchange of keys, remotes, and detailed instructions).
4. **Transaction costs** are the costs incurred by the intermediating platform to facilitate the trade in the home sharing process. These include service fees charged by payment service providers (e.g., Braintree, PayPal). In a broader sense, transaction costs comprise all costs necessary to facilitate a sharing transaction end-to-end (e.g., labor costs, IT costs, and office rent).
5. **Commission fees** are the costs charged by the intermediating platform and incurred by the host and/or the guest in return for coordinating and settling the economic exchange. Commission fees are the primary source of income for home sharing platforms.
6. **Customer service and arbitration** describes the means and processes necessary for dispute resolution between two or more of the three parties involved (guest, host, platform).

In the subsequent sections, we follow the dimensions of autonomy and automation in Fig. 3. As automation and autonomy increase, the change is reflected in the four other characteristics of the platform. We have identified five distinct "blockchainification" stages of home sharing platforms.[3] Figure 2 shows the five types of home sharing platforms including the traditional Airbnb-like version and a hypothetical scenario that we call "BlockBnB"—representing an enhanced version of Airbnb that we use in this chapter to illustrate how incumbent intermediaries could harness blockchain technology to further scale and streamline their operations.

---

[3] For the sake of simplicity, we use the term "platform" for all types of home sharing models. However, technically, a decentralized, peer-to-peer network (stages 3 and 4) constitutes the opposite of a "platform". A platform in the narrower sense of the word describes an intermediating, *centralized* body where user-generated value or content is exchanged by the means of Web 2.0.

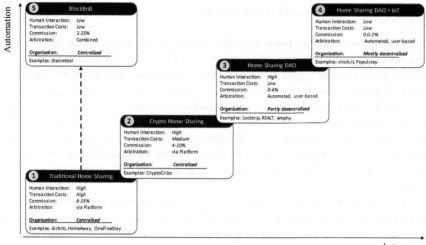

Fig. 2 Stages of blockchainification in the home sharing industry

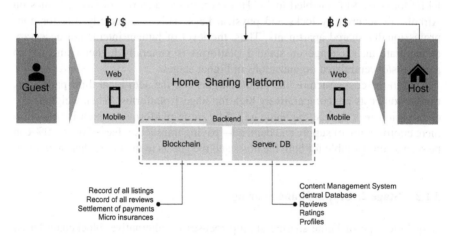

Fig. 3 High-level overview of stage 3 home sharing platform (adapted from LockTrip)

The different stages are not to be understood as discrete, independent manifestations of the same concept. Rather, the boundaries between the stages are blurred, and platforms in the lower stages can evolve to a level 3 or 4 platform. Often, this evolution is predefined in the roadmaps of the startups—for example, by planning the implementation of IoT technology (e.g., smart locks) (Tumasjan 2018).

In the following section, we describe the different stages in detail. Where applicable, we describe selected startups that fall into the respective category.

3.1.1   Stage 1: Traditional Home Sharing

Traditional home sharing platforms like Airbnb, HomeAway, and the more exclusive version OneFineStay do not (yet) utilize blockchain technology in any way. Stage 0 platforms are digital players in a traditional sense, with corporate functions like management, business development, IT, finance, customer service, and a legal department. The organizational structures and the required personnel are among the main cost factors of any traditional home sharing platform. The exchange of apartments and houses is facilitated via fiat currency.[4] The payments are settled through third-party service providers such as Braintree and PayPal (as is the case for Airbnb). These payment providers charge a service fee, which is passed on to the customer of the home sharing platform.

On conventional platforms, human interaction is in many cases still necessary to coordinate arrival times, directions, and the exchange of keys between guests and hosts. In particular, providing the guest access to the home requires logistic effort. More often than not, both the host (or any mandated human being) and the guest have to be present at the same place at the same time to exchange keys and remotes. Theoretically, conventional locks can be replaced by code locks, RFID locks or NFC-enabled locks. However, in the majority of cases, homes on Airbnb are secured by locks and physical keys. This is especially true for non-professionally shared apartments. Thus, the level of human interaction necessary to facilitate an exchange on stage 1 platforms is generally higher compared to platforms/decentralized organizations of higher stages.

Due to the cost structure, the profit margins and the additional third-party fees, transaction costs are comparatively high for stage 1 platforms. When weighing the commission fees against the value added by these platforms—which is limited to mere coordination of supply and demand—paying transaction fees of up to 30% can be seen as unfavorable for both the hosts and the guests in the home sharing market.

3.1.2   Stage 2: Crypto Home Sharing

A specific type of home sharing startup focuses on alternative, blockchain-based means of payment. Stage 2 platforms do not directly employ blockchain technology and smart contracts for process automation. Rather, they accept cryptocurrencies like Bitcoin, either exclusively or in addition to fiat money. By cutting out payment service providers like PayPal, these platforms can reduce transaction costs. Platforms that rely exclusively on cryptocurrencies target a niche market of tech-savvy users who are familiar with the use of cryptocurrencies and possess the necessary wallets. *CryptoCribs* (www.cryptocribs.com) is one example for such a platform. However, due to the strong network effects in the sharing economy, targeting only a small

---

[4]The term "fiat currency" refers to a currency that is issued by a government's central bank and that is not backed by physical commodity. Most modern paper currencies are fiat currencies (e.g., U.S. Dollar, Euro).

fraction of the entire market can be considered a risky strategy. A small fraction of the market participating on the platform means reduced supply in comparison to other platforms, which diminishes the value of CryptoCribs for all users.

CryptoCribs

CryptoCribs was founded in 2017 by UC Berkeley student Erasmus Elsner. In its current stage, CryptoCribs is a centralized home sharing platform that accepts Bitcoin, Bitcoin Cash and Ethereum. Like many startups, CryptoCribs is planning to progress into a fully decentralized peer-to-peer platform over time. CryptoCribs currently lists around 1500 apartments, predominantly in Switzerland and the United States. Prices are stated in BTC, and the website design is similar to Airbnb's. The platform incorporates a standard review system.

In summary, stage 2 platforms are characterized by a slightly higher degree of autonomy and automation (payments are processed without the need for an intermediating third party). The organizational structures, level of human interaction and arbitration follow traditional patterns similar to Airbnb's. No records apart from payment information are secured on a blockchain.

3.1.3 Stage 3: Decentralized Home Sharing Organization

Stage 3 comprises partially and fully decentralized organizations built on a third-party blockchain like Ethereum or a proprietary blockchain. In order to fall in this category, platforms must either be fully decentralized already or state a clear goal to incrementally increase the degree of decentralization. Smart contracts record (nearly) all transactions on the blockchain, including payments as well as reviews and ratings, micro insurance contracts for the duration of the rental agreement, and security deposits (Möhlmann et al. 2019; Wehome 2019).

Lower commission fees, ranging between 0 and 4%, represent the major selling point of stage 3 platforms. Hence, keeping the operational costs low is one of the main motivators for the application of blockchain technology. Startups like locktrip, emphy and REALT attempt to replace human staff with technology (e.g., smart contracts) wherever possible.

A crucial step to reduce the need for human staff in customer service is the implementation of an automated arbitration mechanism. One possible solution is a tribunal mechanism for anonymous, and hence unbiased, arbitration. In the case of a dispute over a rental agreement between a host and a guest, other (highly rated) users are presented with the conflict situation and are asked to cast votes in favor of one or the other party. A smart contract will automatically release the funds (e.g., the deposit held in escrow) to the winning party. The tribunal members receive a small fee in the native token as an incentive to contribute to the arbitration of the dispute.

From an IT architecture perspective, some stage 3 platforms prefer to keep a centralized backend (e.g., databases and content management systems) in addition to the decentralized blockchain layer to store heavier data like pictures and videos. All settlement information is executed and recorded on the blockchain layer. By storing heavy data off-chain, costs can further be reduced. It is cheaper to provision the additional servers and databases for the centralized backend than to store heavy data on a blockchain. A centralized backend also allows these startups to add new, data-heavy functionalities (e.g., AR/VR features) more swiftly.

LockTrip

LockTrip (www.locktrip.com; formerly: Lockchain) is a partly decentralized, open-source booking ecosystem for hotel rooms as well as private short-term accommodations. This startup offers its booking service to guests with no commission fees. Locktrip aims to provide an alternative to platforms like Airbnb and travel metasearch engines such as Priceline, Booking.com,[5] and Expedia. It distinguishes itself from competitors in the home sharing sector by simultaneously targeting the hotel industry and private homeowners. The core element of the project is the LockTrip marketplace. Property owners and hotels can use the one-click solution built into the mobile app and web client to easily transfer listings from competing platforms and make them available to LockTrip users. The marketplace has a "look and feel" that is similar to Airbnb's. All internal transactions are regulated by the "Decentralized LOC Ledger" and governed by smart contracts. All financial transactions on the platform are settled in the native LOC token. However, LockTrip accepts a range of other cryptocurrencies as well as fiat currencies (1–3% conversion fees may apply). It employs a conversion algorithm that automatically converts other currencies into LOC tokens. A hedging mechanism to eliminate the potential risks of token volatility has been developed as well, making the marketplace more suitable for everyday users. Lock-Trip uses blockchain technology and the utility token primarily to increase process efficiency, streamline the renting process, and increase transparency. As of July 2019, LockTrip has listed over 100,000 homes and hotels.

3.1.4 Stage 4: Home Sharing DAO and IoT

Stage 4 platforms are in many ways similar to stage 3 platforms. However, stage 4 platforms take the concept of blockchain automation one step further. By introducing smart locks to the home sharing ecosystem concept, they are able to eliminate the need for human interaction. Homes are turned into nodes of the blockchain network. IoT technology enables these platforms to expand blockchain into the "real world" and turn the home into an element of the decentralized sharing network. Access control smart contracts settle transactions for renting/sharing, booking, and payments. Guests receive a token on their smartphone application, which can be used to unlock the apartment or house via Near Field Communication (NFC) technology. The token will expire automatically once the rental agreement terminates. The same concept can be extended to washing machines, coffee machines, and similar devices. Thus, home owners can, at their discretion, use access control modules to "lock" home appliances and other complementary items (e.g., bicycles). For an additional fee, the

---

[5]Booking.com was acquired by the Priceline Group in 2005.

guest can "unlock" these devices and will be charged on a pay-as-you-go scheme. Friends and family can be whitelisted so that pre-specified people are able to book the home and use appliances at no cost or at reduced rates. Stage 4 networks leverage blockchain and IoT to minimize maintenance and other overhead costs for hosts to accommodate their guests. In such a setting, IoT-enabled devices would be owned or leased and maintained by the property owner, whereas they are paid for on a pay-per-use basis be the guests.

Most stage 4 networks provide an open source infrastructure on which blockchain application modules can be deployed. These modules can be smart locks or other access control clients (e.g., for home automation). Stage 4 decentralized networks are open to third-party modules to run a full node or light client. A light client only synchronizes the block headers of the blockchain without running all the transactions of a block. A series of smart contracts is available for booking, arbitration, review, and identity management. Native tokens (usually ERC20 tokens) are used to incentivize users to participate in the network and foster growth.

Users have grown accustomed to optimized web and mobile platforms. Thus, most stage 3 and 4 platforms put a strong emphasis on mimicking the user experience of Airbnb by building modern, responsive, easy-to-use HTML5 websites, and native mobile applications. Data are stored off- and/or on-chain. Centralized, cloud-based backend infrastructure usually still exists to host data, the website, and the mobile application. Hashes of the stored information (e.g., user reviews) can be kept on-chain to increase the data's integrity.

Slock.it

Slock.it (www.slock.it) is a startup that combines IoT technology and blockchain to create what the founders call a Universal Sharing Network (USN). The company gained popularity and media attention through their prototype of a smart door lock ("slock") that embeds smart contracts into a tangible product (the lock) and is linked to the Ethereum blockchain. An apartment equipped with a "slock" takes on the role of a light node in the USN. The apartment has access to a copy of the blockchain and thus to the current state of ownership rights for the respective apartment. It can be unlocked with a device that carries the appropriate token (i.e., the owner's or the current tenant's smartphone). Slock.it envisions a fully automated Airbnb renting process; the owner of an apartment sets a price for timed access to his/her property, and an interested party can find the apartment on a smartphone application and transfer the required amount plus a deposit (in Ether) into an escrow account. By the rules of a smart contract, the renter is then granted an access token for the agreed rental period (Christidis and Devetsikiotis 2018). Within the USN, Ethereum transactions are required to initiate and to end the rental agreement. To open and close the door, *Whisper* messages[6] are sent between the lock and the renter's smartphone. This helps to prevent scalability issues and increase transaction speed, as renters do not have to await a block confirmation every time they wish to lock or unlock the

---

[6]Whisper is a communication protocol for decentralized applications (https://github.com/ethereum/wiki/wiki/Whisper).

apartment door. After the rental period has ended, if both parties agree to release the funds, the owner receives the payable amount, and the deposit is transferred back to the renter. Slock.it claims that the platform is ideal for integration in vehicle chassis, door locks, gas/electricity meters, and washing machines. Further examples of stage 3 and 4 startups are The Bee Token, Wono, GoEureka, abab.io, Tetarise, The Rentals Token, Populstay, CryptoBnB, Zangll, and Casa.

3.1.5   Stage 5: "BlockBnB"

Airbnb spearheaded the rise of collaborative consumption, which was also fueled by new technologies. Hence, it is plausible to assume that this tech-savvy company will follow up on the recent developments and assess the potential of blockchain technology to benefit its own business. This claim is backed by Airbnb's acquisition of the startup ChangeCoin[7] in 2016 (Carson 2016), as well as Airbnb's Co-Founder and CTO Nathan Blecharczyk's statement on the opportunities of transferrable reputation for the sharing economy. Apart from these examples, there is little to no evidence on how the incumbents are seeking to harness blockchain technology. However, it is conceivable that Airbnb will use blockchain technology to drive its own transformation toward a more cost-efficient and thus profitable platform. For the sake of our analysis, we call this purely hypothetical construct "BlockBnB" (BBNB).

Airbnb payments in the U.S. are processed by Braintree, a payment service provider owned by PayPal. By adopting blockchain technology, BBNB could cut out rent-extracting intermediaries. In order to do so, the company would create an ecosystem consisting of a proof-of-stake public blockchain, as well as centralized data centers for hosting the web application and property listings. In this scenario, it would issue a utility token that is used for all internal transactions. Every user would own a wallet integrated into their user account that holds the tokens. Prices and available funds would be displayed in the BBNB currency or are converted into fiat for a simplified user experience. In the early phase, standard fiat payments would continue to be accepted. However, the use of the BBNB token would be incentivized through lower service fees.

As the BBNB token would not be sold through a token offering and would not need to incentivize early adopters financially through a high ROI, the token's value could track the U.S. dollar for the sake of greater practicality (i.e., lower volatility). The token would be used to pay for rent, commission fees, and third-party services (e.g., cleaning and insurance). As long as the tokens circulate in the BBNB ecosystem, the users would pay no exchange fees and only negligible transaction fees. Only if users buy tokens in exchange for fiat money or decide to "cash out" from their wallet conversion fees would apply. This implementation could not only reduce the total amount of fees but also allow for secure real-time payments through smart contracts. The entire rental agreement, including the deposit payment and insurance fees, could be replicated by multi-signature smart contracts. These smart contracts

---

[7]ChangeCoin was a Bitcoin startup specialized in micro-payment solutions.

would have to incorporate cancellation terms and, optionally, discounts for friends and family members. Arbitration could be automated as well, by relying on tribunals of highly ranked users, who would earn BBNB tokens in return for their efforts. As a result, guests would not have to wait up to 14 working days before being refunded after cancellation or a dispute. Moreover, these measures would lower the overhead costs of BBNB drastically. The lower operational costs could be passed on to the users by lowering the service fees, which enables BBNB to compete with other blockchain-based home sharing startups without sacrificing too much of its own profit.

A public BBNB blockchain could automate not only abstract contractual agreements but also the physical process (e.g., exchange of keys, welcoming guests) of renting out an apartment. By enabling hosts to connect smart locks to the blockchain, BBNB would do away with the cumbersome process of coordinating arrival times between guest and hosts. Apartments could become light nodes of the blockchain network, and the guest retrieves an access token to (un)lock the smart property using his/her wallet app. To complete the check-out process, the guest would provide the host with pictures or videos of the apartment using the BBNB app. The files would be stored on the user's devices and on the Airbnb servers as a precautionary measure in case of disputes. To secure the file and to prevent manipulation, it would be timestamped, and its hash value stored on the blockchain. If both parties agree, the fees would be released by the smart contract, and the deposit returned to the renter. Additionally, a cleaning fee could be transferred directly to a "cleaning smart contract" for increased convenience, and the information on the public blockchain could be made accessible to third parties, such as cleaning services. Knowing the idle times of any given apartment, the cleaning service provider, who is a member of the BBNB ecosystem, could dispatch its staff equipped with temporary access tokens. Again, video-based proof could be requested by owners before they release the tokens from the cleaning contract. The apartment would then be ready to host the next guest. With blockchain technology, BBNB fully eliminates the need for personal interaction between guest and hosts. While this impersonal way of "sharing" certainly would not appeal to all users, it eliminates many of the frictions in today's sharing economy. Furthermore, reviews could be linked to the user's public key and saved on the blockchain. By transferring their profile to other platforms, users could prove their trustworthiness and credibility. A positive reputation earned on BBNB could boost users' success on other sharing economy platforms (e.g., a freelancing marketplace).

Leaving our hypothetical scenario and returning to actual Airbnb projects, one blockchain application that Airbnb is indeed investigating is immutable and transferable reputation (Kar and Wong 2016). Airbnb's Blecharczyk (CTO) once stated that, "within the context of Airbnb, your reputation is everything, and I can see it being even more so in the future, whereby you might need a certain reputation in order to have access to certain types of homes". By following such a transformational path, incumbent home sharing platforms could combat new market entrants and optimize their cost structure.

4   Recommendations for Startups and Incumbents

The largest player in the market, Airbnb, constitutes a stable de facto monopoly in the home sharing business and is one of the largest players in the entire tourism industry (Hartmans 2017). Airbnb benefits from strong network effects (Zhu and Iansiti 2019), high usability, and a strong trust base built on a trusted brand and a large set of user reviews. Airbnb users have built their own trusted brands on the platform based on the reviews and reputation scores received from other users. New market entrants, whether blockchain-based or not, have to reach a critical mass of users to be able to offer any value at all (O'Briant 2018). In general, customers are disinclined to compromise on the variety of supply (e.g., large numbers of homes in different cities), convenience (e.g., easy-to-use-interfaces, mobile apps), and trustworthiness of brands, and thus they are reluctant to support the somewhat idealistic rationale behind new forms of organizations such as DAOs. For an emerging blockchain-based home sharing network, offering lower commission fees and data transparency is not sufficient to compete against the current incumbents or against blockchain-based startups with a similar selling proposition. New platforms will only stand a chance of surviving if they provide true added value in comparison to the established marketplaces and reach a critical mass of users to become self-sustainable. In summary, from our analysis, we derive the following guidelines for new entrants to accelerate growth:

1. Leverage the cost advantages of a blockchain-based backend and keep the commission fees charged significantly below the current market standard.
2. Increase automation and convenience for end-users by incorporating an IoT layer into the sharing platform. Enable integration of third-party smart locks and other connected devices.
3. Employ smart contracts to securely automate as many back- and frontend processes as possible. Keep the data stored on the blockchain light for performance and scalability. Install a centralized (cloud-based) backend to process and store auxiliary data such as images and video.
4. Most existing blockchain platforms lack visibility in the market outside the crypto-sphere. Thus, investments in marketing activities are necessary to attract a critical mass of users. Concentrate marketing activities on cities with high tourism dependency.
5. Put a strong emphasis on the usability and convenience of the mobile app and the booking website. Simplify the use of the crypto wallet and hide blockchain processes from the end-user to reduce the perceived complexity.
6. Implement a hedging mechanism to keep the internal currency stable.
7. Start the operations of the platform by entering an alliance with an existing booking platform. An initial base supply of available homes will help attracting users to the platform and increase its real-world value. Doing so mitigates the risk of a potential collapse of the network, which otherwise would build solely on artificial rewards to grow.

8. Strike an end-user-friendly balance between transaction throughput and censorship resistance of the underlying blockchain and the consensus mechanism. A performant and user-friendly platform is what users expect from any Airbnb competitor.

5 Implications and Concluding Remarks

The implications of our research as presented in this paper are of theoretical as well as practical nature. One the theoretical side, we developed a stage model that can be used to describe different types of emerging blockchain platforms, and to characterize them according their business models and application of technology. We invite other researchers to advance our model and to develop industry-specific versions following the same logic.

On the practical side, we describe and compare the business models of "blockchainified" entrants to the home sharing industry vis-à-vis "traditional" platform businesses. Based on our findings we formulate a set of recommendations for blockchain-based challengers to better overcome the barriers of the platform-based industry.

Furthermore, if we look at how emerging home sharing startups use blockchain technology and consider the economics of the sharing economy, we can conclude that challenging Airbnb as the undisputed leader in the home sharing sector is no easy undertaking. From an end user's perspective, the one major selling point of a decentralized home sharing network is that of the significantly lower commission fees to be paid. In terms of user-friendliness, usability and augmenting services (e.g., insurance, bookable tourist activities), no decentralized platform is yet on par with Airbnb. Users' willingness to sacrifice on these attributes in exchange for cost savings is generally low (Tumasjan and Beutel 2019). However, a large-scale shift of users to a decentralized network is necessary to surmount the network effects in the home sharing sector. Otherwise, no alternative platform will be able to provide significant value to users. Factoring in the low visibility of blockchain platforms outside of the crypto scene and comparatively low legitimacy (Moser et al. 2017), we conclude that it is unlikely that any decentralized home sharing network will reach a critical mass of users to become self-sustainable within the next few years.

Nevertheless, blockchain and crypto-tokens will likely impact the industry as the technology matures. Based on our research, we argue that two types of blockchain-enhanced platforms are likely to make an impact on the home sharing industry. First, we see the integration of IoT devices as a major trend in the sector (Tumasjan 2018). Open sharing networks (stage 3) like Slock.it's USN will allow users to not only monetize idle homes but also expand the concept of 'sharing' to any other needs of travelers (e.g., bicycles, washing machines)—all on the same technological backend infrastructure using blockchain technology. Second, under this wave of technological change, incumbent platforms are likely to adopt blockchain technology to increase internal efficiency and enhance the user experience. A question that remains for future research is how decentralization through blockchain technology will impact the economic mechanisms of the sharing economy in the long-run (Tumasjan, forthcoming). Can decentralized networks co-exist and compete, or will they keep converging to one monopoly in a "winner-takes-all" market?

References

Abrahao, B., Parigi, P., Gupta, A., & Cook, K. S. (2017). Reputation offsets trust judgments based on social biases among Airbnb users. *Proceedings of the National Academy of Sciences of the United States of America, 114*(37), 9848–9853. https://doi.org/10.1073/pnas.1604234114

Airbnb, Inc. (2019). *What is the Airbnb service fee?* Retrieved from https://www.airbnb.com/help/article/1857/what-is-the-airbnb-service-fee?locale=en.

Airbnb Newsroom (2020). *Fast Facts.* Retrieved April 2, 2020, from https://news.airbnb.com/fast-facts/

Balaram, B., Warden, J., Wallace-Stephens, F. (2017, April). *Good Gigs: A fairer future for the UK's gig economy.* Retrieved from Royal Society for the encouragement of Arts, Manufactures and Commerce website: https://www.thersa.org/globalassets/pdfs/reports/rsa_good-gigs-fairer-gig-economy-report.pdf.

Belvaux, B. (2011). The development of social media: Proposal for a diffusion model incorporating network externalities in a competitive environment. *Recherche et Applications en Marketing, 26*(3), 7–22. Retrieved from https://doi.org/10.1177%2F205157071102600301.

Benkler, Y. (2015). Interview by D. Tapscott.

Bothun, D., Lieberman, M., & Egol, M. (2015). *The sharing economy.* Retrieved from https://www.pwc.fr/fr/assets/files/pdf/2015/05/pwc_etude_sharing_economy.pdf.

Brosseau, E., & Penard, T. (2007). The economics of digital business models: A framework for analyzing the economics of platforms. *Review of Network Economics, 6*(2), 81–114. Retrieved from https://s3.amazonaws.com/academia.edu.documents/42649123/The_Economics_of_Digital_Business_Models20160213-7352-b1sx0l.pdf?response-content-disposition=inline%3B%20filename%3DThe_Economics_of_Digital_Business_Models.pdf&X-Amz-Algorithm=AWS4-HMAC-SHA256&X-Amz-Credential=AKIAIWOWYYGZ2Y53UL3A%2F20191117%2Fus-east-1%2Fs3%2Faws4_request&X-Amz-Date=20191117T151411Z&X-Amz-Expires=3600&X-Amz-SignedHeaders=host&X-Amz-Signature=eb98299ef0821498c05510b0be41bc8316eda8bd7758072d22b385b102dd385a.

Buterin, V. (2014). *Decentralized protocol monetization and forks.* Retrieved from https://blog.ethereum.org/2014/04/30/decentralized-protocol-monetization-and-forks/.

Carson, B. (2016). Airbnb just brought on a team of bitcoin experts from a tiny startup. *Business Insider Deutschland.* Retrieved from https://www.businessinsider.de/airbnb-buys-bitcoin-startup-changecoin-2016-4?r=US&IR=T.

Catalini, C. (2017). *How blockchain technology will impact the digital economy.* Retrieved from https://mitsloanexperts.mit.edu/how-blockchain-technology-will-impact-the-digital-economy-christian-catalini/.

Christidis, K., & Devetsikiotis, M. (2018). Design of the blockchain smart contract: A use case for real estate. *Journal for Information Security, 9*(3). Retrieved from https://doi.org/10.1109/ACCESS.2016.2566339.

Dutra, A., Tumasjan, A., & Welpe, I. M. (2018). Blockchain is changing how media and entertainment companies compete. *MIT Sloan Management Review, 59*(1), 39–45.

Eckhardt, G. M., & Bardhi, F. (2015). The sharing economy isn't about sharing at all. *Harvard Business Review.* Retrieved from https://hbr.org/2015/01/the-sharing-economy-isnt-about-sharing-at-all.

Ert, E., Fleicher, A., & Magen, N. (2015). Trust and reputation in the sharing economy: The role of personal photos on Airbnb. *Tourism Management, 55*, 52–73. Retrieved from https://www.researchgate.net/publication/315410754_Trust_and_Reputation_in_the_Sharing_Economy_The_Role_of_Personal_Photos_on_Airbnb.

de Filippi, P. (2017). What blockchain means for the sharing economy. *Harvard Business Review: HBR*. Retrieved from https://hbr.org/2017/03/what-blockchain-means-for-the-sharing-economy.

Frenken, K., & Schor, J. (2017). Putting the sharing economy into perspective. *Environmental Innovation and Societal Transitions, 23*, 3–10. Retrieved from https://doi.org/10.1016/j.eist.2017.01.003.

Friedlmaier, M., Tumasjan, A., & Welpe, I. M. (2018). Disrupting industries with blockchain: The industry, venture capital funding, and regional distribution of blockchain ventures. In *Proceedings of the 51st Hawaii International Conference on System Sciences* (pp. 3517–3526).

Hartmans, A. (2017). Airbnb now has more listings worldwide than the top five hotel brands combined. *Business Insider*. Retrieved from https://www.businessinsider.de/airbnb-total-worldwide-listings-2017-8?r=UK.

HomeAway (2017). *What is the service fee? Paying the fee*. Retrieved from https://help.homeaway.com/articles/What-is-the-service-fee-and-how-does-it-work.

Hülsemann, P., & Tumasjan, A. (2019). Walk this way! Incentive structures of different token designs for blockchain based applications. In *Proceedings of the Fortieth International Conference on Information Systems (ICIS)*.

Jentzsch, C. (2017). *The internet of things is born-slock. It is back!* [Video File]. Retrieved from https://www.youtube.com/watch?v=iRtG_6pYqGE.

Kar, I., & Wong, J. I. (2016). Airbnb just acquired a team of bitcoin and blockchain experts. Retrieved from https://qz.com/657246/airbnb-just-acquired-a-team-of-bitcoin-and-blockchain-experts/.

Kollmann, T., Hensellek, S., de Cruppe, K., & Sirges, A. (2019). Toward a renaissance of cooperatives fostered by blockchain on electronic marketplaces: A theory-driven case study approach. *Electronic Markets*, 1–12. Retrieved from https://doi.org/10.1007/s12525-019-00369-4.

Macrinici, D., Cartofeanu, C., & Gao, S. (2018). Smart contract applications within blockchain technology: A systematic mapping study. *Telematics and Informatics, 35*(8), 2337–2354. Retrieved from https://doi.org/10.1016/j.tele.2018.10.004.

Mazareanu, E. (2019). Monthly number of Uber's active users worldwide from 2016 to 2019 (in millions). Retrieved from https://www.statista.com/statistics/833743/us-users-ride-sharing-services/.

Möhlmann, M., Teubner, T., & Graul, A. (2019). *Leveraging trust on sharing economy platforms: Reputation systems, blockchain technology, and cryptocurrencies*. Retrieved from https://www.researchgate.net/publication/335425931_Leveraging_Trust_on_Sharing_Economy_Platforms_Reputation_Systems_Blockchain_Technology_and_Cryptocurrencies.

Moser, K., Tumasjan, A., & Welpe, I. M. (2017). Small but attractive: Dimensions of new venture employer attractiveness and the moderating role of applicants' entrepreneurial behaviors. *Journal of Business Venturing, 32*(5), 588–610.

Mougayar, W. (2016). *The business blockchain: A primer on the promise, practice and application of the next Internet technology*. Hoboken: Wiley.

Much Needed. (2019). *Airbnb by the numbers: Usage, demographics, and revenue growth*. Retrieved from https://muchneeded.com/airbnb-statistics/.

O'Briant, T. (2018). *What is critical mass? A minimum viable explanation*. Retrieved from https://medium.com/immutable/critical-mass-937355e1f179.

Oliviera, L., & Zalovokina, L. (2018). *To token or not to token: Tools for understanding blockchain tokens*. Zurich. Retrieved from University of Zurich website: https://www.zora.uzh.ch/id/eprint/157908/1/To%20Token%20or%20not%20to%20Token_%20Tools%20for%20Understanding%20Blockchain%20Toke.pdf.

Owyang, J. (2016). *Honeycomb 3.0: The collaborative economy market expansion*. Retrieved from https://www.web-strategist.com/blog/2016/03/10/honeycomb-3-0-the-collaborative-economy-market-expansion-sxsw/.

Piovesan, M. (2018, July 17). A foundation of trust is how the sharing economy thrives: Trust is built on transparency and confidence. If you don't have it, your brand will be hurt. *Entrepreneur Europe.* Retrieved from https://www.entrepreneur.com/article/315809.

Ridester.com. (2019a). *Uber fees: How much does Uber pay, actually?* Retrieved from https://www.ridester.com/uber-fees/.

Ridester.com. (2019b). *Understanding lyft fees for passengers and drivers.* Retrieved from https://www.ridester.com/lyft-fees/.

Schellong, D., Sadek, P., Schaetzberger, C., & Barrack, T. (2019). *The promise and pitfalls of e-scooter sharing.* Retrieved from https://www.bcg.com/publications/2019/promise-pitfalls-e-scooter-sharing.aspx.

Schneck, P., Tumasjan, A., & Welpe, I. M. (2018). *Disrupting the disruptors? An in-depth analysis of the implications of blockchain technology for today's sharing economy.* Working Paper.

Shapiro, C., & Varian, H. R. (1999). *Information rules: A strategic guide to the network economy.* Boston, MA: Harvard Business Review Press.

Slock.it. (2016). *Partnering with SafeShare to create the ad-hoc insurance of the sharing economy.* Retrieved from https://blog.slock.it/partnering-with-safeshare-to-create-the-ad-hoc-insurance-of-the-sharing-economy-77462163ab91.

Slock.it. (2017). *Ethereum computer.* Retrieved from https://slock.it/ethereum_computer.html.

Sundararajan, A. (2017). *The sharing economy: The end of employment and the rise of crowd-based capitalism.* Cambridge, MA, London: The Mit Press.

Swan, M. (2015). *Blockchain: Blueprint for a new economy* (1st ed., Online-Ausg.). Sebastopol, CA: O'Reilly Media, Inc.

Taeihagh, A. (2017). Crowdsourcing, sharing economies and development. *Journal of Developing Societies, 33*(2), 191–222. Retrieved from https://doi.org/10.1177%2F0169796X17710072.

Tapscott, D., & Tapscott, A. (2016). *Blockchain revolution: How the technology behind bitcoin is changing money, business, and the world.* US New York: Penguin.

TaskRabbit Inc. (2019). What is the TaskRabbit service fee? Retrieved from https://support.taskrabbit.com/hc/en-us/articles/204411610-What-is-the-TaskRabbit-Service-Fee-.

Ting, D. (2016). *Why Airbnb and other travel brands are interested in blockchain technology.* Retrieved from https://skift.com/2016/05/12/why-airbnb-and-other-travel-brands-are-interested-in-blockchain-technology/.

Tumasjan, A. (forthcoming). Hype or hope? The emergence of the blockchain and crypto industry. In M. Kipping, T. Kurosawa, & D. E. Westney (Eds.), *Oxford handbook of industry dynamics.*

Tumasjan, A. (2018). Blockchain-technologie und das internet of things: Kurzfristiger hype oder eine symbiose für neue IoT-Geschäftsmodelle? *Industrie 4.0 Management, 34*(2), 29–32.

Tumasjan, A., & Beutel, T. (2019). Blockchain-based decentralized business models in the sharing economy: A technology adoption perspective. In B. Treiblmaier (Ed.), *Business transformation through blockchain* (Vol. 24, pp. 77–120). https://doi.org/10.1007/978-3-319-98911-2_3.

Uber Marketplace. (2018). *Uber service fee: How can pricing serve riders and drivers?* Retrieved from https://marketplace.uber.com/pricing/service-fee.

Upwork Inc. (2019). *Freelancer service fees.* Retrieved from https://support.upwork.com/hc/en-us/articles/211062538-Freelancer-Service-Fees.

Venkatesh, V. (2013). Unified theory of acceptance and use of technology: A synthesis and the road ahead. *Journal of the Association of Information Systems, 17*(5), 328–376.

Wehome. (2019). *Wehome whitepaper: Home sharing on blockchain.* Retrieved from Wehome website: https://wehome.me/download/whitepaper_en.pdf.

Zaveri, P., & Bosa, D. (2019, February 15). Uber's growth slowed dramatically in 2018. *CNBC.* Retrieved from https://www.cnbc.com/2019/02/15/uber-2018-financial-results.html.

Zhu, F., & Iansiti, M. (2019). Why some platforms thrive and others don't. *Harvard Business Review,* 118–125. Retrieved from https://hbr.org/2019/01/why-some-platforms-thrive-and-others-dont.

Patrick Schneck, M.Sc. (TUM) is alumni of the Technical University of Munich and of the ESB Business School Reutlingen. He holds degrees in Management and Technology as well as Industrial Engineering. His research focusses on the implications of blockchain technology for businesses in general and for platform business models in particular. In his work he analyzes the disruptive potential of blockchain technology based on its potential to allow for building new, decentralized networks that are in direct competition with established digital platforms. He currently works as a strategy and IT consultant in business and technology innovation for Capgemini Invent Germany. He advises international clients on their digital transformation journeys and on how to leverage technology to build a faster, more agile and customer-oriented business. He has worked with clients in retail, automotive, public services, and life sciences.

Prof. Dr. Andranik Tumasjan is a professor and head of the research group of management and digital transformation (MDT) at Johannes Gutenberg University Mainz, Germany. In his research, he investigates how the digital transformation impacts management and gives rise to the emergence of new organizational forms, business models, and entrepreneurial opportunities. His current focus is on the potential of blockchain technology for novel business models and organizational forms. He graduated from Ludwig Maximilian University of Munich (LMU) and received his doctoral degree (Dr. rer. pol.) and postdoctoral degree (Dr. habil.) in management from the Technical University of Munich (TUM). As a fellow of the China Scholarship Program, he studied at Nanjing University (China) and was a visiting scholar at Columbia University, New York, and the University of California, Los Angeles. He is a research fellow of the Centre for Blockchain Technologies at University College London. His work has received numerous national and international awards, including Best Paper Awards from the *Academy of Management*, the *Hawaii International Conference on System Sciences (HICSS)*, and the *German Academic Association for Business Research (VHB)*.

Prof. Dr. Isabell M. Welpe is a professor and head of the Strategy and Organization research group at the TU München, Germany. In her current projects, she focuses on the digital transformation of organizations, the impact of emerging technologies such as Blockchain on the economy and organizations and on the future of leadership and work/organizational design. Isabell M. Welpe studied management at the Ludwig-Maximilians-Universität in Munich, Germany and at the Massachusetts Institute of Technology, Boston, USA. In addition, she completed an MSc at the London School of Economics. She has been a visiting professor at the Keck Graduate Institute, Claremont, USA, a postdoctoral fellow at the Carlson School of Management at the University of Minnesota and a post-doc at the Max Planck Institute for Economics. She is a research fellow at the Centre for Blockchain Technologies at the University College London. Her research is covered in the media, such as the Harvard Business Manager, MIT Sloan Management Review, Süddeutsche ZeitungHandelsblattManagerMagazin, Die Welt, BR, and WirtschaftsWoche. Her work has received several national and international awards, including Best Paper Awards from the *Academy of Management (AOM)*, the *Hawaii International Conference on System Sciences (HICSS)*, and the *German Academic Association for Business Research (VHB)*.

Using Blockchain for Online Multimedia Management: Characteristics of Existing Platforms

Bikram Shrestha, Malka N. Halgamuge, and Horst Treiblmaier

Abstract In this descriptive study we investigate the use of blockchain in the online multimedia industry. We analyze the content of 30 peer-reviewed academic publications, white papers and industry websites published between 2016 and 2018 which report the application of blockchain for multimedia management. This includes diverse use cases in the music and advertising industries, healthcare, social media, and content delivery networks. Ethereum was found to be the most popular blockchain and proof of work the favorite consensus mechanism. More than half of the platforms reward their users for content curation and community development. The majority of the platforms have implemented tokens and smart contracts to automate the distribution of earnings or to enable data access. Our study further shows that the majority of multimedia blockchain platforms have already implemented monetization capabilities.

Keywords Blockchain · Multimedia industry · Literature review

1 Introduction

Data generated on the Internet is growing steadily due to facilitated access to technology, an increasing number of applications consuming a lot of bandwidth, and the proliferation of smart devices. The amount of data created in the years 2016 and 2017 alone constituted 90% of total global data in existence at that time, and a future grow rate of 27% per year was predicted in 2018 (Norta et al. 2018). An

B. Shrestha
School of Computing and Mathematics, Charles Sturt University, Bathurst, Australia
e-mail: bikramshrestha777@gmail.com

M. N. Halgamuge (✉)
Department of Electrical and Electronic Engineering, The University of Melbourne, Melbourne, Australia
e-mail: malka.nisha@unimelb.edu.au

H. Treiblmaier
Department of International Management, Modul University Vienna, Vienna, Austria
e-mail: horst.treiblmaier@modul.ac.at

© Springer Nature Switzerland AG 2020
H. Treiblmaier and T. Clohessy (eds.), *Blockchain and Distributed Ledger Technology Use Cases*, Progress in IS, https://doi.org/10.1007/978-3-030-44337-5_14

increase in Internet of Things (IoT) devices, fueled by 5th generation network infrastructure, will further accelerate this trend. This growth has brought numerous data
related threats and management issues related to online content. Tools such as Flash
AIR, Silverlight, Apple HTTP Live Streaming (HLS), Digital Right Management
(DRM), RealNetworks, and Windows DRM are used for license management and
content encryption, but they are unable to verify the ownership of content and detect
fraud (Ma et al. 2018a, b). To address many of the pending problems pertaining to
lack of transparency, privacy, ownership and security, which exist in current online
multimedia management systems, blockchain has been suggested as a decentralized,
tamper-resistant database platform (Ma et al. 2018a, b).

In recent years, a lack of transparency among digital service providers and content
providers has allowed for the poor compensation of artists for their digital work.
Novaes et al. (2018) argue that although existing platforms focus on monetizing
user content, the majority of them lack transparency regarding payment mechanisms
and their underlying algorithms. The incessant increase in consumption of online
multimedia content (Nielsen 2019) has led to a growth in the number of copyright
infringement cases as well as the sharing of fake content using online channels. Such
fake news articles often go viral via social media platforms and are frequently used
as propaganda (Ma et al. 2018a, b). Shang et al. (2018) and Zhaofeng et al. (2018)
point out that the present lack of traceability on media platforms has created new
challenges in identifying responsible persons. Meanwhile, new market segments have
emerged within the data brokerage industry for the monetization of data, and growing
centralization has created a situation where four companies (Facebook, Microsoft,
Apple, Google) have access to the majority of data on the Internet (Novaes et al.
2018). Yet the lack of provision for user consent, numerous data breaches, and the
proliferation of fake news, have altogether led to a lack of trust in Internet giants
such as Google and Facebook (O'Flaherty 2018). This situation has raised interest in
decentralized database platforms, and especially blockchain, as a solution to tackle
issues of data privacy, security, ownership, and transparency.

1.1 Blockchain Functionality

Blockchain is a data structure that consists of blocks of data packages in a chain,
where a block contains multiple transactions that are validated by the network using
cryptographic means (Treiblmaier 2019). This process generates properties such as
anonymity, immutability, and transparency, and thereby enables numerous applications across various industries (Clohessy et al. 2019; Önder and Treiblmaier 2018).
Figure 1 shows the general structure of a multimedia blockchain. Since it is uneco-
nomic to store large files on the chain, multimedia data stored in a database is fed
into a hashing algorithm to create a unique fingerprint ("hash") of a file. This hash
is stored on the blockchain so that anyone who has access to the original file can
check its validity using the hash data. In order to ensure the immutability of the
chain, the hash of the current block includes the hash of the previous block. Altering

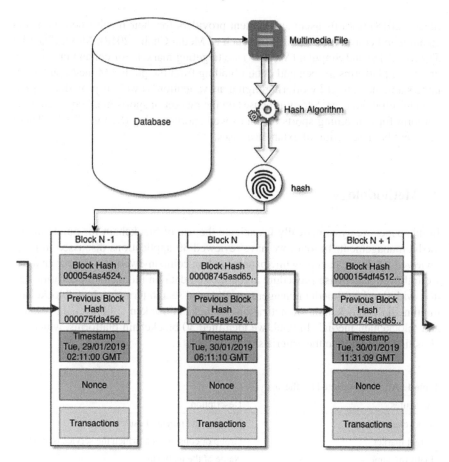

Fig. 1 Data storage on a multimedia blockchain

information would therefore require the recalculation of the hash of all subsequent blocks in the chain.

1.2 Blockchain in the Multimedia Industry

Various blockchain-based platforms such as Opus (2018), imusify (2018) and CreativeChain (2017) have been developed to tackle issues present in the current centralized systems. DataWallet, for example, aims to create a fair and transparent data exchange protocol especially targeting the data brokerage industry (Norta et al. 2018). The Ara content delivery platform uses blockchain to store license transactions for each file (Jiang et al. 2018). Current is a music service platform which rewards multimedia users in exchange for their data and interactions (Novaes et al. 2018). Similarly,

Steem (2018) rewards users and content providers for their involvement in media creation and consumption. Platforms such as Media Chain (2018), MovieChain by Tvzavr (2018) and SingularTV (2018) are targeting markets for content creators by providing platforms to seek and obtain funding from the public. Monegraph (2018) targets a niche market by offering digital art validation as well as providing a platform to sell unique art. Scorum focuses on the market of sports media by creating a platform for consuming sports media as well sports betting (Scorum 2018). These represent but a selection of extant use cases.

2 Methodology

In this paper we systematically investigate the use of blockchain for online multimedia management. In total, we have reviewed 30 applications discussed in peer-reviewed academic papers, white papers, and on company websites. In our analysis we followed a stepwise procedure and collected data on blockchain platforms that deal with data/multimedia management. We used search terms such as 'blockchain multimedia', 'blockchain monetization', 'blockchain token', 'blockchain reward' and 'blockchain media'. In total, we identified 30 blockchain platforms, which we classified according to the criteria shown in Table 1.

Table 1 Attributes selected for the analysis

Attributes	Description
Blockchain use case	Existing and potential use cases
Target market	Group of consumers at which the service is aimed
Platform name	Name of the platform
Underlying framework	Development of a new framework or fork of an existing one
Monetization	Possibility to generate revenue with the platform
Maximum transactions per second (TPS)	The theoretical maximum number of transactions which can be processed per second
Smart contracts	Self-executing programs to automate tasks
Consensus	The set of rules that nodes follow to validate blocks
Token	Name of the token
Token standard	Standards describing the operation of the token
Reward system	Incentives for users who provide feedback or use/provide content

3 Results

The list of sources and the complete results table can be found in the appendix. In the following sections we highlight the most important characteristics of the blockchain-based multimedia platforms. Figure 2 lists the fields in which the platforms operate, with the advertising industry, the music industry, and the healthcare sector attracting the most platforms, followed by uses for researchers, the film industry, and digital content delivery. We found only a single platform within each of the fields: sport media, social media, television broadcasting, art collecting, entertainment, and digital media creation.

Figure 3 shows that the vast majority of blockchain-based multimedia platforms employ the Ethereum blockchain. Three platforms were built upon each of Bitcoin, Hyperledger Fabric, and Graphene, while only a single platform used each of PIVX, Dash, and Neo.

Figure 4 shows the consensus mechanisms being used by the platforms, with proof of work as the most popular consensus method, followed by delegated proof of stake. As blockchain platforms are trying to solve scalability issues, many new consensus mechanisms are being developed and tried out. In total, we found 12 different mechanisms.

In Fig. 5 we list several features of the platforms. 73.33% of them offer a monetization capability, which enables the artists to directly generate revenue from their digital asset. Slightly more than half of them (53.33%) have a system in place which rewards users for their interaction and helps to attract new users (Novaes et al. 2018; Steem 2018). 80% of the platforms apply smart contracts to automate the licensing process as well as reward/royalty distribution.

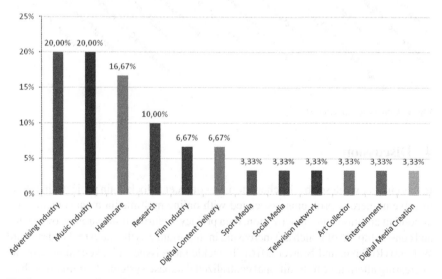

Fig. 2 Multimedia blockchain platform proliferation, by field

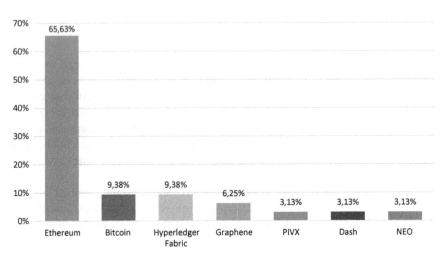

Fig. 3 Blockchain platform underlying multimedia applications

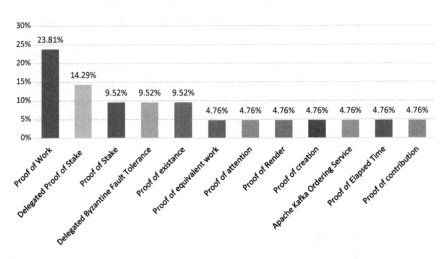

Fig. 4 Consensus mechanisms

4 Discussion

In this chapter we describe the characteristics of recent blockchain projects that strive to solve numerous problems associated with online multimedia management, such as content curation and monetization, data privacy, security, transparency, ownership and censorship, all of which are increasing in importance as the industry heads toward Web 3.0 (Rudman and Brewer 2016). To tackle these issues, blockchain presents an interesting alternative to traditional centralized database systems. Our findings show that the industry has already recognized the potential benefits of blockchain. This

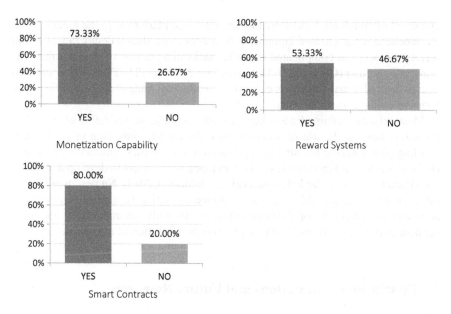

Fig. 5 Features of blockchain-based multimedia platforms

comes as no surprise, since industries depending on multimedia content have, for some time, faced challenges arising from the limitations of centralized solutions (Norta et al. 2018; Media Chain 2018; Opus 2018; AdEx 2018; Emerify 2018). We found Ethereum to be the dominant blockchain on which most multimedia platforms are currently being developed. Ethereum was especially designed as a versatile blockchain platform and has seen strong developer support and constant innovation (Schneider 2014). It has to be noted, however, that Ethereum has been criticized for its centralized development governed by the Ethereum foundation (Voshmgir 2017).

Our results further show that the (equal) largest portion of the researched multimedia blockchain platforms are employed by the music industry. Platforms such as *Current* (2018), *Opus* (2018), *imusify* (2018), Ujo (2018), *dot Blockchain* (2018) and *Musicoin* (2017) are implementing blockchain to solve issues related to digital rights management, royalty distribution, and the fair compensation of artists. In the advertising industry, blockchain platforms are built to remedy problems such as lack of privacy, transparency, unauthorized data mining, and misuse (Norta et al. 2018; AdEx 2018). According to Statista (2017), the cost of digital fraud amounted to $19 million in 2018 and will rise to $44 million in 2022. Consequently, the *AdEx* (2018), *BAT* (2018), *Papyrus* (2018), *AdLedger* (2017), *DataWallet* (2018), and *Lucidity* (2018) platforms apply blockchain technology to address issues faced by the advertising industry. The healthcare industry uses electronic medical records (EMR) to store patients' data, yet the exponential increase in the amount of data being gathered leads to problems of data fragmentation, interoperability, and security (Bogle

2018): all of which are tackled by blockchain-based platforms. In the media industry, blockchain has enabled computing resources to be shared democratically, and thereby to carry out complicated rendering tasks in a fraction of the time that was previously needed (Otoy 2017). Platforms like *TV-TWO* (TV-TWO 2018) strive to disrupt the traditional Television ecosystem, while *Ara* (Jiang et al. 2018) offers new forms of online content delivery.

Most existing multimedia blockchain platforms offer monetization of their digital assets through the use of tokens to ease fundraising, investing or community building. Token enable investment opportunities in the form of initial coin offerings (ICO) or security token offerings (STO) and incentivize users to develop a community (Parker et al. 2016; Belleflamme et al. 2014; Mollick 2014). Numerous platforms offer reward systems enabled by tokens to promote self-governance, quality assurance, and to further develop the community. Additionally, smart contracts automate the distribution of royalties, digital rights, and the allocation of resources.

5 Conclusions, Limitations and Future Research

In this study we give an overview of current implementations of blockchain in the online multimedia industry, which includes sectors as diverse as the music industry, advertising, healthcare, social media, and content delivery. Ethereum was found to be the most popular blockchain on which the majority of platforms were built. Proof of work was shown as the most popular consensus mechanism, followed by delegated proof of stake. More research is needed to investigate other attributes, such as scalability and throughput. Furthermore, we did not evaluate the legal challenges and other implications presented by blockchains. Overall, blockchain turns out to be a versatile platform to develop online multimedia management solutions for existing issues of data privacy, security, ownership, transparency, and monetization. Future research can include additional criteria, select a more comprehensive sample, and elaborate on potential implications the current developments might have for the multimedia industry.

Appendix: List of Sources

No	Citation	Blockchain use case	Target market	Platform name	Underlying framework	Monetization	Max. TPS	Smart contracts[a]	Consensus	Token	Token standard	Reward system
1	Norta et al. (2018)	Advertisement	Advertisement industry	DataWallet	Ethereum	Implemented	–	Smart contract	Proof of work	DXT	–	Yes
2	Novaes et al. (2018)	Music distribution	Music industry	Current	Ethereum	Implemented	–	Ethereum smart contract	–	CRNC	ERC20	Yes
3	Steem (2018)	Social media	Social media	Steem	Graphene	Implemented	10,000	–	Delegated proof of stake	STEEM	–	Yes
4	Media Chain (2018)	Movie funding/DRM	Film industry	MediaChain	Ethereum	Implemented	–	Ethereum smart contract	Delegated byzantine fault tolerance	MDC	ERC20	No
5	Ujo (2018)	Music distribution	Music industry	Ujo	Ethereum	Implemented	–	Ethereum smart contract	–	Patronage badges	ERC721	Yes
6	Monegraph (2018)	Digital art	Art collector	Monegraph	Bitcoin	Implemented	–	Smart contract	Proof of existence	No token	–	No
7	Opus (2018)	Music distribution	Music industry	OPUS	Ethereum	Implemented	–	Ethereum smart contract	–	OPT	ERC23	No
8	Scorum (2018)	E-sport/sport media	Sport media	Scorum	Graphene	Implemented	10,000	–	Delegated proof of stake	SCR	–	Yes
9	imusify (2018)	Music distribution	Music industry	imusify	NEO	Implemented	10,000	NEO smart contract	Delegated byzantine fault tolerance	IMU	NEP-5	Yes
10	Movieschain by Tvzavr (2018)	Movie funding/DRM	Film industry	Movieschain	Ethereum	Implemented	–	Ricardian smart contract	–	ZVR	–	No
11	SingularDTV (2018)	Multimedia	Entertainment	SingularDTV	Ethereum	Implemented	–	Smart contract	–	SNGLS	–	No
12	Creativechain (2017)	Musicians/designers/writer	Entertainment	CreativeChain	–	Implemented	1000	Smart contract	Proof of creation	CREA	–	Yes

(continued)

(continued)

No	Citation	Blockchain use case	Target market	Platform name	Underlying framework	Monetization	Max. TPS	Smart contracts[a]	Consensus	Token	Token standard	Reward system
									Proof of existence			
13	Musicoin (2017)	Music distribution	Music industry	Musicoin	Ethereum	Implemented	–	Pay per play smart contract	Proof of work	MUSIC	–	Yes
14	dotblockchainmedia (2018)	Music distribution	Music industry	dotBlockchain	Bitcoin	Implemented	–	–	Proof of elapsed time	No token	–	No
15	Papyrus (2018)	Advertisement	Advertisement industry	Papyrus	Ethereum	Implemented	1,000,000	Ethereum smart contract	Proof of stake / Delegated proof of stake	PPR	ERC20	Yes
16	Lucidity (2018)	Advertisement	Advertisement industry	Lucidity	Ethereum	Not implemented	–	Smart contract	–	No token	–	Yes
17	Ma et al. (2018a, b)	DRM multimedia	Research	DRMChain	Ethereum	Not implemented	1000	–	–	No token	–	No
18	(Zhaofeng et al. 2018)	Digital art	Research	Artwork DRM	Hyperledger fabric	Not implemented	–	–	–	No token	–	No
19	Ma et al. (2018)	Multimedia	Research	Master–Slave blockchain	Bitcoin	Not implemented	–	–	Proof of equivalent work / Proof of contribution	No token	–	No
20	Medicalchain (2018)	Health record management	Healthcare / Research	Medicalchain	Hyperledger fabric / Ethereum	Implemented	–	Ethereum smart contract	–	MedToken	ERC20	Yes
21	Ekblaw et al. (2016)	Health record management	Healthcare	MedRec	Ethereum	Not implemented	–	Ethereum smart contract	Proof of work	No token	–	No
22	McFarlane et al. (2017)	Health record management	Healthcare	Patientory	Ethereum	Not implemented	–	–	–	PTOY	–	No
23	Emerify (2018)	Health management	Healthcare	Health Passport	Ethereum	Not implemented	–	Ethereum smart contract	Proof of work	HIT	ERC20	Yes

(continued)

(continued)

No	Citation	Blockchain use case	Target market	Platform name	Underlying framework	Monetization	Max. TPS	Smart contracts[a]	Consensus	Token	Token standard	Reward system
24	TV-TWO (2018)	Smart TV content and ad distribution	Television Network	TV-TWO	Ethereum	Implemented	–	Ethereum smart contract	–	TTV	ERC20	Yes
25	Basic Attention Token (2018)	Advertisement	Advertisement Industry	Basic Attention Token	Ethereum	Implemented	–	Ethereum smart contract	Proof of attention	BAT	ERC20	Yes
26	Timicoin (2018)	Health record management	Healthcare	TimiHealth	Hyperledger Fabric	Not implemented	–	Hyperledger chaincode	Apache Kafka ordering service	TMC	–	No
					PIVX				Proof of work			
					Dash				Proof of stake			
27	Jiang et al. (2018)	Content delivery	Digital Content Delivery	Ara	Ethereum	Implemented	–	Ethereum smart contract	–	Ara	–	Yes
28	Otoy (2017)	Rendering Graphic	Digital Media Creation	Render Token	Ethereum	Implemented	–	Ethereum smart contract	Proof of render	RNDR	ERC20	Yes
29	Georgiev et al. (2017)	Advertisement	Advertisement Industry	AdLedger	Ethereum	Implemented	–	Smart contract	–	ALT	–	No
30	AdEx (2018)	Advertisement	Advertisement Industry	AdEx	Ethereum	Implemented	–	Ethereum smart contract	–	ADX	–	No

[a]Several applications did not name the underlying platform. In this case the generic term "smart contracts" is used

References

AdEx. (2018). *AdEx blockchain-based ad network.* Retrieved 12, 2018 from adex.network: https://www.adex.network/.

Basic Attention Token. (2018, March 13). *Basic attention token : Introducing blockchain-based digital advertising.* Retrieved from Basic attention token: https://basicattentiontoken.org/BasicAttentionTokenWhitePaper-4.pdf.

Bogle, A. (2018, July 31). *Health service providers suffer the most data breaches, as overall numbers jump.* Retrieved from abc.net.au: https://www.abc.net.au/news/science/2018-07-31/information-commissioner-health-sector-leads-data-breaches/10052650.

Clohessy, T., Acton, T., & Rogers, N. (2019). Blockchain adoption: Technological, organisational and environmental considerations. In H. Treiblmaier & R. Beck (Eds.), *Business transformation through blockchain* (pp. 47–76). Cham: Palgrave Macmillan.

Creativechain. (2017, Feburary 23). *Whitepaper introduction.* Retrieved from crea: https://creativechain.org/wp-content/uploads/2017/03/Whitepaper-Creativechain-1.2.pdf.

dotblockchainmedia. (2018). *The future is already here.* Retrieved Dec 21, 2018 from dotblockchainmedia: https://dotblockchainmedia.com/main/#technology-1-section.

Ekblaw, A., Azaria, A., John D. Halamka, M., & Lippman, A. (2016, August). *What is medrec?* Retrieved from MedRec: https://dci.mit.edu/assets/papers/eckblaw.pdf.

Emerify. (2018). *Health information token.* Retrieved 12, 2018 from emerify.com: https://www.emrify.com/hit/assets/Whitepaper.pdf.

Ethereum. (2018). *Ethereum: Blockchain app platform.* Retrieved from Ethereum: https://www.ethereum.org/.

Fedorov, A. K., Kiktenko, E. O., & Lvovsky, A. I. (2018). Quantum computers put blockchain security at risk. *Nature: International Journal of Science, 563*(7732), 465–467.

Georgiev, I., Stoyanov, D., & Ivanova, V. (2017). *Adledger.io.* Retrieved from adledger: https://adledger.io/whitepaper.pdf.

Henry, R., Herzberg, A., & Kate, A. (2018, July/August). Blockchain access privacy: Challenges and directions. *IEEE Security & Privacy, 16*(4), 38–45.

imusify. (2018, May 1). Retrieved from imusify: https://imusify.com/whitepaper.pdf.

International Telecommunication Union. (2017, July). *ICT facts and figures 2017.* Retrieved Jan 2019 from itu.int: https://www.itu.int/en/ITU-D/Statistics/Documents/facts/ICTFactsFigures2017.pdf.

ITU. (2018, November 27). *ICT statistics home page.* Retrieved from International Telecommunications Union: https://www.itu.int/en/ITU-D/Statistics/Documents/statistics/2018/ITU_Key_2005-2018_ICT_data_with%20LDCs_rev27Nov2018.xls.

Jiang, E., Kelly, C., Werle, J., Mugavero, T., & Kincaid, V. (2018, October 1). *The blockchain content platform.* Retrieved from ara.one: https://media.ara.one/whitepapers/ara-whitepaper-en.pdf.

Karame, G., & Capkun, S. (2018, August 06). Blockchain security and privacy. *IEEE Security & Privacy, 16*(4), 11–12.

lBelleflamme, P., Lambert, T., & Schwienbacher, A. (2014). Crowdfunding: Tapping the right crowd. *Journal of Business Venturing,* 610–611.

Lucidity. (2018). *Lucidity.* Retrieved from Lucidity: https://lucidity.tech/whitepaperdownload/.

Ma, Z., Huang, W., Bi, W., Gao, H., & Wang, Z. (2018a, August). A master-slave blockchain paradigm and application in digital rights management. *China Communication, 15*(8), 174–188.

Ma, Z., Jiang, M., Gao, H., & Wang, Z. (2018). Blockchain for digital rights management. *Future Generation Computer Systems, 89,*746–764.

McFarlane, C., Beer, M., Brown, J., & Prendergast, N. (2017, May). *Advancing blockchain technology.* Retrieved from Patientory Association: https://ptoy.org/patientory_whitepaper.pdf.

Media Chain. (2018, January). Media chain: A de-centralised blockchain focused on the film industry. Retrieved from https://wxappres.feeyan.com/block/project/3710.pdf.

Medicalchain. (2018). *Medicalchain*. Retrieved from medicalchain.com: https://medicalchain.com/Medicalchain-Whitepaper-EN.pdf.

Mollick, E. (2014). The dynamics of crowdfunding: An exploratory study. *Journal of Business Venturing*, 1–16.

Monegraph. (2018, November). *Overview*. Retrieved from monegraph.com: https://monegraph.com/#Overview.

Movieschain by Tvzavr. (2018, August 15). *Blockchain-based decentralized film distribution platform*. Retrieved from Movieschain by tvzavr: https://www.movieschain.io/whitepaper/.

Musicoin. (2017, October). *Revolutionizing music with the blockchain*. Retrieved from Musicoin: https://www.scribd.com/document/362834077/Musicoin-White-Paper-v2-0-0.

Nielsen. (2019, January 8). *Total album equivalent consumption in the U. S. Increased 23% in 2018* (Nielsen). Retrieved from Nielsen: https://www.nielsen.com/us/en/insights/news/2019/total-album-equivalent-consumption-in-the-us-increased-23-percent-in-2018.html.

Norta, A., Hawthorne, D., & Engel, S. L. (2018). A privacy-protecting data-exchange wallet with ownership- and monetization capabilities. In *2018 International Joint Conference on Neural Networks (IJCNN)*. IJCNN.

Novaes, D., McEvily, N., Panesar, K., Moyer, J., Fisch, R., Pai, A., … Ryan, W. (2018). *A rewarded blockchain enabled multimedia network*

Önder, I., & Treiblmaier, H. (2018). Blockchain and tourism: Three research propositions. *Annals of Tourism Research, 72*, 180–182.

O'Flaherty, K. (2018, October 10). *This is why people no longer trust google and facebook with their data*. Retrieved from Forbes.com: https://www.forbes.com/sites/kateoflahertyuk/2018/10/10/this-is-why-people-no-longer-trust-google-and-facebook-with-their-data/#5c9a22a54b09.

Opus. (2018). *Opus*. Retrieved 12, 2018 from opus.audio: https://opus.audio/whitepaper.pdf.

Otoy. (2017, August 28). *RNDR: Distributed GPU rendering on the blockchain*. Retrieved from Rendertoken: https://files.acrobat.com/a/preview/d442da8a-067e-490f-88cf-2c4511016ff7.

Papyrus. (2018). *Papyrus*. Retrieved 12, 2018 from Papyrus: https://papyrus.global/media/files/whitepaper_en.pdf.

Parker, G. G., Alstyne, M. W., & Choundary, S. P. (2016). *Platform revolution. How networked markets are transforming the economy and how to make them work for you*. New York: W.W. Norton & Company Inc.

Piramuthu, S., Kapoor, G., Zhou, W., & Mauw, S. (2012). Input online review data and related bias in recommender systems. *Decision Support Systems, 53*(3), 418–424.

Rosenblatt, B. (2016). *Watermarking technology and blockchains in the music industry*. Beaverton.

Rudman, R., & Brewer, R. (2016, February 01). Defining web 3.0: opportunities and challenges. *The Electronic Library, 34*(1), 132–154.

Schneider, N. (2014, April 7). *Code your own utopia: Meet ethereum, bitcoin's most ambitious successor*. Retrieved from Aljazeera America: https://america.aljazeera.com/articles/2014/4/7/code-your-own-utopiameetethereumbitcoinasmostambitioussuccessor.html.

Scorum. (2018). *Scorumcoins*. Retrieved Nov 2018 from https://icorating.com/upload/whitepaper/W4UvRqUoZimD7Bn9wdnY4MTzKH5AFcRL5HH4Iccn.pdf.

Shang, W., Liu, M., Lin, W., & Jia, M. (2018). Tracing the source of news based on blockchain. In *2018 IEEE/ACIS 17th International Conference on Computer and Information Science (ICIS)* (pp. 377–381). Singapore: IEEE.

SingularDTV. (2018). *SingularDTV*. Retrieved Dec 21, 2018 from SingularDTV: https://singulardtv.com/.

Statista. (2017, September). *Estimated cost of digital ad fraud worldwide in 2018 and 2022 (in billion U.S. dollars)*. Retrieved from statista: https://www.statista.com/statistics/677466/digital-ad-fraud-cost/.

Steem. (2018, June 28). *Steem: An incentivized, blockchain-based, public content platform*. Retrieved Nov 2018 from Steem: Steem Whitepaper https://steem.com/wp-content/uploads/2018/10/steem-whitepaper.pdf.

Timicoin. (2018). *The tokenized healthcare ecosystem*. Retrieved from Timicoin: https://www.timicoin.io/timicoinwhitePaper.pdf.

Treiblmaier, H. (2019). Toward more rigorous blockchain research: Recommendations for writing blockchain case studies. *Frontiers in Blockchain, 2*(3), 1–15.

TV-TWO. (2018, April 20). *TV-TWO*. Retrieved from TV-TWO: https://tv-two.com/TV_Whitepaper.pdf.

Ujo. (2018). *Frequently asked questions*. Retrieved Dec 21, 2018 from ujomusic.com: https://www.ujomusic.com/faq.

Voshmgir, S. (2017, September 21). Disrupting governance with blockchains and smart contracts. *Strategic Change, 26*(5). Retrieved from https://doi-org.ezproxy.csu.edu.au/10.1002/jsc.2150.

Vukolić, M. (2016). The quest for scalable blockchain fabric: Proof-of-work vs. BFT replication. In *Open problems in network security*. Springer International Publishing.

Weber, R. M., & Horn, B. D. (2017). Breaking bad security vulnerabilities. *Journal of Financial Service Professionals, 71*(1), 50–54.

Zheng, Z., Xie, S., Dai, H. N., Wang, H. (2016). *Blockchain challenges and opportunities: A survey*. Work Pap.

Zeilinger, M. (2018). Digital art as 'monetised graphics': Enforcing intellectual property on the blockchain. *Philosophy & Technology, 31*(1), 15–41.

Zhaofeng, M., Weihua, H., & Hongmin, G. (2018). A new blockchain-based trusted DRM scheme for built-I content protection. *EURASIP Journal on Image and Video Processing*.

Bikram Shrestha is a software developer currently working in the security industry as a full-stack developer. He graduated from Charles Sturt University, Melbourne, Australia in Master of Information Technology with Postgraduate University Medal in the year 2019. He has also done master's in business management with Project from BPP University, London, UK in the year 2016. His research interests include Blockchain, Internet of things and Machine Learning.

Malka N. Halgamuge is a researcher in the Department of Electrical and Electronic engineering, University of Melbourne. She received the PhD degree from the same department in 2007. Since then she has published in areas including wireless communication, life sciences, Internet of Things, big data, and blockchain. She has published more than 110 peer-reviewed technical articles attracting over 1174 Google Scholar Citations with h-index = 19 and her Research Gate RG Score is 35.98. She is an experienced researcher and educator with a demonstrated history of working with highly reputed research institutes in University of California, Los Angeles (UCLA), Chinese Academy of Sciences (CAS), Beijing, China, and Lund University, Sweden.

Horst Treiblmaier is a professor in international management at Modul University Vienna, Austria. He received a Ph.D. in Management Information Systems in 2001 from the Vienna University of Economics and Business in Austria and worked as a Visiting Professor at Purdue University, University of California, Los Angeles (UCLA), University of British Columbia (UBC), and the University of Technology in Sydney (UTS). He has more than fifteen years of experience as a researcher and consultant and has worked on projects with Microsoft, Google, and the United Nations Industrial Development Organization (UNIDO). His research interests include the economic and business implications of Blockchain, cryptoeconomics, methodological and epistemological problems of social science research and gamification. Currently he serves on the board of the "City of Blockchain", an association promoting blockchain and cryptographic technologies. His research has appeared in journals such as *Information Systems JournalStructural Equation Modeling*, The *DATA BASE for Advances in Information Systems, Communications of the Association for Information SystemsInformation & ManagementJournal of Electronic Commerce ResearchJournal of Global Information ManagementSchmalenbach Business ReviewSupply Chain Management: An International JournalInternational Journal of Logistics Management*, and *Wirtschaftsinformatik (Business & Information Systems Engineering).*

Supply Chain Visibility Ledger

Wout J. Hofman

Abstract Improved situational awareness, also known as Supply Chain Visibility, contributes to better decisions with the ability to synchronize processes and reduce costs. It requires data sharing of for instance positions, speed, direction, and estimated time of arrival and—departure at locations of vessels, trucks, barges, and trains. Any two collaborating stakeholders might already be sharing these process 'milestones' in the context of a commercial relation, using a platform. Reception of a milestone by a stakeholder may be a trigger to inform a customer of the progress of its order or can be used to synchronize physical processes. First, this research chapter specifies supply chain visibility in more detail and secondly provides arguments for applying distributed ledger technology. These arguments address on the one hand near real-time share milestones in supply and logistics chains with a broadcast mechanism based on subscriptions and on the other hand large scale distribution and implementation of software on a distributed ledger. The latter raises issues of governance, that will be briefly touched upon. Scientific contributions of this research chapter are in 'state' validation of real-world objects as a means of mining, ontology-based input validation, and interaction sequence specification by a business process choreography.

Keywords Supply chain visibility · Digital Twin · Distributed ledger · Blockchain · Semantic technology

1 Introduction

The lack of or limited situational awareness of the various stakeholders involved in supply and logistics chains causes unnecessary delays and—waiting times, fines imposed by customers for delays, and unnecessary priority shipment for products required by a customer, and stock reduction (Parjogo and Olhager 2012; Urciuoli and Hintsa 2018; Caridi et al. 2014). The latter paper (Caridi et al. 2014), provides a good literature review of definitions of supply chain visibility and potential benefits. Lack

W. J. Hofman (✉)
TNO, The Hague, The Netherlands
e-mail: wout.hofman@tno.nl

© Springer Nature Switzerland AG 2020
H. Treiblmaier and T. Clohessy (eds.), *Blockchain and Distributed Ledger Technology Use Cases*, Progress in IS, https://doi.org/10.1007/978-3-030-44337-5_15

of visibility leads to higher costs, increases the carbon footprint, and contributes to waste. In general, improved situational awareness will contribute to decision making (Endsley 1995). (Near) real-time supply chain visibility addresses these issues.

Supply chain visibility is also relevant to authorities like customs. For this purpose, they developed the concept of 'data pipelines' where data would come available to customs authorities (Heshket 2010). This concept evolved in so-called trusted trade-lanes (Hulstijn et al. 2016), where customs authorities received data from enterprises other than traders on a voluntary basis. The underlying architectures for sharing data in these data pipelines are based on either pushing data to customs authorities or notifying them of data availability (Rukanova et al. 2018).

Thus, there is a clear business case for supply chain visibility to both public and private sector. However, supply and logistics chains can be complex. International supply chains involve many enterprises and authorities, each with their heterogeneous IT systems either tailored Commercial Off The Shelve (COTS) or proprietary developed. Data is duplicated by messages between these systems, including various formats and implementation guides of open standards (Hofman 2018). Many of these systems are not yet able for real-time processing of events generated by physical assets (IoT—Internet of Things). Different solutions are being developed addressing these issues, each with their (proprietary) interfaces. Tradelens and the Electronic Product Code Information System [EPCIS (Global Systems One 2014)] are two examples. Identity mechanisms supported with delegation (iShare 2019) are introduced to access the status of logistics chains. These various solutions have a so-called publish and subscribe (Erl 2005) model in common, for instance in a bilateral collaboration or based on delegations.

This research chapter provides a solution for real time status sharing between all stakeholders in supply and logistics networks by Distributed Ledger Technology (DLT). Subscription mechanisms are based on transactional relations between stakeholders and the associations between the various physical objects, like a container transported by a vessel. Additional rules are specified by which status information is propagated downstream in chains towards the final destination, especially the predicted status to address the aforementioned issues.

First, supply chain visibility is analyzed and illustrated by two use cases. Secondly, the solution is specified illustrated with a first demonstrator. Finally, the relation with available standards is analyzed and conclusions are presented.

2 Supply Chain Visibility

This section introduces supply chain visibility and further generalizes the issues that can be addressed by a Supply Chain Visibility Ledger. The introduction contains some references to typical cases; examples of use case can be found in literature like (Hofman et al. 2018).

2.1 Introduction to Supply Chain Visibility

Supply chain visibility can be defined as 'awareness of and control over end-to-end supply chain information—including insight in sources of data and whereabouts of goods—enabling agile, resilient, sustainable as well as compliant and trusted supply chains' (Wieland and Wallenburg). Other definitions state 'the ability to be alerted to exceptions in supply chain execution' or 'capturing and analysing supply chain data that informs decision-making, mitigates risk, and improves processes' (Caridi et al. 2014). Basically, it supply chain visibility is about improving decision-making by increased situational awareness (Endsley 1995). Supply chain visibility has many advantages in terms of costs and time (Caridi et al. 2014) based on process synchronization. It reduces inventory and contributes to customer service by on-time delivery and providing customer visibility. Process synchronization requires sharing of knowledge of the location of physical objects, and in case these physical objects are transport means, their speed and direction, any relation between physical objects like a container transported by a truck, and a prediction of a time for completing a particular logistics operation. These times can be various, like:

- Transport operations—the following predicted times are relevant:
  - Estimated Time of Arrival (ETA) of a transport means at a location, e.g. a vessel in a port.
  - Estimated Time of Departure (ETD) of a transport means, or the combination of the Actual Time of Arrival (ATA) and a predicted duration of a call of a transport means at a location.

- For transshipment operations, the estimated discharge and loading times of cargo objects like containers of and on transport means are relevant. An estimated discharge time provides for instance an indication for the next transport leg to pick up the cargo objects.
- In case of corridor management of for instance locks in inland waterways or short sea shipping between ports (Lind et al. 2018) data on Estimated Arrival Time at a destination like the next port or hub need to be shared. Based on these ETAs, lock planning and speed of barges or feeders can be optimized, thus reducing fuel consumption and contribute to sustainability.
- In global trade, authorities like customs already get data of transport movements, but also require data on diversions and transhipments of goods, combined with their ETA information. This data is required for risk assessment and planning for customs inspections.

These types are basically relevant for synchronizing different transport operations, or what can be called 'transport legs', of a logistics chain. Any disturbances caused by for instance accidents, incidents, lack of qualified personnel, weather conditions, and maintenance of both on physical assets used to facilitate transport operations and the infrastructure used (e.g. roads and inland waterways with locks), will influence these transport operations. They will cause delays that have to be known to the next transport leg.

Administrative procedures may also cause delays. Examples are missing documents or data of a shipment like a Certificate of Origin, lack of a confirmation by an authority like a customs release, a physical inspection of cargo by a customs authority, and payment of the previous transport leg. Providing authorities and financial institutions supply chain visibility, improves their decision processes, which may lead to less or unnecessary delays (Urciuoli and Hintsa 2018; Caridi et al. 2014), contribute to safety (Hofman et al. 2018), and improve supply chain finance. Relevant stakeholders in these supply chains need to be aware of the status of administrative procedures for continuation of the physical chains. Supply chain visibility may include both data of cargo and their itinerary with estimate times of arrival.

Thus, process synchronization of transport operations also has to meet particular conditions imposed by formal—and financial procedures, optionally providing additional data (Hulstijn et al. 2016), and agreements between stakeholders involved, like specified by for instance the INCOTERMS used in international transport. The INCOTERMS specify for instance which of the stakeholders has to pay for which part of a logistics chain. An example is 'free delivered' mostly applied in eCommerce where a shipper pays transport charges. The other example in this section is on process synchronisation for transhipment in a port and the final one presents the data pipeline perspective for global trade facilitation.

2.2 Generic Functionality to Enable Supply Chain Visibility

It is possible to list various business scenarios in which supply chain visibility plays a role. These scenarios vary in terms of for instance transport modality, cargo type, and the aforementioned INCOTERMS. Generalization leads to the following visibility use cases, where milestone data is shared by events:

1. Transaction progress: informing a customer on the start, relevant changes, and the finalization of a transport order.
2. Leg synchronisation: a coordinator of a (part of a) chain synchronizes adjacent legs in that chain, where stakeholders performing these legs only have a transactional relation with the coordinator.
3. Authorities: re-use of relevant transport data for its particular governance role (piggy backing).
4. Conditions for progress: sharing status information generated by stakeholders like customs and financial institutions, where this status information is a relevant condition for further action.

These use cases are related, especially the first two. For instance, an event with a milestone received by a customer from its service providers ('transaction progress') may result in generation of an event by that customer acting as coordinator to another service provider ('leg synchronization'), and an event to its customer ('transaction progress'). Further progress might depend on some status information, e.g. a release notification, and authorities may have to be informed.

The following figures visualizes these two variants, one for transaction progress and another for leg synchronization.

Figure 1 shows that reception of an event for transaction progress may trigger leg synchronisation, generate an event to one or more authorities, and potentially inform a customer of the progress of its transaction.

One of the issues that needs to be addressed by a solution, is that a service provider may report transaction progress of a container, whereas a customer has only knowledge of pallets and not of the container that transports these pallets.

Figure 2 shows that reception of a change from a customer can result in a change to one or more service providers. This change may have to be made visible to an authority. For example, if a shipper informs his forwarder to change the destination of

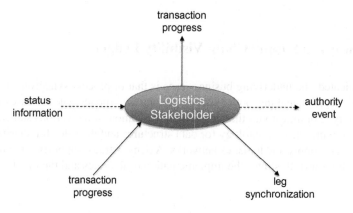

Fig. 1 Triggering by transaction progress

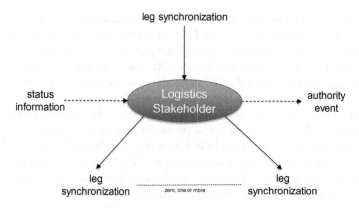

Fig. 2 Triggering by leg synchronization

particular cargo, the port of discharge may have to change to a port in another country, resulting in providing an update to another customs administration for incoming cargo.

In the case of Figs. 4 and 5, status information is either used by the logistics stakeholder itself, e.g. with regards to the previous leg, or must be forwarded to a service provider. There could also be a rule that one or more status information events have to be combined to generate another one, for instance a commercial—and a customs release that are combined a release. The latter release can be shared with a carrier.

Firing an authority event will be triggered by an event; authorities will have to specify the milestones (and references to data sets) they want to receive.

Reception of such an update for leg synchronization may result in zero, one or more updates to service providers as shown in the figure.

These cases will be elaborated further; they provide requirements to the various interfaces. The end of this section will give a summary of these cases.

3   Towards a Supply Chain Visibility Ledger

Like indicated, the underlying business case is that of process synchronization and improved decision making, both by authorities and enterprises. The use cases demonstrate the type of milestones that might be shared amongst the various stakeholders. This section presents an ontology for data structures and the rules for sharing these milestones in supply and logistics networks. A demonstrator supporting the use case of direct transport illustrates the implementation of the rules and the ontology.

3.1   General Concepts

Conceptual, transactional relations formulate the subscription to events. A transactional relation is defined in two ways. First, a customer and a service provider share an order like shipment of cargo, a service provider informs a customer of the status of that order by sharing relevant milestones. Relevant milestones are those of direct transport, potentially extended with intermediate locations relevant to the customer like the location of border crossing or an (air)port where responsibility for transport is handed over (see the use case of port transshipment). The second type of transactional relation is based on an enterprise providing data like a customs declaration to an authority and waiting for status information of that authority. The data will have a unique identification, e.g. a Movement Reference Number for a customs declaration, and contains identifications of one or more physical objects subject. In this proposal, an enterprise acts service provider and an authority as customer.

Secondly, the concept 'Digital Twin' is introduced (Boschert and Rosen 2016): a Digital Twin is a data representation of any physical object, e.g. a container, a truck, a vessel and a product. Any subscription, either an order or a declaration, considers at least one Digital Twin. The concept 'Digital Twin' will be elaborated when specifying an ontology as a basis for data structures in the ledger.

3.2   The Supply Chain Visibility Choreography

The interaction choreography (Object Management Group 2011) of a customer and service provider is depicted as sharing events based on relevant order—and declaration data. In practice, every service provider can be a customer in its turn, by outsourcing parts of an order or bundling orders. Outsourcing is outside scope of the Supply Chain Visibility Ledger. It requires a so-called control tower (Hofman 2014).

The Supply Chain Visibility Ledger does not support ordering, which means that customers and service providers need to enter relevant order data. Eventually, a physical device or a human will generate an event, indicating that a milestone has passed, e.g. a container has been loaded on a truck or a vessel. This event must be linked to an order, where that order can be related to another order by a subcontracting relation or to the itinerary of a transport means.

Figure 3 shows the high-level choreography supported by the Supply Chain Visibility Ledger. It consists of three activities: management of orders that serve as subscriptions to events, itineraries establishing a link to physical transport of cargo contained in orders by a transport means, and events that provide details of milestones relevant to customers. These events might update orders and/or itineraries, for instance indicating that an order has been completed or an itinerary is ended. This choreography allows that events can be stored independent of an order or an itinerary:

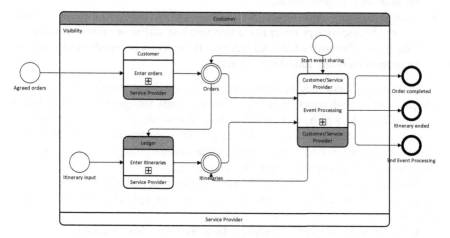

Fig. 3 Choreography supported by the supply chain visibility ledger

a scanning device or human generating the event is not aware of the existence of such an order or itinerary.

First of all, a high-level description of the choreography for orders and itineraries will be given. Secondly, a more detailed specification of the event choreography is provided.

The choreography to register orders basically consists of two steps, namely a customer submitting an order to the ledger and a service provider confirming the order, thus establishing a subscription. Of course, an order may also be rejected if there is no transactional relation. The confirmation of a subscription can be given in three ways, namely a service provider confirming the order directly, e.g. a forwarder confirming that an order with a shipper exists or linking an order to an itinerary. Linking an order to an itinerary depends on the business processes of a service provider that has impact on that of a customer. We distinguish two ways of handling itineraries, namely:

- Itinerary-to-order. The itinerary is established by planning software for assigning orders to a transport means, resulting in an itinerary of that transport means (also known as trip for a truck). As part of the itinerary flow, an itinerary can be stored on the ledger, automatically relating cargo of orders to that itinerary.

  Since a service provider can store this type of itinerary to the ledger before an order has been stored by a customer, that customer will not receive any events with milestones before storing an order with the relevant cargo. To prevent this latter option, the itinerary must contain an order reference in addition to cargo identification(s).

  This type of itinerary is completed if all cargo has been transported. It might never end, if the planning is updated during its execution, meaning for instance a truck just drives (indefinitely) and transports cargo. This would be relevant to especially autonomous transport means.

- Order-to-itinerary. An itinerary like a voyage scheme, flight or timetable of a train is stored by a service provider like a shipping line, airline or railway undertaking to the ledger. During booking and ordering, the itinerary is available to a customer. An order is therefore linked to an itinerary.

This itinerary has a lifetime spanning either geographical or in time. For instance, a voyage ends at its destination. A vessel can have a new voyage at that destination. A flight or timetable, which is scheduled periodically like daily or weekly, will end at a certain time. Whether or not it is replaced by another one depends on the agreements of the service provider with one or more infrastructure managers and/or hubs, like slot allocation at an airport or path allocation for trains.

A state diagram of orders and their cargo represents the possible milestones, which are considered relevant for the current version of the supply chain visibility ledger (Fig. 4).

In this version of the ledger, an order starts once it has been loaded on a transport means. Intermediate positions of the cargo can be given GPS sensors on either cargo or transport means, e.g. the Automatic Identification System (AIS) of vessels and

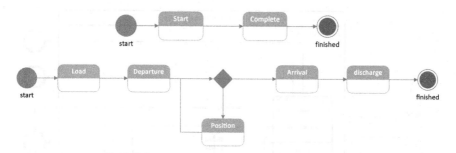

Fig. 4 State diagrams of orders (top diagram) and their cargo (bottom diagram)

barges can generate their position. A future version of the ledger might also support order picking and packing as milestones.

An itinerary can also be represented by a state diagram, see Fig. 5. The underlying assumption of this state diagram is that a transport means always starts by loading cargo at some location at initiation of an itinerary, which is only the case for order-supporting-itinerary. Furthermore, the state diagram assumes that at a location, discharge takes place before loading new cargo. This is not always the case, for instance loading and discharge of containers on a vessel can be in parallel.

Whereas the previous states, which represent milestones, represent the actual state of a transport means at its itinerary, there are also other states relevant, namely:

- Future states: these represent the future state of a transport means during its itinerary. Normally, the Estimated Time of Arrival—and Departure (ETA/ETD) are considered, but also predicted deviations of positions can be given, based on any planned or unplanned activity in the infrastructure. These deviations are the basis for delays and, potentially, changes in the places called upon during the itinerary.
- Data sets: at loading and discharge, data representing the physical state of the cargo at hand over to a carrier and by a carrier to the next leg operator, e.g. a consignee, is represented by a data set. This data set should contain all relevant data required by authorities, like dangerous cargo details required by infrastructure managers.

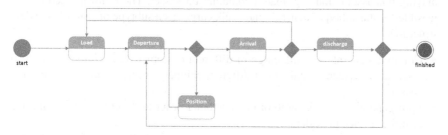

Fig. 5 State diagrams of an itinerary

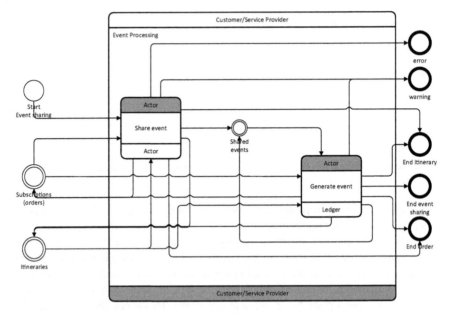

Fig. 6 Choreography for sharing events

The ledger can contain a reference (a link) to a data set, e.g. a transport document, like a waybill or CMR (road transport), and a customs declaration.

Figure 6 shows the choreography for sharing events. The reception of an event with a milestone by a service provider.

Events can be submitted by any actor, either in its role as customer or service provider. Each actor, e.g. an organization or a Digital Twin (see data structures), can have both roles, where in general a Digital Twin will have the role of service provider. Having received an event may also indicate the completion of one or more orders and/or an itinerary.

In an ideal situation, everyone uses the Supply Chain Visibility Ledger. Associations between any two Digital Twins are stored by an event submitted by the actor making this association, e.g. load a container on vessel. The following actions are feasible for the subtype 'general' and 'bulk cargo' as a subtype of 'cargo' (see data structures):

- Combine general—or bulk cargo of different customer orders into one order to a service provider, containers of different shippers are transported by the same vessel,
- Split general—or bulk cargo of one customer order to different orders with one or more service providers.
- A combination of both, namely splitting general—or bulk cargo of one customer order to different orders and combining it with general—or bulk cargo of other customers orders.

These actions impose additional validations for completing an order. For instance, an order where cargo is transported by two or more transport means, is completed when all cargo is delivered at the agreed location. An actor can submit an event to the ledger in its role as customer or service provider, as shown in Fig. 6 by 'share event'.

Each new event stored at the ledger will contain a reference to one or more objects, e.g. a transport means and/or its cargo. Having received an event of a transport means, e.g. its arrival at a location, may generate a new event for cargo to be discharged at that location. A service provider might also submit an event with a milestone, for which a condition is not yet met, e.g. there is not yet a release. In case cargo is loaded, but not yet departed, a notification a new event will be generated to the service provider that departure is not yet allowed. In case cargo is departed, an event indicating a warning will be generated and potentially other stakeholders will have to be informed.

The role of the actor submitting the event should be part of the event, resulting in the following actions:

1. If a service provider submits an event to the ledger, an event is shared with a customer based on a confirmed order only if the place of a Digital Twin in an event equals the place of acceptance,—delivery or some intermediate place mentioned in the customer order. A transport means or cargo object of an event can only be linked to customer orders that are not yet completed. In case a cargo object can be associated to two (or more) orders, it can only be associated to the one that is either not yet completed, or where the timestamp of the milestone given by the event is within the time interval between time of acceptance and—delivery and the place is either the place of acceptance or delivery of an order. This case represents that the same container is transported from a port to the hinterland that can re-appear the same day in the port.

   A warning is generated in relation to conditions (see for instance 'release'). Another warning provides an indication of delays or deviations that are not in line with an itinerary and/or an order. A delay indicates that a milestone is not within its agreed time period, e.g. a transport means arrives too late at a location. A deviation means that a location will be called upon by a transport means, which is not given in the original itinerary. Especially when cargo is discharged at that location, a warning will be generated to a customer. An error represents absence of an itinerary of a transport means and/or absence of cargo in an order. In the latter two cases, the event may be stored temporarily and processed at a later stage when an itinerary and/or order are entered.

2. If a customer shares an event to the ledger, this event should relate to cargo of an order that serves as subscription. The event is directly accessible by the service provider. There are different cases like a forwarder sharing a custom— and a commercial release with a carrier or a shipping line sharing a commercial release with a terminal. In both cases, the event must contain uniqueness of its provenance, customs and a bank respectively. A carrier can thus only pick up a container after a terminal as authenticated the customs release. Record integrity of the releases needs to be provided.

An event submitted by a service provider or customer is always stored in the ledger. It can trigger a new event, either submitted to a service provider or a customer, unless an error or warning is detected. In its turn, this new event is also stored and can trigger generation of a new event. Whenever it is not possible to generate a new event, the process of sharing events ends. It means that none of the following conditions can be met that are implemented by 'generate event':

1. Event is received by a customer. The following rules are validated for generating a new event:
   (a) The receiving customer acts as service provider in an order that contains the Digital Twin of the received event. A new event is generated to that customer. The condition is formulated as: <u>if</u> The Digital Twin in the received event occurs in an order of that customer in its role as service provider <u>and</u> (<u>if</u> (the milestone is departure and the place in the event place of acceptance in the order <u>and</u> the time of the milestone is in the period mentioned in the order) <u>or</u> (the milestone is arrival and the place of the event is the place of delivery in the order <u>and</u> the time of the milestone is in the period mentioned in the order) <u>or</u> the milestone is pass and the intermediate place is in the order) <u>then</u> generate new event to the customer of the order.
   (b) The Digital Twin is associated with another Digital Twin that appears in one or more order. There are two cases identified for these orders (they can be formulated in more detail like the rule before):
       (i) The receiving customer acts as customer. The only relevant situation for generating a new event is where the milestone of the received event is arrival at place of acceptance in the next order. In case the milestone is an ETA prediction, the next leg represented by the order can be informed in case the ETA does not fit with the time period for start of the next leg.
       (ii) The receiving customer acts as service provider. The service provider will generate a new event to a customer as described by the first part of 'share event'.

2. Event is received by a service provider. If the service provider also acts as customer, i.e. it has outstanding orders with other service providers, the event will be shared with those service providers that have the place of acceptance or—departure and the Digital Twins that are concerned as part of the order with them. The places of arrival and—departure can be given as places of call of an itinerary. The time of release also has to fit with the period mentioned in the order.

Sharing a release like a customs—or commercial release is only feasible if that release refers to a particular place, for instance a terminal. Thus, it is not sufficient to specify only a release milestone, but also where the release takes place and what objects it concerns.

3.3 Data Structures—Digital Twin

The data structures for the interactions are based on an ontology of all data that can be shared. The concept of 'Digital Twin' (Boschert and Rosen 2016) is core to this ontology: a Digital Twin is a representation of any physical object in the real world with information. As the following figure shows, transport means, and cargo are the main subtype of Digital Twin. Cargo in its term has the subtypes of equipment (e.g. containers, trailers), general cargo consisting of number and types of packages (e.g. pallets), bulk cargo (e.g. liquid bulk like palm oil) and transport means (e.g. a truck with its trailer on a ferry or railway wagon). A Digital Twin has an identifier like a container number or Automatic Identification System (AIS) identification. A business transaction, which is an instance of a business service, has a unique identification and so will have orders and events. Actors have one of two roles in a business transaction: customer or service provider. The role can be modelled by a property of the association or as a separate list of potential roles, since other roles like shipper, forwarder, and carrier can act as customer and/or service provider.

Figure 7 shows the high-level ontology, the so-called upper ontology, for supply chain visibility. It includes business services representing data shared between any two stakeholders in a business transaction. An order is part of this business transaction

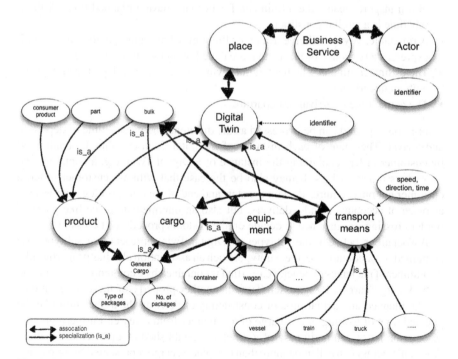

Fig. 7 Ontology for supply chain visibility

data, representing the progress in a choreography representing ordering and planning. An order can be on transport, thus containing at least data of the subtype 'Cargo' of Digital Twin, or on buying and selling, thus containing the subtype 'Product'.

Each Digital Twin has an association with 'place', where place represents physical locations like terminals, warehouses, (air)ports, and distributions centres. Two types of places are foreseen for transport: the place where transport starts (place of acceptance) and where the service is completed (place of delivery). In some cases, these places have different names like port of loading and discharge for sea transport or pickup and drop off for road transport.

An itinerary is represented by the ordered set of places called upon by a transport means, where the order is defined by a time sequence. In many cases, this time sequence of a places of call for a transport means has a unique identification like a trip—, voyage—or flight number. In some occasions, the actual transport means can be added later to an itinerary, for instance a trip can be assigned at a later stage to a particular truck. By modelling an itinerary as a Digital Twin, such a unique identifier an be assigned. Since an itinerary has no additional data, it is not further specialized into a subtype in the ontology.

Additionally, an intermediate place is required like border crossing place. Each of these places is represented by an association with the following properties:

- An agreed or planned time with an uncertainty expressed by a period. A timetable of a transport means like a train can for instance have a planned time. A flight schedule is a similar construct.
- A timetable, voyage scheme, route, or flight may have a unique identification. It expresses a sequence of places that are called upon by a transport means.
- The estimated time at which a Digital Twin will be arrive or depart from a place, with an uncertainty.
- The actual time of arrival or departure.

A turnaround period can be expressed as the difference between a time of departure and arrival. The route of each instance of a Digital Twin can thus be configured by customer orders containing the instance of a Digital Twin, e.g. a container and its various transport legs. It may also be the case that within a customer order, a customer not only requires data on the start and end of the transport leg, represented as place of acceptance and—delivery, but also an intermediate place like place of border crossing, for instance to decide on the customs procedure at crossing.

Associations between the subtypes of Digital Twin represent that subtypes are contained by or contains another subtype. Such an association also has properties like the number of packages of general cargo that is contained by a container or the volume of bulk cargo carried by a vessel. Time is another property of these associations, i.e. the planned and actual time of constructing or deleting the association like the planned time of loading or discharge of a container from a vessel. Furthermore, the association is (or can be in case of a itinerary) established at a particular location. Since an itinerary can call upon more than two places, cargo represented by associated

Digital Twin must be linked to a particular place. This place is mentioned in an order, either as place of acceptance or—delivery.

Primarily, the milestones 'arrive', 'depart', 'construct' or 'load', or 'delete' and 'discharge' are foreseen. The construct and delete milestone will be made specific to an association:

- Pack and unpack products to general cargo;
- Stuff or stripping of general cargo in container(s);
- Load or discharge cargo from a transport means.

Secondly, milestones like ETA or release are identified, where a customs can provide a customs release and another stakeholder a commercial release based on payment of transport charges by a bank.

This ontology is the basis for three data structures representing orders, itineraries, and events. Basically, three operations can take on these data structures, namely create a new instance (a so-called post operation), update an existing one (put operation), and retrieving data (get operation). Each operation is linked to an activity in the choreography. For instance, an actor can post an event in event processing, whereas another actor can get new events. Data can not be deleted from a ledger, due to its immutability. Only the state of a data entry can be changed, e.g. to rejected.

For implementation purposes, the conceptual data structure is simplified and specific elements for processing are included. The subtypes of Digital Twin can be 'type of Digital Twin' and 'place of acceptance' and '- delivery' can become properties of a Digital Twin. The milestones are part of the implementation structure.

Figure 8 shows the implementation structure (x: data is required; o: data is optional). This latter structure allows visibility of all types of Digital Twins, including sharing their milestones. Also, the provenance of milestones has to be traceable. A hash of the event is inserted, where the hash is encrypted with the private key of the one that has submitted the event. Since such an event can have a relative low amount of data, a generated string can be inserted if is used to calculate the hash. There can be multiple conditions to an order, like commercial—and customs release. These conditions are the basis for a warning, see before. The table of the implementation data structure also includes a state variable for an order and an itinerary. The Digital Twin or cargo state is represented by a milestone shared by an event.

The implementation data structure has an entry for 'Relation to data' with a URL, the type of data (e.g. purchase order data), and its technical representation. In the conceptual model, such a purchase order contains product data and represents the progress of the collaboration between a buyer and seller.

A purchase order can be modelled as a lower ontology based on the one shown in Fig. 5 or as a set of rules on data requirements represented for instance in SHACL (World Wide Web Consortium 2017). Figure 7 is not complete, it can be extended by the association between products and general cargo, representing despatch advice data.

Conceptual structure					Implementation structure - general			
Data properties	Order	Itinerary	Event		Data element	Order	Itinerary	Event
Actor					Actor			
customer	x		x		customer	x		x
service provider	x	x	x		service provider	x	x	x
identifier	x	x	x		identifier	x	x	x
Digital Twin					state	x	x	
Identifier	x	x	x		milestone			x
Subtype	x	x	x		timestamp			x
Digital Twin - place of acceptance					encrypted hash			o
alternative role	x		x		provider of the hash			o
planned time (window)	x				Digital Twin	x		x
estimated time			x		Identifier	x	x	x
actual time			x		Subtype	x	x	x
Digital Twin - place of delivery					No. of units			x
alternative role	x		x		Start of an acitvity	x		
planned time (window)	x				place	x		
estimated time			x		time window	x		
actual time			x		Completion of an activity	o		
Digital Twin - intermediate place					place	x		
alternative role	x		x		time (window)	x		
planned time (window)	x				Intermediate			
estimated time			x		Place	o		
actual time			x		time window	o		
Place(s)					Place(s)			x
Place	x	x			Place		x	
planned time (window)		x	x		time		x	x
estimated time					Speed (transport means)			o
actual time					Direction (transport means)			o
General cargo - equipment	o		o		Condition(s)	o		
number of packages			x		Relation to data			o
planned stuffing time (window)	x				URL to data			x
actual stuffing time			x		Type of data			x
planned stripping time (window	x				Data representation standard			x
actual stripping time			x		Digital Twin associaton (s); related to places	o	x	o
Cargo - transport means	o		o		Identifier	o	x	x
planned loading time (window)	x				Subtype	x	x	x
actual loading time			x		time	x	x	x
planned discharge time (window	x							
actual discharge time			x					

Fig. 8 Conceptual—and implementation data structures

3.4 Ledger Technology Functionality

There are two important requirements to implementation of the supply chain visibility functionality by ledger technology, namely transactional confidentiality and data semantics.

Till now, we have not presented any functionality that is specific to implementing supply chain visibility by ledger technology. However, utilizing ledger technology requires transaction confidentiality. Whereas all data can be encrypted and only decrypted by a recipient, the fact that any two stakeholders share data is already sensitive. It allows detection of commercial relations between any two stakeholders.

Transaction confidentiality is therefore an important feature of a Supply Chain Ledger. It considers two aspects, namely the ability that only an intended recipient is able to read the data (Hofman et al. 2018) and it is impossible for unauthorized users of the ledger to trace back which users shared particular data. Transaction confidentiality makes the ledger completely private, thus supporting commercial sensitivity. Each user has a keypair acting as its identity that is verifiable. Transaction confidential is achieved by a user, which we will call submitter and is intending to share data with another user, generating a new identity, i.e. keypair 1. Payload data is published to the ledger via this new identity, where the data and a signature created by the submitter are encrypted with a symmetric key. Details for unlocking data, the so-called payload unlocker, are shared with an intended recipient by creating yet another identity, i.e. keypair 2. Each recipient also creates a new identity, i.e. keypair 3, for receiving the data. The payload unlocker contains keypair 1 and a signature of the original submitter of the data proving the integrity of the symmetric key, where the signature is made by encrypting the symmetric key of keypair 1 by the private key of the submitter. The public key of the submitter can also be shared in the payload unlocker but could also be shared otherwise.

A second important requirement to ledger technology is the separation of data structures and software code. So-called smart contracts contain data structures, which means that any updates in data structures and their semantics would result in new software code. By separating them, software code can be more generic, and code and data structures can be maintained and shared via a ledger separately. The data structures can be represented as SHACL (World Wide Web Consortium 2017) and validated using standard software components. A rule could be for instance for events that if the type of Digital Twin is 'container', the 'identifier' should have a particular format (4 letters, nine digits, and a check digit based on an algorithm), meaning that the software can validate container numbers given by an event. Another rule would be that the event should at least contain one Digital Twin of type cargo or transport means and their subtypes. These SHACL rules are stored on the ledger and can be accessed by anyone. Thus, data structures are separated from software code of the APIs provided by the Supply Chain Visibility Ledger.

3.5 *Potential Functional Extensions*

The proposed Supply Chain Visibility Ledger supports physical actions represented by milestones. Since IoT enables not only location-based services, but also other types of services like monitoring the condition of cargo, the milestones can be extended. Cargo conditions can for instance be detected by temperature sensors to signal that the temperature exceeds a maximum or is lower than the minimal allowed setting which can be relevant to the quality of the cargo, shock sensors that can be used to trace potential damage to packages, seals that signal unauthorized opening of the cargo, especially containers, and weighing assets that detect the actual gross weight of cargo, for instance at loading a container on a vessel. The ledger can be used to share these sensor readings.

In this research chapter, the ledger supports milestones that reflect the start and completion of an order between a customer and service provider, i.e. the place and time of acceptance and delivery. This order is used as a subscription mechanism to events and represents in fact the access policy of an enterprise. Since orders can differ, this access policy must be dynamic. Such access policies may be extended with intermediate places for which milestones are required. A service provider can decompose a customer order in various transport legs and the customer might require to be informed of the status of each leg. Additional settings can be given in the order or can be considered as configurations of the ledger by a customer.

Although we have mentioned them, authorities' requirements are not yet incorporated in the functionality. Authorities can have access to milestones shared by events, where both the milestones and the relevant data accessible through links can be mandatory. For instance, a customs authority could formulate its requirement to receive all milestones for container movements of those containers that will arrive in the first port of call (customs at entry and are discharged in a port under its responsibility. These container movements include any diversions due to changes in voyage schemes of vessels. Where the access policies of enterprises are dynamic, those of authorities will be static and should be derived from regulations. The authority access profiles will only change when regulations change. These types of extensions based on dynamic and static access policies require further elaboration.

4 Discussion

Like stated, the previous specifications are technology independent, but impose particular requirements to ledger (and potentially other) technology. This section briefly discusses on the one hand the advantages of using ledger technology for developing the Supply Chain Visibility Ledger and on the other hand potential extensions of the Supply Chain Visibility Ledger. The ledger is also positioned in a context with other IT solutions for handling storing data, managing orders, and decision support of enterprises and authorities.

4.1 Advantages of Applying Ledger Technology

Ledger technology consists of a (n immutable distributed) data layer with software providing API functionality. The data layer consists of a set of (interoperable) nodes of a given technology, e.g. BigChainDB, Ethereum, or Hyperledger Fabric.

A first major advantage of ledger technology is that the data layer replicates (almost) immediately data across all nodes. For instance, a customs release token only has to be published once and is immediately available to a carrier and stevedore, based on their contractual relations with their customers. In case many platforms are used by relevant stakeholders, such a token needs to be distributed to all relevant stakeholders or these stakeholders have to regularly have to poll whether or not a token is available and they are also allowed to access this token by delegation (iShare 2019). Applying ledger technology will speed up logistics operations.

Having the data in a ledger, not only provides an immutable log and audit trail that could serve as a proof in case of conflicts, but also makes it possible to post events independent of an order or itinerary. It supports sensors and scanners providing milestones that are relevant to an itinerary and/or order, without these sensors or scanners storing data of these orders. Thus, a leger with the proposed interfaces optimally supports Internet of Things (IoT). Having all relevant data in a ledger also provides the opportunity to automatically generate additional events. The ledger functions as a type of broadcasting solution based on subscriptions.

Creating a global supply chain visibility ledger also implies that each stakeholder has one interface with that ledger. It only needs to connect once and is able to share data in a controlled manner with all others connected to the ledger. This fully supports the idea of what is called 'plug and play' developed by the Digital Transport and Logistics Forum (Digital Transport and Logistics Forum (DTLF) Subgroup 2: Corridor Information Systems, 2018).

Furthermore, the data layer is also applied for distributing software, what is called 'smart contracts' in case of Ethereum. The same software providing supply chain visibility APIs is available to all end-users of the ledger. One of the main requirements to technology is global support, i.e. all logistics stakeholders and authorities should be able to use the same solution. Ledger technology supports this requirement.

Another advantage is that the nodes of the data layer can be installed in all domains, e.g. an individual authority can install a node, authorities of one country can share a network of nodes, and a logistics stakeholder or an IT service provider can install such a network. An IT service provider might offer this (sub)network to Small and Medium sized Enterprises (SMEs) and provide all relevant functionality to these SMEs with a business model. Thus, each user can run its own network of nodes and act as ledger steward. This network of nodes is robust, meaning that if one of many nodes fails, the network and functionality and data are still available. Such a network of nodes needs to consist of at least three nodes. In case the number of nodes is low, performance of the network might decrease due to failure of one node.

Separation of concerns based on layering is also an important advantage of applying ledger technology. Whereas the nodes store and distribute the data, the software providing the API functionality can be developed and validated by a small group of individuals. Of course, these APIs execute operations on data stored in the ledger, which implies that the structure of the data stored in a ledger has to be downwards compatible; any update of a data structure needs to support the previous version or else new API functionality has to be distributed resulting in what could be considered forks. Downward compatibility allows end-users to gradually upgrade their functionality. Separation of concern supported by the software distribution mechanism is a great advantage over more traditional platform solutions, where each platform will have to upgrade their APIs themselves.

Finally, the nodes all store the data encrypted. It means that someone providing a node does not have access to the data, unless a ledger steward also acts as end-user.

4.2   Infrastructure Governance

A supply chain visibility ledger is a digital infrastructure (Tilson et al. 2010) with specific features (see the previous pages). Governance defines the scope of the application of such an infrastructure. In general, the governance principles for a network-based infrastructures development should consider (Ostrom 1990; Andereis et al. 2004):

- Defining Boundaries—The boundaries of the information structure and those individuals or groups with rights to infrastructure resources should be clearly defined.
- Balancing the Benefits and Costs of Resource Usage—Operational rights specifying the types of infrastructure resources that a user can access should be directly linked to local needs and conditions concerning work practices, available technologies, information, and/or money inputs.
- Managing and Sanctioning resource—A system monitoring resource image should be implemented by the users themselves. Users who violate rules should receive gradual sanctions (depending on the seriousness and context of the offence) from other users and/or official accountable to these users (i.e. by constitutional right holders).
- Devising and Modifying resource Usage—Users should have rights and modify the rules determining the use of infrastructure resources. These rights should not be imposed by external authorities (e.g. the state).
- Conflict Resolution mechanism—Users and their officials should have rapid access to low-cost, local area arenas to resolve conflict among users, between users, and between their officials, and infrastructure providers.

These aspects consider resources as crucial, being for instance the supply chain visibility ledger. The boundaries are clearly specified by the supply chain visibility APIs. Resource usage will be governed by on the one hand technology, i.e. the API functionality with potential restrictions imposed by one or more stakeholder (groups), and on the other hand the rules for accessing the resources, i.e. valid attestations for identity provisioning like having a registration by international accepted bodies like the Chambers of Commerce, financial creditability and a valid bank account. From a technical perspective, standardization and adoption of open standards, i.e. standardization of supply chain visibility data structures,—choreographies specifying the sequencing and functionality of APIs, and the APIs themselves, can be of value. Having open standards stimulates innovation. Internet standards are a very good example illustrating innovation by open standards where applications utilizing the Internet drive adoption. These standards could be transformed into open source software, that can be implemented directly or via distributors by organizations, thus creating business models like that Redhat (Krishnamurthy 2005).

4.3   Infrastructure Technology

There is also the issue of different providers using different technology, including the application of different blockchain technology like Ethereum, BigChainDB or Hyperledger Fabric. For instance, a commercial platform provider may develop a solution based on an Enterprise Service Bus (Erl 2005). Such a solution will apply the publish/subscribe mechanism of the technology and implement business logics. A platform itself can be offered as a cloud solution. Another approach would be to extend the reference architecture of the International Data Space (Dalmolen et al. 2019) with the required functionality. For this purpose, specific application components can be developed and distributed via a type of Appstore. The IDS reference architecture can be implemented by many providers, leading to different IDS networks based on peer-to-peer data sharing with IDS connectors and one or more Appstores. Although the IDS reference architecture has implemented some type of separation of concerns (layering), its software distribution is separate from the infrastructure.

In case there are many of these platform providers, different IDS networks, or different ledger technology applied, these different solutions have to become interoperable to provide global supply chain visibility. There are at least two issues to be addressed in these implementations. The first is that of technical interoperability:

- IDS networks. The protocols for interconnection of IDS connectors are standardized. The only issue is to discover the proper connector of a customer or service provider. Therefore, the IDS brokers serving as registry have to be interconnected. It requires standardization of (meta)data stored in the various brokers.
- Platforms. The registries of platforms need to be interoperable to discover which platform is used by which user.
- Ledger technology. Ledger technology can be made technically interoperable by implementing the appropriate technical standards. Besides sharing user registrations amongst each other, API software should also run on different ledger technology.

Secondly, solutions of different providers based on different or identical technology need to be functional interoperable, namely at business level. Supply chain visibility services need to be identical for all users. Services provided to end-users have to be interoperable at a functional, business level, preventing any loss of data. IDS connectors need to implement the same application component for supply chain visibility, preferably of the same developer, or platforms must provide the same supply chain visibility service. There are solutions for having different providers of IDS application components or platform services, like validation and certification. This will require additional overhead (and governance) to implementation of supply chain visibility.

In case the supply chain visibility ledger is based on a variety of ledger, first of all this technology has to be interoperable (Hardjono et al. 2019). A ledger of a given technology implicitly supports real time distribution of software providing the API functionality, i.e. the software is part of the blockchain, where the software is agreed by the majority of the stakeholders. There are two relevant aspects to be addressed. The first is a governance issue. Bitcoin has solved governance by its mining solution and a small group of developers posting new software, i.e. smart contracts, to the network (Bohme et al. 2015). Differences in smart contracts lead to so-called forks that are considered as new crypto currencies with their network of nodes, miners, and developers. For (global) supply chain visibility, a similar type of governance has to be installed to prevent forking (although one might consider forks for localisation of the functionality, forks focussing on a particular modality, or forks supporting a particular type of cargo (containers, commodities, etc.)). The second issue is the support of API software by different ledger technology. For instance, Ethereum has its programming language, whereas BigChainDB can support different types of programming languages.

4.4 Interoperability Between Different Technology Solutions—Visibility Standards

The design assumes an ideal world, where all users integrate with one Supply Chain Visibility Ledger. These users can be enterprises and authorities that require and share milestones of the physical processes. In the real world, we will have many Supply Chain Visibility Ledgers and—Platforms, each with their users and business model. Enterprises that do business with each other, can use different ledgers or platform and authorities don't wish to integrate with all ledgers and platforms. First, authorities will develop their ledger or platform, secondly, privately operated ledgers have to configure the proper subscriptions for authorities, and thirdly, all ledgers and platforms have to be interoperable, i.e. they have to be able to share data. The latter consists of two parts:

- Technical interoperability—the ledgers and platforms have to be able to communicate with each other.
- Functional interoperability—the ledger—and platform services have to be identical to allow users to share events. Functional interoperability requires agreement on the configuration of subscriptions and events with milestones.

Technical—and functional interoperability has to be standardized and adopted by each ledger—and platform provider, see before. There are already (proprietary) supply chain visibility interfaces like the Open Trip Model (OTM[1]), Tradelens,[2] and the Electronic Product Code Information System [EPCIS (Global Systems One, 2014)]. These interfaces differ in functionality, e.g. OTM stems from road transport and expands to other modalities, Tradelens supports visibility of container transport by sea, and EPCIS is generic and needs to be configured with semantics. They are

---

[1] www.opentripmodel.org.
[2] https://docs.tradelens.com/.

incompatible and a proposal is to develop one standard based on these inputs. Any implementation choices also need to be represented as options, like the provenance of a milestone.

In general, the public—and private domain all have their different systems. The implication of having several Supply Chain Visibility solutions in the private domain is that the public domain will develop its own solution. This latter solution will have to be interoperable with private domain solutions, both technical and functional for all modalities and all subtypes of Digital Twins. It requires harmonization of milestones and data semantics.

An alternative solution would be to construct a layer of nodes operated by enterprises, authorities, and service providers. These nodes can be based on different technology solutions and technical interoperability constructs an immutable distributed database. A common understanding of a conceptual approach as taken in this research chapter for implementation of functionality with agreements between all stakeholders will automatically provide functional interoperability of these nodes. The same infrastructure can be used by public and private sector stakeholders and provide real time supply chain visibility. The construction of such a global supply chain visibility ledger requires a clear governance structure. Governance requires active participation of both authorities and supply and logistics enterprises.

5 Conclusion and Further Work

Distributed Ledger Technology (DLT) can reduce complexity and automatically provide supply chain visibility to all stakeholders in a controlled manner by generating events and warnings based on events posted by physical devices (sensors, scanners). Complexity reduction is achieved by avoiding that individual stakeholders need to develop, implement, and maintain software for processing incoming events and generating new events. Based on various use cases documented in literature, this research chapter formulates general requirements for supply chain visibility. These requirements are transformed into conceptual specifications resulting in data structures and proposals for a limited set of APIs to support supply chain visibility. The conceptual specifications are developed by applying BPMn Choreography, state diagrams, and ontology modelling.

Since the specification is technology independent, this research chapter presents arguments for applying ledger technology. Governance is one of the main issues for any technology implementation of the functionality. Applying ledger technology instead of any other type of technology provides the opportunity to create a global, neutral supply chain visibility infrastructure that can be applied by both the public— and the private sector (one might also have a separate public—and private sector implementation that is synchronised). Applying ledger technology also makes it possible to create a broadcasting solution where only subscribers are able receive particular events.

In case ledger technology is applied, transaction confidentiality and a separation of data structures and software code need to be implemented. This research chapter briefly presents results of previous work on these topics, discussed in various other papers.

This research chapter presented a conceptual specification of functionality of a supply chain visibility ledger. A demonstrator of this ledger needs to be developed to create awareness of the potential of Distributed Ledger Technology. It can also be an instrument to further develop, validate, and improve specifications of an open supply chain visibility infrastructure and support the discussion on governance of such an infrastructure. Validation of the demonstrator and extending the functionality can be in close collaboration in different use cases with users, both business and authorities. The validation would lead to formalization of the choreography, the semantic model, data structures for all interactions, and various implementation choices that have to be made.

References

Andereis, J. M., Janssen, M. A., & Ostrom, E. (2004). A framework to analyze the robustness of social-ecological systems from an institutional perspective. *Ecology and Society, 9*(1), 18.

Bohme, R., Christin, N., Edelman, B., & Moore, T. (2015). Bitcoin: Economics, Technology, and Governance. *Journal of Economic Perspectives, 29*(2), 213–238.

Boschert, S., & Rosen, R. (2016). Digital twin—the simulation aspect. In P. Hehenberger & D. Bradley (Eds.), *Mechatronics future* (pp. 55–74). Cham: Springer.

Caridi, M., Moretto, A., Perego, A., & Tumino, A. (2014). The benefits of supply chain visibility: A value assessment model. *International Journal of Production Economics*, 1–19.

Dalmolen, S., Bastiaansen, H., Somers, E., Djafary, S., Kollenstart, M., & Punter, M. (2019). Maintaining control over sensitive data in the Physical Internet: Towards an open, service oriented, network-model for infrastructural data sovereignthy. *International Physical Internet Conference (IPIC2019)*. Londen.

Digital Transport and Logistics Forum (DTLF) Subgroup 2: Corridor Information Systems. (June 2018). *Enabling organizations to reap the benefits of data sharing in logistics and supply chains— executive summary.* Von Digital transport and logistics forum: https://ec.europa.eu/transparency/regexpert/index.cfm?do=groupDetail.groupMeeting&meetingId=4855abgerufen.

Endsley, M. R. (1995). Toward a theory of situation awareness in dynamic systems. *Human Factors: The Journal of the Human Factors and Ergonomics Society, 37*(1), 32–64.

Erl, T. (2005). *Service Oriented Architecture—concepts, technology and design*. Prentice-Hall.

Global Systems One. (2014, May). *Electronic Product Code Information System (EPCIS) version 1.1.* Abgerufen am 27. 10 2017 von www.gs1.org.

Hardjono, T., Lipton, A., & Pentland, A. (2019). Toward an Interoperability Architecture for Blockchain Autonomous Systems. *IEEE Transactions on Engineering Management*.

Heshket, D. (2010). Weakness in the supply chain: who packed the box? *World Customs Journal, 4*(2).

Hofman, W. (2014). *Control tower architecture for multi- and synchromodal logistics with real time data.* Breda: ILS.

Hofman, W. (2018). *Towards large-scale logistics interoperability based on an analysis of available open standards. Interoperability for enterprise systems and applications.* Berlin: Springer.

Hofman, W., & Rajagopal, M. (2015). Interoperability in self-adaptive systems of multiple enterprises—a case on improving turnaround time prediction at logistics hubs. In *6th IFIP International IWEI2015*. Nimes.

Hofman, W., Spek, J., & Ommeren, C. V. (2018). Applying blockchain technology for situational awareness in logistics—an example from rail. In *International Physical Internet Conference IPIC2018*. Groningen.

Hulstijn, J., Hofman, W., Zomer, G., & Tan, Y.-h. (2016). Towards trusted tradelanes. In *International Conference on Electronic Governance* (S. 299–311). Cham: Springer.

iShare. (2019, April 4). *iShare Scheme v1.9*. Von https://ishareworks.atlassian.net/wiki/spaces/IS/pages/70222191/iSHARE+Schemeabgerufen.

Krishnamurthy, S. (2005, January 18). An analysis of open source business models. In J. Feller, B. Fitzgerald, S. Hissam & Karim Lakhane (Eds.), Von making sense of the bazaar: perspectives on open source and free software. MIT Press: https://ssrn.com/abstract=650001abgerufen

Lind, M., Watson, R. T., Ward, R., Bergmann, M., Bjørn-Anderse, N., Rosemann, M., et al. (2018, September 9). Digital Data Sharing: The ignored opportunity for making global maritime transport chains more efficient. *Unctad Transport and Trade Facilitation Newsletter*.

Object Management Group. (2011). *Business Process Model and Notation Specification 2.0*. Von https://www.omg.org/spec/BPMN/2.0/abgerufen.

Ostrom, E. (1990). *Governing the commons: the evolution of institutions for collective action*. Cambridge University Press.

Parjogo, D., & Olhager, J. (2012). Supply chain integration and performance: The effects of long-term relationships, information technology and sharing, and logistics integration. *International Journal of Production Economics*, 514–522.

Rukanova, B., Henningsson, S., Henriksen, H. Z., & Tan, Y.-H. (2018, March/April). Digital Trade Infrastructures: a framework for analysis. *Complex Systems Informatics and Modeling Quarterly (CSIMQ)*, 1–21.

Tilson, D., Lyytinen, K., & Sørensen, C. (2010). Digital Infrastructures: the missing IS research agenda. *Information Systems Research*, 1–12.

Urciuoli, L., & Hintsa, J. (2018). Improving supply chain risk management—can additional data help? *International Journal of Logistics Systems and Management, 39*(9), 741–761.

Wieland, A., & Wallenburg, C. M. (kein Datum). The influence of relational competencies on supply chain resilience: A relational view. *International Journal of Physical Distribution & Logistics Management*, 300–320.

World Wide Web Consortium. (July 2017). *Shapes Constraint Language (SHACL)*. Von World Wide Web Consortium: www.w3c.org/tr/shacl/abgerufen.

Wout J. Hofman is a senior researcher at TNO with 35 years of experience in interoperability and ICT for transport and logistics. Before joining TNO in 2006, Wout was a consultant and partner of a Dutch consultancy firm, later taken over by Deloitte. He worked on interoperability and data sharing for all modalities, sea (the Port of Rotterdam), road, rail, and inland waterways. He received his Ph.D. at Technical University of Eindhoven and Erasmus University of Rotterdam on the topic of control tower architecture (1994). He has been and still is responsible for IT in various EU (FP7/H2020) funded projects on international trade facilitation, inlcuding the Connecting European Facilities (CEF) Federated Action. Wout has been consultant to EC DG TAXUD on development of the Transit System and EC DG JAI on the current Schengen information system. Currently, Wout supports EC DG MOVE for realizing seamless data sharing in the logistics and the Dutch Ministry of Infrastructure and Water management on realizing the Digital Transport Strategy. In his role as scientific lead, he performs research on applying blockchain technology to achieve these objectives. Wout has published over 100 scientific papers and is author of three books.

Printed in the United States
by Baker & Taylor Publisher Services